THE POETICS OF APPEARANCE IN THE ATTIC KORAI

MARY STIEBER

THE POETICS OF APPEARANCE IN THE ATTIC KORAI

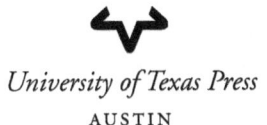

University of Texas Press

AUSTIN

This book has been supported by an endowment dedicated to classics and the
ancient world and funded by the Areté Foundation; the Gladys Krieble Delmas
Foundation; the Dougherty Foundation; the James R. Dougherty Jr. Foundation;
the Rachael and Ben Vaughan Foundation; and the National Endowment for the
Humanities. The endowment has also benefited from gifts by Mark and Jo Ann
Finley, Lucy Shoe Meritt, the late Anne Byrd Nalle, and other individual donors.

◯ The paper used in this book meets the minimum requirements of
ANSI/NISO Z39.48-1992 (R1997) (Permanence of Paper).

Library of Congress Cataloging-in-Publication Data

Stieber, Mary C. (Mary Clorinda)
The poetics of appearance in the Attic korai / Mary Stieber— 1st ed.

p.   cm.
Includes bibliographical references and index.
ISBN 978-0-292-74236-9
1. Kore statues.   2. Polychromy—Greece—Athens.   3. Votive offerings—
Greece—Athens.   4. Athena (Greek deity)—Cult.   5. Inscriptions, Greek.
6. Acropolis (Athens, Greece)   I. Title.
NB94 .S74   2004
733'.3—dc21
2003011966

Excerpt from Euripides, *Iphigenia in Tauris,* trans. Bynner, from *The Complete
Greek Tragedies,* vol. 3, ed. Grene and Lattimore, reprinted by permission of the
University of Chicago Press. © 1956 by The University of Chicago.

For John

Give them my hands and circle round and dance
And always try to be the loveliest,
Under my mother's gaze,
In my unrivalled radiance of attire
And in the motion of my hands and feet,
While my embroidered veil
I would hold closely round me as I danced
And bowed and hid my cheek
Under the shadow of my clustering curls.

EURIPIDES, *Iphigenia in Tauris* 1145–1150
(TRANS. W. BYNNER)

CONTENTS

LIST OF ILLUSTRATIONS

The illustrations follow page 222.

20. Acropolis Museum 682 *(back view)*.
21. Princess of Amarna, from the family of Amenhotep IV (Akhenaten), New Kingdom, Egypt, limestone, Musée du Louvre E 14715.
22. Acropolis Museum 687 *(detail)*.
23. Acropolis Museum 673, kore from the Acropolis of Athens, marble.
24. Acropolis Museum 600, kore from the Acropolis of Athens, marble.
25. Acropolis Museum 683.
26. Acropolis Museum 681 *(detail)*.
27. Acropolis Museum 682 *(detail)*.
28. Acropolis Museum 594.
29. Acropolis Museum 682 *(detail)*.
30. Acropolis Museum 680 *(detail)*.
31. Acropolis Museum 674 *(detail)*.
32. Acropolis Museum 686 ("Euthydikos' Kore") *(right side)*.
33. Acropolis Museum 685 *(three-quarter view from front)*.
34. Acropolis Museum 616 *(right side)*.
35. Acropolis Museum 682 *(detail)*.
36. Acropolis Museum 683 *(detail)*.
37. Acropolis Museum 598, kore from the Acropolis of Athens, marble.
38. Acropolis Museum 598 *(detail)*.
39. Acropolis Museum 598 *(detail)*.
40. Kore from Attica ("Berlin Kore"), marble, Staatliche Museen zu Berlin, Preussischer Kulturbesitz, Antikensammlung 1800.
41. Bearded head with tiara from Herakleia Pontica, Turkey, marble, Museum of Anatolian Civilizations, Ankara 19367.
42. Head of a man ("Sabouroff Head"), Athens or Aegina, marble, Staatliche Museen zu Berlin, Preussischer Kulturbesitz, Antikensammlung 308.
43. Decadrachm ("Damareteion") of Syracuse, Sicily, silver, Museum of Fine Arts, Boston 35.21.
44. Acropolis Museum 609 (lower half of "Euthydikos' Kore").
45. Acropolis Museum 670 *(detail)*.
46. Kore from Merenda, Attica ("Phrasikleia"), marble, Athens, National Archaeological Museum 4889.
47. Kore statuette from Sparta, bronze, Staatliche Museen zu Berlin, Preussischer Kulturbesitz, Antikensammlung 7933.

ACKNOWLEDGMENTS

This book owes it origins to my doctoral dissertation of 1992. However, ten years later, my thesis about viewing the Attic korai, my thinking about it and about them, and the evidence brought to bear upon the argument have undergone such significant modification and expansion as to have resulted in a completely different work.

At various stages of the project's history, friends and colleagues have offered help and advice in a number of different ways; I would like to thank a few of them here: Carmen Arnold-Biucchi, William A. P. Childs, Marie Mauzy, T. L. Shear Jr., R. R. R. Smith, Brian Swann, Diane Harris-Cline, and, most of all, John Walsh. All errors are my own.

While I was an Associate Member of the American School of Classical Studies at Athens, supported by a Kress Fellowship from Princeton University, the staff at the Acropolis Museum courteously allowed me to visit its storerooms in order to view the korai not on display. Thanks and appreciation are also due to the editorial staff at the University of Texas Press, especially Humanities Editor Jim Burr and Managing Editor Carolyn Cates Wylie, and to freelance editor Kerri Cox Sullivan.

Boreas has kindly allowed me to reuse in revised and updated form material from my 1996 article titled "Phrasikleia's Lotuses," which forms the basis of Chapter Five. I thank the University of Chicago Press for allowing me to reproduce the portion of the chorus from Euripides' *Iphigenia in Taurus,* captured in elegant translation by Witter Bynner, which serves as the epigraph to the book.

MARY STIEBER
The Cooper Union for the Advancement of Science and Art

LIST OF ABBREVIATIONS

Where not obvious, abbreviations used for ancient authors and works are those found in *LSJ*.

AA   *Archäologischer Anzeiger*
AAA   *Athens Annals of Archaeology*
AB   *Art Bulletin*
ABFV   J. Boardman, *Athenian Black Figure Vases* (New York, 1974)
AJA   *American Journal of Archaeology*
AJP   *American Journal of Philology*
AM   *Mitteilungen des Deutschen Archäologischen Instituts, Athenische Abteilung*
AMA   E. Langlotz, W.-H. Schuchhardt, and H. Schrader, *Die archaischen Marmorbildwerke der Akropolis*, 2 vols. (Frankfurt am Main, 1969 [orig. pub. 1939])
ArchEph   Ἀρχαιολογικὴ Ἐφημερίς
ARFVA   J. Boardman, *Athenian Red Figure Vases: The Archaic Period* (London 1983)
BCH   *Bulletin de correspondance hellénique*
BICS   *Bulletin of the Institute of Classical Studies of the University of London*
BSA   *Annual of the British School at Athens*
CEG   P. A. Hansen, *Carmina Epigraphica Graeca* (Berlin, 1983)
CR   *Classical Review*
DAA   A. E. Raubitschek, *Dedications from the Athenian Akropolis: A Catalogue of the Inscriptions of the Sixth and Fifth Centuries B.C.* (Cambridge, Mass., 1949)
FGrH   F. Jacoby, *Die Fragmente der griechischen Historiker*, 15 vols. (Berlin and Leiden, 1923–1958)
GSA   J. Boardman, *Greek Sculpture: The Archaic Period* (London, 1991)

GSC   J. Boardman, *Greek Sculpture: The Classical Period* (London, 1985)

HSCP   *Harvard Studies in Classical Philology*

IG   *Inscriptiones Graecae* (Berlin, 1873–)

JDI   *Jahrbuch des Deutschen Archäologischen Instituts*

JHS   *Journal of Hellenic Studies*

LSJ   H. G. Liddell, R. Scott, and H. S. Jones, with R. McKenzie, *A Greek-English Lexicon* (Oxford, 1968)

NC   *Numismatic Chronicle*

OJA   *Oxford Journal of Archaeology*

PCG   R. Kassel and C. Austin, *Poetae Comici Graeci* III.2 (Berlin, 1983–)

PMG   D. L. Page, *Poetae Melici Graeci* (Oxford, 1967)

RE   A. Pauly and G. Wissowa, *Real-Encylopädie der classischen Altertumswissenschaft*, 83 vols. (Stuttgart, 1894–1980)

TAPA   *Transactions of the American Philological Association*

TrGF   B. Snell, R. Kannicht, and S. Radt, *Tragicorum Graecorum Fragmenta* I– (Berlin and Göttingen, 1971–)

YCS   *Yale Classical Studies*

ZPE   *Zeitschrift für Papyrologie und Epigraphik*

THE POETICS OF APPEARANCE IN THE ATTIC KORAI

CONCEIVING REALISM IN
ARCHAIC GREEK ART

It has been suggested that this image of a modest young girl [Acr. 670] . . . was a more or less direct portrait of a living model. And it is true that the most beautiful faces of Attic korai—those which are not, like some others, merely mediocre copies of genuine master-pieces—present, despite their superficial resemblance, a variety of shapes and expressions that is not merely the fruit of the sculptor's imagination. An exceptional instance of this is Kore 643. The face, under the loops of hair that crown it like two folded wings, seems imbued with poetry like a distant echo of Sappho's verse. So typically Attic in its openness to the light, so spiritually and physically indi-vidual with its slightly crooked smile, this face refuses to be consid-ered simply a member of a stylistic family and rebels against the dawning severity of the age.[1]

Those who have found themselves at one time or another face to face with the veritable chorus of marble maidens from the sixth century B.C., whose Archaic smiles seem to breathe life into the stony stillness of the archaeo-logical museum that houses them, will understand why Jean Charbonneaux found poetry in appearances. For the korai from the Acropolis of Athens are extraordinary, strange figures from a pre-Classical past whose com-bined presence is pure poetry, a poetry whose poetics is but skin deep, so to speak, rooted, as it is, in the maidens' physical demeanors. At face value, and in the face of the korai themselves in their present home in the Acropolis Museum, the above remarks are simply a straightforward re-sponse which might occur to anyone viewing these famous images for the first time or for the hundredth time, who, for a moment, chooses to forget what he or she may have been taught to think about these statues and instead respond to what is actually seen and felt in their presence. And yet, beneath the apparent naiveté of the above remarks lies an iconoclastic view of a much discussed and analyzed group of ancient images, which, because they are well known, many assume they know well, a view that is seldom expressed in the ever-expanding body of scholarly literature on Archaic Greek art.

There are some fifty-six marble votive korai from the Athenian Acropolis preserved in various states of fragmentation, a selection of which is on view in the Acropolis Museum, while the rest lie in its storerooms.[2] They represent young women in a range of scales, from under life-sized to well over, elaborately dressed, coiffed, and accoutered, and carved and painted with great skill, care, and expense. They were dedicated to Athena, the patron goddess of the citadel, in the sixth and early fifth centuries B.C., a period encompassing both the latter years of the Peisistratid tyranny and the early years of democracy; the dedicants came from both inside and outside the aristocracy.[3] Alone, any one of them might go unremarked, but together, like a chorus, is how the korai make their strongest impression, since together is, after all, the only way they were ever meant to be seen. Together they once stood on the Archaic Acropolis; for nearly twenty-four centuries, they lay buried together; and so it is fitting that together they confront, and bewitch, the modern-day museum visitor. And, unlike some other famous sculptures which first saw the light of day on the Athenian Acropolis, the korai have been spared separation and relocation; the Attic light under which they were intended to be seen still falls on them, if only through the museum's windows. These statues, much scrutinized, much admired, much written about, and yet still as mysterious as any to have survived from the ancient world, are the subjects of this study.[4]

Contrary to the impression conveyed by the introductory quotation, the Acropolis korai are not usually regarded as individualized representations of young women but as examples, if rather fine, of a generic type, counterparts to the Archaic images of young men, the kouroi. This, however, was not always the case. The earliest observers, like Henri Lechat and Franz Winter, writing at the turn of the century, shortly after the korai's discovery during the excavations of the Acropolis in the 1880s, allowed themselves to effuse at length about the statues' individuality and life-likeness. But these first impressions were short-lived. A different interpretation of these images has prevailed in subsequent scholarship. Arguably, the most influential study of the korai has been Gisela Richter's 1968 monograph, *Korai, Archaic Greek Maidens: A Study of the Development of the Kore Type in Greek Sculpture*. Adapting a methodology that she had already applied to convincing effect in her equally influential monograph on the kouroi,[5] Richter arranged all of the korai, including the Acropolis examples, primarily according to her conception of an advancing naturalism evidenced by the sculptor's increasing ability to render volume and three-dimensionality and to break through the limitations imposed by the shape and dimensions of the block. That Richter's groupings of the korai as well as the methodological principles on which they are based have emerged substantially intact after more than three decades suggests that her chronology as well as its premise is sensible and therefore likely to be correct.[6] As a sign of the resilience of Richter's methodologies, and serving as well as a tribute to her work, Claude Rolley, in a major recent French-language survey of Archaic and Early Classical art, devotes a portion of a chapter to a critique of Richter's approach.[7]

However, a less fortunate result of Richter's hold on the scholarly literature has been that all of the korai, regardless of quality, are first and foremost thought of as examples of a fixed, predetermined type; in other words, what unites them is privileged over what differentiates them. The wording of Richter's own subtitle acknowledges its focus on this aspect of the korai.[8] The notion of the korai as types has remained firmly entrenched, resistant to new ideas, in spite of much subsequent scholarship that has sought to expand the parameters of the discourse on these images. In this study, while neither directly assailing nor undervaluing Richter's schemata, I present an alternative way of viewing the Acropolis korai which I believe has not been seriously entertained since the late nineteenth century and even then not fully explored: that these statues display a concern for a kind of individuality, for a mimetic modality that can even be considered realistic, and that this modality is not necessarily exceptional for the age in which the korai were created. Thus, "conceiving realism" applies both to the existence of an Archaic *mentalité* that is sympathetic with the idea of mimetic realism and to the subtle charge to the reader to conceive of the possibility that realism is present in a style of art in which it is almost never thought to be present.[9]

It may be useful to pursue, for a moment, an analogy with a style of art which, like the Greek Archaic, is not often associated with realism but perhaps should be: Analytical Cubism of the early years of the twentieth century. It is no accident that styles as dissimilar as Archaic Greek, Romanesque, tribal, and early Modern are discussed in nearly identical aesthetic terms. These styles do share many qualities, including a notion of mimetic realism and even portraiture that is fully functional in a nonclassical, nonnaturalistic idiom. Analytical Cubist portraits, for example, are effective as conveyors of a set of individualistic characteristics that coalesce into a distinct personality, while at the same time being difficult to decipher from a formal point of view—in other words, they are abstract. Yet, in spite of the arcane formal language of its presentation, it is unlikely that the art dealer D.-H. Kahnweiler might be known any better or more satisfyingly than in Picasso's portrait of 1910.[10] A sufficient number of informative details are present; the viewer has but to put them together. A photograph of another sitter, Wilhelm Uhde, and Picasso's 1910 portrait of the same are often reproduced side by side for comparison.[11] Since only the essential particularized features of the man are reproduced, the painting conveys a more potent image than the somewhat characterless photograph, even though the latter is more easily legible.

It is a mistake to assume, as is commonly done, that photographic reality represents the highest degree of realism achievable in a work of art and that photography should be the gauge by which all other realism in art is judged. It is fair to say that mimetic realism was an achievable goal in periods and places that did not know the paradigm offered by the photographic replica. Furthermore, the optical correctness of photography has itself been regarded with suspicion from the very beginning of its history. Apollinaire, who knew photography, nonetheless recognized the unique placement of the new Cubist modality in the centuries-old quest for artistic realism when he remarked in a program note to the 1917 production of Erik Satie's ballet *Parade,* with Cubist sets and costumes by Pablo Picasso: "This realism, or this Cubism, *whichever you prefer* [my emphasis], is what has most deeply stirred the arts during the last ten years."[12] Apparently realism and Cubism were thought of as synonyms by the creators of the style, among whom was Apollinaire, a notion that is every bit as astonishing at the beginning of the present century as it must have been at the beginning of the last. Similarly, a notion that bemused Classical Greeks and eludes the modern viewer, that Archaic Greeks thought of the figures that they produced as nothing other than realistic, went just as surely unquestioned by the original viewers.

MIMETIC REALISM

The term "mimesis" in its nominal, adjectival, and adverbial forms appears throughout this study; its usage must be clarified. Mimesis is the *act* of imitating nature; mimetic realism is the *result.* Mimesis is generally thought to be etymologically derived from mime, a dramatic artform, a derivation which attests the fact that the mimetic act has never been confined to the visual arts.[13] Successful mimesis results in lifelikeness, or trueness-to-life, sometimes to an astonishing degree. However, in part because of its origins in the art of acting, there is always an inherent deceit, or counterfeit, associated with the product of the successful mimetic act. A mimetic object may be a perfect facsimile, but it is never the real thing. A mimetically realistic work of art invariably signals trickery; it invites comparisons with nature and carries overtones of accomplishing the impossible or the unlikely, of matching or even besting nature. When used of the visual arts, mimesis should not be equated with naturalism, since naturalism refers to a stylistic mode rather than an act. Naturalism can aid in the achievement of mimetic realism, but it is not essential to successful mimesis, and above all should not be considered a synonym for either mimesis or realism, but rather one choice among many as a means of access. "Mimesis" (as the act) and "mimetic realism," or simply "realism," (as the visual result) shall be used largely interchangeably of the phenomenon which this study explores. Thus far the crux of the present argument may be stated as follows: Some Archaic works of art are not necessarily very naturalistic but they are realistic, in that they are successful essays in mimesis. The fact that they are not very naturalistic does not automatically disqualify them from being realistic.

Naturalism and realism are not synonymous terms or concepts, although they often are treated as if they are. Naturalism can be said to indicate the degree to which a work of visual art successfully matches, visually, what most human beings would agree to be the actual appearance of nature or physical reality. In other words, the naturalistic work of art is one that matches what is seen as judged by the same eye that sees it. It is therefore directly dependent upon the way we see, upon optics; therefore naturalistic art can be said to be optically correct. The closer a work of art is to optical correctness, the more like natural appearances it seems. The eye is the arbiter, rather than the intellect or the emotions. With this said, it must be cautioned that what most human beings agree to be naturalistic can change from place to place, from era to era. Even idealized images can and should be regarded as naturalistic if they seem to represent appearances correctly at any given time and place.

Classical Greek art and all the arts of the Classical tradition are almost exclusively naturalistic; in fact naturalism can be said to be the chief distinguishing characteristic of Classical styles of art. Yet the character of naturalism itself changes even during the narrow course of the Classical period proper, between the time that Polykleitos (mid–fifth century B.C.) was working and the time of Lysippos (second half of the fourth century B.C.). On the contrary, with the great exception of the Amarna period, Egyptian art is almost never described as naturalistic, although much of it comes quite close to being naturalistic in the way that Classical art is. This is because *contrapposto*, what we have come to regard as the essential

ingredient of naturalism, as a result of the Classical artist's virtual obses-
sion with it, is absent from Egyptian art.

There is little justification for discussing Archaic art in terms of strict
fidelity to natural appearances, or naturalism; it may even be a little unfair. To do this would be to diminish what is best about Archaic art, to
wring the life out of it, to disregard what it does better or different than
the art of later periods. It may be many things, awkward, clumsy, funny,
strange, just plain wrong, but it wears its freshness well over a longer period of time than does the Classical. Its naiveté could be seen as a reflection of the tendency of Archaic Greeks to see and name things and parts
of things for what they are, not for the qualities which make them what
they are, a presocratic construing of the world which Alexander Mourelatos
has called "the naive metaphysics of things."[14] Unlike the Classical, which
all too soon degenerates into what might be called an academic style,
Archaic art may be formulaic, but it never becomes academic. The style
seems impervious to the organic theories about the development and de-
cline of forms which have been applied with varying degrees of success to
other historical styles. And, most important, I would argue that Archaic
art, at its highest levels of execution, is capable, in its way, like the best
Analytical Cubism of Picasso and Braque, of attaining realism in spite of
its less than perfect naturalism. While the history of Western art would
include a number of nonclassical styles which would repeat this feat, it
would never be repeated in the Graeco-Roman period.

Optical correctness (= naturalism) is not the only "correctness" in the
visual arts. The term "realism" has both a broader and a far more complex
visual and conceptual frame of reference than does the term "naturalism."
All works of art which are naturalistic are not necessarily also realistic, and
works of art which are realistic need not also be naturalistic. In other
words, to say that naturalism is optional in a realistic work of art is neither
the paradox nor the contradiction in terms that it may at first seem. What
then is realism? The very word "real*ism*" inherently implies that it may be
something like reality but never reality itself; therefore we must seek a
definition that is exclusive to the making of art and which will involve
artifice to some degree or other, since artifice and its consequence, artifactuality, the means and the end, are what set art apart from nature. We
have seen the inadvisability of preserving the notion that realism in any
style or period of art is commensurate with naturalistic depiction. Any
definition should then be broad enough to apply both to naturalistic styles
of art and to nonnaturalistic styles of art, and therein may lie the greatest
obstacle to conceiving realism for the modern mind.

This study proposes and proceeds on the premise that the essence of realism in any work of art lies in the accretion of information and meaning provided by accumulating layers of *detail*. These details may be stylistic or iconographic, intellectually erudite or philosophical, subtle or overt, aesthetically or extra-artistically inspired; the more of them there are, the more realistic an image will seem to the viewer. Realism in a work of art can be as simple as this: If more lines are inscribed in a length of flowing drapery, whether or not those lines conform to prevailing notions of optical correctness or reality itself, that drapery will appear more realistic than if fewer lines were indicated; the rendering of drapery in the Parthenon pediments compared with the pediments of the Temple of Zeus at Olympia may be cited to illustrate the point. Or it may be as complicated, if we may again turn to a useful postclassical example, as the following: It has been shown that Michelangelo turned to ancient physiognomic theory to formulate his image of David, noting that the similarly youthful and audacious Alexander the Great was deemed leonine in appearance and that the lion was also the ancient symbol of Florence; thus, Michelangelo's marble colossus has flowing, leonine locks.[15] These, along with additional references and allusions which result in a highly complex, distinctive, and erudite iconography, make Michelangelo's portrait of David more realistic than, say, an image of David from a medieval manuscript which conveys little more information about the biblical giant-slayer than that he was a boy with a sling.

Whether of a formal or an iconographical nature, the more information given about the subject of a work of art, the more realistic the results are likely to be judged to be. It will be noted that little of this is directly related to reality itself, even in the form in which it is best known, nature, or the visible world. This allows, then, images of people who cannot necessarily have been seen by the artist, such as gods, mythological and biblical figures, and, in some cases, the dead, to be considered realistic as well. Rather than being copied, nature is imitated, in Aristotle's sense, as if the artist is a quasi-divine creator.[16] This is mimesis. As does nature, so the artist, starting with his knowledge of the characteristics of something, applies his technical skills and "brings to life" (that is, mimes) a convincing portrayal detail by informative detail. He may or may not be "matching" visually, but he is "making," to use E. H. Gombrich's well-known terms. A simplified version of the intellectual progression that leads to mimetic realism might go something like this: man; man with beard; man with beard and fine wavy hair; man with beard, fine wavy hair, and wart, and so on.

Thus defined, realism is then the exact opposite of idealization. For to idealize is to simplify, while to render realistic is to complicate. Idealization involves a reduction in visual information and a subsequent raising of the evidence of artifice; consequently there is a reduction in the range of possible meanings conveyed about the subject of the artwork, in other words, in the very details that lead to an impression of realism. Artifactuality is given more conceptual space than nature. The more the work of art is inflected by artifice, at the expense of informative details which can be verified by consulting nature or, in lieu of that, memory, the farther from mimetic realism it drifts. It is a long-held truism that idealization is the predominant characteristic of Greek art as a whole, that Greek art through-out its history concerned itself more with the universal than with the par-ticular. It is also true, however, that even in its most paradigmatic form, the art of the High Classical period, this art never ceases to betray a con-cern for realism at some level.[17] Arguing that a form of realism is present in a style of art in which it has not often been sought leads to the startling but inevitable conclusion that some degree of realism is seldom altogether absent from a work of figural art, reflecting something elemental and abid-ing about the practice of making images, of the act of imitating nature, in Aristotle's sense. Just how powerful is the association between image-making and the generation of life is demonstrated by the fact that creator gods like Hephaistos, Athena, Prometheus, and the Egyptians Ptah, Imho-tep, and Khnum are all metaphorical artisans, just as real-life artisans are metaphorical creators.[18] These self-referential conflations become so in-tertwined that the term "metaphor" no longer aptly describes them; they are quite simply truth.

THE POETICS OF APPEARANCE

Proceeding from the notional definition of realism just articulated, this study proposes a new way of viewing the Attic korai.[19] In gathering to-gether ancient evidence, both visual and verbal, both direct and indirect, that these statues are highly individualized, mimetically realistic—on the terms just outlined—representations of Archaic young women, my conclusions challenge some of the most venerable and most tenacious truisms about ancient art, that the korai, like their male counterparts, the kouroi, are no more than types, that they represent idealized images of female beauty, and that these characteristics would seem to preclude any possibility that the statues could be realistic. Through primary evidence, the reader will be introduced to a way of conceiving realism in pre-Classical Greek art and, more specifically, to conceiving it in the korai under discussion.

It will be seen that the expression "poetics of appearance" in the book's title alludes both to the methodology of applying the evidence of literature to a consideration of the question of realism in Archaic visual arts, and to the conclusion that physical appearance, in the form of dress, gait, bearing, and accoutrements, especially in the case of women, is paramount in any perception of realism in the art of this period. It should be noted that the use of the term "poetics" has little directly in common with a current theoretical approach called "cultural poetics," which involves an appropriation of the term whose fitness for the use to which it is being put might in fact be debatable but which has proved a useful designation to describe the shared interests of an interdisciplinary group of scholars among whom the label and the loosely defined endeavor have found acceptance.[20] Poetics, however, as the title of Aristotle's treatise indicates, refers quite simply to the ways and means of poetry. I am using the term in its traditional sense, with a twist. The lovely physical appearances of the korai are and have always been judged to be no less than poetic and, more literally, I enlist actual poetry to aid in elucidating them.

The study opens with a historiography of the statues, in other words, a brief synopsis of the written history of the korai, including a discussion of the evolution of aesthetic appreciation in modern times which has resulted in the general consensus, challenged in this study, that the statues are idealized, generic, and repetitive types. In addition it is argued that the early descriptions of the korai, written when much of their painted polychromy was still in place, now form an essential part of the statues' historiography. Chapter Two consists of visual analyses, supplemented by information now available only through the early descriptions, which reveal that, rather than homogeneity, distinctiveness is their most salient characteristic. The korai are justly celebrated for their elaborate coiffures, each distinguishable from the next by its particular arrangement of a combination of crimps, braids, and curls. The variety of their garments and other accoutrements is also commonly acknowledged. However, all of this evidence is rarely treated as a sign of the degree of intentional, calculated differentiation among the statues. Even less frequently appreciated is the fact that faces and figures are also individualized. This chapter treats the purely visual characteristics, that is, the materiality of the korai.

Chapter Three adduces literary and archaeological evidence to suggest that an untheorized, but nonetheless intentional, conception of likeness in art that borders on portraiture existed in the pre-Classical period, but that it manifested itself in ways that are not entirely consistent with modern expectations. It cannot, however, be overemphasized that my proposition that the korai are mimetically realistic images does not stand or fall on the conclusion that the korai are portraits of real individuals; the very notion of portraiture is too fluid a concept to be applied systematically to the arts of all periods and places, and is especially problematic in the case of unnamed statues like the Acropolis korai. For these reasons, when the term "portrait" is used in this study, it is usually enclosed in quotation marks to indicate that it is being applied with qualifications. Chapter Four contextualizes the korai through an examination of the relevant written material, including poetry, literature, and history, which, as a verbal parallel to the korai figures, similarly reflects on the demeanor and appearance of young women in the Archaic period. This evidence will complement the visual evidence presented in Chapter Two and broaden the base of support for the thesis that the korai represent mimetically realistic images of Archaic women.

Poetry will again provide the comparanda in the final chapter, a single case study of a completely preserved Attic monument, the kore Phrasikleia with its inscribed base, which, unlike the Acropolis group, all of which served a votive function, was made to mark a grave. Once more interweaving verbal and visual evidence, this funerary image is systematically decoded to disclose the synthetic likeness that it was arguably intended to be.

THE KORE AS TYPE

What does all of this imply, ultimately, about the kore as a type in comparison with the kouros? Quite a bit, actually. It has long been noticed that the kouros type is more numerous and has a wider distribution over the Archaic Greek world than does the kore,[21] a fact which suggests that the male form was always a more versatile format whose range of perceived usefulness was more flexible than the female. The kouros' nudity offered a virtual *tabula rasa* of interpretation imposed or deduced by the maker, the patron, and the viewer which lent itself neatly to acclimation to the occasion and locale, whereas the dressed kore automatically accrued some degree of iconographical specificity, intentional or not. Not surprisingly, given the potential, as well as the constraint, of greater iconographical specificity, the kore was more restricted in use and in distribution. The great majority were votive; merely a handful were certainly funerary, Phrasikleia being the outstanding extant example. And by far the most and finest korai occur on the Acropolis of Athens. Thus, the phenomenon of "kore" may be said to be particular, if not necessarily exclusive, to the Acropolis of Athens.

At first glance, one could assume that the ideological framework of the Acropolis group was extraordinary because the statues themselves are extraordinary. But the context for korai on the Acropolis is the type's primary context and only appears exceptional when it is assumed that the kore is exactly analogous to the kouros. Because the Acropolis is the *locus classicus,* so to speak, of the kore in the High Archaic period, its function there should logically be regarded as the referent for its function elsewhere. The Acropolis kore is the norm for the type, not the exception, thereby paradoxically rendering, if one follows the argument to come, mimetic realism the norm for the type rather than the exception. The paradox is that, while the kore is still, by later artistic standards, a type, the limited and specialized case of its principal occurrence being on the Acropolis of Athens allows, unlike the kouroi, for the narrowing of the possibilities of its meaning to the determinant(s) of its specific function on the Acropolis. This use, as it turns out, is perfectly in keeping with the kore's pre-Acropolis history.

It is generally acknowledged that the Acropolis korai, and the kore as a type, are genealogically descended from a seventh-century B.C. statuary prototype which flourished first on the islands and in Asia Minor. It has long been suspected, and in a few cases certified, that islanders might even have sculpted the Attic examples; Phrasikleia, for one, certainly was made by Aristion of Paros. These early korai were votive and arguably meant as representations of a worshiper, who is occasionally named; none appears to be a goddess.[22] Their intended function as *Stellvertreter*[23] ("place-takers") is virtually certain. As the type gained a foothold on the Acropolis, the simpler style of the earlier images, which limits any perception of mimetic realism, was superseded by the advanced Archaic style, which offered new scope for aesthetics and the exploitation of iconography. What is missing on the Acropolis are names, for any number of reasons, but the function of the kore as place-taker was carried over. The marker of name is replaced by the marker of visual individualization and differentiation.

Although, or perhaps because, the Attic korai are among the most well known and beloved of all ancient works of art and have been studied for so long by so many, a fresh interpretation of them is overdue. These statues have sometimes been the victims of their fame, with the result that they are seldom viewed with true objectivity, independent of the vast scholarly apparatus which has grown about them over the many decades since their dramatic recovery. In fact, so accustomed are we to the "official" modern views of the Acropolis korai that it may be by now impossible to revisit them without the encumbrance of scholarship that these images trail behind them as they do their flowing chitons, and it may be presumptuous to suggest that one may begin to find one's way to interpretation simply by looking and trusting, in the manner of the earliest commentators, in the judgment of the eye. Unlike the viewers of the late nineteenth century, viewers of the present may not enjoy the luxury of seeing these statues and commenting upon them for the first time in their long history, or of an honest, dispassionate scholarly response. But as long as these statues are there for the looking, the urge to understand them will prove irresistible to some. In offering a new way to view the korai, as an alternative or as a complement to the traditional interpretations, it is hoped that some of the ideas presented in this study, as with previous studies both grander and more modest which likewise fail to explain them completely, may find a place in the historiography of these magnificent images and, perhaps more important, in the minds and eyes of those who continue to want to look at them. At best, if it compels the first-time viewer or the recurrent viewer to take another, longer look at the Attic korai, this study will have served its purpose.

CHAPTER ONE

HISTORIOGRAPHY

The history of the korai from the Athenian Acropolis may be written in the following summary fashion: They were created and erected during the sixth and early fifth centuries B.C. They performed their duties as votives to Athena on the Acropolis until 480/79 B.C., when the Persians sacked the citadel, burning and desecrating the statues and buildings that adorned it.[1] The korai, damaged or not, were subsequently buried in "graveyards" on the very Acropolis upon which they had once stood, discarded as evidence of barbarian impiety, and perhaps also as stylistically obsolete remnants of an earlier era; the ancient testimonia about Daidalos leave little doubt that the Archaic style was regarded as old-fashioned in the Classical period and thereafter.[2] The so-called Propylaia Kore (Acr. 688) was one of the last to be made and the very last to be discarded; it was built into the foundations of the Periclean Propylaia as late as 438/7 B.C.[3]

No extant ancient author mentions the Acropolis korai. The statues lay alongside one another in their graves until the citadel was excavated in the 1880s, when they emerged from the ground in great hoards and in remarkable physical condition, their polychromy still vibrant, giving the impression that they had been interred as sacred objects.[4] It is tempting to speculate that the statues were treated as if they had once been alive, as if as a group they constituted a comprehensive record of the range of female beauty valued in the period, and as if there was a concern that future excavators should recognize their ancient importance.[5] The response to the freshly unearthed statues was immediate: The korai were admired. The korai were talked about. The korai were written about. They were placed in the Acropolis Museum, where they have been admired, talked about, and written about ever since.[6]

The korai's historiography begins with the first words written about the statues, their inscriptions. Their status as votaries is certified by the content of the inscriptions that were carved directly onto the columns and square pillars upon which the statues stood.[7] The bases which contain

the inscriptions were found separated from the statues they once supported. A large number of inscriptions can, however, be associated with
korai rather than with other types of votive on the Acropolis; the characteristics of a hole for a plinth, for example, can reveal the size of the statue
and whether it was male or female, although very few of them can be
attached securely to specific examples. While there are material remains
of some fifty-six korai from the Acropolis, just sixteen bases are able to be
associated with extant korai or fragments, according to A. E. Raubitschek,
whose edition of the inscriptions remains fundamental.[8]

The Archaic votive inscriptions from the Acropolis follow the same
generic formulae for dedications whether they accompanied a representation of a human figure or a functional object such as a vase. Raubitschek
summarizes the components of the formulae for the prose inscriptions,
the great majority of which consist of a selection from among seven elements composed in a variety of formulaic combinations. The elements, in
the order of their importance, are: the name of the dedicant; the verb
indicative of the act of dedicating; the name of the deity; the patronymic
(the dedicant's father's name); the dedicated object in one of its forms,
"ἀπαρχέν" ("first fruits") or "δεκάτεν" ("tithe"); the ethnic (name of the
dedicant's tribe) or demotic (name of the dedicant's deme); and the
dedicant's occupation. Raubitschek adds that only twenty-three inscriptions, which he lists, contain elements other than these seven.[9] Some are
in verse; others are not. The verse inscriptions follow much the same pattern; however in twenty-five cases, a version of "τόδ' ἄγαλμα" ("this object, statue, or gift") is the direct object of a verb.[10] The inscriptions can be
as simple as "so-and-so dedicated" or as elaborate as "so-and-so dedicated
to Athena this tithe from his possessions." Rarely, the artist's name is included. In the final analysis the dedicatory inscriptions from the Athenian
Acropolis are not particularly informative about the objects they document. There are no proper names used of the images to help with
identification; they are referred to only in an abstract sense to label their
purpose. This situation, the "naming" problem, has perplexed scholars
who would otherwise be inclined to see the Acropolis korai as individualized representations. If they are individuals, why are they not named?

A couple of possible explanations present themselves. First, there is the
evidence provided by Pausanias for the existence of a tradition of dedicating portrait statues on the Acropolis which did not require the addition of
memorializing names to make clear their dual function as portrait images
and dedications. To regard the korai as "portraits" in the usual meaning of

the word would probably be going too far, although some writers have not been so reluctant. However, the following evidence for the possible existence of portraiture on the Acropolis is relevant to the korai if, as I am arguing, they are to be considered highly individualized images which might have been taken in their time for unnamed likenesses of real Athenian women. During his visit to Olympia, as Pausanias (5.21.1) is trying to make sense of the different types and functions of the multitude of objects which he sees in the Altis, he compares the situation there with Athenian practice, apparently already having seen on the Acropolis objects similar to what he sees at Olympia. Pausanias is deliberate with his terminology, using the same terms to describe and differentiate the practices at both sanctuaries:

> From this point my account will proceed to a description of the statues [ἀνδριάντων] and votive offerings [ἀναθημάτων]; but I think that it would be wrong to mix up the accounts of them. For whereas on the Athenian Acropolis statues [ἀνδριάντες] are votive offerings [ἀναθήματα] like everything else, in the Altis some things only are dedicated in honour of the gods, and statues [ἀνδριάντες] are merely part of the prizes awarded to the victors. The statues I will mention later; I will turn first to the votive offerings, and go over the most noteworthy of them.

Still at Olympia, Pausanias (5.25.1) adds: εἰκόνας δὲ οὐ τιμῇ τῇ πρὸς τὸ θεῖον, τῇ δὲ ἐς αὐτοὺς χάριτι ἀνατεθείσας τοὺς ἀνθρώπους, λόγῳ σφᾶς τῷ ἐς τοὺς ἀθλητὰς ἀναμίξομεν ("The statues which have been set up, not to honor a deity, but to reward mere men, I shall include in my account of the athletes"). Here he calls the portrait statues εἰκόνας, and to indicate that these εἰκόνας are the ἀνδριάντες of the earlier passage, and vice versa, he spells out clearly that they are "to reward mere men." It is safe to say that, in this case, by ἀνδριάντες Pausanias means portrait statues as opposed to generic votive images, whatever their form or their time of creation. Pausanias seems to be saying that, while a name on a portrait statue at Olympia would be *pro forma,* in order to mark its special function as a victor's prize, it would be superfluous or perhaps even inappropriate to name someone on the Acropolis, where a portrait statue can be considered, at most, one subcategory of votive image, the qualities which make it a portrait incidental to or subsumed beneath its function as a votive.

While the situation at Olympia is more complicated,[11] what Pausanias is implying about dedicatory traditions on the Acropolis is clear, simple, and potentially relevant to the present discussion. It is highly probable that the korai now on view in the Acropolis Museum would have been buried long before Pausanias' visit. Yet the possibility—while remote, as we shall see presently—remains that remnants of the korai were still there, although it is not central to the point. It is well to keep in mind that, during his visit to the Acropolis, Pausanias (1.23.4) admits that he is not mentioning everything he sees on the citadel. It is also important to note that, in Pausanias' time, there was a strong tradition of dedicating on the Acropolis statues of maidens of noble birth who had had the honor of being chosen to serve as *arrhephoroi,* living on the Acropolis for a year in order to perform secretive rites for Athena Polias at the festival called the Arrhephoria.[12] The parents and sometimes also the girl's brothers were dedicants and the girl was always named.[13] Pausanias might have seen some of these statues.

It is regrettable that Pausanias is not more forthcoming about the history of dedicatory practices on the Acropolis; his subject in Book 5 is, after all, Olympia. But here, as elsewhere in his work, Pausanias is exhibiting his characteristic conscientiousness about matters historical. As at Olympia, where he begins his commentary somewhere in the seventh century B.C., in his brief digression on Athens he likely means to imply that the Athenian practice described in summary fashion has a comparably long history. Pausanias could have known this history himself or, if he did not, he would have been careful to consult a proper source. At least two Hellenistic Greek authors, Heliodorus of Athens and Polemon of Ilium, wrote treatises on the votive objects on the Athenian Acropolis.[14] Furthermore, since the function of votive dedications persists with little change throughout Classical antiquity, and the forms that votaries take may change but not their purpose, any description of ancient votive practices permits extrapolation backward. Thus we may conclude the following about the Acropolis korai from Pausanias' comments: it is possible that, since Pausanias implies that there is a tradition of statues representing mortals—that is, portrait-type statues on the Athenian Acropolis—and that the individualizing qualities of these statues might be overlooked, as they were equivalent to votives, and probably carried inscriptions indistinguishable from ordinary votive inscriptions, the korai could have been examples of such individualized, portraitlike dedications, and if Pausanias had either seen or heard about any korai, he would probably have referred to them as *statues* (ἀνδριάντες), according to his scheme.[15]

A second explanation for the paucity of information afforded by the Acropolis inscriptions may lie in the very nature of early inscriptions. An early Greek monument delivers its message by way of two equally nonlingual media which archaeology may preserve: the artifact or art object and the inscription, the visual and the written, which sometimes occur together and thereby invite comparisons about the degree of efficacy of each—*ut pictura poesis*. In the case of the Acropolis korai the term "generic" so often applied to them is actually more appropriate to the epigraphy than to the statues. The dedicatory inscriptions from the Archaic Acropolis betray little or none of the same wealth of informative detail that permits the statues to be called mimetically realistic, as we shall see. One or more artisans will have spent months producing a statue to which, in most cases, nothing more than a brief, formulaic inscription was appended. However well the letters are formed and just what they tell us about the stylistic history of the epigraphist's *technē* are separate matters; even when in verse, the Acropolis inscriptions cannot be considered poetry and, as far as their content is concerned, they are scarcely worthy of the art of inscribing or of the artistry of the statues which stood over them.

Raubitschek noticed this phenomenon and attributed the somewhat disappointing formulaic repetition of these inscriptions to the methods of production: "These short inscriptions can hardly have been the work of real poets, but rather of the sculptors or stone-cutters themselves . . . How many and which elements were to be included in the epigram probably was a matter for the dedicator to decide; he may have had the choice between various model epigrams which were offered by the artist or his stone-cutter."[16] Raubitschek observes that the "considerable uniformity" of the dedications is consistent with a pattern of dedicatory inscriptions that occurs throughout the Greek world in this period. This is not surprising, he concludes, in the light of the fact that many foreign artists worked at Athens, bringing with them their idiosyncratic repertoires of artistic practices, and, if indeed the artists themselves composed the inscriptions, uniformity would be expected as well when differing clienteles are served by the same group of artists.[17] It is plausible that Archaic epitaphs were conceived and executed in the atelier.[18] It is also possible, though less likely, that the dedicant himself composed the epigram. But in the end it must be acknowledged that works of art are not defined or given further meaning by inscriptions like these.[19] On the other hand, Phrasikleia's epigram, to be discussed later, significantly augments the visual evidence to enlighten the meaning of the work of art which it serves.

It is ironic that if the korai from the Acropolis had not been associated with the Acropolis inscriptions, scholars might have permitted themselves more freedom in their interpretations of the visual evidence unfettered by the authority of the written word. For such is the supremacy of the authority habitually granted to written words over images that it is commonly held that, in certain periods and places, such as the ancient Near East, when mimetic realism is assumed, perhaps unfairly, not to be a concern, only the inscribed name rendered an image a portrait regardless whether the image itself resembled the person portrayed. However, this theory can prove difficult to uphold even in its best test case, Egyptian art. When a pharaonic portrait was reused by a later pharaoh, great care might be taken in transforming the portrait's physical appearance, both face and figure, into that of the new pharaoh, inasmuch as this was technically feasible. An example is provided by a seated portrait of Amenhotep III in the Louvre which was methodically recut into a portrait that more accurately reflected the physical characteristics of the fuller-figured Ramesses II. Arielle P. Kozleff describes in detail how this metamorphosis was accomplished; her description makes for illuminating reading.[20] The common presumption that attributes greater semiotic power to the written word shortchanges the equally well documented power of the sculpted image when it stands alone as the conveyor of meaning.

It is fair to say that, as the Archaic period was neither prehistoric nor fully historic in its patterns of written documentation, it may be best not to expect too much from the Acropolis inscriptions. In spite of increasing general literacy, orality was still central in Archaic society much as it had been in the Dark Age.[21] Homer had recently been committed to writing for the first time, if one adheres to the traditional attribution to the Peisistratids of the earliest transcription of the poems.[22] Documents were few, by comparison with the Classical period. Widespread use of prose was just developing. All Greek literature prior to Thucydides' history was composed or written to be comprehended orally, all drama, iambic, lyric, and elegiac poetry, epic. Even Herodotus' history was written to be declaimed. Whether written inscriptions with statues were the exception and not the rule, or whether they were the rule, their usage was not as regularized or institutionalized as would later be the case. Since the Athenians in this period were not generally literate, a statue alone may have spoken more fully than an inscription to the passing viewer; to argue otherwise is to underestimate the prestige of the visual image in a society that is not wholly literate. This would account for the limited range of words and phrases on the inscriptions that do accompany statues, and for the use of the first person, as if the statue itself were speaking to the passerby. The so-called dialogue epigram is a type of inscription, most often funerary, that adopts a conversational tone as if the monument itself were accosting the passerby; it boasts of the decedent's character and manner of death, if it was a noble one, and asks the living to remember the dead, as in the epitaph of the kouros named Kroisos.[23] Not everyone would have been able to read an inscription. Most would, however, have been equipped to pass judgment on the aesthetic effects of a statue, visual literacy being a more universal phenomenon than lettered literacy even today.

Between their likely burial sometime shortly after 480/79 B.C. and their excavation in the 1880s, there is virtually no history to write for the korai. The ancient sources mention in passing some survivors of the Persian holocaust, but korai are not among them.[24] Yet there is no need to assume that Archaic images, or the Archaic style itself, were completely banished and banned from the Acropolis immediately after the Persian Wars, as the *terminus ante quem* provided by the so-called *Perserschutte* ("Persian destruction debris") would imply, if rigidly enforced. It seems that some religious sculptures were set back up, their desecrated state likely intended as a further reminder of barbarian impiety, already in evidence everywhere on the Acropolis. This was the category of statues of which isolated examples were still visible in the second century A.D. when Pausanias (1.27.6) visited the Acropolis, where he noticed some "old figures of Athena" by the Erechtheum, "no limbs of which indeed are missing, but they are rather black and too fragile to bear a blow. For they too were caught by the flames when the Athenians had gone on board their ships and the King captured the city emptied of its able-bodied inhabitants." One of these statues may have been the figure known as Endoios' Athena (Acr. 625).[25] It is not out of the question that some korai also made it through the flames and destruction essentially intact.[26] It seems that the very few images of divinities that survived were preserved and rededicated. If the Acropolis korai were representations of divinities, we should probably expect that they, too, would have been preserved instead of buried; that they evidently were not begins to argue against the possibility that they are representations of divinities.

A few secular images may have also survived. Pausanias (1.28.1) was surprised to see a statue of Kylon, the would-be tyrant, when he visited the Acropolis; it is possible that this work was genuinely Archaic. Pausanias speculates that Kylon was not being honored for his aborted coup attempt of ca. 630 B.C., but rather he was immortalized for the physical beauty for which he was renowned. The knowledge and appreciation of that beauty would have been prerequisites for the making of a portrait statue, and these would have dimmed with the years, making it likely that the statue was made sometime in the Archaic period. There was also a bronze lioness dedicated, according to Pausanias (1.23.2), who saw it, by the Athenians at the end of the Peisistratid tyranny to commemorate a woman whose name was Leaiana ("Lioness"), a mistress of one of the tyrant-slayers who was tortured by the surviving tyrant, Hippias. Lucian (*Im.* 4 and 6) mentions a statue of "Sosandra" that stood on the Athenian Acropolis by the sculptor Kalamis (fl. second quarter of the fifth century). One of its characteristics, according to Lucian, who, in search of a description to match the beauty of Panthea, mistress of the emperor Lucius Verus, attributes the qualities of a number of famous statues to her, was its "solemn, inscrutable smile" (τὸ μειδίαμα σεμνὸν καὶ λεληθός), a characteristic feature which is associated with Archaic rather than Classical art.[27] This statue sounds at least stylistically Late Archaic, roughly contemporary, perhaps, with the latest of the korai from the Acropolis, Acr. 686 and 688. It has been thought that the statue of Aphrodite by Kalamis which Pausanias (1.23.2) says was adjacent to the bronze lioness is this Sosandra.[28]

While it seems that only the most significant of Acropolis dedications were preserved after the Persian destruction, there could have been additional survivors. Pausanias (1.23.4) makes it clear that there were monuments standing on the Acropolis that he does not describe: "I do not want to write of the less distinguished portraits" (τὰς γὰρ εἰκόνας τὰς ἀφανεστέρας γράφειν οὐκ ἐθέλω). Could korai have been among these εἰκόνας τὰς ἀφανεστέρας? If any Archaic korai were seen by Pausanias but regarded as "portraits" of an early, primitive style, this, not to mention the fact of their being dedications of lesser individuals, some of whose families were not aristocrats, might have caused them to be ranked among the "less distinguished." Alternatively, ἀφανεστέρας could connote "less certain" or "more doubtful"; in that case, the incomplete information on the inscription, or the lack of inscription, could have dissuaded the cautious Pausanias from drawing conclusions about them.

There is some, albeit slim, archaeological evidence for the history of the Acropolis korai after the Persian encounters. It has been suggested that Acr. 269 (Lyons Kore) was available for scrutiny during the Roman era.[29] The Acropolis inscription that uses the word "kore" to refer to the object dedicated and which may be dated, according to Raubitschek, to ca. 480 B.C., allows for the possibility of a kore dedicated soon after the Persian destruction.[30] Then there is the strange provenance of Acr. 688, which, while it cannot have been seen by Pausanias, was discovered among the foundations of the Mnesiclean Propylaia that were constructed as late as 438/7.[31] Since it was not buried in the debris of the Persian destruction, it must have lain out in the open or stood in place until this date. The least of the korai in quality, one of the smallest and the only one to have suffered the indignity of being built into a wall, Acr. 688, with its vaguely Classical style represents the last gasp of a once ubiquitous Archaic artform. That one of them was being used as building material rather than being treated to the reverential burial that the earlier, larger, and finer examples had earned indicates that the kore's format and purpose were finally obsolete only as late as 438/7, significantly later than the traditional date of ca. 479 (which hinges on the idea of *Perserschutte*), and allows for the remote possibility that some korai remained standing on the Acropolis during and after the Classical period.

The historiography of the korai is resumed in modern times, as reflected in a vast bibliography which has centered primarily on the following: (1) relative chronologies and dating; (2) regional styles, sculptural schools, places of origin of carvers; (3) traditions and innovations of dress and hairstyles; (4) the inscriptions; (5) whom or what the korai represent; (6) what they mean. In addition the Acropolis korai have figured in several studies of Archaic polychromy.[32] Regarding the identification and meaning of the korai, the subject of the present study, a number of theories have been proposed, falling into four categories: (a) particular goddesses (Athena, usually, on the Acropolis); (b) heroized or other mythological figures; (c) priestesses or young women or girls in the service of the deity, such as *kanephoroi* (processional basket-bearers) or *arrhephoroi;* (d) generic pleasing images, ἀγάλματα ("delightful gifts"), to the deity. Of the above only "c" and "d" allow for a high level of individuality or for the possibility that some of the korai may represent likenesses of living, mortal women, which, just because they are unnamed, need not be assumed to have been intended for anonymity.

The two theories about the identities of the korai which have gained the most currency are what we shall call for convenience the "divinities" theory and the "agalmata" theory. The latter has always had a kind of all-purpose appropriateness. In his recent monograph on the Athenian Acropolis Jeffrey Hurwit characterizes the essence of the theory: "Traditionally, *korai* have been considered generic maidens—embodiments of an aristocratic ideal beauty, anonymous girls meant simply to adorn the sanctuary space and so please Athena."[33] Andrew Stewart puts it somewhat differently: "For [the archaic spectator] they were surely just a 'delight,' pure and simple, their satisfactions so interlaced and conventionalized within the genre that everybody gained and no one needed to question further."[34] An interesting variation on the theory has recently been presented by Robin

Osborne, who, noting that the term "agalma" is not (with one exception) used in dedications of kouroi, associates the kore-as-agalma with "the world of exchange of precious objects," which, of course, included women. Consequently, Osborne argues, "it is not just appropriate but inevitable that *korai* be used to mark the relationship between *men* and the gods," and, when confronted by the male viewer, korai serve to draw men's attention to "the world where dressing up in finery, offering gifts and offering them in a particular manner, where women matter."[35] As Osborne's comments make clear, some material support for the theory can be found in the inscriptional record from the Athenian Acropolis: the expression ἄγαλμα (or alternatively, τόδ᾿ ἄγαλμα or τὸ ἄγαλμα) does occur, as we have already seen, in the votive inscriptions from the Acropolis but only occasionally, yet only a very few of the inscriptions which include the term accompanied korai.[36] And before too much significance is attributed to the written word, we should recall that all of the Acropolis inscriptions are formulaic and the individual components of the formulae as well as their combination in any given inscription are not as informational as we might like and, furthermore, may have been randomly selected.

Part of the appeal of the agalmata theory is that it does not necessarily conflict with other theories of identification. The concept of a statue as delightful gift to a divinity constitutes one of the more venerable ideas about images to be encountered in the ancient world. Statues and the aesthetic quality of delight or pleasure are so intertwined in Greek thought that the term ἄγαλμα eventually becomes the most common word for statue, especially of a divinity. The reasoning is simple: if an image is delightful to look at, it honors the deity by its appearance and becomes a source of continual pleasure for the deity. This can be true whether the statue is a votive or a cult image, or whether it is meant to represent the divinity or the worshiper; both kinds of votives are attested in the Archaic period. It may be worth noting that, in this case, the naming of an object is motivated by an abstract concept that is descriptive of its primary function. An intangible quality is metathesized into a name for a concrete object. The naming process begins with an idea. As a word for a statue, agalma is a *mimēma* of the intangible quality, that is, delight or pleasure, most closely associated with an image. Naming by likeness, as Cratylus seems to be saying in Plato's dialogue (*Cra.* 434a), is preferable to and etymologically more likely than naming by chance sign. The term "agalma" is intriguing in that it incorporates a notional dimension to the naming by likeness. And the idea of delight or pleasure remains a cornerstone for the creation, use, and reception of statues for much of antiquity.

The term is used of real women in literature. Helen of Troy is called a gentle "agalma" of riches at Aeschylus' *Ag.* 741; Iphigenia is an "agalma" of Agamemnon's house at *Ag.* 208; both might be considered possessors of beauty of the same nonidealized form which is found in the korai. In Euripides (*El.* 175, 192) both Electra and the chorus are able to capture with a single abstract term, ἀγλαῖαι ("splendid vanities"), the materialistic essence of the typical array of jewelry and accoutrements worn by well-born young women, the sort of things which Electra misses in her present state and which the sympathetic chorus offers to lend to her.[37] The Acropolis korai wear just such an array in the form of earrings, necklaces, and brace-lets, including, on Acr. 269, a pair of dangling earrings, in this case carved, although actual metal attachments are documented in the group.[38] We shall return to such imagery and its literary comparanda in Chapter Four.

Whether or not ἄγαλμα and ἀγλαῖα belong to the same family of words may be arguable, but the contexts in which they are used are comparable. The adornment of an already lovely young female body with a panoply of exquisite accoutrements, especially if made of precious materials, results in a creature of even greater delight, one to satisfy both gods and mortals. In the case of statues a third conceptual layer is implied. The marble im-ages are themselves beautifully carved and painted objects; the young women represented are in the prime of their youth; and they (both statue and "girl") are outfitted with ornaments, carved, painted, or real. Thus the statues become in and of themselves agalmata, a status more suitable to objects than to persons. Viewed in this way the kore as a type may be regarded as the product of an attempt to personify an abstract condition peculiar to females which is parallel to that which is sometimes identified as *kalokagathia* ("comeliness/nobility") in the kouros.[39]

Even the modern viewer finds it easy to be persuaded that the korai are agalmata in this, the earliest and most etymologically correct sense. Sim-ply put, since they are votive offerings and are delightful in appearance, the statues are by definition delightful gifts, regardless either of whatever other meanings or allusions may have been intended by their creators and commissioners and attached to them in ancient times, or of whomever, if anyone, they represent. But in the end the agalmata theory can offer only a partial explanation for the korai's existence. It is significant that, from the beginning of their modern history, among those who have seen or written about the korai, most have posed and addressed the question of who they are. For there is a specificity about the appearances of these figures that is hard to ignore and which is not entirely explained by the undeniable fact of their being agalmata. A brief overview shall reveal that, throughout the history of scholarship on the korai, a certain tension is evident between the intuitive recognition of the particularized physical appearances of the statues and the received wisdom that mimetically realistic images are not found in Archaic art. Again and again the details of polychromy, dress, hairstyles, and accoutrements are tallied, and their variety noted, but when it comes to making a judgment about the statues' identities, most commentators have retreated to the neutral territory of the agalmata theory.

Among those who have been willing to acknowledge that the korai are something more than agalmata, most of the interest has centered on whether they represent goddesses, nymphs, or lesser divinities, and if so, which ones. This is the essence of the "divinities" theory.[40] Since it is the Acropolis and they are statues of females, the primary candidate should be Athena. Then, however, the fact that there are no evident attributes associated with this goddess on any of the korai would need to be explained. Oddly enough it seems as if the divinity theory should have been eliminated early on. One of the earliest observers and admirers of the Acropolis group, Henri Lechat, realized that in order to be goddesses the statues must have attributes, absent among the korai, and they should look generically divine, that is, all relatively like each other, and they do not.[41] Yet in spite of his inability to discern attributes and his observing with obvious admiration the breadth of the statues' individuality, Lechat ultimately retrenched behind a variant of the agalmata theory.[42] But merely by calling attention to the problem posed by the absence of attributes, Lechat had immediately identified the most telling category of evidence against the divinities theory, but he also understood a more subtle point, that the individuality is a sign that, if the korai are goddesses, they cannot all be the same goddess, since they look so different. Any subsequent attempt to assign a divinity to each kore would therefore require a wide range of divinities to be represented, resulting in a situation that is far more complex, problematic, and, finally, implausible than it need be.

There are exceptions, however. In spite of the absence of obvious attributes, two statues in particular, the small-scaled Acr. 679 (Peplos Kore) (fig. 1) and the colossal Acr. 681 (Antenor's Kore, dedicated by the potter Nearchos and signed by the sculptor Antenor) (fig. 2),[43] have periodically been identified as goddesses; they remain the best candidates for divinity among the korai. Brunilde S. Ridgway, the most formidable advocate of the divinities theory, has put forth an attractive proposal that the Peplos Kore is a sixth-century statue mimicking a seventh-century cult statue of a goddess such as Artemis or Aphrodite.[44] Ridgway is to a degree convincing because, in the case of Acr. 679, what might be considered archaic costume for the time, Doric peplos, when Ionic chiton and himation were the prevailing fashion,[45] and the rigid, *xoanon*-like stance are seen in combination with an advanced sculptural style and technique. The small scale and the understated, nearly imperceptible nuances in the modeling of the forms make the Peplos Kore more akin to Late Archaic works like the Kritios Boy and the male torso Acr. 692, as well as the horse Acr. 697, than to earlier korai and to the Rampin Rider, with which the statue is often stylistically associated.[46] No one has put it more accurately than Humfry Payne, who first drew attention to the numerous subtleties which reward the keenest observer of Acr. 679, when he concluded that "when one considers . . . the power of the peplos, even in much later sculpture (at Olympia, for instance), to substitute its own architecture for that of the body, the independence of the body beneath the dress of this statue is really remarkable."[47] It is undeniable that Acr. 679's apparently late style contrasts sharply with the archaizing garment and the "statuesque" posture. However, rather than being evidence of an earlier date, as is often believed,[48] these archaisms could be signs of an intentional imitation of an older statuary type in order to make it clear to the viewer that a statue rather than a live body is represented.

It is instructive to compare the representation of an Archaic statue on a red-figured kalpis by the Kleophrades Painter, which shows Cassandra seeking refuge from Ajax beside an old-style statue of Athena which, as has frequently been pointed out, looks very much like the Peplos Kore.[49] It is true that Acr. 679 wears a more complicated series of garments than the simple peplos shown in the two-dimensional example. There would be greater opportunity for the kind of expansion of detail that leads to realism in a monumental statue-in-the-round than on the irregular surface of a vase on which the depiction of a statue is but one element in an elaborate pictorial narrative. And further, one must not be misled by the apparent depiction of the feet of the statue on the vase as one in front of the other, something which does not occur in the Peplos Kore. By contrast, the majority of the Late Archaic korai from the Acropolis are depicted as if in motion, a point to which we shall return. The body of the pictured statue is frontal, while the head and feet are shown in profile, a device likely borrowed from Egyptian art and thereby an additional token of archaism; no sign of one leg being placed in front of the other can be detected beneath the peplos.

In addition to the archaizing dimension to the *wechselseitig* ("side-changing")[50] pose of the figure, there is a more mundane explanation: the painter has avoided foreshortening in his depiction of the feet. Drastically foreshortened feet required by a fully frontal view are both difficult to bring off and exceedingly ugly even when they are; for these reasons, they are a rarity on Archaic pots, as is full frontality in general. Just how hapless less-than-masterful foreshortening can appear is evident in the rare examples attested in Egyptian wall painting of artists' attempts to deviate from the canonical modes and depict a figure, usually a member of the under classes, in action as if from a single point of view.[51] Few draftsmen, ancient or modern, have possessed the skill of a Michelangelo to make every occurrence of foreshortening an occasion for beauty. Finally, on the vase, the manner of representation adopted for the statue is being set in contrast with the later style of the live protagonists of the scene; without doubt, it is to be read as a representation of a statue, an image of an image, leading to the conclusion that Acr. 679 might be read this way as well. Pausanias (9.40.3–4) mentions, among a list of works by Daidalos that were extant in his time, a small *xoanon* (wooden statue) of Aphrodite at Delos that did not have feet but ended in a squarish "schema." The association of squareness in a statue with age and divinity is perpetuated, perhaps, in images like the Peplos Kore and the statue of Athena on the Kleophrades Painter's vase.

In an article constituting the most sustained argument for the divinities theory to date, Ridgway amasses a body of ancient evidence about the use of distinctive headgear as an indicator of divinity in order to make a case that the metal rods found emerging out of the heads of some sixteen korai, usually identified as the remnants of *mēniskoi* ("little crescent-moon-shaped umbrellas"), once held attributes, now lost, which would have certified the statues' divine status.[52] This time she focuses on Acr. 681, which, she argues, once wore an elaborate helmet like those seen on contemporary Panathenaic amphoras and later in the chryselephantine statue of Athena Parthenos by Pheidias.[53] Although Ridgway brings an impressive amount of comparanda to her argument, in my view she assumes too much in her final assessment of the entire corpus of korai as a result of the admittedly strong case made for Acr. 681: "It is therefore time to view *all* Akropolis korai in this light. To say that they represent goddesses or divine beings is to do no more than extend to these luxurious marble offerings the same interpretation that is routinely given for any terracotta statuette found in a sanctuary."[54] Some may be reluctant to take the leap of faith necessary to accept that the existence of the only iconographical indication that the Acropolis korai represent divinities must be argued by absent evidence. Hurwit, however, follows Ridgway in believing that the Peplos Kore, by virtue of a hole pierced through her right hand, is either Artemis (if she held an arrow) or Athena (if she held a spear), and that

Antenor's Kore "almost certainly" wore a helmet and thus must represent Athena.[55] It may be significant that, in a monograph on the Athenian Acropolis, Hurwit approaches the important question of the identities of the Archaic korai with some trepidation, not the least revealed by his brevity on the subject; he finally implies rather than argues that the remaining korai which retain portions of metal rods, in Hurwit's view, evidence of a helmet, may also represent Athena.

If one rejects Ridgway's interpretation of the broken and twisted metal rods that are still to be seen jutting from the heads of some korai, the identification of their purpose remains a persistent question. The commonly accepted interpretation, that they are the remnants of *mēniskoi,* though not completely convincing, at least has the virtue of being less problematic than others. The ancient evidence for *mēniskoi* seems straightforward enough. In one of Euripides' genre vignettes (*Ion* 106–108, 177), Ion lists among his daily chores putting to flight with his arrows the birds who "harm the sacred dedications" in the sanctuary of Apollo. This passage has been used together with other literary evidence like Aristophanes' *Birds* 1114–1117, which appears to testify that statues on the Athenian Acropolis carried bronze μηνίσχοι ("little moons") over their heads as a means to limit the damage to the marble images as a result of continual bird droppings, in support of a theory that the korai from the Acropolis were once outfitted with small bronze parasols attached with rods to their heads.[56]

While it may never be proved, this remains the most popular and the most compelling explanation for the problematic existence of the metal rods. First, it would make sense to devise a means more efficient than the one mentioned in *Ion* to protect expensive objects like the korai from the damage wrought by birds. Second, as a picturesque trope it does not interfere with the impression of real life; young women would have carried parasols to protect themselves from the sun in order to preserve the desirably feminine, pale color of the skin. And third, the literary evidence is strong enough to corroborate both the problem (the vignette from *Ion;* the shooting itself cannot be taken seriously) and the solution. It is true that the metal rods are difficult to account for; but while I am not altogether convinced that they are remnants of *mēniskoi,* or if *mēniskoi* even existed outside of the comic venue of Aristophanes, to my mind no better explanation for their presence has emerged to date. Finally, the obligation to explain the function of the metal rods on some of the korai as a feature specific to korai is lessened by the fact that other votive statues on the Acropolis were also outfitted with them, including such well-known images as the Rampin Rider, the Blond Boy, and the Kritios Boy, as well as non-Acropolis funerary monuments of mortals such as Kroisos and Aristodikos.[57]

Even if one were inclined to accept the divinities theory, unconvinced that the metal rods are the remnants of *mēniskoi,* the very scarcity of potentially divine attributes among the korai, if they are goddesses, seems incongruous. By the late sixth century B.C., Athenian artists and their patrons appear to have become interested in creating individualized iconographies for divinities. Just at this time Athena and other gods begin to be represented with specific attributes. Athena always wears an Athenian-type helmet on Athens' coins, and a Corinthian-type helmet on the coins of Corinth. She appears with full iconographical regalia in the Gigantomachy pediment, formerly thought to have been built during the Peisistratid tyranny but now convincingly dated down to the Kleisthenic period.[58] The gorgoneion puts in an early appearance in sculpture in Angelitos' Athena at the end of the Archaic period and the beginning of the Early Classical; it had appeared even earlier in vase-painting.[59] On the contrary, we associate a dearth of attributes with the Classical period rather than the Archaic; the respective assemblages of deities on the friezes of the Parthenon and the Siphnian Treasury may be compared.

All in all, in the Late Archaic/Early Classical period, artists appear to be searching for ways to specify rather than to generalize—all the more reason for attributes to be on the korai, if they were meant to be regarded as representations of divinities. Thus it would seem logical that the proponents of divinities theories, if they are to make their case convincingly, be compelled to explain why attributes or traces of their onetime existence are not evident for the majority of the Acropolis korai. When all is said it seems the more difficult position. On the other hand, those who favor the agalmata theory, which leaves open the possibility that the statues reflect the appearances of mortal women, whether universalized or particularized, find themselves in the comparatively comfortable position of engaging the korai on the basis of what is there rather than what is not.

Most of the scholarly opinions about the Acropolis group of korai that have been expressed over the years, including those which favor a version of the divinities or agalmata theories, acknowledge in some fashion that variation is one of the figures' most salient characteristics. This circumstance proved ultimately too troublesome for Lechat, for one, who found himself circling his marble subjects and always ending up face to face with the puzzling presence of variation where sameness would be required (if one deity is represented), and searching for alternative explanations. With few exceptions, however, most of the time the variation has been seen in the areas of hairstyles, dress, and accoutrements, where there are potential alternative explanations for it, rather than in physiognomies, both faces and figures, in which case deliberate particularization would appear to be the only explanation, aside from that default category, stylistic differences. Variation in the physiognomies of the korai is either ignored or, when reported, treated in a perfunctory manner as if without substance, unprovable and nothing more than personal observation which has little relevance to the important questions of identity and meaning.

It is no surprise that the earliest observers and commentators were most often inclined to see individualization, physiognomic and otherwise, among the figures. Struck at once, as these first modern viewers were, by a variety and high degree of individuality in the sculptures that was atypical for Archaic art, or so they presumed, the first questions to be raised after the discovery of the korai centered not on issues of chronology, styles, and influences, but rather on whom they represent. The polychromies of the statues, which were vibrant and detailed upon emergence from the pits and which would be instrumental in conveying this impression, would soon fade, permitting subsequent viewers only a fraction of the visual record that was available to their predecessors, for faded polychromy adds up to missing evidence for distinctiveness and deliberate variation. Moreover, these early scholars, confronted with statues most of which had not been seen since ca. 479 B.C., and charged with the task of conveying first impressions, enjoyed a freedom from the weight of accumulated scholarship that was not to be available again. Later writers would be left with potentially insurmountable liabilities, including an incomplete evidentiary record and the disadvantage of having to measure their own instinctive impressions of the statues against the authority of a body of inherited opinion that was becoming weightier and at the same time narrower in scope.

Considering the relative consistency of the responses of the early writers on the korai, it is surprising that only one, Lechat, took the individualization seriously enough to explore it at length. In the early 1890s Lechat wrote a series of articles on the Archaic sculptures in the Acropolis Museum.[60] One was devoted to the polychromy of the korai and included a section on the "interpretation of the statues" which directly assays the issue of portraiture.[61] Lechat's conclusion, however, was negative. Even the korai whose dedicants are named (Acr. 680, 686) provide no real evidence, Lechat admits, that permits the conclusion that they are likenesses of "the dedicant's wife or daughter." Faced with insufficient evidence for any definitive answer to the question of identification, Lechat with some reluctance ends by articulating a generalizing aesthetic for the statues, although he stops short of calling them agalmata. In spite of multiple published attempts to come to terms with their individuality, for Lechat, the identities of the korai, including the broad question of whether they represent divinities or mortals, remained "une grande incertitude."[62] Yet the issue, not to mention the faces of the korai, continued to haunt him. A few years later, in his books on Attic sculpture before the Persian Wars from the Acropolis Museum (1903) and Attic sculpture before Pheidias (1904), Lechat confronted the problem again, this time with more zeal, trusting, apparently, his own first impressions, and not having fully convinced even himself in his earlier articles that the korai cannot be portraits.[63]

In the earlier of the two books Lechat wrote a chapter on "the question of portraits" among the Acropolis korai that remains the most earnest and most thorough scholarly treatment of a topic which admittedly few others have chosen to pursue.[64] He selected Acr. 674 as a case study for a protracted qualitative exposition of its characteristics in an effort to convey to an audience as yet unfamiliar with the recently excavated statue and in want of adequate color photographs the extent of the individualization that he saw in the image and the distinct, lifelike personality he detected. However, even after a vivid and convincing characterization of the statue, Lechat once more concluded that, granted that individuality is the most outstanding physical characteristic visible in the korai, because neither 674 nor any of the others bears the name of a particular Athenian woman in an inscription, they cannot then be portraits. In the end he sacrificed a plausible, well-argued theory based on secure visual evidence by yielding to the absence of supporting epigraphical evidence. In the habit of privileging written evidence over visual Lechat was not alone in his day nor would he be out of place in ours. Because Lechat's approach to the korai did not gain followers, it appears iconoclastic, but only in retrospect. Lechat's early work on the korai stands as an important precedent for the present study. His barely checked impulse to call the korai portraits based on first impressions is still worthy of attention, since he saw the sculptures in their full polychromy. And while I would not insist on the correctness of the notion that portraiture, as we know it, exists among the Acropolis group, preferring, if one needs a concrete label, to consider them more moderately as intentional likenesses, I empathize with Lechat's persistence in trying to demonstrate the validity of a theory inspired by his first impressions of the newly excavated statues.

While Lechat's work constitutes the most sustained scholarly effort to date to identify and articulate the degree of mimetic realism that is visibly evident in the Acropolis korai, he was not alone in pondering this apparent realism and its meaning. In 1886, the very year of the discovery of the "sensational find" of korai on the Acropolis, Maxime Collignon was suggesting that Archaic sculptors, in direct contradiction to what was being said about the lack of naturalism in their products, were instead "what in our day would be called realists," and that "there is no nearer approach to nature in art than in the marbles of this period." Collignon went further to claim, perhaps overreaching, but not entirely without credibility, that Archaic masters "copied from life" and, of their creations, that their "very exaggerations . . . are a pledge of truth."[65] A few years later, after he had been able to study the newly excavated korai, Collignon would ask of them, "Ces images sont-elles des portraits?" ("Are these images portraits?") Ultimately, he would answer in the negative; like others before and after him, Collignon, his earlier positivism on the matter notwithstanding, was unwilling or unable to conceive of the possibility of mimetic realism in the korai, all the while cataloging an impressive list of their individualities.[66]

Similar views are expressed by another early observer, Franz Winter, who made some brief but remarkable and seldom-cited comments on the Acropolis korai in a Habilitationsrede titled *Über die griechische Porträtkunst* from 1894.[67] He includes the recently excavated korai among examples of Archaic sculptures which betray an interest in qualities that may be associated with portraiture. His reasons for considering the Acropolis korai, as well as some other Attic kouroi, "Porträtstatuen" are worth reviewing. Winter dispenses with those korai which "durch die Zugabe von Attributen als Göttinnen charakterisiert sind" ("through the addition of attributes are characterized as goddesses"), although he does not specify which he has in mind, and concentrates instead on those which are neither representations of "Kore" or "ein ideales Ehrengefolge der jungfräulichen Burgöttin" ("a group of generic attendants of the maiden city-goddesses"); presumably, *arrhephoroi* or *kanephoroi* are what he has in mind here. From these korai, that is, the majority of the Acropolis group, which represent "bestimmte Personen" ("specific persons"), Winter concludes that "Wir lernen . . . die Töchter aus den Häusern des athenischen Adels kennen" ("We get to know . . . the daughters of the houses of the Athenian aristocracy"). He goes on to take note of the "Vershiedenheit nach Stoff und Zuschnitt" ("differentiation in material and style") among the members of the group, which he sensibly associates with the emulation of real life.

Winter further observes the individuality of the "Köpfe" ("heads") of the korai, from which "keiner dem andern gleicht" ("no one resembles another").

Winter iterates a point made at the beginning of my own study, that it is only through viewing the entire series together that one is able to gain the correct impression of how these statues were viewed in antiquity, and it is this consolidated view that results in an "almost unsettling" impression of lifelikeness which is driven by the condition of differentiation: "jeder sein so bestimmtes individuelles Gepräge hat, dass man sich *beim Anblick ihrer langen Reihe* [my emphasis] unter dem Eindruck solcher Fülle von Lebendigkeit fast beunruhigt fühlt" ("each has its own so distinctly individualized character that one, *on looking at the entire series,* almost feels disquieted by the impression of such a profusion of lifelike animation"). Winter concludes his remarks on the korai by pointing out the qualitative differences between the Acropolis group of korai and the bulk of preserved Archaic sculpture, evidence of the work of "bedeutende" ("significant") as opposed to "unbedeutende" ("insignificant") artists, although I believe he unfairly rates their workmanship far above that of "eine beliebige Grabstele" ("a typical grave stele"), of which many are also of high quality. But Winter is right to maintain that "das Urteil über den Kunstcharakter einer Zeit richtet sich nicht nach den schwachen, sondern nach den starken Leistungen" ("the assessment of the character of the art of a period is determined not by its weak achievements but by its strong"), and to consider the Acropolis the obvious source for the best work, or what I would call the avant-garde of the age.

Wilhelm Lermann, in a monumental work of 1907, *Altgriechische Plastik: Eine Einführung in die griechische Kunst des archaischen und gebundenen Stils,* devotes a great deal of space to the recently excavated Acropolis korai. His extensive treatment of hairstyles, facial features, and dress, and especially his detailed, early analyses of the statues' preserved polychromies, accompanied by twenty color plates, will contribute to the presentation of the visual evidence in Chapter Two. Here we are interested in Lermann's consideration of the question of type versus individuality, or what he calls "Typik und Porträthaftigkeit," among the members of the Acropolis group.[68] Lermann, like Winter, sees more individuality in the faces than in the bodies of the korai. Perhaps unfairly, he finds the bodies "lifeless" ("Aber welche Leblosigkeit in diesen Körpern!" ["But what lifelessness in these bodies!"]), succumbing to a still-prevalent prejudice that there can be no realism without naturalism. His admiration for the skills of Archaic artists is tempered with a certain disappointment that their technical expertise appears to fall short of an overall conception of how a human body is constructed ("den Eindruck eines lebendigen Organismus" ["the impression of a living organism"]), noting how rarely among the korai the parts relate felicitously to the whole. By way of an example, Lermann points to the high quality and convincing naturalism of the preserved feet of some korai by comparison with the relative crudeness of arms and hands, speculating, with a degree of credibility, that the latter might have been entrusted to an assistant, although the opposite would seem more logical.

In spite of his reservations about the sculptors' capabilities, Lermann wisely steers his thinking clear of assumptions about Archaic types, positing this sort of stylization, idealization, and abstraction in the art of the later period rather than the earlier. He finds it paradoxical that, with their consuming, almost finicky concern for the particularizing detail, the makers of the korai were not able to achieve true portraiture, even though, as he seems to suggest, they might have been aiming for likeness to the "model." These artists, according to Lermann, were too occupied with surface decoration, missing the greater realities beneath and squandering an opportunity to create a true likeness, which eluded their grasp despite their formidable technical skills. Notwithstanding his reservations about the limitations of Archaic "realism" (my word, not his), it is significant that, throughout his lengthy discussion of the Acropolis korai, Lermann speaks freely, even offhandedly, of "models." In an echo of Collignon, he writes: "In dieser reifarchaischen Zeit hält sich vielmehr der Künstler möglichst an sein Modell" ("in this late phase of the Archaic period the artist adheres closely to his model as much as is possible"); and, specifically of Acr. 686: "das Individuelle des Modells drängt sich bei dieser Figur so stark hervor" ("in this figure the individuality of the model thrusts itself strongly forward").

In a 1938 article on the Parthenon Paul Graindor took up the question of the identity and function of the Archaic korai from the Acropolis.[69] Struck, as was Lechat, to whose work he refers, by a persistent impression of individuality, Graindor is tempted to believe that the makers of the korai "aient cherché à en faire des portraits" ("would have sought to make them portraits") and, like Lechat, he dismisses the idea, at least "au sens moderne du mot" ("in the modern sense of the word"). Graindor carefully considers the range of alternate identifications, rejecting one after the other, first, the notion that they are priestesses of Athena, since the korai are too young to be priestesses, who held their position for life, and second, that they are divinities, following Lechat's argumentation. Graindor ultimately settles on a version of the agalmata theory, with an interesting slant. The statues cannot be simply the "porteuses d'offrandes" ("bearers of offerings") to which they had been reduced by an earlier scholar, according to Graindor, since their persons are far more elaborately ornamented than the meager offerings some of them held. A male dedicant, as Graindor deduces, could offer one of two things to the goddess on the Acropolis, either an image of himself (e.g., Acr. 624, the "Moschophorus") or a representation of a female servant. The korai cannot, of course, be images of their male dedicants. Graindor finally settles on highly individualized generic "servantes de marbre" ("marble servants") which were created, conceived, and dedicated to serve the patron goddess of the Acropolis in perpetuity. For literary support of his identification of the Acropolis korai as servant-figures for Athena, he cites Euripides' *Ph.* 220–221, where a chorus of young women wishes, in retrospect, that "just like *agalmata* made of worked gold, I might have become a servant of Phoebus' at Delphi." The reader will be reminded of Near Eastern precedents, such as, possibly, the statuettes from the Abu Temple at Tel Asmar and, more certainly, the vast numbers of *shwabti* figurines populating New Kingdom tombs.

Writing in 1939, in the introduction to his catalogue of the korai in *Die archaischen Marmorbildwerke der Akropolis,* Ernst Langlotz concludes, as had Graindor, that the statues' youth and "unverhohlene Koketterie" ("unabashed coquetry") would speak against their identification as "Bildnisse von Priesterinnen" ("likenesses of priestesses"). He further illuminates the korai's "Körperlichkeit" ("corporeality") by identifying many of the qualities which had struck earlier viewers, although in somewhat more abstract terms: "Alle Koren zeigen die Heiterkeit ungebrochenen Daseins und die vitale Diesseitsfreude der Jugend, nicht nur im Antlitz mit seinem berückenden Lächeln. Auch Haltung und Gebärde sind von sapphischer Anmut, bisweilen sogar von anakreontischer Verspieltheit." ("All the korai display the cheerfulness of an inviolate existence and the vigorous joy of being alive appropriate to their youth, and not only in the face with its captivating smile. Their bearing and gestures are Sapphic in their gracefulness, while also being Anacreontic in their playfulness.")[70] But instead of finding evidence of mimetic realism per se in the qualities he enumerates, Langlotz attributes to all Archaic "Menschenbilder," including the korai, a commonly expressed, vaguely Platonic notion of idealization which allows them to be conflated with gods and thus permits a view into the early Greeks' notions of godhood.[71] Yet, because of these life-giving and true-to-life characteristics, whose authenticity is supported by the poetry of the age that deals with the lives and habits of young aristocratic women, Langlotz believes that: "Man muss sich diese griechischen Mädchen durch die Vasenbilder und die Gedichte dieser Jahre vergegenwärtigen, um die Koren als sinnlich bewegte, lebende Menschen ihrer Zeit zu sehen, wie sie die Mitlebenden entzückt haben." ("One must view these Greek maidens through the lenses of contemporary vase-painting and poetry in order to see the korai as convincingly animate, living people of their time, just as they charmed their original audience.")[72]

It may or may not be noteworthy that the minority view of the korai is seldom expressed in English. An exception is George Karo, a German archaeologist specializing in the Bronze Age, whose Martin Classical Lectures at Oberlin College resulted in the publication of *Greek Personality in Archaic Sculpture* in 1948. Perhaps the fact that he was not an Archaic specialist emboldened Karo to observe of the Acropolis group: "The variety and the individual character of all these korai are amazing: no two are alike, each has a personality of her own, the first impression as one enters their rooms in the Acropolis Museum is that they are portraits." While his instincts tell him that they could be portraits, so "amazing" is their individuality, Karo, in common with many others, appears instead to have allowed his assumptions about Archaic art to prevail over what he felt in the presence of the statues. He continues: "This is not the case, of course, individual portraits begin far later in Greece. But all these maidens are individual studies in personality, and that adds historical importance to their artistic charm."[73] It seems somewhat unjust to reduce the individualities of the Acropolis korai to "artistic charm," but Karo's sentiments are not misplaced. Karo unfortunately did not permit himself the opportunity to speculate further about what he thought he saw; his brevity suggests that by the time he penned his remarks there was already in place an established tradition of reluctance to allow the visual evidence of the statues' physical appearances to stand on its own as a significant clue to the identity and the meaning of the statues, a tradition that would pick up momentum during the second half of the twentieth century.

It should be clear by now that the early historiography of the Acropolis korai reflects a shared impression that there is a strong sense of individuality on display in these statues. But each of the writers discussed above sought and ultimately found grounds on which to check the impulse to conclude that some members of the group can and should be thought of as early manifestations of mimetic realism or even portraiture, primarily, it seems, on account of preconceived notions about Archaic art. However scattered and incompletely articulated, though, these views have always been aired, and occasionally still are. Most recent is Nikolaus Himmelmann in his important 1994 study, *Realistische Themen in der griechischen Kunst der archaischen und klassischen Zeit*. In the course of considering the subject of Archaic portraiture, Himmelmann introduces the issue of the Acropolis korai as portraits. He acknowledges of Archaic statues that even the modern viewer may wonder at these "unbewusste Lebewesen, vegetative Gebilde" ("living creatures lacking only consciousness, vegetative entities" [?]), with "unbändige Vitalität" ("boundless vitality"), but cautions that, in spite of these qualities, it is misguided to seek "personalities" (Persönliches) behind such images.[74] If personalities are suspected, according to Himmelmann, this is not "evidence" (Aussage) given by the statue itself, but rather it is due to the personal style or "touch" of the artist ("die Handschrift des Künstlers, die verschiedenen Werken ein gemeinsames Gepräge gibt" ["the 'signature' of the artist, which gives distinct works a common character"]). This point leads Himmelmann to remark upon the initial scholarly reception of the korai, noting that the first archaeologists to view the newly excavated statues were somewhat carried away by their impressions ("verblüfft von der Vielfalt scheinbar individueller Formen in Gesichtern und Körpern" ["dumbfounded by the variety of apparently individual forms in faces and bodies"]) and mistakenly believed that what they were seeing were "persönliche Bildnisse" ("personalized depictions").[75]

Himmelmann's interest, however, lies in inscribed portraits, some of which shall be discussed in Chapter Three, so he does not linger on the korai. But the term *Stellvertreter* ("place-taker"), which he seems not to regard as substantial enough a criterion for portraiture, is nonetheless well applied, if indirectly, to the Acropolis korai to describe their function as votaries. By this we might infer that Himmelmann considers the korai almost, but not quite, portraits, while admitting that they appear incidentally to be "unbewusste Lebewesen, vegetative Gebilde" partaking of the "unbändige Vitalität" of Archaic images. If the argument from silence can be applied here, it may be significant that Himmelmann does not mention the possibility that they represent anything other than human beings.

Closest to my own approach to the korai is Lambert A. Schneider, who, in a groundbreaking study, *Zur sozialen Bedeutung der archaischen Korenstatuen,* brings together evidence provided by literary descriptions of young women participating in public festivals and relates it to the physical appearance and demeanor of the Archaic kore as a type.[76] Some of the literary evidence collected by Schneider will be adduced in Chapter Four, although it shall be interpreted somewhat differently. While Schneider's approach is sound and long overdue, his overall conclusion that the Archaic korai are "Wunschbilder" ("ideal images"), and, ultimately, generically ideal figures in spite of the realistic details that he is keen to document, seems at odds with the evidentiary material that he presents so thoroughly.[77] Schneider is led astray, I think, by treating all korai from every period and region as representatives of one and the same phenomenon in Archaic art, whereas I have limited this study to the Athenian korai because, with few exceptions, they can be assumed to reflect a common function, purpose, and attitude, because they are numerous, and because, on the whole, they represent the qualitative best of the kore type. Yet, since much of the information presented by Schneider points in the same direction as the present study but results in a slightly different conclusion, his work has nonetheless served as a valuable precedent and must be so acknowledged.

Two peripheral interpretations by R. Ross Holloway are worth mentioning, not only because they are not often cited in the literature on the korai, but also because they get to the statues' reason for being, even if they do not presume to venture very deeply into the discourse on mimetic realism with which we are currently engaged. The earlier of the articles proposes, with plausibility, that the Parthenon frieze does not represent the Panathenaic procession, but rather an attempt at a visual reincarnation in two-dimensional relief of the appearance of the Archaic Acropolis. This is accomplished, according to Holloway, by incorporating images evocative of examples drawn from the repertoire of types of votive dedications which had populated the Archaic Acropolis before the sacks and burial of the Persian debris, rendering the Classical frieze a veritable restoration of those lost monuments. Holloway associates specific figures and figural types on the Classical frieze with actual votive monuments from the Archaic Acropolis: The male figures leading sacrificial animals on the north and south friezes, with the Moschophoros (Acr. 624); the water jug–carriers on the north frieze, with the bronze hydriae which were dedicated on the Acropolis; the six riders of the north frieze who wear a "barbarian" costume in the form of a long-sleeved chiton, with the Persian Rider (Acr. 606); and, of course, the maidens of the east frieze with the Archaic korai.[78]

The korai have always been compared to the frieze maidens, who also carry things in their hands, but no one else has made such an explicit connection between them. Following Holloway's lead, we may note further that the line of continuity between old and new, pre-Persian and post-Persian, is extended in three-dimensional form as well in the caryatids of the south porch of the Erechtheum, to which the Archaic korai have also always been compared. It may be no coincidence that the Erechtheum caryatids were referred to as "korai" in their day.[79] A pattern of visual retrospection on the Acropolis may be traced from an Archaic votive statue like Acr. 593 (Pomegranate Kore), who holds a ring-shaped object, possibly a wreath or crown, in her right hand, through the maidens from the east frieze, who carry phialai in their right hands, to the Erectheum maidens, who also once carried phialai in their right hands.[80]

In the later of the two articles Holloway attempts to answer the question, "Why was the kore type chosen so overwhelmingly for the major sculptural dedications of the late sixth and first two decades of the fifth century on the Athenian Acropolis?"[81] Richter had noted in passing that the majority of extant korai come from the Acropolis, but did not attempt to draw conclusions on this point.[82] The fact remains that, as Holloway's article reminds us, while we think of the kore type as being ubiquitous in the Archaic Greek world, the densest gathering of them, and the best representatives of the type, are those from the Acropolis. When one thinks of "kore" one thinks of the Athenian Acropolis. The Acropolis korai are "the" korai. The type has to have had some exclusive significance there. Holloway does not discuss the appearances of the statues and makes no definitive statements about type versus individuality, although it is clear that he does not think the korai are portraits. Turning to the Acropolis dedicatory inscriptions, Holloway discovered that the "vast majority" of dedications adopts language that refers to wealth and success, rather than to "public recognition or agonistic achievements," which were the most common motivations for aristocratic Acropolis dedications, and concludes by this evidence that the majority of korai would have been dedicated by successful members of the nonaristocratic merchant class. Holloway thus proposes a social solution to the question of "Why korai?": the kore represented a "generalized figure of good omen, suitable for dedications recording financial prosperity."

If Holloway's appealing theory is correct, then the kore was the favorite dedication of the "nonaristocratic commercial class of Athens," among them a surprising number of artisans, and held meaning for that class in particular, serving as a testimony to its "success" and "aspirations." Such an interpretation of the written evidence complements the interpretation of the visual evidence being presented in this study. As the chosen emblems of the individual success and prosperity of a new and rising class, which owed its existence to Solon's reforms of the first quarter of the sixth century B.C., the korai from the Acropolis make more sense as personalized images. We cannot say with certainty that all of the korai were dedications by the business class, since only sixteen have been securely associated with inscriptions. Holloway seems to proceed from the assumption that, since more than half of the documented Archaic statues or statuary groups from the Acropolis are korai, and since the randomness of the preservation of inscriptions should match the randomness of the preservation of statues, and since the majority of dedications are of a nonaristocratic type, then it is likely that the numerically superior statuary type may be associated with the numerically superior class of inscription. However, if some of the korai represent either *kanephoroi* or *arrhephoroi,* they would have to be aristocratic dedications, since these groups drew upon the daughters of aristocratic families.[83] At the very least Holloway's thesis allows the kore on the Acropolis to be treated as a reflection of nonaristocratic values, rather than exclusively aristocratic, as is usually assumed.[84]

Whether aristocratic or nonaristocratic, the Acropolis korai are examples of expensive private dedications being put to the service of very public display. Under such circumstances, it would be difficult to imagine that the competitive instincts of the ancient Greeks were not aroused in a quest for a unique particularizing mode of representation. There is evidence to suggest that the most prominent sculptors of the day were engaged in the production of private votives; the Athena Lemnia of Pheidias, regarded in antiquity as the "one most worth seeing" of Pheidias' works (Paus. 1.28.2), is an outstanding example of a private votive in the guise of a divinity rather than a mortal.[85] Aileen Ajootian has recently suggested that Praxiteles and his relatives, as well, did "votive portraits," of whose appearance we can know nothing, but which seem in fact to have been considered a kind of specialty for this family of Athenian sculptors of the fourth century B.C.[86] While we know few of their sculptors' names, it is clear that most of the korai from the Acropolis are also from the hands of master artisans. The Acropolis korai could be rare examples of early Greek portraits of private individuals, knowledge of whose existence may be reflected in Aeschylus' *Ag.* 416 (εὐμόρφων δὲ κολοσσῶν, "well-shaped statues"), most likely a reference to portrait statues of Menelaus' absent wife Helen which decorated the couple's house.[87]

If the Acropolis korai were intended as surrogates for their dedicants, in common with the majority of ancient votive images, whether or not the place-taker is the same as the dedicant him- or herself, it is hard not to think of likenesses of some form or another. The general remarks of A. David Napier concerning the early history of portraiture focus on the votive surrogate as effecting a "binding correspondence" with the "spirit" to whom the votive is dedicated. Napier reasons that, on account of this relationship, individuality in the form of "pictorial identification" becomes paramount and, as a result, "invariably portraits will predominate over generic types."[88] It is true that, while women did dedicate votives on the Acropolis, with one possible exception, no woman dedicated a kore.[89] Yet this has not prevented them from being considered *Stellvertreter.* Christiane Sourvinou-Inwood, while she does not use the word "portrait," believes that "votive korai represent young female worshippers, but are not always representations of the dedicator, which is why males can dedicate korai statues." She continues: "To present an image of oneself as a votary was clearly one choice open to those dedicating votive statues. To present an image of a beautiful *parthenos* as a votary was clearly another option open to a male, perhaps even if he did not have a daughter whose image this statue could be deemed to be."[90] In other words there is no reason to assume that the dedicant of a female statue would need to be the very female whose likeness is imitated in order for the statue to perform successfully its votive function. In the case of a man or an older woman being the dedicant, any young woman might serve as model or source of inspiration, whether daughter or other relative who is sufficiently specified in physical appearance for the resultant image to be distinguished among a large group of similar images which functioned similarly in the same space. The array of prosopographical information provided by the Acropolis inscriptions as a whole makes clear the participation of relatives in the votive act; relatives codedicated votives and dedicants dedicated votives on behalf of their relatives,[91] patterns which allow plenty of room for the possibility that votives could also *represent* relatives.

This overview of the historiography of the korai from the Acropolis has given precedence to a nonconventional viewpoint which, though less frequently expressed as the twentieth century progressed, nonetheless demonstrates that the conventional consensus that the korai are simply idealized, generic, repetitive types, whether goddesses, mortals, or simply agalmata, has been challenged before, if not with full conviction. It remains to mention a couple of interpretative options for those who are unconvinced that the korai may be mimetically realistic images, actual likenesses, or even some form of early portrait, but who, like the writers whose views have been addressed, find themselves unable to disavow the particularization evident among them. Neither of these options contradicts the proposition that the korai are mimetically realistic images of Archaic young women, but they may be thought of as representing differing levels of acceptance of the proposition.

The first option is that the human was conflated with the goddess, or made to seem godlike.[92] Divine beauty can be made visible only through observing the best that the human form has to offer; thus, the array of female beauty on display in the korai reflects the array of real-life beauty in the sixth and early fifth centuries B.C., if not the faces of real women. An artist intent on achieving perfect female beauty does not need to imagine it; some real people do possess it. The second option is that the korai do represent generic dedications to Athena in the form of personifications of female attendants to the goddess dressed in their festival garb, and that is all they were meant to be, with the qualification that the sculptors based their representations on the living features and the individual and distinctive *kosmos,* or ornamental accoutrement, of young women they knew, or even that real women modeled for these generic dedications and their features in all their dissimilitude and imperfection appear inadvertently in the finished statue. The practice of using models, whether from memory or from life, inevitable as it would be in any event, and the variety that results from it, would serve the purpose of setting off one person's expensive dedication from another, but would not require that the particular model was meant to be recognized in the final product, only the recognition that a model was used. This option has the advantage of allowing for the *content* of korai to be universalized, but the *form* to be particularized.

CHAPTER TWO

THE REALITY OF APPEARANCES

What it looks like, that is, its appearance, speaks first and most authentically about any artifact. When that artifact is also a work of art, the significance of appearance is intensified. The importance of a reckoning of the actual appearances of the Acropolis korai cannot be overstated, since the deceptively paradoxical "reality of appearances" is the most solid reality upon which any work of art, ancient or modern, rests. In the case of an ancient work, judging by appearances becomes an obligation. As a visual object, and in the absence of written addenda, an assessment of its meaning and its value is dependent upon what we can see. What we can see is all that we can know for certain about an ancient artifact or artwork, especially if it is uninscribed or if its inscription is minimally informative. Of those categories of evidence which might be brought to bear on any ancient art historical problem, the visual, the literary, the epigraphical, and the archaeological, it is the visual which offers the most compelling testimony for the interpretation of the art in question as well as for the larger cultural implications which could follow from this interpretation.

What their statues look like, that is, the reality of statues' appearances, tells us much that is valuable and perhaps otherwise irrecoverable about what Archaic Greeks thought, how they approached life and the making, using, and regarding of images, and likely something of their physical selves and their psyches. The tenses of the verbs in the previous sentence are not incidental. What their statues *look* like in the present is testimony to what existed in the past. In the case of the Acropolis korai the reality of appearances leads directly to an apprehension of the appearance of reality in art, for the realism of the korai reveals at least one form reality can take in art produced during the Archaic period. Stated another way, the appearances of the korai show how reality can be made to appear in the art of the Archaic period.

It is the physical appearances of the Acropolis korai which provide the most authentic testimonies to the success of the mimetic act which produced them; again, the paradox of the reality of appearances. In this study

I intend "physical appearance" to allude not only to the category of foren-
sic evidence about what the statues look like, but also to a particularly
Archaic Greek way of publicly presenting one's femininity which would,
it is fair to say, not be out of place in the twenty-first century of the modern era. In other words, how a woman looks, a great part of which concerns the degree to which she is able or unable to exploit her natural
endowments, including her youth and robust good health signaling her
capabilities for childbirth, as well as her personal taste, skills in weaving,
and the expendable wealth of the male relative to whom she is bound, is
the measure of who she is, how she is known, and how and with what she
shows herself to the outside world. There may never have been a time or a
place in history when physical appearances did not matter for women;
whether beauty, youth, or health is the preferred condition being measured and evaluated, the physical body and when adorned, the manner in
which it is adorned, are the external signs of it.[1] When, in an Attic grave
inscription from the middle of the fourth century B.C., a dead woman,
Dionysia, is singled out for praise on account of admiring her *husband*
more than clothes or jewelry, it is clear that the quantity and quality of a
woman's accoutrements formed an integral part of her public persona as
well as her personal self-esteem.[2] In that they accent contemporary values
for women, disclosing what those values were, appearances are marked
signs. What we seek in the korai is no less than a semiotics of physical
appearances.

The following analyses make no attempt to catalogue all of the visual
evidence or assemble it in the form of a database for further shuffling,
prognostic probing, and ultimate vivisection, a lifeless format, it would
seem, through which to substantiate the trueness-to-life of a group of
ancient sculptures. The demonstration of mimetic realism involves more
than a list of comparative details and cannot be gauged solely by such. In
order to demonstrate that realism—in the guise of an accumulation of
significant meanings provided by multiplying layers of informative, atypical
as well as typical details—could have been a goal for sculptors of the Archaic period, it would not be enough simply to demonstrate variety, or
even individualization, among the korai. The presence of variety among
the Acropolis korai, as we have already seen, has always been noted by
observant viewers, some discovering it through archaeologically rigorous
documentation (Richter) and others through an attempt to explain the
impression of realism which these korai as a group are thought to convey
(Lechat), but its implications have not been fully explored.

Variation in itself is an obvious means for artists intent on communi-
cating realism to attain that end. Nature, being various in its forms, would

require of the artist as imitator a comparable stock of forms at his disposal. Variation is often a reliable clue that mimetic realism is what the
artist had in mind, even when his efforts are not quite successful, because
it does provide more information on a literal level, if without nuance.
However, when a large group of monumental statues produced for the
same location and purpose is under consideration, there may be alternate
explanations for the presence of variety. One artist might desire his product to look distinct from those of his peers in the interest of competitive
rivalry or he might want to indulge in virtuosity for its own sake, both of
which are likely in ancient artisanal practice, as evidenced, for example,
by the taunt "as never, Euphronios" inscribed on a red-figured amphora
by a rival painter, Euthymides.[3] Or one patron might have more money
to spend on his or her votary than another; this would likely result in his
or her statue being larger, more elaborately carved and painted, and accoutered with a broader array of precious materials, such as bronze or
glass. The point is that variety can in many instances be explained on one
or more grounds other than intentional mimetic realism. Yet, regardless
of whether the direct inspiration was economic or artistic, the result is the
same, an increase in the degree of perceptible realism among the statues as
a group. If more money was allotted for the making of a statue, and a
more realistic image resulted, then it might be assumed that more money
provided an excuse for the artist to indulge to a greater degree his, and
perhaps his patron's, interest in a mimetically realistic votive image to
serve more forcefully than another the purpose for which it was intended,
continuous veneration of the deity to whom it was offered.

Mimetic realism in the korai as manifested in the evidence of physical
appearances permits discovery through two separate analytical approaches
which are interwoven throughout this chapter: first, through a typological
approach which cuts across the material in documenting those particularized features of individual korai which are noteworthy witnesses for variation, and second, by focusing at greater length on how these features function as indicators of individuality in specific examples. The categories to
be treated include eyes, noses, mouths, skin tones, composite physiognomies, hair, garments, accoutrements (headdress, footgear, jewelry), and
general body structures. Some of this visual evidence can be verified today
by a visit to the Acropolis Museum. For what can no longer be autopsied,
that is, those once polychromed features which have faded or disappeared
since being re-exposed to light, it is imperative to consult the published
observations of the excavators, as well as the early Acropolis Museum cata-

logues, graphic reproductions, and the like to help to reconstruct what has been lost.[4] It will become apparent that the early studies of the Acropolis korai reviewed in the previous chapter are now part of the statues' otherwise irretrievable history and thereby significant evidentiary sources for all subsequent interpretation of these statues; in short, these studies have moved beyond their status as secondary sources and have joined the ranks of primary sources on the korai and, as such, have become an essential part of the statues' historiography.

An overview of the physical appearances of the Acropolis korai, feature by feature, will reveal that particularization is a conspicuous presence in the group, and that, when the results are assessed, the statues will be seen to be in many respects as different from one another as they are alike in their common kore format. Skeptics may counter that the most noticeable characteristics of the korai are not those on which attention is focused here, but rather those characteristics which typify Archaic art all over the Greek world, such as the bulging almond-shaped eyes, incorrectly rendered, the high cheekbones, the frozen smile—in other words, those stylistic traits which make Archaic art Archaic. However, if one seeks to discover the intentions of the Late Archaic artistic avant-garde that Attic art represents, regardless of the regional origins of its sculptors, he or she must be ready to look beyond these common features. What the Acropolis sculptors did in addition to or in spite of these inherited Archaic mannerisms and motifs is more significant for this study than how they adhered to type. Therefore, throughout the following we shall focus on the atypical rather than the generic or typical, while acknowledging that the typically Archaic is by no means absent in the Acropolis group.

EYES

The korai exhibit as broad and as various a range of eye color, some of it successfully naturalistic, some not, as occurs in real life. At present the most common color of irises is red, which is contrary to nature as we know it now, as surely it was in the sixth and fifth centuries B.C. But there is an explanation. Because red is an essential component of formulae for achieving numerous other colors which occur in nature, it is the most used and most frequently preserved pigment in antiquity.[5] All of this red should not be regarded as intentional; it is as often the case that red is all that remains of a mixture of hues originally combined to make diverse hues and tones of brown, formulae which may also have included blue and yellow pigments in varying amounts and intensities. Furthermore, red paint, stain, or dye is the most tenacious of colors. Discussing the effects of strong sunlight on colors in her still-useful dissertation of 1947, Penelope Dimitriou observes that "red is the color least affected by light."[6] It is also possible that in some cases the preserved red once served as a kind of underpainting or foundation,[7] in a process something like the system of glazing in oil painting, for other colors which have proved more fugitive.

"Red" eyes in the korai are usually paired with red hair. Then as now it can require a substantial amount of effort and outlay of expensive pigments to achieve a desired hue; it is not surprising that the same color is put to double or triple representational duty once a good-quality sample is produced. While some of this red hair was likely originally intended to be a hue or tone of brown, resulting in matching hair and eye color, as is often the case in nature, there are also instances of apparent attempts to differentiate between eye and hair color on an individual kore. Of the irises whose polychromy is still visible, the preserved reds are far from uniform, ranging, according to various opinions, from light red ("Hellrot") (Acr. 686) to ochre-red ("Eisenrot") (Acr. 679), to brown-red (Acr. 673), to brown with traces of black and dark red (Acr. 684).[8] This variation thereby suggests that the artists were seeking to articulate various hues and tones of brown and dark blue to violet, which would require a red additive to a predominantly blue pigment base.

But while it is the predominant color, red is by no means the exclusive color of eyes. Acr. 683, according to Guy Dickins, the compiler in 1912 of the earliest Acropolis Museum catalogue, had yellow-ochre pupils when excavated; Langlotz, writing in 1939, concurs.[9] Today the eyes of Acr. 683 (fig. 3) appear to be red surrounded by brown for the iris and blue for the pupil. On the whole Dickins saw more yellow-ochre features than any other cataloguer, probably because this color was visible in the early years after excavation but not thereafter. Rather than concluding that Dickins' color perception is faulty, as has occasionally been implied, it is preferable to suppose that, of all colors, those in the yellow-ochre to olive-green portion of the spectrum fade most quickly.[10] Regardless of the original coloration, it may be deduced even from the present appearance of kore 683's eyes that the polychromer, who could have been a different person from the sculptor—since it is highly likely that, in the Archaic period as later, differently trained artisans were responsible for the carving of statues and their painting[11]—went to some trouble to represent irises of a dis-

tinctive, unusual hue that was difficult to achieve by means of the colors
he had at his disposal.

Perhaps for similar reasons, Acr. 681 had eyes of either inserted or
inlaid purple glass with inset eyelashes; Acr. 682 had much the same
arrangement.[12] Acr. 674 has remarkably dark eyes and eye sockets, still
today much as described by Langlotz, with black brows and eyelids, chestnut brown irises surrounded in black, with black pupils (fig. 4).[13] Acr.
688 has gray-blue irises with incised outlines.[14] The incision may be either
for visual emphasis or for technical purposes, to contain the freshly applied wet color;[15] the much larger and more expensive kore Phrasikleia
(fig. 46) also has incised irises that echo the circular incisions that decorate her peplos. A puzzling ancient term used of Athena's eyes has been
associated with kore 688.[16] Pausanias (1.14.6) describes the statue of Athena
next to the Hephaisteion in Athens as having "γλαυκούς" ("glaucous")–
colored eyes; γλαυκῶπις ("glaucous-eyed") is a common epithet of Athena
in Homer, but no one is precisely sure what it means, or whether it refers
to eye color at all.[17] Acr. 688 does not, in anyone's judgment, represent
Athena, but the unusual coloration is nonetheless evocative of Athena's
epithet.

A first impulse may be to explain these exceptional instances of eye
color in the korai as evidence of a patron getting more for his money;
logically, the higher the price, the larger the statue, the finer and more
extensive the carving and polychromy, and the more numerous the additions in expensive precious materials. There are, however, korai just as
elaborate as the ones mentioned above which do not have eyes of precious
material, whereas if this premise were valid, they might be expected to do
so. Such apparent incongruities, however, are relatively common among
the Acropolis korai and not easily explained; for instance, Acr. 682, by all
accounts the most ostentatious of the group, has carved buttons on the
sleeves of her chiton while those of smaller, less impressive-looking Acr.
684 were of added precious material. Perhaps, in the case of the exceptional eyes, the desire was to achieve a naturalistic hue which could not be
adequately rendered in paint. All in all it is a tribute to the skill and re-
sourcefulness of the Acropolis artists that such a naturalistic range of eye
color was achieved, for the most part, with success.

As for the general configuration and disposition of eyes, it must first
be acknowledged that most of the Acropolis korai are outfitted with typically Archaic-looking eyes. Yet there may be noticed a few examples of
structural differences, in which there is an evident effort to individualize
eye structures by the addition of details that, while not always successful

essays in naturalism, nonetheless betray a sense of striving toward mimetic realism despite the usual Archaic formal constrictions. Acr. 643, 672, and 686 have incised wrinkle lines on their upper eyelids, in the latter two cases originally painted red.[18] Acr. 696 (fig. 5) has eyes which are nearly Classical in form, with convincing eyelids and tear ducts. In fact many of the korai have eyelids. It is odd that some of the very latest, like Acr. 688, do not have proper eyelids; one wonders whether an individual sculptor developed an idiosyncratic way of rendering eyes and his whole workshop then produced them that way, or whether this is due simply to the inferior quality of this statue. In the light of the variety in evidence, it is tempting to speculate that at least some of the generic, or typical, qualities that recur among the Acropolis korai are a result of the whole group having been carved by a relatively small number of artisans, since, judging from the overall high quality of the work, which has often been noted, only the most skilled seem to have been employed for works which were intended for the Acropolis.

A kore may have her eyes set at an acute angle, their lids partially closed, her head bowed, her gaze slightly downcast, perhaps in a gesture of modesty, perhaps as if to assure herself that she is not stepping on her skirts, or perhaps as a concession to the viewer, who would often find him- or herself substantially below the statue's gaze. Acr. 674 (fig. 6) may be the most striking example of the trope on the Acropolis.[19] Ellen Reeder has recently collected evidence to show that Greek women were expected to incline their heads and lower their eyes in the presence of men as evidence of their *aidōs* ("modesty") and *sōphrosynē* ("discretion"), both sexual and social, although she does not mention the korai in this context.[20] Meeting of eyes between male and sculpted female would suggest an overtly erotic situation comparable to that of real-life eye contact.[21] This would offer a sociological explanation for the prominence of this combination of features among the Acropolis korai, which are all of the appropriate age group for relations with men, that is, marriage.[22] But downcast eyes are not the only type to be seen among the korai. A kore may have aligned eyes, chin parallel to the ground, and look straight out at the viewer (e.g., Acr. 672, 681, 684, 686 [fig. 7], 688). Any or all of these and combinations thereof may represent optical refinements, conventions, inherited types, or simply the sculptor's continuing struggle with naturalistic representation, or they may be a meaningful feature. In most instances the positioning of the eyes was probably not intended to convey additional mimetic information about the particular young woman depicted, but we cannot be sure. Variety alone speaks on behalf of intentional individualization.

NOSES

So few of the Acropolis korai have their noses intact that it is difficult to characterize them one way or another. Generally speaking, preserved noses are broad-bridged and square. Some, however, have narrower, softer bridges (Acr. 672, 674 [fig. 4]); others appear to be aquiline or "Roman" (Acr. 673, 674, again). Acr. 682 has the most distinctive nose of all; it is long, pointed, nonidealized, distinctly nonclassical, almost mannered in style, and not especially flattering, as has been noted. The honesty of its portrayal suggests that this singular feature was captured "from life."

MOUTHS

While the preserved reds of hair and eyes must be weighed carefully on a case by case basis, the case of lip color is less complicated. Many of the korai have lips painted red, which is true to life. Yet again differing shades and hues are preserved. For example, in the opinions of various observers, Acr. 686 (fig. 7) has "hellrot" ("light red") lips, while 679's are "eisenrot" ("ochre-red") or "hochrot" ("high-red"), distinct, according to Lermann, from the "Ziegelrot" ("brick-red") of the hair and eyes.[23] An exception is Acr. 674, which, since no early writer comments on lip color, seems never to have had traces of red on the lips, around which an engraved outline is faintly visible today. Their color, however, can be surmised to have been quite dark, based on the evidence of this kore's skin coloration (olive) and eye coloration (chestnut brown).

The shapes and structures of mouths are various and therein true-to-life; only a few examples need be mentioned. Acr. 682 has a pronounced dimple in the middle of the lower lip and the upper lip is fuller than the lower; Acr. 674 has a thin, delicate upper lip and a broad, flat lower lip; Acr. 643 has lips very close to each other in size and shape. As in real life, a kore's lips may be rounded or angular, pretty or plain; some lips enhance the looks of the portrayed; others appear to spoil an otherwise attractive countenance.

Against the notions of variety and individualism, it could be countered that most of the korai feature the Archaic smile, which bestows upon all of them alike a generic combination of youthful happiness, seductiveness, and vigor. The smile, for all that has been written about it, may never be explained. Attempts range widely, addressing it from the point of view of both form and content; most theories about the smile are plausible and in one or more of them may lie the correct answer, if there is one.[24] Regarding its form, the smile could have served as a means to approximate natural appearances before the intricacies of the structure of the human mouth were formally resolved. Or alternatively it may have represented an optical refinement of sorts; to be sure, some of the korai's smiles do not appear so obvious when they are viewed from below.[25] In general it seems that there is a correlation between korai looking down, the smile, slanted eyes, and very high, prominent cheekbones. The fact that these features often occur together might be a sign of the sculptor's attempt to take into consideration the viewer's perspective.

Smiles on Archaic funerary statues are easier to explain. In a funerary context, as in the gold masks from the shaft graves at Mycenae, a smiling face would reassure the living that the dead is enjoying a happy afterlife, in short, that death is not really final. Something similar could be extended to votive statues which could be smiling at the mere prospect of an afterlife granted by the gods. If the kouroi Cleobis and Biton in the Delphi Museum smile because they died young, having just performed the noble deed which rendered them, according to Herodotus (1.31), the second happiest of all men, could not the korai be smiling because they *are* young and happy? At the very least, the fact that not all of the Acropolis korai smile, as we shall see, implies that one explanation may not fit all occurrences of the smile among the members of the group.

In any accounting of the Archaic smile the debt owed to Egypt, certainly formal and possibly also conceptual, must be dealt with. In Egyptian art, facial expressions are rare, and should in most cases be interpreted in the light of the standardization of anatomical parts that was required of all artisans in the employ of the king. Exceptions are few. Ankh-haf of the Old Kingdom does look as if he is sad or pensive, Middle Kingdom kings like Sesostris III and Amennemes II do appear to be anguished and uncertain, and sobriety and confidence are worn on the faces of Old Kingdom kings like Chephren in the same way that age and honor are worn in the sculpted faces of Romans of the Republic. New Kingdom kings such as Ramesses II more often wear a benign expression, even a happy one, suitable to the more optimistic and cosmopolitan tenor of the Empire. It is the latter representations which seem to have struck early Greek artists most strongly, perhaps through accidental affinities of taste or through the effect of their larger numbers. Smiling pharaohs, especially from the New Kingdom, are commonplace. The Thutmosids of the Eighteenth Dynasty are regular smilers, as is Ramesses II of the Nineteenth, but no pharaoh smiles more broadly or more often, and apparently for better reason, than the Sun King, Amenhotep III, also of the Eighteenth Dynasty.[26]

Whatever the precise iconographic purpose in its mass proliferation in portraiture of the New Kingdom, this expressive feature is not entirely unknown in the Old Kingdom, where a faint trace of a smile seems to offer additional physiognomic demonstration of Pharaoh's sublime sovereignty. That, on the other hand, Middle Kingdom pharaohs almost universally frown, with even greater expressive effect, would seem to reinforce the idea that the smile was meaningful in Egyptian art. Given the strength of the hieroglyphic tradition and its continual significance in Egyptian two- and three-dimensional art, the smile could have functioned as a glyph of sorts, in Egypt and subsequently in Greece. William A. P. Childs has recently made the appealing observation that, like the extended left leg of kouroi which signifies the quality of mobility, the Archaic smile functions as a sort of hieroglyph for "speech."[27] In the ancient Near East the smile is not confined to Egypt. Farther east, among Mesopotamian examples, female votives smile, perhaps because they are represented in the act of beholding the deity in continual worship and apparently liking it.[28] As votives to Athena the Acropolis korai could smile for much the same reason. The smile in Archaic Greek art may represent a formal borrowing only, having been adopted from the Near East with its meaning partially or completely detached, or it may have carried with it real meaning, if imperfectly understood, for the Greeks.

But it is hard not to attribute additional conceptual significance to such an expressive feature. The most common suggestion for explaining the smile is that it imparts a sense of aliveness to an image that is lacking due to less than perfect naturalism; some have even argued that the smile is the only feature which animates these statues, otherwise held rigid and inert within the stiff Archaic format. While this theory, in my view, is inadequate as an explanation for all Archaic smiles, it does have particular resonance among the Acropolis group of korai. It is true that, while it is not a prerequisite for lifelikeness in these images, the smile perpetuates an illusion of animation in all senses of the word which cannot help but enhance the overall impression of lifelikeness.

I have often wondered whether there is a connection between the emphasis on the mouth as the source of animation, if this is what is meant by the Archaic smile, and the Egyptian "opening of the mouth" ceremony performed when the mouth of the cult or funerary statue is touched by the same special tool that is used symbolically and literally to open the mouth of a mummy, permitting entry into the afterlife. This rite was essential for "vitalizing" a statue so that it might properly perform its duties as a place for the manifestation of the nonphysical entity for whose habitation it was intended.[29] In Egypt the funerary statue is a repository for the dead person's *ka*-spirit for eternity; this is why one Egyptian word for "sculptor" translates literally as "he who keeps alive."[30] While there is always a strong idealizing component in an Egyptian royal portrait, the statue was in some senses meant to look as much like the depicted in real life as possible, since, theoretically, at least, the *ka* would have to mistake the image for the real body in order to be deceived into taking up residence there.[31] There is a possibility that the close kinship between statues and life that is well documented in Greek literature has its roots in Egyptian ideas about death, the afterlife, the role of the sculptor, and the function of statues, including the opening of the mouth. Greeks could have become aware of this curious ritual either by observing it or seeing it represented. The ceremony is depicted on the walls of New Kingdom tombs; in some cases the statues are shown with a smile.[32] We know that Greeks revered things Egyptian both for their awesome antiquity and their perceived sacredness (e.g., Hdt. Bk. 2; Plato, *Laws* 2.656d–e). It is not inconceivable that some level of acquaintance with and emulation of the ancient Egyptian custom of regarding the mouth as the seat of life is reflected in the Archaic smile. The neoplatonic idea that the eyes function as something like a mirror of the soul as well as a kind of portal might be compared.

Although it is doubtful we can ever know what the smile originally meant to Archaic Greeks, a sensation of vivacious well-being is one of its effects in the korai, whether intentional or not. The smile also adds to the seductiveness of the figures. Most, I think, would agree that the korai are meant to be seductive, and some might agree that they are seductive, both as artworks and as representations of nubile young women. Aphrodite herself is "laughter-loving" (φιλομμειδής) in Homer.[33] The goddess of love smiles (μειδιαίσαισ') in Sappho's ode (fr. 1.14), and the poet herself smiles sweetly in the famous apostrophe to Sappho by her compatriot Alcaeus (fr. 384), ἰόπλοκ' ἄγνα μελλιχόμειδε Σάπφοι ("violet-haired, holy, sweetly-smiling Sappho"). According to Bruno Gentili this pithy verse "expresses, as eloquently as one might hope for from a contemporary and a poet, the sacral dignity that linked Sappho to the divinities she worshipped and the grace she conferred on the forms of love."[34] The korai could be portrayals of young women in love, sculptured versions of comparable imagery in Sappho. A smile can bestow grace, in real life or on a statue. But whether it is grace, love, or something else, in conveying an illusory sense of personality, temperament, or mood, the smile makes the korai seem more real, more empathetic. The smile fills an essential role in the mimicry of life. All said, the Archaic smile remains an enigma, permitting the conclusion that the most self-evident explanation may in the end be the best one: like the smiles of Leonardo's *Mona Lisa* and Watteau's *Pierrot*, as well as a host of other enigmatic smiles in the history of art, the Archaic smile is destined always to remain suggestive, rather than fully revelatory, to the appreciative viewer. Full revelation would answer too many questions, including the major one about whether these statues are the products of art or of nature.

Most of the Acropolis korai smile, but they do not all smile in the same way. If one looks deeply enough, and is willing to use his or her imagination, character traits will seem to emerge from beneath the formal barrier of some of the korai's Archaic smiles. The inscrutable expression of kore 674 (fig. 4), which barely qualifies as a smile, might be contrasted with the soft, beguiling openness of kore 696's expression (fig. 5), and the coy, seductive grin on the face of kore 616 (fig. 8). All three korai smile just perceptibly and each is rendered more lifelike by her smile, but the expressions of two (696, 616) may be read while that of the third (674) remains impenetrable. The smile of kore 616 suggests that she could be a young woman in possession of a ready sense of humor, in contrast to the more reserved appearance of kore 696, beneath whose lips one might picture perfectly formed white teeth, displayed only on rare occasions for the pleasure of a fortunate few. The coarse and smug pursed cupid's bow mouth of kore 661 (fig. 9) is unmistakably repugnant; this kore seems to be a woman whose smile would come slowly, grudgingly, and perhaps at someone else's expense; with this look, it is not difficult to imagine a person whose language could be as indelicate as the contours of her lips. As in real life, the smiles of statues can, on occasion, be less than pleasing. On the other hand, an aura of solemnity surrounds kore 670 (fig. 14) that is unbecoming to a youth in part because of a smile that seems wistful and bittersweet rather than joyous, while kore 683's (fig. 3) taut, resolute Archaic smile suggests that a certain matter-of-factness could characterize the depicted's attitude toward life. Although entirely subjective, this sort of exercise is nonetheless useful for establishing the presence of particularity or difference among the occurrences of a feature which is commonly cited as a symptom of uniformity in Archaic art.

Some korai have only a trace of the Archaic smile, or none at all. Scholars, following Richter's example, have traditionally arranged the korai in a relative chronology on stylistic grounds, including the degree to which they smile. In this scheme Acr. 674 smiles only slightly, so is thought to be later than most of the others, but earlier than 686 (fig. 7), the "pouter," which is rightly judged to be latest of all because it also exhibits a cluster of traits associated with the new Early Classical style. Added to the list of korai with late traits is Acr. 688 which, in spite of careless craftsmanship and small size, exhibits more features of the Early Classical style than any other Acropolis kore, including the absence of a smile. However, the smile may not be a foolproof indicator of chronological differences. There are examples of korai which show no trace of the new style and yet hardly smile at all (e.g., Acr. 672 [fig. 10]). Acr. 684 (fig. 11) and 685 (fig. 12) also have latent Early Classical features, with full chins, aligned eyes, and an apparent relaxation of the facial muscles, but otherwise appear in full High Archaic regalia, in comparison with the more simplified and stylized rendering of the costume of kore 686, which truly presages Classicism. These two korai smile slightly to not at all, depending on the viewing angle. Both have aligned eyes, but while 684 looks straight out at the viewer, 685 looks down, away, and, ultimately, inward, giving her an overall more Archaic appearance, despite the advanced style. In sum it may be said that, among the members of the Acropolis group of korai, the smile may serve purposes other than, or in addition to, chronological ones, and is best treated as a stylistic choice whose potential significance is to be explained on a case by case basis.

Whether they smile or not, the Acropolis korai are wonderfully expressive creatures. Acr. 686 is the only kore actually to frown, as opposed simply to not smiling. But there is no need to attribute significance to this rare, mild display of seriousness. Archaic Greece is not a period in which tumultuous times are mirrored in physiognomies, as in Middle Kingdom Egypt, when a worried look on a pharaoh's face may reflect domestic turmoil or external threat to the world he inhabits and over which he presides. On the contrary, the configuration of facial features in Archaic Greek art has not been crystallized into an iconography. In exhibiting even this expression, however, kore 686 distances itself from the majority of bland, expressionless Early Classical statues with which it is sometimes grouped and allies itself instead with the other Acropolis korai in the tradition of Archaic expressiveness.

This expressiveness, either subtle or overt, plays an important role in encouraging some viewers of the korai, beginning with Lechat, to imagine that they are in the presence of distinct personalities, since it adds another dimension of information to heighten the impression of aliveness for the observer who is willing to be deluded. In this light, the Archaic smile, which is sometimes cast aside as a meaningless convention that, if anything, obstructs the achievement of naturalism or realism in Archaic art, is taken to be a primary ingredient of expressiveness and empathy, contributing to a sensation of illusionary aliveness and ultimately to mimetic realism. Yet it is unlikely to be what could be called, for lack of a better term, a "typified" motif, with typification referring to the practice of overrefining subject matter to the point where it eventually becomes sterile in meaning, really a sort of subspecies of idealization, which can and usually does occur where idealized imagery of one kind or another is preferred—and this is not true of the Archaic period, which was still an age of broad experimentation with the possibilities of mimesis.

Because it cannot be ascertained whether or not the Archaic smile is an artist's convention, and since it cannot be considered a typified motif, the smile fits best in the category of inherited type on the basis of its ubiquity throughout the Archaic world. For this reason, its presence in a work of art of the Late Archaic period in Attica was probably taken for granted, its original meaning, if there ever was one, forgotten. The Archaic smile was clearly optional at the time of the creation of the Acropolis korai. Therefore, it is possible that the iconographical content of the smile is negligible in the Late Archaic period. With the burden of meaningful significance set aside, at least some of the korai can smile by choice and in their own distinct, mimetically accurate ways.

SKIN TONES

The inventory of facial features would not be complete without mention of skin tones. Alcman praises the "silver complexion" (ἀργύριον πρόσωπον, fr. 1.55) of the much-desired Hagesichora. We know that later Greeks attributed significance to the colors of women's complexions.[35] It would not be surprising if differences in skin tones were represented in art, when feasible. This may have occurred in the korai. Early observers noted that Acr. 683 (fig. 3) and 674 (fig. 4), two korai which have similarly dark eye coloring and hair coloring, also had olive-toned nude parts to complement these features; although the skin coloration on both is now very difficult to detect, an overall impression of duskiness still pervades the appearances of these two korai.[36] On the other hand, Acr. 684 still retains a yellow patina on the face with traces of red on the cheeks,[37] and, as expected, this kore's looks are generally brighter in comparison to the other two. Lermann, Langlotz, and Valentina Manzelli all see red in Acr. 674's nostrils and ear cavities.[38] Likely there were additional instances of this kind of particularization and variation of skin coloration whose evidence is now lost.

As these effects would have been laborious to achieve, there must have been a reason for them. Theoretically, at least, the nude parts of korai could have been left white, which was considered the appropriate skin color for women on contemporary black-figured vases as well.[39] Even on vases, however, where the technical possibilities are severely limited, some, like the Amasis Painter, find ways to indicate differences in skin tone; most female flesh is depicted in added white, but some is simply outlined, perhaps to suggest a more normal appearance rather than the ideal, or perhaps to distinguish goddess and mortal.[40] Richter, followed by others, has argued convincingly for the painting of flesh tones in Greek marble sculpture, which she describes only as "pink or buff," but these colors are hardly representative of the full range of flesh coloration visible in real life in a Mediterranean land.[41] To represent subtle differences in skin tone may have been one of the most difficult tasks the Archaic polychromer set for himself. In comparison with the naturally textured surfaces of carved hair, accoutrements, and drapery, the glassy smooth nude areas would present the polychromer with a more difficult challenge, making it less surprising that the effects were ultimately fugitive.[42] If the variations in skin coloration still evident in some of the korai are deliberate and not an accidental by-product of final buffing or some other technical process, then the apparent attempt at variation of skin tones, a detail whose method of execution and effect in the finished images cannot have gone without comment in antiquity, even if it is scarcely visible now, argues most forcefully for the existence of intentional mimetic realism in the statues.

How were customized skin tones achieved? One answer might be provided by the ancient technical process called γάνωσις, which has occasionally been associated with the question of skin tones among the korai and may, in fact, be relevant to it.[43] The primary sources for this practice are Pliny (*NH* 33.122), Plutarch (*QR* 287), and Vitruvius (7.9.3–4). The Delian temple inventories from 279 B.C. include sponges, nitre, oil, linen and wax, and perfume for the κόσμησις (here, "finishing touches") of a statue, any or all of which might have been used for *ganosis*.[44] These later sources do not refer directly to its application in Archaic sculpture, but we should probably assume that *ganosis* was an important stage in the finishing process in earlier periods as well.[45] The etymological association of γάνωσις with the verb γανόω ("make bright" and, metaphorically, "delight") hints as to the purpose of the practice. According to Pliny, in order to protect the coloration of surfaces polychromed with minium (red-lead) against the adverse effects of sunlight and, curiously, moonlight, a mixture of heated Punic wax (*NH* 21.84 gives a recipe) and oil was applied, reheated, and finally burnished, a process which Pliny equates with the polishing of marble (sicut et marmora nitescunt). Pliny does not specify whether by "marmora" he means statues exclusively or whether he means to associate the process with polychromed rather than "naked" marble, but the safe inference is that polychromed marble statuary is included in Pliny's generalizing statement.[46]

Plutarch's colorful ἐξανθεῖ ("loses its bloom"), used specifically of polychromed statuary, seems to imply the same motivation behind the practice of *ganosis*. Vitruvius, however, while his description of the process matches Pliny's virtually verbatim, and is likely his source,[47] appears to be suggesting a slightly different motivation. Always concerned with optical effects and the technical refinements necessary to accomplish them, Vitruvius seems to be saying that infusing the surface of a marble statue with the wax/oil mixture ameliorates the effect of strong natural light, which tends to reduce the visible *intensity* of polychromy.

Such differences among the ancient sources regarding *ganosis*, while admittedly minor, suggest that its purpose was not entirely understood; hence also the confusion among modern scholars as to its precise function. Pliny, by including moonlight as well as sunlight, unwittingly drops a clue that color intensity, which would be reduced equally, if differently, by both sunlight and moonlight, is the primary motivation; he does not, however, fully comprehend the aesthetic dimensions of the process. Vitruvius, on the other hand, seems to be fully aware that the primary motivation for the process was aesthetic.

Both of these ancient explanations, aesthetic and practical, make sense in regard to the korai.[48] All statues placed outdoors would have required protective measures of some sort; the possibility that *mēniskoi* were used to shield the korai from bird-droppings has already been discussed. Homer (*Od.* 3.408) refers to a polished stone throne that is outside the gates of Nestor's palace at Pylos as "glistening with oil," as if to draw attention to both the practical motivation as well as the aesthetic by-products of artificially enhancing the natural shine of marble. In the case of statues, surface shine does more than embolden the natural assets of the stone; it heightens for the viewer the impression of aliveness. Marble lends itself well by nature to the attainment of the aesthetic condition of shine; for this reason it has always been the preferred stone for figural sculpture anywhere that it is available.

For anything other than real light or a rare few phosphorescent substances to shine as if of its own accord is of course an optical illusion. When even a little light shines on most marbles, especially when carved into a three-dimensional form with multiple and varied exposed surfaces, it penetrates the stone to a certain depth before reflecting back to the observer, with the result that the light seems mysteriously to emanate as if from within, as if the stone object is emitting its own light instead of reflecting it. The effect is quite different from the harsh, instantaneous reflection of light on the surface of metal. To the eye conditioned by modern science, marble's dense crystalline structure connotes the absence of life, so removed is it both in time and in aspect from the organic materials which we know to have formed it. What caught the ancient eye, however, was what this stone does with light. The Greeks called marble μάρμαρος because it gleamed and sparkled, and for these reasons it might have seemed alive. In fact ancient thoughts and intuitions about the origins of minerals and the terms in which they were expressed often reached beyond mere metaphor. Marble and other rocky deposits were viewed as growing things which garnered their life substances, like plants, by way of a system of "roots" and even quarrying a rock face did not necessarily "kill" the stone.[49] The quality of shine thus adds vividness to a sculpture, thereby increasing the sensation of illusionary aliveness and making of it an empathetic object to behold. It is no accident that shine and delight are linguistically and conceptually conflated in the cluster of words surrounding γάνωσις and also those associated with ἄγαλμα. Ganymede, whose name derives from γάνυμαι ("brighten up, be glad or happy") and who served as a continual source of delight on Olympus, especially for Zeus, is a living example of γάνωσις.

But there might be an additional explanation for the use of *ganosis*, at least among the korai. Ernest Gardner long ago had suspected that it was used purposefully to color the exposed flesh parts of the statue.[50] Richter disagrees: "Practical experiments do not bear this out." She observes as well that, when such coloration was desired, the nude areas of ancient sculptures routinely were polychromed along with the rest of the statue; no special process was needed.[51] While Richter does argue forcefully for the polychromy of the nude parts of marble statues, she does not believe that *ganosis* added anything to the overall effects of skin-tone variation. Others, however, have maintained that in the Archaic period *ganosis* was applied directly to the naked marble.[52]

Despite Richter's and others' convictions, it remains a possibility that the "slip" or "glaze" which appears to have been applied to the faces of some of the Acropolis korai could be evidence of *ganosis* used not only for the more general purposes mentioned by the ancient sources, but also specifically for the purpose which Gardner suspected, and that, through variation in the number of times the process was carried out and in the intensity of the materials, a variety of skin tones approximating nature could be achieved.[53] And if *ganosis* of a statue was needed for other, more practical reasons, its beneficial side effects could have been exploited simultaneously, including the fortuitous simulation of the subtle differences in skin tones that mimic real life, and the enhancement for the viewer's pleasure of the sensation of aliveness by an artificially induced shininess supplementing and transfiguring the marble's own. The fugitive nature of the effects of *ganosis* would account for the rarity of its preservation in extant statuary and for its subsequent disappearance in the korai which still showed signs of it shortly after excavation. Moreover, only the most heavily applied treatments of *ganosis*, which might have resulted in a darker complexion, would have preserved evidence for the early observers to see.

If Gardner is correct, as I believe him to be, the visual effects produced by applying *ganosis* to the skin areas of marble statues of the earlier periods would approximate those lifelike effects which would be achieved later, especially among the Romans, by means of a higher degree of surface polish, which accounts for the coloristic effects in Roman non-polychromed portraits and, for example, in the soft, translucent flesh of the Hermes by Praxiteles, possibly a Roman copy.[54] Similar effects were sought and achieved in Egyptian sculpture by juxtaposing a highly polished area, usually skin, beside an unpolished.[55] At any rate, if the process of *ganosis* accidentally produced the distinctive coloration of the skin of some korai, then we might expect variations in skin tone to be common rather than rare, since all alike would have received the treatment.

COMPOSITE PHYSIOGNOMIES

Thus far the features of the korai have been treated as separate typological units. But no catalogue of the constituent parts of a physiognomy can fully account for their cumulative effect. Simply put, some of the korai are pretty of face, others are not.

Acr. 682 (fig. 13) has been considered either beautiful in its ostentatiousness or grossly unattractive, by modern standards. The latter view should not be immediately discounted, since Acr. 682 does look distinctly different from any other kore; if she is beautiful, she represents a kind of Archaic beauty different from what we are used to seeing. If she is not beautiful, Acr. 682 would represent one of the rare moments in Greek art when women were allowed not to be comely. Casting objectivity aside, it is hard to believe that the young woman depicted here was as admired for her natural beauty, such as kore 696 would seem to have been, as she was for her possessions and her regal, statuesque bearing. However one assesses their beauty, kore 682's features are unorthodox for a Greek statue of any period. Her head is too large, her neck too long, her face too square, her forehead too high, her nose too sloping, her chin too pointed, and her bones generally too prominent. The eye sockets are far from expressionless even without the glass inlays, which would only have increased their penetrating, gorgonlike effect. With a look that would seem to remind any viewer that his or her proper place is beneath the lady's piercing, unwavering gaze, both literally and figuratively, this kore's demeanor deviates from the norm of the properly deferential attitude seemingly displayed by the majority of Acropolis korai.

By contrast Acr. 670 (fig. 14) appears a shy, introverted creature, with pale, fine, ethereal, and understated looks, exhibiting an expression full of graciousness and gentleness. Even in black-and-white photographs, this kore gives the impression of being fair of hair and skin. One imagines a personality as sweet and unchallenging as the perfect oval of a face with its fleshy, rounded contours, the structure beneath nearly imperceptible, the cheekbones flattened uncharacteristically for an Archaic statue, and the muscle tone soft. Kore 670's small almond eyes with their angular setting appear as if lined with kohl, contributing to a somewhat exotic appearance.

Kore 683 (fig. 3) is less comely than either 682 or 670. She has a nose that is short, stubby, and unrefined; her eyes are large and graceless in their contours, her ears are outsized, her forehead is narrow and receding, and the face which houses her features is too small and round to display all of them attractively anyway. Yet kore 683's expression is optimistic and forthright.

Acr. 687 (fig. 15), a statue of lesser quality than those just mentioned, nonetheless has some distinctive features, including puffy, full cheeks which appear to be fleshy and malleable rather than firm; their uneven surface, as well as the general impression of fullness in the lower face and the prominent smile, suggested the appearance of "dimples" to Dickins.[56] Kore 683 has a prominent cleft chin, while kore 671 has a very long, broad chin, a feature shared by kore 680 (fig. 16). In fact Acr. 671 and 680 look like sisters, as do 670 and 673 (fig. 23), although sizes differ. Acr. 674 (fig. 4) has a moon-face, full and plump at the bottom, with a narrow, shallow forehead, its skin smooth and impermeable, emerging resplendent beneath a Gothic arch of dense, heavy hair, while Acr. 696 (fig. 5) has a high, broad forehead, capped but not dominated by her finer, lighter hair, her fair skin stretched taut and smooth, her cheeks and lower facial structure generally sleeker and less fleshy than Acr. 674's. Acr. 674's face seems boneless, whereas Acr. 696 has cheekbones reminiscent of Greta Garbo; both are beautiful, but one is crepuscular while the other is caught by the full light of the day, and each, in a different way, is a perfect example of how female beauty in an Archaic Greek statue may not necessarily conform to a single ideal.

Critics may choose to explain away the variant facial appearances of the Acropolis korai as evidence of stylistic idiosyncrasies dictated by places of origin and personal styles of individual artists. The precise number of "hands" in evidence among the Acropolis korai is unlikely ever to be determined to everyone's satisfaction, but the consistently high quality of these pieces, in my view, begins to suggest that there are very few. The presence of common or typical elements would seem to me also to be diagnostic for reducing the pool, thereby allowing the atypical elements to function meaningfully, as I am suggesting, as evidence of an individual artist's repertory of mimetically realistic signs.

It is possible that these faces, unnamed but not necessarily anonymous, should be considered intentional likenesses. This deduction is justified by the abundant evidence of attention to individualization of physiognomies, inviting the observant viewer, somewhat in the fashion of a *repoussoir* device, to participate in an artful illusion, in this case, by imagining the unpictured, the distinct personalities behind the lifelike faces. *Repoussoir* is less often associated with sculptures than with paintings, especially still lifes, in which an object appears to extend out into the viewer's space, suggesting an "invitation" to the viewer to "enter" the illusionistic space or to participate otherwise in the illusion. The idea of a *repoussoir* device as a means of illusionism in painting goes back to the earliest extant still lifes from Pompeii and Herculaneum. However, such a device can also function in a sculpture in the form of an extended limb or other object, or even an oblique glance of the eyes, as happens with the Kritios Boy. In the korai, as in many Archaic standing figures, the extended arms which held the offering played the same role as the *repoussoir* device does in the painted still life, effectively bridging the gap between the viewer's space (that is, real space) and the space occupied by the work of art (that is, portrayed space). I am suggesting that something comparable happens with the intentionally and specifically likened faces of the Acropolis korai, which beckon the viewer, as if promising him or her a deeper, more intimate level of acquaintance.

Some may be tempted to reject the notion that the korai are likenesses on the grounds that the term implies portraits of specific individuals and the korai are not historicized, that is, named, an issue which, as we have seen, has been regarded as problematic from the beginning of the modern history of the Acropolis korai. But the view that an image must be historicized in order to be considered a portrait of any sort cannot be sustained in these cases, since it underestimates the range of responses to human creativity in a period in which it was the rule not to record things rather than to do so. A likeness of this type might be considered a "cognitive likeness," if I am correct in interpreting the term "Ersatzähnlichkeit" ("substitute likeness") used by Nikolaus Himmelmann, a writer who is notoriously difficult to translate, which he defines as those classes of depictions "in denen Ähnlichkeit nicht wörtlich genommen werden darf, etwa bei den Bildnissen halb oder ganz legendärer Personen, deren wirkliches Aussehen nicht bekannt sein kann" ("among which likeness may not be taken literally, as, for example, in the case of representations of partly or fully legendary persons whose actual appearance cannot be known"). Himmelmann elaborates on these imagination-based depictions, or "die sog. Phantasieporträts" ("the so-called fantasy portraits"), which, as he claims, "werden aber durch eine Art Ersatzähnlichkeit gekennzeichnet, individuell wirkende realistische Formen, die der Betrachter seinem Porträt-begriff entsprechend unwillkürlich mit der betreffenden Person verbindet" ("are given characterization through a sort of substitute likeness [consisting of] effectively individualized realistic forms which the observer instinctively connects with the concerned person in conformity with his or her idea of what constitutes a portrait [of that person]").[57] Himmelmann, of course, does not make a connection with the Archaic korai, but, thus defined, his concept seems applicable *in reverse* to unnamed Archaic likenesses on the terms in which I am characterizing them. In a way comparable to Phantasieporträts of individuals whose "likenesses" may not be knowable and the fact of their being likenesses must be taken on faith, in the case of uninscribed Archaic "portraits" in which likeness is sensed, it is the absent *names* that must be accepted on faith.

On the other hand, if a name is attached to a statue, as is the case with the kore Phrasikleia, then it must be considered a likeness whether or not it is regarded as functioning successfully as such by modern standards. For *intent,* as Himmelmann notes, is a key feature of likeness.[58] This is portraiture by default, even if we cannot know who is depicted, a category of likening that is merely mimetic and nothing more, because appearances are everything they seem to be. We have seen how some early writers on the korai have concluded, in spite of their impressions as viewers, that achieving likeness is impossible in the korai, since the essential component parts of the face are not fully naturalistic. It is well to recall that, as I have argued, the degree of naturalism is incidental to realism, a premise which must be accepted in order for realism to be conceived (and conceivable) in Archaic art. Moreover, there is no doubt that the sculptors of the Acropolis korai were capable of a high level of naturalistic representation when the search is extended away from the face into areas which are less conspicuous, more "Morellian."[59] These sculptors' capabilities regarding naturalism can readily be judged impressive if the viewer seeks out the few examples of feet which have been preserved, both attached and unattached to korai, among them the left of Acr. 672 (fig. 17).[60] In the faces of the korai, however, the artists apparently strove for distinctiveness and a sense of liveliness and animation, which is more than naturalism alone can convey.

HAIR

The korai from the Acropolis are nearly as famous as Roman matrons for their hairstyles, which are noteworthy for the diversity of color, texture, abundance, and arrangement. In lieu of a visit to the Acropolis Museum, a perusal through Richter's *Korai,* Payne and Young's *Archaic Marble Sculpture from the Acropolis,* or the plates of *AMA* will suffice to persuade the reader that no two hairstyles are exactly alike. Acr. 682 (fig. 13) is the most elaborately coiffed, exhibiting at least six distinct styles of curls, crimps, and braids.

But the manner of wearing the hair is not the whole story; the character of hair changes from kore to kore. Character or quality of hair may best be judged in black-and-white photographs in which, irrespective of style and color, hair seems, as in life, to have texture, density, and vitality. Just how much of the abundant hair exhibited by the korai is real and how much of it is enhanced through the use of wigs or false plaits or curls is arguable. Most Archaic hairstyles seem too incredible to be believed to be composed only of naturally growing hair, making it likely that much of

what is depicted in the statues betrays evidence of the use of hair exten-
sions of various kinds in real life.[61] This is especially to be noted at the
forehead of some korai, where the pattern of hair runs counter to reality,
and where no evidence of a hairline can be detected (Acr. 678, 684 [fig.
11], to cite just two examples), which may reflect an attempt to differentiate between cut and uncut front hair or the addition of a hairpiece. If
Evelyn B. Harrison is correct about the significance of sculptured representations of differing lengths of hair in Greek art, then cut or uncut front
hair of korai could allude to a difference in age.[62] The use of wigs by both
men and women was routine in Egypt, at least among royalty, as attested
by actual hairpieces made of human hair that have survived and by the
detailed pictorial record for the specifics of royal hairdressing among both
men and women.[63] Possibly Greeks did much the same.

That the combination of natural and enhanced hair can be rendered
seamless and agreeable in real-life practice is demonstrated by present-day
fashions. But in the case of the korai we cannot know for sure. Elizabeth
Bartman has recently argued that the abundant hair on display in portraits of Roman women is in most cases the sitter's own.[64] The evidence of
the Acropolis korai demonstrates that, like Roman women's, a young
woman's hair—whether or not it was all hers—appears to have been a
primary focus of her looks, a means to indulge her vanity. It is conceivable
that, in the Archaic period, bountiful hair could have been among a young
woman's most prized possessions, a natural treasure that she need only
arrange more inventively than another to surpass the other in the perennial contest of feminine looks. All of this seems to disappear in the Classical period, when hairstyles become simpler.

The differences in character between the hair of Acr. 674 and that of
Acr. 696 have already been pointed out. Some korai, like Acr. 683 (fig. 3),
have extremely thick hair with neat, blunt ends, which appears as if it is
naturally straight, and therefore artificially crimped. Acr. 687's (fig. 15)
hair is inconsistent in quality. This kore seems to have a thick head of fine
hair, which is plausible; however, the hair is suspiciously full at the top
and front and less abundant at back and sides, which could be an indication of a top-heavy wig. Kore 595 is odd in having the remnants of long
locks in front but no signs of hair at the back, which is not unfinished but
fully rendered with folds and pleats; the head is missing, making it impossible to tell how the hair was arranged.[65] Her hair cannot have been covered by her mantle, as in Acr. 688 and 671, since she wears it diagonally
rather than straight across her shoulder.

Another standard feature, the triangular area formed by the neat separation of the locks between front and back, is treated variously among the korai. In Acr. 674 this space appears to have been left blank, most conspicuously on her proper right side, where the empty triangle is larger; however, it is possible that what now looks awkwardly unresolved might once have been clarified with polychromy. The very different treatment of this problematic area in Acr. 684 (fig. 18) shows just how much attention to mimetically realistic detail the Acropolis sculptors are capable of demonstrating; the area is filled with deeply incised wavy lines which represent with perfect sense the meticulous brushing back of the thick segment of the hair that falls behind. It is instructive to compare the ways in which Egyptian artists treated similar representational challenges. In the case of separate segments of hair in complex hair and wig arrangements, the segments are differentiated by clearly blocking out the separate masses and then varying the pattern used to represent the character of each, as, for example, in the block statue of the scribe Rey from the Nineteenth Dynasty.[66] On the other hand, the triangular area over the shoulders is seldom successfully resolved in Egyptian painting and sculpture. This is especially evident in the massive wigs worn by Middle Kingdom women, in which there is no attempt to represent sensibly the brushing back; instead, the hair is shown as if cropped to accommodate the shoulder, which is unlikely to have been the practice in real life.

The hair of korai 594 (fig. 19), 673, 680, 682 (fig. 20), and 1360, among others, terminates in an untidy line in the back, frizzing at the unbound ends as does fine, naturally curly or wavy hair. This could either be a true-to-life detail or possibly another Egyptianizing turn, or even both at once. I wonder whether this unusual feature of some korai reflects an underdeveloped interpretation of a fashionable and popular wig style worn by New Kingdom Egyptian women, as well as some men, in their portraits, knowledge of which could have affected Archaic Greek styles of wearing and representing hair. This special type is often referred to as the composite wig; an actual example made of human hair is in the British Museum.[67] In Egyptian artistic representations, the wig appears to be composed of two or three different textures and gradations of hair, as in the youthful Louvre princess (fig. 21) probably from the reign of Tutankhamen, who wears the wig in the form of the child's side-lock, where the hair is worn long at one side only, and short or shaved on the other. Encasing the head itself is a hairpiece consisting of a skullcap of cascading, layered curls which fall over the hairline in a manner which could not be duplicated with real, growing hair. The middle tier or layer consists of a thick grouping of fine braids, sometimes arranged in threes. In the case of the Louvre princess the braids seem to originate from within the skull-cap. The lowest tier or layer of the composite wig appears to be a wispier, thinner, but still braided version of the middle tier, possible evidence of the wearer's real hair beneath the two artificial layers.

It is worth considering the possibility that the similarities between the fullness and the complex, overlapping arrangements of hair or hairpieces, a style which would not survive the Archaic period, in Greek korai like Acr. 682, Acr. 684, and Phrasikleia may be explained as an Egyptianizing trend in both the wearing and the representing of hair, especially among females. If this is the case, then the wispy fringe of hair which character-izes the undermost layer of the Egyptian wig may suggest a model for the thin, straggly wisps of hair which appear at the bottom edge of the long hair of the korai mentioned above and others and which at times cannot be accounted for otherwise. Both the Egyptian and Greek examples could, of course, accurately reflect similar ways of wearing hair in real life at different times and places with or without contact. But in the Greek ex-amples the apparent artificiality of the arrangements, the frequent incon-gruity of the ways of representing hair combinations, the unlikely fact of the simultaneous occurrence of fine and coarsely textured hairs and full and sparse hairs on the same head, and the fact that the Archaic, the most extravagant of Greek hairstyles, is relatively short-lived, would seem to reflect an emulation of a model coupled with incomplete understanding of either the actual styling or wearing of hair or, more likely, of the ways of representing hair.

Regarding the colors of hair among the korai, there is an array of shades and hues of blonde, brown, and red. Much the same circumstances which were introduced in the discussion of eye colors are applicable as well to hair, suggesting that, even though red is again the most commonly visible color, the preserved hues are again diverse enough to testify that artists aimed at imitating in pigment the subtle variations they perceived in the colors of real-life hair.[68] This conclusion would have even more justifica-tion in the case of hair color, since a much wider spectrum occurs in nature. Nevertheless, there are at least three possible alternative explana-tions for the various states of polychromy visible on the hair of the Acropolis korai which need to be addressed. Lermann believes that the range of tones and hues of deep reds to yellow-reds is not a sign of intentional variation of brown but is due to differing states of preservation, citing the "richtiges Blondhaar" ("proper blond hair") of Acr. 687 (fig. 22) as the exception that proves the rule.[69] But this explanation is rendered less likely by the fact that the majority of Acropolis korai have a common history, both pre- and postexcavation. It is true that if one follows Richter in spreading out the korai over seven or so decades, then the differing shades and hues of preserved hair colors could be attributed to their respective lengths of exposure to the sun in antiquity. Others, however, more sensibly contend that the bulk of the Acropolis group is so unified as to suggest that they were produced concurrently with each other within a relatively short period of time. Second, individual observers use different language to describe the same color. However, the fact that Lermann and Langlotz, for instance, employ such a wide variety of color language to describe the preserved polychromy of the korai is itself a testimony to a lack of uniformity, whether or not their choices of color terms coincide in every instance. Third, and most serious, is the fact that no two batches of mixed pigments ever result in exactly the same hue; however, when identical formulae are used, as is likely in Archaic Greece, differences are virtually imperceptible unless the resulting colors are directly juxtaposed. Finally, supporting the idea of intentionally varied polychromies is the fact that the range of preserved color of lips is considerably narrower than that of hair and eyes, as expected, since there is less variation in lip color in real life.

Unlike eyes, some of this red may have represented true red hair. Acr. 685 has blue-red or crimson hair and eyes, Acr. 640 has wine-red hair, and Acr. 649 has carmine red hair, with a blue "gleam," according to Langlotz; all were probably originally shades or hues of brown, as indicated by the presence of blue.[70] On the other hand, the hair of Acr. 696 (fig. 5) has been characterized as "lively red" and that of Acr. 662 was once, according to Dickins, "the most brilliant red preserved in the museum";[71] both might indicate an original true red. Acr. 679 also could have had true red hair, because its preserved color is the same as that of her garments, suggesting that either the kore had red hair or brown clothing, the former more likely. There is some disagreement about the hair color of the darkly beautiful Acr. 674 (fig. 4), attesting to its complexity. Dickins and Dimitriou see red and yellow components, while Langlotz sees only red.[72] Elaborating upon this kore's hair, Dimitriou believes that the colors she sees represent deliberate variations in the intensities of red, almost as if to suggest natural highlights.[73] A more satisfying resolution may lie in Vinzenz Brinkmann's recent suggestion regarding kore 674's hair that the color was applied in two distinct layers in order to achieve the desired "chestnut brown": "Die untere Schicht Ziegelrot, darauf ein dunkelbrauner Ocker. In der Zusammenwirkung der Farben ergibt sich ein Kastanienbraun." ("The lower layer [is] brick red, and on top of it [is] a dark brown ochre. A chestnut brown results from the combined effect of the colors.")[74] If Brinkmann's provocative conclusions about Acr. 674 are correct, it is clear that hair colors of korai could be painstakingly customized.

Rare, but represented, are blondes, also of varying hues and shades from strawberry to platinum, as in real life, as well as in the myths and poetry which reflect real life; both Homer (Achilles and Menelaus have epithets which refer to their hair color) and Sappho (fr. 98a) attest to the occurrence of blonde or tawny hair among the ancient Greeks, which both poets treat as a rarity. Acr. 605, 639, and 664 have yellow or yellow-ochre hair.[75] The hair of Acr. 612 has red and yellow components.[76] Most striking of all, and still vibrant today, Acr. 687 (fig. 22) has ochre-red and yellow hair, whose intense coloring has run down onto her cheeks, leaving a rust-colored stain.[77] Interesting are Acr. 673, 680, 686, and 684—the last, it will be recalled, with a yellowish patina on her face and red cheeks—which, while being quite elaborate otherwise in their sculpted details and polychromy, show no visible traces of color on their hair.[78] These may have been the fairest of the fair, or, alternatively, one could argue that there must have been an unusual pigmentation in the hair, since, unlike the majority of the korai, its components were completely fugitive. Acr. 676 also has virtually colorless hair with only an occasional trace of yellow visible today.[79] It is fair to point out that Acr. 693, a Nike figure, also has yellow hair,[80] suggesting that the choice of hair coloring for statues intended for the Acropolis could sometimes be simply a matter of taste or, from a practical point of view, a reflection of the availability of pigments. However, it remains a fact that yellow hair is a rarity; for this reason alone it is tempting to infer that the percentage of its occurrence in female statues on the Acropolis is largely a reflection of the percentage of its occurrence in real life.

GARMENTS

Clothing and the manner of wearing it are as various as hairstyles. No two korai are clothed exactly alike. And, as with hairstyles, some of the clothing arrangements are so complex and, on occasion, so baffling as to defy attempts to explain and categorize them. The controversies over the number and kind of garments worn by individual korai are ongoing. Since the disparate garments and their multiple combinations and decorations have been catalogued and photodocumented in the standard publications on the korai, in particular, Richter's *Korai,* much supplemented and corrected by the work of Ridgway, it is not necessary to review all of this complex and controversial material. The fact of its tremendous variety remains uncontroversial.[81] Hurwit captures the spirit of the Acropolis korai, if somewhat underestimating them, when he suggests that their sculptors "were little more than virtuoso dressmakers" and that "the young women were high-fashion models there only to display clothing that had an existence of its own."[82] In any discussion of the clothes worn by the Acropolis korai it is important to keep in mind that these are representations of garments, not real garments; thus, a certain degree of artistic license or, less often, representational inadequacy must be accepted when assessing the styles of dress. As mimetically realistic as the garments of the korai are, they remain artist's renderings of reality, and as with any work of art, to whatever degree it aims or does not aim at mimetic accuracy, artifice is to be expected and respected; it is art's prerogative, after all, to be artificial.

Once again the debt to Egypt must first be dealt with. While Greek and Egyptian women dressed quite differently, the former choosing colorful woven fabrics, the latter preferring plain white garments for most of their history, distinctive ways of representing drapery are shared on occasion. Greek korai are admired for the fineness of their garments which, at least according to the sculptors, cling sensuously, if unnaturally, to their youthful bodies, revealing more than they hide. As attractive as this formula is in the hands of the Greek sculptor, it is clear that there was a certain economy of carving involved in the creation of such works that can be attributed, at least in part, to the sculptor's inexperience with the medium and unwillingness to attempt to carve freestanding elements of draped material that would have rendered his sculpture truer to life, as Richter noticed. It also allowed him a kind of halfway license in that he did not have to conceive or carve a nuanced representation of naked flesh, which likely was unacceptable anyway.

Egyptian models could also have served as an influence, however, providing an aesthetic justification for the shortcuts in conceptualizing and carving a monumental, clothed figure in stone. Clinging fabrics are the style of choice for Egyptian royal women, as demonstrated in paintings, sculptures, and reliefs, suggesting that, because they are represented uniformly in both two- and three-dimensional artforms, the images accurately reflect real-life practices. In Archaic Greek art, on the contrary, female dress is portrayed somewhat differently in vase-painting, where it is generally less streamlined and more self-sufficient, and in sculpture, where it does not stray far, if at all, from the body; relief, as expected, falls somewhere in between. The clinging look in Egypt ranges from the Old Kingdom, exemplified in the double portrait of Mycerinus and Khamerer-nebty,[83] where the taut, athletic, and rather masculine figure of the king's chief wife is reminiscent of the youthful athleticism and slight builds of the Greek korai, all the way through the New Kingdom, when styles of draping the transparent linen fabric become loosened somewhat from the body but ever more risqué, as in the linen garment of Nefertiti open from the Empire waist down, seen, for example, in the Stele of the Amarna Dogma.[84]

The standard Ionic costume, the chiton/himation combination with the himation diagonally splayed over one shoulder and across the chest, comes as close to being typical as any style of dress on the Acropolis, but there is nothing typical about the ways of arranging the two garments. One variation on the arrangement of the himation can be seen in Acr. 611 and 678, where it is stretched high and straight across the chest and falls in a symmetrical arrangement down the front and back; Ridgway suggests that this type is made in two pieces.[85] Another variation occurs in Acr. 673 (fig. 23), where the himation is draped across the chest, over the proper right shoulder and pinned up at the left shoulder. A handful of the "stuff" appears to have been grabbed and pulled slightly forward over the garment's upper border at the chest, creating a small pouch. The wrap then cascades in pointed arches around the body. Acr. 600 (fig. 24) also adopts this style.[86] The ubiquitous scarves worn by fashionable modern French women come to mind.

Acr. 602, 670 (fig. 14), 671, and 683 (fig. 25) all wear a style of dress that departs significantly from the standard Ionic combination. There are two ways of explaining the upper portion of this dress. It could be, as some claim, either a very long chiton that has been pulled up and over a belt to form a *kolpos,* or pouch, that reaches to the thigh, or a short, blouse- or sweaterlike garment, the chitoniskos, worn over some sort of a skirt or shift, not unlike modern-day "separates"; the latter seems more likely.[87] Over her "sweater," Acr. 671 wears a third garment, the epiblema, a capelike wrap of apparently heavy fabric that covers the tresses at the back; this young woman seems dressed for cooler weather.

Even the standard format itself holds some surprises. Kore 685 (fig. 12) wears the chiton/himation combination normally, but the skirt portion, while clinging and form-revealing as expected, appears to be made of a slightly weightier fabric, more drapable than linen. In this kore the char-acteristic discrepancy between the fine, crinkly appearance of the upper portion of the linen dress and the smooth, transparent lower portion seen in many korai who wear the chiton is more pronounced than usual, as if to signal different fabrics or weaves. Even among such obvious diversity, some ways of dressing can be said to be rarer than others. Ridgway calls the dress of Acr. 615 "surprising," in that it exhibits "a change in the arrangement of the himation which foreshadows Classical, rather than Severe, attire, and displays pouches and folds for which no rationale can be found."[88]

The polychromal decorations of the garments of the Acropolis korai constitute the statues' most attractive but ephemeral attribute. This polychromy is in a perpetual transitory state. It makes of the statues a *vanitas,* bestowing upon them an aura of intriguing decay, like that of the colorful peeling facades of Venice, for those persons captivated, as viewers of earlier monuments always seem to have been, by the visible evidence of very great antiquity and the ruinous traces it inevitably leaves behind in an object wrought by human hands. From a more clinical point of view, the polychromy may also be in the end the korai's most valuable attribute, the extent of its preservation among the members of this group being unparalleled among ancient works of art.

Polychromed sculptures and architecture were the norm in ancient Greece, yet the aesthetics of ancient polychromy are all but lost on the modern viewer, whose experience can only be sporadic and incomplete. The often reproduced recreation of the Peplos Kore with its original polychromy from the Museum of Classical Archaeology, Cambridge, serves as a somewhat unsettling reminder of the fact that ancient Greek statues were painted.[89] Yet it is surely unfair to make judgments based upon modern recreations like this. Much of the reason this image is so unsatisfying is because it is merely informative; its aesthetic qualities cannot and were not intended to compete with the original. Better to judge from the originals, in spite of their rather poor condition. It is instructive to recall that the first modern viewers of the statues were awed at once by their polychromy. Of all of the polychromed statues and architecture from antiquity, the Acropolis korai, as a group, are among the very few works of art which retain enough of their original polychromy to give a real impression of the aesthetic effects of painted statues. In fact the use of polychromy on Greek statues was not completely understood until the excavation of great quantities of original Archaic statuary on the Acropolis, a large percentage of which were korai, provided unequivocal testimony.[90]

Speaking for the lost art of weaving and for the artistry of the weaver nearly as eloquently as the actual items might have, had they survived, the variety of woven garments worn by the korai make for a fitting display on

the Acropolis, the citadel of Athena, the patron goddess of textile production. Since the diversity of painted/woven decorations among the statues
does not need to be argued, and the visual evidence even in its present
state speaks well enough on its own behalf, just a few general comments
on the phenomenon are in order. For the solid colors of chitons, there
were shades and hues of red, blue, and green. A "curious soft lavender
gray," a very rare color, no longer visible, was seen on "two narrow bands
which decorate the girdle" of the still lavishly polychromed Acr. 594 soon
after the statue was excavated, according to a report by Russell Sturgis in
Harper's New Monthly Magazine of 1890. Sturgis himself acknowledges
that the color is difficult to distinguish in his accompanying engraving,
and adds that this color was found only on this kore and "on only one
other of all this collection," although he unfortunately does not name the
other kore he has in mind.[91]

Sometimes, when choosing a chiton color, the color of the hair seems
to have been considered; Dimitriou noticed that "red was chosen for chitons as a contrast to yellow hair of korai instead of the usual blue or more
rarely malachite green chitons of korai with red hair."[92] The attention to
tasteful, flattering contrast is likely to reflect more than just a decorative
decision on the part of the polychromer. It likely alludes to real-life patterns of dressing. Today, women with red hair still usually do not wear
red, since the respective hues might not necessarily harmonize well; dyed
red cloth or thread will always be brighter than even the brightest of red
hair, making the latter, surely the most prized possession of the woman
who has it, then as now, seem lackluster by comparison. The fact that
certain colors of clothing suit certain hair colors and complexions, while
others seem to detract from or draw all the color out of them, appears to
have been a concern for the tastefully dressed Archaic Greek woman as
well. Red or blonde/tawny hair, with its attendant coloration of the complexion, as an uncommon occurrence and an undeniable asset, perhaps
even a status symbol for both men and women, would have inspired its
possessor to seek ways to emphasize rather than diminish the striking
visual impact of the unusual coloration. Again the korai stand as documents for real-life practices.

Of the polychrome motifs which decorate the individual garments,
none appears to duplicate another. I have often wondered whether vase-
painters carried out what is in essence a miniaturist's task. A great deal of
this, the most intricate of polychromal work on the statues, may still be
appreciated in the museum today, but most, it seems, has been lost since

excavation, and we must turn to earlier publications with modern artists' firsthand renderings to appreciate fully the extent of differentiation among the patterns. Lermann in 1907 published what are now invaluable large hand-colored plates based on artists' renderings of the polychromal patterns which were still apparent in the early years of the twentieth century. Richter's *Korai* may be consulted for black-and-white renditions of these colorful patterns which adorn vestments and headdresses, thereby documenting the apparent uniqueness of each.[93] A small lekythos by the Amasis Painter depicts real-life peploi-makers at work with their products on view displaying a similar heterogeneity of woven patterns.[94] Additional comparanda from vase-painting include a cup by Makron showing Demeter wearing a cloak covered with parallel horizontal figured friezes of various subjects, a format which, as Elizabeth Barber sensibly suggests, was most likely used for the Gigantomachy on the Panathenaic peplos;[95] and the skyphos attributed to the Penelope Painter showing Telemachos and his mother in front of a loom containing a cloth in the process of being woven with an impressive figured frieze.[96] An amphora by Exekias shows the Dioscuri at home with their parents, with Leda wearing an elaborately woven peplos; on the other side is the famous scene of Ajax and Achilles playing dice.[97]

It is impossible to characterize these ornamental designs *en masse.* In that there is no typical design among them, the variety and apparent exclusiveness of the designs are reminiscent of Scottish tartans. Among the outstanding examples, Acr. 683 wears a chitoniskos whose surface is decorated in places with a white palmette pattern of exquisite, filigree-like workmanship, impossible to see in photographs.[98] Yet still today, when the natural light strikes the kore's proper right sleeve just so in the Acropolis Museum, rendering the design visible, it is an astonishing apparition. On the chiton of Acr. 681 (fig. 26) the rosettes scattered around the area of the calves are not cursorily hand executed like those on Late Corinthian pots; this decoration was incised and then painted, which suggests the use of mechanical devices in order to maintain precision and regularity. The decoration of the left sleeves of Acr. 681 and 682 (fig. 27) are eloquent witnesses for the artistry of the polychromer as of the weaver. The smooth shoulder of the chiton of Acr. 686 once bore the traces of a chariot-frieze no longer visible. Dimitriou described the frieze with great clarity in 1947; since she cites no source, one assumes that she was able to see it for herself: "at neckline, [a] maeander accompanied by painted figure frieze of chariot race within black outlining bands, once painted figures on dark-stained (originally blue) background; red on horses' manes, tails, bridles and reins."[99] A woman arriving at the wedding of Peleus and Thetis on the François Vase wears a peplos woven with an elaborate pattern of chariot-friezes, which may be compared with Acr. 686;[100] Demeter's elaborate cloak on the cup by Makron also contains a chariot-frieze. These and other representations on vases, along with the evidence from Acr. 686, suggest that the models for these "tapestry" gowns were taken from real-life garments woven for and worn by wealthy women. Barber comes to the same conclusion as I do, namely, that it was the textile patterns which influenced the painters and sculptors, rather than the other way around.[101]

But, lest one prefer to believe that some of these patterns were the inventions of encaustic painters, Barber, a weaver herself, made an informative discovery in attempting to replicate on her own loom the diverse techniques used for creating the ubiquitous running spiral motif versus the Greek meander, which she believed to be a squared-off version of the running spiral whose angular edges were dictated by the particular weaving technique. Barber was able to reproduce both to prove her theory, but in the process found that, in replicating the meander, she "couldn't seem to get rid of a bit of white warp showing at intervals along the edge of the meander," and realized that "it was a necessary and unavoidable evil of the technique." Later, while she was observing kore 594 (fig. 28) in the Acropolis Museum, Barber noticed "little white ticks all along the edge" of the meander which prominently decorates the border of the woman's chiton. Based on her own firsthand experience, Barber concluded: "There is no way that an artist 'thought up' that imperfection in the weaving: he was looking at real cloth."[102]

The prominence accorded to the *paryphē,* a term used to refer to the flattened or pleated central vertical strip or border of the chiton, which is visibly swept to one side by the pulling gesture, suggests that it is a particularly important feature among the members of the Acropolis group (e.g., figs. 28, 29, 30, 31). The Greek verb παρυφαίνω ("weave at the border"), whether derived from the noun παρυφή or the other way around, suggests that the border or hem of a garment was a significant area for the weaver, perhaps a locale in which to display the fullest extent of her skills. That this was so is reinforced by Philostratos (*Im.* 2.28), where the term comes to mean simply "excel in weaving."[103]

It is tempting to speculate, though impossible to prove, that individualized *paryphē* ornaments could have served as "signatures" of some kind, whether of the hand of the artist or as a sign of the identity of the depicted. Major vase-painters of the Geometric period like the Dipylon and Hirschfeld Masters consciously incorporated signature ornamental lozenge chains into the complex network of concentric geometric designs which decorated the surface of the pot, thereby revealing their hand to the careful observer and enabling archaeologists to assign individual works to the masters or their workshops.[104] On the korai, however, this signature, if it indeed is one, need not be assumed to be that of the polychromer. A *paryphē* design may have served as a mark of distinction among families much as tartans do among the Scots; one might also think of a Roman toga's purple stripe, the *clavus,* a sign of rank for senators and equites. To attach iconographical significance to ornament on textiles would parallel its use in Greek architecture, where the exclusive application of a specific ornamental pattern to each of the various types of molding may be intended to allude to a reiteration of the shape of the profile of the individual molding or to the original organic source of inspiration.[105] Whether or not the choice of ornamental designs for the borders of the dresses of Acropolis korai was as systematic as this, the fact that each appears to be exclusive adds yet another particularizing dimension to the conglomerate of meaning deduced thus far from the statues' appearances and further enhances the impression of mimetic realism.

But there is an additional dimension to this mimesis. The eye is drawn to the *paryphē,* partly because it is held up as if on exhibit in the left and, occasionally, the right hand of the korai who display the gesture, and partly because it is frequently more ornately polychromed than any other segment of the drapery. The purpose of the gesture in real life need not detain us; we shall return to it in Chapter Four. From an aesthetic point of view, the highly decorated surface forces the eye to assess the configuration of the disturbed fall of the *paryphē* and serves to suggest animation in two ways. A sensation of fleeting, flickering movement is provoked as the eye travels across any heavily ornamented surface. A high degree of sculpted ornamentation, especially when combined with vivid polychromy and real metal attachments, as in the korai, can create an overall sensation of shimmering, an illusion of surface movement. David Summers' characterization of Cicero's definition of ornament in rhetoric might just as usefully be applied to statues: "It added brightness and life to the words corresponding to things, thus creating an artificial analogue to the vividness of things really present." Summers, continuing his characterization of Cicero, speaks of "the function of ornament as sensuous surface."[106] Ornament—as sensuous, tactile surface, as the figured language of the sculptor's art, as universal vivifying principle, as the vehicle for artificial glitter and nonmetallic shine, as the agitator of contours—on its own can create a sensation of aliveness in a stone image. But the polychromed border itself, in some of the korai, is pulled into a loose sigma shape whose sinuous path stirs the eye, in another way, to apprehend "movement."

ACCOUTREMENTS

Much of what has been said about hair and garments also applies to the accoutrements worn by the Acropolis korai. The degree of elaboration or expense involved in the execution of a kore's accoutrements is not always proportionate to the statue's size. Techniques vary; some accoutrements were carved only, some were carved and painted, some were added in another material. Among headgear, poloi (Acr. 269, 696 [fig. 5]), fillets, or taenia worn around the head or over a portion of the hair at back (e.g., Acr. 678, 684 [fig. 18], 686 [fig. 32]), highly decorated stephanai (alternatively referred to as diadems) reminiscent of wedding headgear (e.g., Acr. 674 [fig. 4], 680, 682, 683, 685 [fig. 33]),[107] and what appear to be form-fitted caps, most likely a variant of the typical stephane (e.g., Acr. 616 [fig. 34], 670, 671, perhaps also 686),[108] occur in a range of shapes, sizes, configurations, materials, and polychromed decorations.

Of the korai with preserved feet, some are barefoot, some shod.[109] Worthy of special notice are the complex and highly ornamental sandals worn by Acr. 682 (fig. 35), as with every other aspect of this kore, carefully rendered in every detail, and the unusual but not unique red cloglike shoes worn by Acr. 683 (fig. 36).[110]

Acr. 269 wears carved dangling earrings that look like something one could purchase today in the Athenian Plaka. Acr. 686 appears to wear no jewelry, perhaps reflecting the simplicity of the developing Early Classical style. Also contributing to the overall sense of particularization in the statues, and supplying further information of perhaps a personal nature, are the proffered gifts, now mostly missing, which most of the korai held in an extended arm or clasped. Some held out both arms (Acr. 615) while others used the nonproffering hand to pull aside the skirts (Acr. 674). Of the very few which have the offering preserved, Acr. 680 (fig. 16) extends an apple or a pomegranate.[111] Acr. 683 (fig. 25) enfolds a rather large bird against her waist. These objects, representing an array of small vessels, small animals, and fruits, are in keeping with the kore's function as *aparchē* or *dekatē* and serve to amplify the kore's role as an agalma for the goddess by in effect doubling the offering. When they appear in an extended hand they also serve the additional function of *repoussoir* devices. Thus these korai hold a tiny, inflected image of themselves, an abbreviated hieroglyph, a simple rebus of their function, and they invite the viewer to partake also of this joy in their youth, their beauty, and their good fortune.

It is unquestionable that accoutrements, which include real and depicted jewelry, headgear, and items of clothing, are fundamental to the generation of an Archaic likeness. An Archaic Greek could not buy a skirt or suit off the rack or jewelry over the counter; each item of his or her dress was handmade and consequently one of a kind. Perhaps in part as a result of the lack of uniformity inherent to handmade objects, a desirable commodity once again in our own age of mechanical reproduction, material possessions served as an important means of defining oneself in Archaic Greece and of proclaiming one's status to one's peers and others; a comparable prestige accorded to the outward signs of manual facture is reflected in the status today associated with so-called couture as opposed to ready-to-wear women's garments.

Bodily accoutrements were so intimately connected with an Archaic Greek's public and private image that he/she took the best of them to the grave. There these goods would serve as signs of an individual's uniqueness, long after the remains had decomposed, giving notice to the denizens of the underworld and the gods of the heavens, as well as to mortal posterity, that he or she had not only existed but had lived well and nobly. The possessions that gave people meaning in life gave them meaning in death, testified to their existence and their personhood, and allowed them to be distinguished from other members of their *genos* ("clan") and of the human race. It may be no mere coincidence that what we know about the ritualistic process of final κόσμησις of a statue, which probably included the accoutering of the image with attached ornaments along with surface finishing, buffing, *ganosis,* and general maintenance—which involved washing and the use of perfumes—suggests that it is reminiscent of the rites of burial.[112] All statues, not just funerary images, resonate with the reality of Archaic life and Archaic death. A statue's permanent condition of suspended animation, or so it seems, permits it to perform decorously in both worlds, the here and the hereafter, that of the living and that of the corpse. Mimicking the real women they stand in for, the korai have been objectified, literally and figuratively, like their accoutrements, for the viewing pleasure and the instruction of men, women, and gods. While their precise meaning may be lost to us, the accoutrements of a kore may be said to represent the personal iconography of the depicted, mirroring the iconography of signs that she might take to her grave. Such signs and symbols, even when they are forced to remain uninterpreted, contribute to the reality of appearances in a statue.

GENERAL BODY STRUCTURES

The physical builds of the korai are as differentiated as the other aspects of their appearances that have been discussed. The korai vary in size and scale from substantially under life-size to well over, yet proportions may be compared and contrasted irrespective of differences in actual size and scale. There can be no doubt that life-size scale elicits greater empathy from the viewer, resulting in an enhanced sensation of lifelikeness. However, in the Acropolis korai, it is likely that the choice of size more often had a practical basis, the amount of money the dedicant wished to spend on a statue. This circumstance makes the issue of relative scale largely irrelevant to the question of mimetic realism.

All of the korai seem to be precocious young women, as Langlotz suspected with his "unverhohlene Koketterie."[113] They are not demure, even though they are frequently so called; rather, they flaunt their strong bodies (Langlotz' "Körperlichkeit") and, along with them, their latent sexuality just as the kouroi flaunt theirs. The buttocks of the korai, while nominally clothed, are nearly every bit as revealed, prominent, and sexualized as they are in the males. And the message offered by the women is a comparably egoistic one. In place of pride in military or athletic exploits and able physiques goes confidence in one's family and in one's unique feminine desirability, in essence, evident pride in and display of the very things which mark the differences among women in Archaic times: richness of dress, abundant hair, youth and physical beauty, but most important, the overt signs of female robustness with obvious implications for the woman's capacity to endure the physical strains of frequent childbirth.

The young women depicted are of the same, marriageable age group, that is, teenagers. However, as in life, where one adolescent may have already developed the fully formed body of an adult while another retains longer her prepubescent build, some korai give the impression of having physically matured at an early age, while others seem to be approaching maturation more slowly. Acr. 680 (fig. 16) seems too voluptuous for a young woman; she is also broad-shouldered and narrow of hip, which lends her figure a top-heavy, matronly appearance. On the other hand, Acr. 594 (fig. 28) is small shouldered and bosomed, but heavier in the hips and thighs, giving her a disproportionately bottom-heavy appearance, which is especially evident in the three-quarter view from the back (fig. 19). No matter how one evaluates Acr. 682's looks (fig. 13), because she is tall, well developed, and physically imposing, this kore appears significantly older than the others. Acr. 598 (fig. 37) has a Michelangelesque physique, with exceptionally broad shoulders (fig. 38) and stocky, muscular legs (fig. 39). Acr. 670 (fig. 14) has a feminine build, broader of hip and with more fat than muscle in her legs. She also has the small, high, pointed breasts of a youngster while Acr. 682 has a large, womanly bosom. Acr. 675 is full-bosomed although petite in her proportions, a characteristic which is not affected by actual size (small), and in possession of narrow, sloping shoulders and a disproportionately large head. Acr. 685 (figs. 12, 33) is tall and well proportioned, with fine, feminine-looking shoulders, a medium-sized bosom, narrow waist with hips swelling in proportion, and long, slender legs. Neck lengths are also varied. Acr. 674 (fig. 6) has the swanlike neck of a dancer; Acr. 683 (fig. 3) has a short thick neck; Acr. 682 has a neck that is "abnormally long," as Richter noted.[114]

If kore 685 seems merely tall, Acr. 682's height is flaunted, lending this kore an aura of palpable energy, of imperious presence, and of being in control of her surroundings. From the remnant of her *mēniskos* to the long, elegant toes of her slender, sandaled feet, this figure exudes power, magnificence, and strength of character. If Socrates needed an answer from the painter Parrhassios about how the artist goes about the depiction of character (Xen. *Mem.* 3.10.3–5), he might have looked no further than Acr. 682, had it been available, in which sheer height contributes mightily to the illusion of personal formidability. Exceptional height was what impressed the Athenians about Phyē, causing them to mistake her for Athena, if we are to believe Herodotus' (1.60) anecdote about Peisistratos' final, triumphal entry into Athens, and the sole reason, we must assume, that they were willing to be duped into concluding that the girl who stood beside the tyrant in his chariot was, in fact, their patron goddess.[115] Perhaps because gods, goddesses, and heroes are large and tall, height (μέγεθος) is one component of a common formula for female beauty in Greek poetry, the other being "form" (εἶδος), as at *Od.* 5.217, where the pairing is used of Calypso.[116]

The impression of above-average height has little to do with kore 682's being among the largest of the korai in actual size, for size and scale can be two different things; kore 683, with her squat proportions could be said to be of the same relative scale as Acr. 682. By contrast, Acr. 670's body is plumper and more feminine as well as shorter, broader, and smaller-boned than 682's. Whereas an impression of overall angularity dominates in 682, kore 670 seems curvilinear by comparison. Robustness, as has already been noted, is a common trait in the Acropolis korai, but kore 670 departs from the norm with a figure lacking in muscle; she seems womanly enough but more suited to a sedentary lifestyle. With dainty step, it seems as if kore 670 has just politely excused herself from a Chardin painting, while kore 682 has extracted her presence from a Dürer engraving only with reluctance. Kore 670, with her soft, underdefined forms, seems unprepared for immortality in stone while kore 682 appears statuesque as if by divine ordinance.

At the other end of nature's spectrum falls Acr. 683 (fig. 25), the "strange little kore"[117] which has with some justification been considered a representation of a dwarf.[118] The statue's scale is not inconsistent with the majority of Acropolis korai, yet everything about the young woman depicted is reduced in proportion almost to the point of grotesqueness. Actual size contributes little if anything to the impression of diminution that is this kore's most prominent characteristic. This could be a very young girl, but she has breasts and hips, and her hands and feet are quite large. Extreme youth, at any rate, is not the response this statue leaves with the viewer. If anything she seems old beyond her years; Graindor, evidently taken aback by kore 683's unusual appearance, even among a group of statues that stand out for their portraitlike individuality, offered this startling but apt encapsulation of it in 1938: "L'une d'elles a même l'air d'une vieille fille" ("One of them even has the air of an old maid").[119] If she is a dwarf, which is not out of the question, her visibly small stature would have betrayed the fact of her questionable aptitude for reproduction, a surprising thing on the Acropolis, where muscular fitness of a kore is presented as if another accoutrement.[120]

Virtually all who have written about Acr. 683 have commented that this kore looks "realistic" compared with the others, implying that 683 is different in conception from the remainder of the Acropolis group, which at face value seems unlikely. While it is by no means clear whether kore 683 should be regarded as an intentional representation of a dwarf and thus a rare instance of genre-type realism in Archaic art, it does seem the most obvious explanation for the statue's remarkable physical characteristics. Dwarfs were respected and deemed worthy of sculptural immortalization in Egypt, especially in the Old Kingdom; at the very least the dwarflike appearance of Acr. 683 could be argued as another instance of Egyptianizing in Archaic Greek art. This kore has long been associated with a base containing an inscription recording a dedication by two people, a man, Lysias, and a person of uncertain, but more likely female gender, Euarchis, so, perhaps, a husband and wife. This base features two sockets for marble statues; the larger fits the plinth of Acr. 683, while the other statue is lost.[121] When Raubitschek observes that kore 683 "has its right foot advanced" instead of the more usual left because "the statue is part of a group," without further explanation, it is assumed that he means a real group, as opposed simply to a double dedication, with some attempt at integration of the two figures other than symmetry, which is out of the question because of the size differential.[122] If this is the case, then it is important to consider whether the second, smaller statue might have altered the visual impression of the scale of kore 683, and how it might have contributed to the meaning of the whole dedication.[123] One suspects another genre-type image, perhaps close in appearance to 683, but there is no way of knowing.

This chapter has assembled a broad spectrum of physical evidence visible or once visible among the korai from the Acropolis in order to argue that there is mimetic realism in the representation of appearances. But mere tabulation aside, we have also seen how individual features may coalesce in these statues, as they do in life, to give an overall impression of a depicted person's looks, status, and, on occasion, personality. From head to foot, the Acropolis korai are as dissimilar as real women are. The persistence of this dissimilarity strengthens the possibility that, in many of the korai, the sculptor intended to evoke a likeness of a special female human being, with a singular demeanor and a particularized image of herself and her position both in her family and in society, even if the statue itself is not given a name, and even if it was not strictly modeled—to use a term and concept borrowed, surely inappropriately, from the modern art academy—"from life."

It cannot be overstressed that this is a realism solidly anchored in the vocabulary and semiotics of the physical appearance of the body in its entirety. Archaic likeness is not focused on the face alone. The theory of a portraiture centered on the face to which we are accustomed developed primarily because Aristotle and his followers began to read signs of character in the configuration of the face, whereas the conversation of Socrates and Parrhasios on the artistic representation of character recorded by

Xenophon (*Mem.* 3.10.1–5), in which it is significantly not restricted to the face, may reflect earlier beliefs. In the Archaic statue the whole image is engaged in the generation of likeness, every part conscripted for its potentially informative effect, toward the forging of an impression of authenticity. The physical appearances of the Acropolis korai reflect the feminine looks and comportment that were valued in real life, the same system of values which is articulated in poetry, as we shall see in Chapter Four. It need not be inferred from this that the statues are then to be regarded as generic or idealized, but rather that they are based squarely in the context of observable reality, where individual women find common, socially acceptable ways of presenting themselves, but nonetheless are able to distinguish their personal styles and appearances from that of their peers and competitors by attending to the details.

In the final analysis the sculptors of the Acropolis group may have reached beyond mimetic realism. An artist's ability to combine in distinctive ways individualized features with inherited typical ones into a unified, coherent, and often inspired view of a person by way of his or her physical attributes—in other words, to seek reality through appearances—is, as it turns out, what characterizes the best and most successful portraits from any age. Just as, theoretically, at least, a simple list of the qualities or physical characteristics of a person could be considered a verbal "portrait" of that individual, while there can be no question of naturalism or lack thereof, so too the Acropolis korai, where the visual markers are just as clear and far more integrated, though lacking in naturalism, might be considered "portraits" of individuals, unnamed but not, by implication, nameless.

CHAPTER THREE

THE IDEA OF LIKENESS

The reality of appearances, as we have seen, is an authoritative reality. The disclosure of mimetic realism among the members of the Acropolis group of korai by means of visual evidence alone in the previous chapter significantly ameliorates the hindrance posed by the absence of names, which has heretofore obstructed their being interpreted as representations of young women. A rationale for this mimetic realism must now be sought. Even though the korai cannot be considered full-fledged portraits in the traditional sense of the term, since they cannot be identified with specific, named individuals, it remains to consider whether these statues might nonetheless exemplify tentative, incompletely articulated incursions into the genre of portraiture, early efforts to address the idea of personal likeness in a representation of a human being, in acknowledgment of the deep, long-standing ideological connection between likeness and representation.

Any successful attempt at mimicking the physical characteristics of a particular thing, whether a person, an animal, a place, or an object, to such a degree as to make it recognizable as that particular thing may be considered a likeness. A likeness of a person concentrates almost exclusively on the outer, visible, and therefore verifiable evidence of his or her appearance, as well as wealth, status, or position within the community, the public persona rather than the private self—in short, the very things which are on display in the korai. It is well to recall that the etymological force behind εἰκών, the most common later Greek word for portrait, is the verb *εἴκω (ἔοικα, found throughout Homer, "resemble, be like"); the noun, then, preserves the essence of a *formal* coincidence of likeness between subject and artifact, as if likeness were more important than any other element in a portrait, and as if likeness alone allowed an image to be considered a portrait. If it can be shown that a nontheoretized idea of likeness resembling something very like portraiture was conceivable in Archaic Greece, then the mimetic realism visibly evident in the Acropolis korai would make sense as a by-product of the social and cultural milieu in which the statues were commissioned, made, and viewed. This chapter explores the ancient evidence for the existence of that idea.

There are strong indications that the most basic concept behind the "true" portrait, likeness, was understood and accepted well before fully developed portraits with secure historical identifications are found in Greece.[1] In three separate passages Pliny associates the very beginnings of the figurative arts of both painting and sculpture (modeling) with the making of a likeness. In the first (*NH* 34.35), he links the art of modeling with portraiture: "It will be better to speak of the origin of the modelling of portraits [similitudines] when we treat of the art which the Greeks call πλαστική, as it is earlier than statuary." His later accounts of the arts of painting and modeling both begin with similar anecdotes, which reveal an early connection with the idea of creating a likeness:

> The origin of painting is obscure, and hardly falls within the scope of this work. The claim of the Egyptians to have discovered the art six thousand years before it reached Greece is obviously an idle boast, while among the Greeks some say that it was first discovered at Sikyon, others at Corinth. All, however, agree that painting began with the outlining of a man's shadow. (*NH* 35.15)

Pliny (*NH* 35.151) offers further anecdotal information about the origins of portraiture when he opens his narrative of the art of modeling with a more detailed account of some form of portrait made from clay by Boutades of Sicyon:

> Of painting I have said enough and more than enough, but it may be well to add some account of clay modelling. It was by the service of the selfsame earth that Boutades, a potter of Sicyon, discovered, with the help of his daughter, how to model portraits [similitudines] in clay. She was in love with a youth, and when he was leaving the country she traced the outline of the shadow which his face cast on the wall by lamplight. Her father filled in the outline with clay and made a model; this he dried and baked with the rest of his pottery, and we hear that it was preserved in the temple of the Nymphs, until Mummius overthrew Corinth.

Whether or not there is any historical truth behind these charming stories, they do at least reveal that the idea of likeness-making is venerable. As Pliny understands it, the common impulse which led to the discovery of the arts of both painting and modeling was the desire or need to make an image like enough to a living person to stand in his place. In other words, the initial impulse to make figural images and the impulse to make portraits were, in Pliny's account, one and the same.

Also attesting to the great antiquity of the art of portraiture, Daidalos, the myth-historical sculptor of uncertain date and legendary skills, is credited by Diodorus (1.97.6) with a self-portrait: "The very beautiful propylon of the temple of Hephaistos in Memphis was also built by Daidalos, who became an object of admiration and was granted a statue of himself in wood, which was made by his own hands and set up in this temple."[2] However exact this image was as a likeness, it must have been credible by the standards of the day. For the name of Daidalos, it seems, became, among other things, synonymous with accurate likeness in works of art. The association between likeness and Daidalos is reiterated in a preserved fragment of Aeschylus' satyr-play *Theoroi* (or *Isthmiastai*) (*TrGF* 3, fr. 78a), a chorus of satyrs marvels at "Daidalic likenesses" (τὸ Δαιδάλου μ[ί]μημα, v. 7) of themselves with which they have just been provided, perhaps by Daidalos himself. Struck, above all, with the close resemblance between "portrait" and subject, the satyrs declare that the resemblance is so nearly perfect that the only thing lacking is speech (v. 7), something which is often said later about the works of Daidalos, and go on to deduce, remarkably, that the images are true enough to life to deceive their own mothers (vv. 13–17).[3] If, as is likely, what is said about Daidalos reflects what was said and thought about real-life artisans, by Aeschylus' lifetime, creating a successful likeness was already considered to be fully within the capabilities and conceptual horizons of contemporary artists. It is well to recall that the tragedian lived ca. 525–456 B.C., had his first tragedy produced in 499, and would have seen the Acropolis korai *in situ* and quite possibly witnessed the floruit and demise of the type and the burial of its finest exemplars.

Theodoros of Samos (fl. mid–sixth century B.C.) is credited by Pliny (*NH* 34.83) with having made one of the earliest self-portraits after that of Daidalos:

> Theodoros, the maker of the labyrinth at Samos, also cast a portrait of himself in bronze, famed as a wondrous likeness [similitudinis], and also celebrated for the extreme delicacy of the workmanship. The right hand holds a file, while three fingers of the left hand support a tiny team of four horses, which is now at Praeneste, so small that the team, marvelous to relate, with chariot and charioteer could be covered by the wings of a fly which the artist made to accompany it.

The description would suggest that there was a genre-element to this like-ness, and that iconographical signs carried much of the meaning and bore a great portion of the informational load that would enable the subject of the likeness to be recognized and identified.

Portraiture of what might be called the genre-type—that is, its essen-tial features tend toward caricature—is rather common in early Archaic literature, drawing upon a tradition that goes as far back as Homer. Homer does not attempt a portrait of Helen's nonidealized beauty in the *Iliad;* Zeuxis, after all, needed five beautiful virgins to serve as models for his painted rendition of Helen, whereas Homer needed only to refer to the misery of the current war to convey the power of Helen's physical pres-ence, in lieu of describing her, as Gotthold Lessing long ago observed.[4] But Homer does deliver a convincing verbal portrait, which borders on parody, of Helen's diametrical opposite, Thersites (*Il.* 2.216–219), perhaps indulging in this ignoble little ekphrasis because genre-type realism lends itself more readily than nonidealized beauty to exposition, both verbal and visual, not to mention being more entertaining to produce and to listen to:[5]

> This was the ugliest man who came beneath Ilion. He was bandy-legged and went lame of one foot, with shoulders stooped and drawn together over his chest, and above this his skull went up to a point with the wool grown sparsely upon it.

In this same tradition the Lyric poet Alcaeus (fr. 429) portrayed Pittacus, statesman and lawgiver of Mytilene, as "drag-foot" (σαράποδα and σάρα-πον), "because he had flat feet and trailed them behind him"; "chap-foot" (χειροπόδην), "because of the cracks in his feet, which they called 'chaps'"; "prancer" (γαύρηκα), "since he was always prancing around"; "pot-belly" (φύσκωνα, cf. also Alc. fr. 129.21) and "big-belly" (γάστρωνα), "because he was fat"; "dusky-diner" (ζοφοδορπίδαν), "since he did not use a lamp"; and "well-swept" (ἀγάσυρτον), ironically, "since he was slovenly and dirty."[6] Whether or not any of these things were true, it is clear that Alcaeus did not like the man, whom he considered to be a tyrant, and was able to use the inherently vituperative language of genre-type realism against him.

The philosopher Critias of Athens (480–403 B.C.), criticizing the seventh-century poet Archilochus of Paros for being indiscreet enough to reveal his own iniquities in his poems, provides a literary portrait of Archilochus that is in essence a summary of the latter's purported self-revelations. While it does not attempt to describe Archilochus physically, as that information was most likely not to be discovered in the poet's oeuvre, it does offer an unvarnished, genre-type character profile that is typical for the Lyric age:

> Otherwise, if he [Archilochus] had not published this view of himself in Greece, we should not have known either that he was the son of Enipo, a slave-woman, nor that he left Paros because of poverty and destitution and went to Thasos, nor that when there he was on bad terms with the inhabitants, nor that he vilified friends and foes equally. Moreover, we would not have known that he was an adulterer, nor lustful and violent, if we had not learnt it from him, and—most disgraceful of all—that he threw away his shield. So that Archilochus was not a good witness for himself, leaving behind such a reputation and such a name.[7]

While Archilochus does not seem to have described his own physical appearance in unflattering terms, he does describe (fr. 114) his ideal military commander in genre-type imagery which might better be called veristic, since it is a form of idealized ugliness:

> I don't like an army commander who's tall, or goes at a trot,
> Or one who has glamorous wavy hair, or trims his beard a lot.
> A shortish sort of chap, who's bandy-looking round the shins,
> He's my ideal, one full of guts, and steady on his pins.[8]

These accounts encapsulate the often brutal and, one suspects, somewhat exaggerated realism, much of it stereotypical and formulaic, that characterized poetry and life in some areas of Greece at the close of the Dark Age and the dawn of the Archaic. For "Archilochean poetry," as Gentili believes, "was a poetry genuinely concerned with real life and everyday experience."[9]

That these genre-type verbal "portraits" may represent a legitimate reflection of the capabilities and intentions of contemporary visual artists rather than merely an early Archaic literary trope is given support by Pliny's account of the circumstances surrounding the creation and public exhibition of an unflattering but accurate "portrait" of another Archaic poet, Hipponax (fl. mid- to late sixth century B.C.):[10]

> Hipponax was conspicuous for his ill-favoured countenance, which incited the sculptors [Boupalos and Athenis] in wanton jest to display his

portrait [imaginem] to the ridicule of their assembled friends. Incensed at this Hipponax lampooned them so bitterly that, as some believe, they were driven to hang themselves. This, however, cannot be true, for they afterwards made in the neighbouring islands, as for example, in Delos, a number of images of the gods.   (*NH* 36.12)

One may be reminded of a droll remark attributed to the renowned American portraitist John Singer Sargent: "Every time I paint a portrait, I lose a friend."[11] Even a professional portraitist did not, it seems, always please his patrons by representing them accurately; apparently Sargent's customers were not expecting their portraits to be likenesses of themselves and were surprised when they were.

As for Pliny, he wisely refrains from passing judgment on the accuracy of Boupalos' and Athenis' portrait of Hipponax according to the standards of his own day; he simply reports the story as he heard or read it, editorializing only to add that he does not believe it. However, it is significant that his disbelief does not stem from skepticism about the levels of mimetic realism and likeness realizable in "portraits" from the Archaic period, but from the fact that he knows of the existence of other, later works by these two sculptors, a fact which would appear to undermine the plausibility of this version of their deaths. What strikes modern readers as either a startling revelation or an anachronism, that realistic portraiture of the genre-type existed at this early date, Pliny takes for granted. In writing a history that unfolds on the basis of who did what first and when, Pliny was well aware of what would have been within the scope of the two Archaic sculptors' abilities. Statues by them were on view in the Rome of Pliny's day, where they served as acroteria atop the temple of Apollo on the Palatine and "indeed in almost all the temples built by the god Augustus," according to Pliny (*NH* 36.13). There is no reason to assume that Romans could not distinguish nuances of Greek sculptural style; they were perfectly familiar with the distinction between Archaic and Classical, not only through examples of Etruscan art, much of which imitates Archaic Greek, but also through authentic Greek examples.[12] If mimetic realism in the form of accurate, recognizable similitude would have struck Pliny as remarkable and out of chronological sequence, it seems likely that he would have commented.

The force of this anecdote lies in the recognition that, whatever Archaic realism consisted of, in this instance it was impressive enough by the prevailing contemporary standards to initiate the sequence of events described by Pliny. While it is now generally acknowledged that the stated targets of iambic poets' invectives as well as the circumstances which ostensibly inspired them are not necessarily to be regarded as historical, and that the genre has many conventional features, it nonetheless remains significant that realism is the predominant theme of iambic poetry. Regarding the historicity of the Pliny anecdote, Ralph M. Rosen has recently collected the sources for the historical verification of the existence of Boupalos and Athenis and regards them as real figures, although he somewhat inexplicably maintains that the testimonia, including Pliny's, about their quarrel with Hipponax, are "utterly unreliable."[13]

As it was apparently the cause of so much damage, it is worth considering what this portrait might have looked like, if it ever existed. That it was mimetically realistic enough to convey with such convincing effectiveness a specific, identifiable likeness to a sixth-century B.C. audience is certain. What features were selected for emphasis and the manner in which they were conveyed, the "ingredients," so to speak, are matters for speculation. Since humor was intended, and visual humor of any era is seldom subtle, especially with regard to body parts, accurate physical resemblance to its subject may have been incidental. Whatever struck the contemporary audience as humorous must have reminded them of what they already knew to be true about Hipponax' physical appearance. The man and his likeness would not need to have been seen side by side.

The Archaic smile could easily have been exploited as caricature, something which happens, perhaps unintentionally, in several very fine statues from the period, including the Berlin Kore (fig. 40). One or more of the horrific yet at the same time risible features of the ugly Gorgon sisters, commonly depicted in early temple pediments and on vases of the period,[14] could have been incorporated in a composite image that would have struck the right chords in an audience accustomed to poking fun at funny-looking people. While the extant apotropaic gorgons on temples are by no means intended to be risible and in fact are not, the vocabulary of forms was there for the taking. The stubby, ill-proportioned legs, the fat round face, the lolling tongue, and so on, were established motifs in the artist's repertory. To get a rough idea of what a clever Archaic sculptor might have made of Hipponax, one might compare a red-figured kylix in the Vatican showing a dwarfish, bearded, and balding cripple who is seated and conversing in earnest with a fox who is also seated. This almost certainly represents a scathing, comical, but possibly quite realistic depiction of Hipponax' contemporary, Aesop.[15]

Whatever they consisted of, the iconographical clues as to the subject and target of the likeness of Hipponax were surely not subtle; the details were all that was needed for the message of the image to be conveyed. Granting that an image like this might be considered no more than a caricature is not to concede to those who would claim that a caricature is not a likeness, since caricature in itself presupposes some understanding of the concept of portraiture. The caricaturist takes aim at the individualizing feature rather than the generalized, exaggerating it for satirical effect, and presupposing a general or popular recognition of the likeness at which the caricature is aimed. A satyr's face in itself is not, strictly speaking, a caricature. Socrates portrayed with a satyr's face is a caricature, and the fact that all caricature is not necessarily unflattering is attested by the encomium on the satyrlike "beauty" of Socrates by Alcibiades in Plato's *Symposium* (215a–216a).[16]

Another Archaic portrait very likely of the genre-type is attested by Herodotus (1.51.5). Once again it does not appear to have been regarded as unusual for its time, the second half of the sixth century B.C., since Herodotus mentions it without comment in a catalogue of costly objects dedicated by King Croesus of Lydia in an effort to influence the oracle at Delphi:

> And Croesus sent many other dedications that were not inscribed [οὐκ ἐπίσημα] along with these [already mentioned], [including] both circular silver bowls and especially [καὶ δὴ καί] a golden figure [εἴδωλον] of a woman, three cubits high, which the Delphians say is a portrait [εἰκόνα] of Croesus' baker-woman.[17]

At three cubits (ca. four and a half feet), that is, nearly life-size, and of gold, one understands Herodotus' use of καὶ δὴ καί ("especially").[18] A key phrase for interpreting this passage is οὐκ ἐπίσημα. Some take the phrase to mean "undistinguished" or "of no great importance"; however, this is unlikely, since silver bowls and "especially" a golden portrait statue are hardly trifles. Furthermore, to conclude that the golden figure was undistinguished would then render senseless the force of καὶ δὴ καί used to introduce it. What instead distinguishes this group of objects from the previous ones narrated is that the others were inscribed, while these are not,[19] and these, being uninscribed, might be missed as dedications by Croesus, but among them is an unusual object, the baker's golden image.[20] By using two different words to refer to the image, Herodotus makes clear that in his mind all εἴδωλα were not εἰκόνες, that is, not all statues or representations should be considered portraits unless one has further information about them such as an inscription or, in the present instance, the word of an informed source. It comes as no surprise that, as this passage suggests, with very early portraits it was not always visually obvious whether a statue, even an expensive one, was a "representation" or a "portrait"; Herodotus needed the Delphians to tell him that this particular εἴδωλον was meant to be an εἰκών.

It is significant that Herodotus does not challenge the opinion of the Delphians about the identification of the baker's portrait, whereas a few lines earlier (1.51.3) he had challenged the validity of an inscription:

> In addition Croesus sent four silver casks, which are in the Corinthian treasury, and two sprinklers for lustral water, one of gold, the other of silver; the former has the name of the Lacedaemonians engraved upon it, and they claim to have presented it. But this is not true: Croesus presented it along with all the rest, and some Delphian (I know his name but will not mention it) cut the inscription to please the Lacedaemonians.

Apparently an inscription can be questioned, whereas the spoken word which confirms a long-standing tradition of interpretation is so credible as to be accepted as a correction of the written word. In this case the evidence which gave rise to the spoken statement is itself likely to be based upon a combination of hearsay, subjective impressions, and memories, or perhaps even on visual evidence alone—all evidentiary categories which, with the exception of the last, will strike the modern mind as somewhat insubstantial. It is well to recall in this context that the inscriptions which accompanied the korai from the Acropolis provide little evidence about the images for the viewer. In their case, too, it is tempting to speculate that word of mouth alone could have assumed the role of disseminating and preserving the information about their identities.

Early Greek portraiture was not limited to displays of realism of the genre-type. The realism of nonidealized beauty is also attested in early portraits. Kylon made an unsuccessful attempt ca. 630 B.C. to seize the Acropolis of Athens and become tyrant, an event and its aftermath which resulted in a curse being placed upon the Alcmaeonid family throughout the Archaic and Classical periods. Pausanias (1.28.1) saw his portrait statue on the Acropolis and commented on it as follows:

> Why they set up a bronze statue of Kylon, in spite of his plotting a tyranny, I cannot say for certain; but I infer that it was because he was

very beautiful to look upon, and of no undistinguished fame, having won an Olympian victory in the double foot-race, while he had
married the daughter of Theagenes, tyrant of Megara.

Since Pausanias says nothing to indicate otherwise, we may assume that
this statue was roughly contemporary with Kylon's floruit. Moreover, it
would seem likely that the accurate memory of the man's physical beauty,
the only plausible reason for the honorific portrait, as Pausanias deduced,
would not survive many generations, lending further credence to an Archaic date.

From Herodotus (2.182.1) comes the story that Amasis, the sixth-century B.C. Egyptian king noted for his philhellenism, and a contemporary
of King Croesus of Lydia, had not one but three likenesses (εἰκόνες) of
himself made—one of them, apparently, "from life" (εἰκασμένην)—which
he dedicated at various shrines around Greece:

> Amasis further showed his goodwill to Greece by sending presents to
> be dedicated in Greek temples; to Cyrene he sent a gold-plated statue
> [ἄγαλμα] of Athene and a painted portrait of himself [εἰκόνα ἑωυτοῦ
> γραφῇ εἰκασμένην]; to the temple of Athene at Lindos, two statues in
> stone and a remarkable linen corslet; and to the goddess Hera in Samos
> two likenesses of himself [εἰκόνας ἑωυτοῦ], in wood, which until my
> own time stood behind the doors in the great temple.

Again, Herodotus mentions these early portraits without surprise or commentary. He definitely saw two of them and even clarifies their out-of-
the-way location for anyone else who might wish to see them, if they are
still there to be seen. As an Egyptian, Amasis was accustomed to portraiture; the great pharaonic tradition to which he was heir accounts for Amasis'
reliance on the medium of sculpture to disseminate his likeness around
the sanctuaries of the Mediterranean. However, from Herodotus' unre-
flective recollection of it one might conclude that portraiture in this period was commonplace even among Greeks. If it were a purely Egyptian
phenomenon, Herodotus typically would have drawn attention to its
quaintness and explained its purposes for the benefit of his Greek readers,
as is often his practice when recounting something strange. His silence in
this regard is significant; it is as if he assumes that the idea of portraiture
was familiar to his audience.

In Athens Pausanias (1.21.1–2) saw a portrait of Aeschylus of uncertain
date. He uses his own judgment, based presumably upon the style of the

statue, to ascertain whether it is contemporary with the playwright, concluding that it was not:

> In the theatre the Athenians have portrait statues [εἰκόνες] of poets, both tragic and comic, but they are mostly of undistinguished persons [τῶν ἀφανεστέρων] . . . the likeness [εἰκόνα] of Aeschylus is, I think, much later than his death and than the painting which depicts the action at Marathon.

Even though it refers to portraiture from as late as the death of Aeschylus in ca. 456 B.C., which is just beyond the time frame of this study, the passage is illuminating on several counts. First, it confirms that a painting of the Battle of Marathon contained a contemporary likeness of Aeschylus, which allows Pausanias to know what he looked like; the tragedian, it will be remembered, fought at Marathon. Second, it suggests that the style of the Late Archaic/Early Classical period was unmistakable. Third, it reveals that "undistinguished" persons, a group which might include women, could also be the subjects of portraiture. Incidentally, this passage also shows Pausanias to be a discriminating and critical viewer and on that account one whose opinion on stylistic and other subjective matters is to be valued, although he is not always treated with the respect he deserves by modern scholars.

The Archaic likenesses discussed thus far have survived only in the form of literary anecdotes or topoi. We now turn to actual extant examples of works of art. We may begin with a brief discussion of the few preserved Archaic funerary masks, which by their very nature present evidence of an interest in likeness. If, as seems obvious, the practice of putting mimetic masks on corpses before burial is ultimately borrowed from Egypt, where its intention was clearly to preserve the appearance of the decedent's visage, then some degree of intent to liken is even more certain. Gold and silver funerary masks discovered in the graves of aristocrats in the Thraco-Macedonian region, though far removed in circumstances and in geographical location from the Attic korai, are their exact contemporaries, as they date to the last decades of the sixth century B.C. and early fifth, and may be cited as further evidence of Archaic interest in likeness-making.[21] To an even greater degree than the more famous Mycenaean examples, which also were found with inhumed remains, those from Thrace/Macedonia appear to be true death masks, that is, molded directly onto the face of the deceased. As such, some degree of mimetic realism is to be assumed. And, as with the Mycenaean examples, because they are death masks, they cannot be considered works of art. However, the masks are worth citing as a concrete demonstration of Archaic interest in the idea of likeness in a context, that is, memorialization and perpetuation of the dead, for which the appropriateness of the highest attainable levels of mimetic realism had already been certified for centuries in the Mediterranean world.

Among the earliest monumental examples, the late-seventh/early-sixth-century B.C. pair of kouroi from Delphi, Cleobis and Biton, now in the Delphi Museum, arguably were intended as likenesses of the two heroized Argive youths mentioned by Herodotus (1.30–31).[22] Herodotus has the Athenian wiseman Solon answering a query by King Croesus of Lydia about who is the happiest of men, hoping to hear himself named. Solon proceeds instead to name an Athenian, Tellus, and, when pushed further by Croesus, as second happiest, Cleobis and Biton, which prompts him to tell the story of the two sons who yoked themselves to an ox cart and conveyed their mother the nearly six miles to the temple of Hera in time to participate in a festival that she otherwise would have missed. Herodotus also records, again through the mouth of Solon, that, following upon their exploit and subsequent deaths, at their mother's request statues of the two were made by the Argives for dedication at Delphi. There are inscriptions associated with the two kouroi which indicate that these are indeed the statues mentioned by Herodotus.[23] As they may be seen today in the museum, except for minor differences which are virtually undetectable, the two kouroi look like twins, which they are often assumed to be, understandably, since the brothers were probably quite close in age. Herodotus, however, though he does not specify their respective ages, does not call them twins. In nude male statues, to isolate the meaningful details which could have been intended to convey a composite message of mimetic realism is not without its perils. In the special case of Cleobis and Biton, however, the Archaic smiles have a slim chance of being iconographically significant; they are, after all, the second happiest of men! But to be fair, early "portraits" like these, which display little visual evidence for particularization, are perhaps better classified simply as representations of distinct individuals. However, that they were intended to be portraits cannot be denied, since the information provided by an appended inscription must be included in any accounting. With what we have before us, Cleobis and Biton might at most be judged "cognitive likenesses," in Himmelmann's terms.

The fragmentary Geneleos group from the Heraion at Samos of the mid–sixth century B.C. has been characterized as a portrayal of a gathering of real individuals who are named in accompanying inscriptions.[24] The group consisted of six figures on a platform, all facing the viewer in a row, all sumptuously robed, and likely the members of a single family. While the sexes and ages of the figures are not unambiguous, the following description of the composition of the family seems likely: The mother, "Phileia," sits on a throne; the artist's signature, "Geneleos made us," appears on the preserved lower section of her body. Standing to her left are, in order, a son, the smallest and therefore the youngest member of the family; three daughters of varying ages, which are suggested by slight variations in their heights, weights, and hairstyles, although only one is substantially preserved, one whose name is lost, the other two called "Philippe" and "Ornithe"; and at the other end of the monument, Phileia's corpulent, reclining husband, who identifies himself as the dedicant, of whose name only the last part is preserved: $-\alpha\rho\chi\eta\varsigma$.

As far as can be told, given the state of preservation, it appears that the artist or workshop was concerned to some degree with individualization, although for the most part this partakes as much of iconographical details as of physiognomic differentiation. The dedicant is a languorous, reclining figure with fleshy, prominent breasts, which have suggested to some that he is in fact a woman, and a sagging belly, which may be read as "wealthy older man," the latter a conventional feature probably borrowed from Egyptian art, where, for nearly three thousand years scribes, for example, are portrayed with sagging bellies to symbolize their age, their high-status jobs, and their sedentary lives. But this gentleman is also shown leaning on a wineskin and holding a bird or, as recently proposed, a drinking horn, informative details which would have added their meanings to the cumulative effect of the "portrait" as a whole.[25] A new restoration by Elena Walter-Karydi shows the young boy with a double flute in his left hand, enhancing the symposium-like or festival atmosphere which she identifies as the "theme" of the dedication.[26] Whether or not this identification is correct, or even if in fact the piece has a theme, the naming of the individuals again makes it certain that this monument was meant to be a group "portrait" of particular persons whose association with one another made sense enough to convey significance to the family itself, to the ancient visitor to the sanctuary, and to the goddess for whom the dedication was made, Hera. And while one would not suspect, owing to their poor state of preservation, that these images once demonstrated the same degree of attention to the details of physical appearance that is seen in the Acropolis group of korai, it would be unfair to deny the members of the Geneleos group the status of intentional likenesses just because they do not display a comparable level of mimetic realism. The same purpose, association with specific individuals, is achieved through more formulaic visual means, and, unlike the Acropolis korai, the statues are named.

Whether funerary, honorific, or dedicatory, monuments conceived and financed by private individuals or groups seem a logical place for portraiture to begin to take hold. But late in the sixth century, in Athens, an unexpected new context for the erection of public portrait statues was supplied by a political event: the murder of the Athenian tyrant, Hipparchos, which opened the way to democracy in Athens. Pliny (*NH* 34.17) surmises (nescio an) that the Athenians inaugurated the custom of setting up statues in honor of men at the public expense in 509 B.C. with the bronze portraits of the Tyrannicides, Harmodios and Aristogeiton, by the Archaic sculptor Antenor, who also made Acr. 681.[27] Much about the Tyrannicides' portraits and their subsequent history is uncertain. The Archaic group was carried off by Xerxes in 480/79 B.C. and later restored to the Athenians by a Hellenistic king; Alexander, Antiochus, and Seleucus are all credited with this deed in the ancient sources.[28] In the interim the images of the revered twosome were replaced by another set, executed in the new style, by the Early Classical sculptors Kritios and Nesiotes.

Pausanias (1.8.5) appears to have seen both groups during his visit to the Athenian Agora; his phraseology, I think, makes it clear that he is looking at more than two statues: "Of the portraits, some [οἱ μέν] are the work of Kritios, but the old ones [τοὺς δέ], Antenor made." The fact that Greek illustrations and Roman copies of the statues suggest that only one pair of Tyrannicides was available for copying is something of a mystery.[29] Raubitschek has argued that Antenor's group was erected "several years after the battle of Marathon," that Kritios and Nesiotes worked in Antenor's studio, and that the pair's replacement of the earlier group was "merely a copy" of Antenor's in the same style.[30] This would mean that Antenor worked in an Early Classical style, which is not out of the question, judging from the style of Acr. 681. However, if, as I believe, the original group was genuinely Archaic, given the choice of which group to copy, Antenor's group would be less likely to have been preferred, since Classical Greeks and especially Romans did not in general favor Archaic art. Adding to the confusion Pliny (*NH* 34.70) mistakenly attributes a stolen group of Tyrannicides to the fourth-century sculptor Praxiteles.

None of the originals survives. We know what the later group looked like thanks to copies, the most complete being the large-scale examples in the National Museum, Naples.[31] What the Archaic statues looked like remains, however, a subject of ongoing controversy. It is often assumed that, while there is evident individualization in the second group of Tyrannicides, the group by Antenor would have been no more than two undifferentiated kouroi.[32] To judge by the evidence of Acr. 681, this is unlikely. Although 681, as we have seen, is one of the two Acropolis korai which present the strongest cases for divine status, and it is true that the face of the statue seems to be less particularized than many of the others, kore 681 is one of the largest, finest, and most elaborately polychromed of the korai and by one of the most eminent sculptors of the day. We should probably imagine that Antenor found comparable ways to distinguish the two Tyrannicides. Regardless of what can be said about their appearances, the important point is that Antenor's Tyrannicides should be regarded as examples of commissioned Archaic portraits roughly contemporary with the korai and by a master who also worked on the Acropolis.

Another example of an Archaic "portrait" that takes aim at likeness is the recently published marble head of a bearded and mustachioed man wearing a Persian tiara or cap from Herakleia Pontica, now in the Museum of Anatolian Civilizations, Ankara (fig. 41). The head has been dated to the 530s B.C. by Ekrem Akurgal, who considers the image to be a portrait, idealized, but nonetheless a portrait, of a satrap, king, or tyrant in the employ of the Great King, not a Persian but an Anatolian Greek, made by a Greek sculptor. He calls the image "das älteste idealisierte Porträt eines kleinasiatischen Potentaten" ("the earliest idealized portrait of a potentate from Asia Minor").[33] As its dating is based in part on a stylistic comparison with Acr. 679, which itself is one of the korai most difficult to date, it is perhaps best to dispense for the present purposes with any attempt at absolute dating and simply regard the piece as High Archaic.

Stewart, in his review of the publication in which Akurgal's article appeared, correctly recognized the importance of the head for "students of early portraiture."[34] It is my impression from photographs that the claim of idealization is hard to justify; indeed Akurgal's vivid characterization of the individualization of the features would seem to belie his own assessment.[35] In addition to the particularized headgear, the man's ragged beard and moustache are naturalistically rendered; the mouth sneers more than it smiles. Akurgal compares it to the Sabouroff Head in Berlin (fig. 42) which also may be introduced as evidence for a category of Archaic image-making that has much in common with portraiture, and about which Martin Robertson has said: "[It] seems to me nearer to a portrait than any other work [with the exception of the Boxer Relief in Athens] surviving from archaic Greece."[36] The newly identified Herakleia satrap "portrait" displays no feature equivalent to the unusual stippling treatment of the head and facial hair which lends the Sabouroff Head an air of exoticism. As well it lacks the Sabouroff Head's gaunt cheeks and long, expressionistic face, and possesses little or none of that head's enigmatic expression. But there can be no mistaking the intent of the Greek artist who, charged with the task of portraying a self-important provincial potentate in a mimetically accurate way, and drawing upon Oriental iconography and Greek technical ingenuity, arrived at this distinctive early example of intentional likeness.

The Herakleia "portrait" joins the body of material evidence emerging from the fringes of the Greek world, and probably made by Greek artisans, that offers corroboration of the literary testimonia for the existence of a category or categories of image-making very like portraiture at a period far earlier than has been thought to be the case. Numismatic material, in spite of its small scale, adds significantly to the picture, and to it we now turn. Somewhat later in the fifth century, Anatolian Persian coinages "of Greek style" appear, bearing the individualized heads of Persian satraps. John Boardman cautions that these distinctive images "give the appearance of portraits, but may not be more than shrewd Greek characterizations of the typical Persian governor." Boardman acknowledges, however, that these coins are "often taken to be important documents in the early history of true portraiture in Greek art," adding that they were "executed certainly by Greeks for foreign patrons."[37] While this could imply, although Boardman himself does not say so directly, that a foreign demand for particularized images inspired the Greeks to the mimetic realism which led eventually to genuine Greek interest in portraiture in the fourth century,[38] I am arguing instead that the idea of likeness by its very nature implies an interest in portraiture and that this already existed in Greece at a much earlier date.

The Herakleia satrap wears headgear much like the one worn by Themistocles on the coins that the exiled Athenian statesman minted at Magnesia on the Maeander, which he governed, by the authority of Artaxerxes I, from about 466 B.C. until his death ca. 460. As it is, the Themistocles coins are not far in date from the last of the Acropolis korai, and since they are now commonly recognized, along with the contemporary satrap images on coins, possibly Greek work, as among the earliest examples of portraiture in Greek art, they are worthy of consideration. About a dozen of these coins have been identified—tetradrachms, didrachms, and fractions on the Attic standard—with Themistocles' name appearing as the obverse legend around either a heroized standing male figure or a helmeted male head.[39] It is possible that the full-standing figure represents Apollo, though this is unlikely, since the word "Themistocles" encircles him; the portrait bust, however, can be none other than Themistocles himself. H. A. Cahn and D. Gerin are convinced that these images depict "Themistocles, the man":

> On both coins Themistocles seems to wear a tight bonnet, which is unusual as headgear. He avoids presenting himself in oriental attire, for example with a kidaris, attribute of authority of a Persian governor. . . . If we are right, the two coins show the first portraits on a coin. We should not expect an individual likeness. The style is sub-archaic, the features show a sort of smile revealing a fine and ironic expression. But the fact fits the man. According to Plutarch Themistocles was "impetuous; by nature sagacious and by election enterprising, carried away by his desire for reputation, an ambitious lover of great deeds."[40]

At least two portrait statues of Themistocles seem to have been erected during his lifetime, one in Magnesia (Thuc. 1.138.5) and the other at Athens (Plut. *Them.* 22.1–2).[41] In addition to these there are other documented portraits of Themistocles, but it is not clear in each case when exactly they were made.[42] The inscribed Ostia herm, representing the only extant sculpted portrait type of Themistocles, may be a copy or an adaptation of one of these statues.[43] Its Early Classical style would favor the conclusion that it represents an authentic reflection of a contemporary portrait of the statesman. But while the Ostia herm is often regarded as a faithful copy of a rare early "true" portrait type,[44] the evidence for multiple portraits of Themistocles seems instead to show that public portrait images were an acceptable and not particularly unusual occurrence by the time of Themistocles' prime, and that Classical Greeks were already acquainted with the practice. Furthermore, it would seem logical to conclude that portraiture cannot have been a startling new phenomenon in the 470s and 460s if so many portraits of one man were regarded as acceptable. When in the hands of later rhetors an unflattering comparison between modern (fourth-century B.C.) Athenians and those of the High Classical period became a topos, the criticism incorporated rhetoric about Themistocles' being punished for making himself seem greater than his fellow citizens; perhaps this had something to do with his interest in portraiture.[45]

A contemporary parallel is found in the coinage of Alexander I of Macedon (ruled ca. 498–454 B.C.). N. G. L. Hammond has observed that an armed, mounted man on the obverse of coins which began to be minted under Alexander I shortly after the Greek defeat of Persia in 480/79 shows an increasing attention to particularized detail between the 470s and the 450s.[46] For Hammond, this "was probably the first coin ever which portrayed a reigning king."[47] It is possible that the increasing concern for realism, or what Hammond calls "consistency in portraiture," in the obverse device on the coins between Doris Raymond's groups I and II is due to Alexander's having set up portrait statues of himself at both Delphi and Olympia in the meantime.[48] The coins with the purported portraits show a man armed with two spears either standing beside or astride a large horse, whose size cannot be ignored, as it dominates the face of the coin. Hammond describes the group: "Clean shaven, [the man] wears a cloak (*chlamys*), a flat, wide-brimmed hat, and a band (comparable with a diadem) with its ends hanging behind his neck. . . . The large horse, so important for the cavalryman, was specially bred in Macedonia, probably from Persian stock, which had been evolved to carry a heavy-armed cuirassier."[49] Raymond speaks of "a touch of realism" as she begins a lengthy excursus on the wealth of detail, differentiation, and even signs of attempted naturalism in the obverses of the series.[50] This is precisely the kind of informative detail that, in my view, leads to an impression of mimetic realism.

But it was not only men who were regarded as important enough to be portrayed on coins in the Late Archaic/Early Classical period, the prime years of the "Greek versus barbarian" mentality which culminated in but did not end with the victories in the Persian Wars. A woman from Greek Sicily, Damarete of Syracuse, played a remarkable part in these struggles, and it was to portraiture that her people turned to memorialize the woman and to honor her role. By the late sixth century B.C., tyrants controlled Sicily. At Gela and Syracuse it was the Deinominids who ruled. Kleandros was the first of the tyrants to establish himself at Gela in 505; Hippocrates was his brother. Both tried unsuccessfully to conquer Syracuse. Gelon, Hippocrates' general and the son of Deinomenes, took over the reign in 491 and successfully annexed Syracuse, moving his capital there from Gela in 485. It is well to recall the situation at Athens at this time. Peisistratos had finally seized power in 547, after two previous, unsuccessful attempts; by 510 the Peisistratid tyrants had either died or been murdered or exiled. Tyranny was gone from Athens by the time it began in Sicily.

Gelon fought and defeated the Carthaginians in 480 at the Battle of Himera on the same day, as tradition has it, as the Battle of Salamis, which freed mainland Greece from another barbarian threat.[51] Gelon's wife, Damarete, of the Emminid family, contributed to her husband's war effort when he became short of money by collecting her own jewelry and that of other Syracusan wives. After Himera Damarete involved herself directly in the peace negotiations. At the request of the Carthaginians she intervened on their behalf in order to achieve the ransom of the prisoners held by her husband, a requirement for the conclusion of the peace. In appreciation for her actions the Carthaginians gave Gelon's wife a "crown" of one hundred gold talents,[52] which she turned into silver and coined. Gelon died soon after Himera in 478/7; his brother Hieron succeeded him in Syracuse while another brother, Polyzalos, whom Damarete later married, succeeded him at Gela. A special decadrachm or large-denomination coin, intended for circulation, was minted by Hieron, Damarete's brother-in-law; the coin was known thereafter in her honor as the Damareteion (fig. 43).[53]

Among the many questions asked about this large, scarce, and beautiful coin, one has direct bearing on the present argument: Is the image on the obverse meant to be a portrait of Gelon's wife or just a grander version of the head of the goddess Arethusa, which decorated the obverse of the smaller Syracusan coin, the tetradrachm? I would argue that the visual evidence strongly suggests that the woman's physical traits, restricted, by the exigencies of the coin, to her head and neck, are sufficiently particularized to reflect reality observed and translated by the coin artist, whom we might call the Damareteion Master. We have no way of knowing what Damarete actually looked like, but at this early date iconographical signs, functioning much like attributes for the gods, were indicators of individuality, and must be included in estimating the degree of mimetic realism apparent in the image. Specifying details include the shimmering, quivering hair, full of life and movement, and the multiple-scalloped treatment of the hair over the forehead. Two bands beneath the crown hold the chignon in place. The tendril at the ear and the tiny wisp of hair that can be seen in *schiaccatto* relief on the other side of the face may also be noted. All of this is played against the smooth, taut skin of a handsome, youthful visage of a woman about the age of 25 or 30, revealing an artist with an impeccable sense for the structure of the human face. Both pupil and iris are clearly differentiated, shown open at the inner corner, but in a three-quarter view that acknowledges perspective although not as accurately as a profile eye would, as well as a real eyebrow, separate from the line of the nose. The open, full, not entirely flattering mouth, lips forming a half-smile, half-sneer, opens to reveal the teeth. The unobtrusive bump on the ridge of the nose, and the flaring nostril, combined with the upturned lip, give the impression, perhaps unjust, of a haughty, arrogant attitude. The array of jewelry, including the pendant on one of the neck-laces, but particularly the earrings, corroborate the ancient testimonia of Hesychios and Pollux that Damarete was associated in the public mind with jewelry. The "crown" is shown.

The preceding articulation of details, all clearly visible despite the small scale of the image, could be considered evidence for at least four levels of intention. First and most straightforward, the Damareteion is a likeness of Damarete. Second, if not a full likeness, the image could be understood as a representation of Damarete's public persona, given her service and the visual details in the image which would be legible to a well-disposed populace fully aware of them and in a position to read them. Third, the face of the real woman is conflated with that of the goddess, Arethusa. And last, an otherwise generic image of Arethusa is intentionally inflected with Damarete's features, or else the opposite, a "portrait" of Damarete is unintentionally inflected with Arethusa's iconography and form, perhaps because the artisans were accustomed to engraving Arethusa in the dies. Each of the alternatives still allows for the possibility of differing degrees of likeness for those who would be reluctant to consider these images "true" portraits.

Is the message too strong for the medium? The Sicilian tyrants did not hesitate to treat the devices on their coins as propaganda-bearers of ex-plicit content. From the beginning the obverse type of the Syracusan tetradrachm showed a quadriga driven by a charioteer, probably to be associated with the equine interests of the Sicilian tyrants. The tyrants openly promoted themselves and their successes on their coins. After win-ning the mule cart race at the Olympics of 480 B.C., Anaxilas of Rhegium had a mule cart stamped on his coins.[54] There is little reason not to con-sider the quadriga's appearance on Syracusan obverses likewise a generic representation of a specific autobiographical/historical event. The coins became known worldwide, and along with them, the propagandistic mes-sages of the tyrants.[55] There would seem to be, then, for Hieron of Syra-cuse, no clear obstacle to incorporating a likeness of his brother's famous and popular wife temporarily on his coinage, likely at the people's urging, and under the conditions specified by the Carthaginians who provided the money. If it was done tastefully and unobtrusively and if the image did not confound expectations too drastically, it could only enhance Hieron's own stature. To adorn a unique issue of decadrachms which the populace knew to have been struck in Damarete's honor with a likeness of the woman in the guise of the nymph Arethusa seems a natural thing to do given the exceptional circumstances. It would remind the wide audi-ence among which the coins circulated of Damarete and her deed while scarcely interrupting the continuity of the imagery on this coinage; one would have to examine the large coin closely to notice the details which would betray that the female represented was not exactly Arethusa. The Damareteion may thus be regarded as an erudite portrait, analogous to those of the Cubists, requiring of the viewer some previous knowledge about the life of the person depicted, in this case, about the jewelry episode and the crowning of Damarete.

The discussion thus far has centered on individual occasions of attested or extant likeness-making or "portraiture." What follows is more general in documenting broader ancient customs, traditions, and situations which required or permitted the use of some form of "portraiture" at an early date. There is ample testimony from both Pausanias and Pliny that portrait statues of Olympic victors were being set up at Olympia and elsewhere as early as the latter half of the seventh century B.C. Just a few of the testimonia need be mentioned. Having finished his description of votive offerings at Olympia, Pausanias (6.1.1) begins his description of portrait statues, as promised earlier (5.21.1); but before doing so, he digresses to explain why he will not be mentioning every statue that he sees, which is, as we have seen, the same practice that he employs on the Athenian Acropolis. Pliny (*NH* 34.16) observes the following about portrait statues at Olympia, although he does not provide an exact date for the institution of the practice: "The ancients did not make any statues of individuals [effigies hominum] unless they deserved immortality by some distinction, originally [primo] by a victory at some sacred games, especially those of Olympia, where it was the custom to dedicate statues [statuas] of all those who had won, and portrait statues [ex membris ipsorum similitudine expressa] if they had won three times. These are called iconic [iconicas]."

Pausanias, however, mentions "portraits" (εἰκών, ἀνδριάς) of sixth-century victors without noting whether or not they were τρισολυμπιονίκεις. Pliny's statement has engendered much discussion centering on the question of the origins of portraiture in Greek art. As early as Gotthold Lessing's essay *Laocoön* (1766) Pliny's apparent distinction between "aniconic" and "iconic" portraits was thought to allude to a distinction between type and individuality in portraiture, and, for some, to suggest that the latter was a later development.[56] This is not the time to engage this controversial issue. However, it must be pointed out that argumentation like that of W. W. Hyde amounts to circular reasoning: "Nowadays all scholars agree that Pliny's word [iconicas] refers to portrait statues. However, Pliny's dictum about the right of setting up portrait statues is certainly open to doubt. It can not have been true of monuments erected before the fourth century B.C. when portrait statues were rare. Portraiture was a form of realism and was a product of the later period of Greek art, especially after the time of Lysippos."[57]

At Olympia Pausanias (6.15.8) saw an "old" statue of a Spartan, Eutelidas, who won double victories in the boys' wrestling and pentathlon contests in 628 B.C.; the inscription was faint. It is true that a little later (6.18.7) he claims that Praxidamas of Aegina and Rexibius of Opuntia were the first athletes to have their statues (εἰκόνες) dedicated at Olympia, respectively in 544 and 536 B.C. He also notes that these were of wood and much worn. Since the statue of Eutelidas is also called an εἰκών, there can be no question of distinguishing different types of images. Even if Eutelidas dedicated his portrait as an adult, his would still be earlier than the others. Perhaps this minor inconsistency is due to the fact that Pausanias felt it necessary to separate portraits of men and of boys, or perhaps it reflects information from two different traditions. Either way it is certain that the practice of dedicating portrait statues of victors originated in Archaic times.

In the marketplace of Phigalia in Arcadia Pausanias (8.40.1) saw an inscribed portrait of a pancratiast who had won three victories by 564 B.C. He recognizes that this statue is very old and stylistically primitive by his standards: "It is archaic, especially in its *schema;* the feet are close together, and the arms hang down by the side as far as the hips"; in other words, it was a kouros, but again, in spite of this and the fact that the inscription had "disappeared on account of time," he has no trouble identifying it as a portrait of a particular man (ἀνδριάς), the pancratiast Arrachion. The portrait statues of Damaretos, a victor in the race in armor in 520 B.C., and of his son, the pentathlete Theopompos, were also seen at Olympia by Pausanias (6.10.4–5), along with an inscription naming the Argive sculptors, another Eutelidas and Chrysothemis, as the makers of both. A bronze tablet containing this very inscription has now been discovered, its date of ca. 500 B.C. confirming the Archaic dates of the images and the accuracy of Pausanias' account of these monuments, with just one, for our purposes, inconsequential, error in transcribing the inscription.[58] Thus the tradition of portraiture appears to have been well established at Olympia throughout the Archaic period. Except to note in passing that their inscriptions are worn, the statues are "old" and therefore of a different style from subsequent figural images dedicated in the sanctuary, Pausanias treats the Archaic victor's images that he sees in the same way that he treats the others, simply as portraits, without offering a judgment upon the degree of realism or the success of the likeness.

In a recent treatment of the concept behind the victor's statue at Olympia and other forms of victory "announcement," Leslie Kurke observes that, from the beginning, the emphasis in the statues was on perfect similitude (although she does not use the word "portrait" or even "similitude"). She assembles a variety of ancient evidence to show just how similar similitude was. According to Kurke the earliest preserved inscription that can be associated with one of these monuments (*CEG* no. 394, from the first half of the sixth century B.C.) trumpets the fact that the image is "equal in height and thickness" to the victor. Citing later testimonia, Kurke suggests that the drive toward similitude eventually extended to recreating in the statue the precise stance of the victor "at the moment he won and was heralded."[59] Although the force of Kurke's argument lies elsewhere, in bringing together this evidence she has contributed to the dialogue on the question of mimetic realism in the early history of portraiture in Greece.

But portraits were not limited to athletic dedications. In a later publication Kurke notices a strange parallel between the right to set up victors' statues at Olympia and another early occasion for setting up a portrait statue, this time as a form of punishment.[60] The custom seems to have been instituted during the lifetime of Solon. According to Aristotle (*Ath. Pol.* 7.1 and 55.5), having to dedicate an expensive statue served as a penalty for breaking the so-called Archon's oath sworn on the herald's stone in the Athenian agora (Plut. *Sol.* 25.2). Having mounted the stone, which was covered with the remains of sacrificial victims, the archon-to-be swore neither to take bribes nor to transgress any other laws, on penalty of "dedicating a golden statue." Plutarch supplies the information that the golden statue is to be set up at Delphi and be of the same "measure" or "weight" as oneself (ἰσομέτρητον), both of which Plato (*Phdr.* 235d–e) confirms, adding, significantly, that it is to be "of oneself" (ἑαυτοῦ). Kurke calls the practice "bizarre," and so it may be, but for our purposes it does document the use and acceptance of portraiture, apparently with some degree of complacency, if portraits were considered equally apt for reward or penalty, as early as the first half of the sixth century B.C.

Another early use of a type of image-making that partakes of some aspects of portraiture is documented at Sparta. Herodotus (6.58.3) tells of a funeral custom among the Lacedemonians of making effigies of kings who were slain in battle to carry in procession: "If a king is killed in war, they make a statue [εἴδωλον] of him, and carry it to burial on a richly draped bier." These would probably be those kings whose bodies could not be retrieved from the battle site, like Leonidas, whose fate at the hands of Xerxes after the Battle of Thermopylae Herodotus reports (7.238.1):

"After this conversation Xerxes went over to the battlefield to see the bodies, and having been told that Leonidas was king of Sparta and commander of the Spartan force, ordered his head to be cut off and fixed on a stake." The purpose of the custom is clear. When the king's body was retrievable, the body itself was brought home to honor; when it was not, an effigy was deemed an adequate substitute. As with other figural imagery directly associated with burial rites, such as masks, some element of intentional mimetic realism must be assumed. These effigies were obviously put together quickly and, like the simple death masks from Mycenae and Thrace, they need not be regarded as works of art. Yet one would imagine that the greatest effort was expended to make them resemble the original as closely as possible, perhaps incorporating a death mask, when the head was available, which was not the case with Leonidas, and actual clothes and accoutrements owned by the deceased. While there is no way of judging how realistic these hastily prepared images needed to be, it is clear that the effigies performed their stated function, being accepted as convincing substitutes, and therefore we should assume that at least a minimal likeness was achieved.

Also worthy of mention is a familiar ancient conceptual phenomenon, the subject of much interesting theoretical discussion of late, that almost certainly lies behind most if not all examples of early likeness-making. The conceit of a statue standing in place of a real person and occasionally speaking, by way of an inscription, on behalf of that person or of his/her image is attested from the very beginnings of sculptural production in Greece. A passing remark by Herodotus neatly encapsulates the phenomenon. Close to the end of the floruit of the Acropolis korai, we know of the existence of two sculpted likenesses of Alexander I of Macedon, whose coinage has already been discussed. The Macedonian king dedicated two gold statues of himself, one at Delphi and one at Olympia, shortly after Xerxes' defeat in 479.[61] The one at Delphi is of interest because of the way it is introduced by Herodotus (8.121.1–2), describing a dedication by Greeks of the first fruits from the booty seized at the naval battles of Salamis and Artemision. He tells us that this dedication was eighteen feet high and holds the beak of a ship in its hand; we may infer from Pausanias (10.14.5), another likely reference to the image, that it was a figure of Apollo, possibly of bronze. Herodotus locates the statue in the sanctuary—although one would not think that an eighteen-foot statue holding the prow of a ship would be easy to overlook!—by telling the reader that it stands very near the "golden Alexander" (ὁ Μακεδὼν Ἀλέξανδρος ὁ χρύσεος). It is curious that no word for statue is used. While it would be obvious that the referent is an actual image in the case of an inscription accompanying a monument, the oral/verbal medium alone does not as readily tolerate such ellipses.

I believe that the apparent off-handedness of Herodotus' remark is telling for our purposes, that is, for assessing the degree of success in producing a convincing likeness that sculptors were capable of achieving by 479 B.C., the end of the Archaic period. Until one hears/reads the attributive adjective ὁ χρύσεος, one assumes that a reference to a real person, Alexander of Macedon, is intended. If Herodotus felt the need to append an adjective in the attributive position in order to clarify that he did not mean the real Alexander but rather the "golden" one, the two must have resembled each other enough to be confused, even if only absentmindedly. In addition this allusion indicates that the golden Alexander was a very famous statue, more famous, at any rate, than an eighteen-foot Apollo holding the prow of a ship, and an easily identified image of the Macedonian king. It is remarkable that Herodotus orients his readers in the overcrowded sanctuary not by telling them to look for a colossal bronze statue, but by telling them that it was near the golden Alexander. While it might strike the modern reader as somewhat ludicrous, the anecdote does attest to the fact that a very well known Late Archaic/Early Classical dedication at Delphi went unquestioned as a portrait.

That statues were thought of as place-takers, or *Stellvertreter,* for real persons is well documented from an early date by monuments, both votive and funerary, that carry inscriptions. A warrior's ghost often loiters at his tomb in Greek vase-paintings;[62] a funerary portrait statue would offer the "ghost" a permanent "house," on the Egyptian model. That the notion of statue as place-taker was interpreted with absolute literalness is clear from stories like one that Pausanias (10.18.5) relates which reveals that the gods themselves apparently could be fooled:

> The men of Orneae in Argolis, when hard pressed in war by the Sicyonians, vowed to Apollo that, if they should drive the host of the Sicyonians out of their native land, they would organize a daily procession in his honor at Delphi, and sacrifice victims of a certain kind and of a certain number. Well, they conquered the Sicyonians in battle. But finding the daily fulfillment of their vow a great expense and a still greater trouble, they devised the trick of dedicating to the god bronze figures representing a sacrifice and a procession.

Although little is known about the relationship between Argos and Sicyon in the Archaic period, this event is thought to have occurred around the time of the First Sacred War over Delphi, generally dated to the 590s B.C., or somewhat later.[63] Fooling divinities would presumably require as high a level of mimetic accuracy as Archaic artist/creators were capable of attaining. An artist's rendition of a person or an event standing in for the real-life person or event must have been so commonplace by the Classical period that Euripides felt free to treat it with a degree of irreverence at *Ph.* 220–221, when the chorus of maidens from Tyre wishes that "just like *agalmata* made of worked gold, I might have become a servant of Phoebus" (that is, at Delphi).[64] The irony is that, while it is well known that votive statues replace and sometimes even replicate the worshiper, in the imaginations of Euripides' chorus, living persons replace and replicate statues. The custom of statues replacing people had long been in place; in the iconoclastic world of Euripides' plays, there is much to bemoan if people are now being enlisted to replace statues!

Of the numerous extant examples of Archaic *Stellvertreter* which could be cited, a well-preserved Attic example from the later sixth century is provided by the monument of Kroisos in the National Museum, Athens (NM 3851), which, speaking through an accompanying epitaph, accosts the passerby with the following: στε͂θι : καὶ οἴκτιρον : Κροίσο / παρὰ σε͂μα θανόντος : hόν / ποτ' ἐνὶ προμάχοις : ὄλεσε / θο͂ρος : Ἄρες ("Stand and pity beside the grave monument of dead Kroisos, whom, at one time, while fighting in the front ranks of battle, raging Ares destroyed").[65] The *kouros* that stands in place of the man is one of the most splendid of Archaic statues, and its size and the quality of its conception and execution suggest that it should be considered an intentional likeness.[66]

Since it retains evidence of a *mēniskos,* it is unlikely that Kroisos' image featured a separately attached bronze helmet, although this attribute might be expected in a warrior's monument.[67] However, his head is fitted with a kind of skullcap which was presumably worn between the hair and the helmet to control the hair and to make the wearing of the helmet more comfortable. Alternatively, this "cap" could be inspired by the type of headdress with which Diomedes is outfitted in the *Iliad* (10.257–259), a simple smooth leather headpiece called by the *hapax legomena* (a word that appears only once in extant Greek) καταῖτυξ, set in striking contrast to the elaborate boars'-tusk helmet worn by Odysseus that is described immediately thereafter, and perhaps worn alone in battle.[68] In this case, it would be an archaizing touch.

The anatomy of Kroisos is typical neither for a real man nor for a *kouros.* His hips are broad and rounded and his lower body is more developed than his upper, a proper build, it would seem, for performing the duties of a hoplite warrior, which would require lower body stability to maintain one's position in the phalanx, and upper body agility to wield and use both spear and sword while holding the shield in the left hand at the same time. This is a body in which fitness for a particular style of warfare, hoplite, is proclaimed by its outward form. But also in Homer (*Od.* 17.225; 18.67–68, 74), great size (μεγάλη) in a man's thighs is equated with great strength. Thus Kroisos' image is an amalgam of military prowess, past and present, evoking both old-fashioned Homeric glory and modern hoplite efficiency, both the individualism of Iliadic valor and the anonymity of the phalanx. Whether or not the dead man looked at all like the kouros who stands in for him is less important than the evident attempt to specify in his "portrait" the life's work which culminated in a noble death, in other words, the central fact of the man's existence. Not his face but his body is the essence of a warrior's portrait. Kroisos' nudity, for some reason, always seems bolder than that of other kouroi. This is nudity as a form of mortal dress, flaunted by those who possess a real-life physique that is, in Homeric terms, ἔξοχον ἄλλων ("better than all the others").[69] As we shall see again in the case of Phrasikleia, and as it was for centuries in Egyptian funerary art, life, rather than death, is the primary theme of one's tomb.

An epigram from Amorgos, an island in the Cyclades, dated to around the middle of the fifth century B.C., speaks in similar, if less glorious, tones, of a dead woman, evidently young, since she refers to her mother: ἀντὶ γυναικὸς ἐγὼ Παρίο λίθο ἐνθάδε κεῖμαι | μνημόσυνον Βίττης, μητρὶ δακρυτὸν ἄχος ("Here I stand, of Parian marble, instead of a woman, a memorial of Bittē, a tearful woe to her mother").[70] The accompanying image is lost. The wording of this inscription is unexceptional for the time; the tradition of statues "speaking" on their own behalf had long been an established trope. But there are a couple of nuances: The verb κεῖμαι may be associated both with the dead woman and her sculpted image, as if both were speaking; in reference to the former, it could be interpreted to signify "lie buried," while, in reference to the latter, the memorial, it could be interpreted as "set up," and thus "stand." At a secondary level the meaning of ἀντὶ γυναικός ("instead of a woman") could be analogous to the language of Phrasikleia's epitaph, to be presented fully in Chapter Five, that is, the young woman, Bittē, who should be called a κόρη rather than a γυνή, did not reach womanhood because she died before marriage. Her marble effigy, which, regardless of actual age, likely depicted a fully developed young woman, comparable in apparent age to the Acropolis korai, must then suffice in place of real womanhood for eternity, just as the name "kore" must stand in place of marriage and motherhood for Phrasikleia. The marble Bittē becomes a *Stellvertreter* for the real Bittē, an ideological substitution which is not perfect, of course, but evidently as satisfactory a solution as was available in Archaic Greece to the survivors of a family member's premature death. The "speaker" seems to want to assure the passing viewer that, though it is unfortunate that Bittē herself has died and cannot be present in the flesh, she has fictively been re-embodied in the substantive, permanent medium of Parian marble for all who pass by to admire, recognize, empathize with, and remember, likely in that order.

Typical for this type of epitaph, there is no word in Bittē's inscription that refers directly to the sculpted image, such as εἰκών. There are a number of reasons why the presence of εἰκών or a synonym might have been superfluous to the successful reading of the image as an intentional likeness. First, the form of the monument, that is, figure accompanied by inscription, presupposed some degree of likeness at least since the time of Nikandre's dedication from Delos, mid–seventh century B.C. The genitive case alone (e.g., "of Aristodikos") was enough to confirm that it was both an image of and a memorial to the named individual. Second, the image itself, by visual means alone, might have demonstrated that it was a "portrait" or intentional likeness to a degree that its appearance "spoke" efficiently enough on its own behalf and would require no further restating in the inscription, in the manner of the Acropolis korai. Third, the poetry of the inscription is simple and direct; its minimalist message is delivered with the utmost expediency and clarity, while the statue said the rest. In an inscription which claims "I am somebody," to engrave the additional letters required to say "I am a likeness of somebody" would seem excessive. In the case of Bittē the phrase ἀντὶ γυναικός affirms the identification of the image as a stand-in for the dead woman. A portrait- or statue-word would have constituted an ideological or conceptual barrier between the sculpted image and the real person whose logic, it seems, would have been questioned by a contemporary audience accustomed to this type of memorial. This was the case too with Herodotus' "golden Alexander," and could explain why he left out the statue-word in his brief allusion to that image. In either instance the insertion of εἰκών or something like it would have interfered with the viewer's literal identification of the statue with the subject.

Those who choose to believe Aristotle (*Topica* 140a21–22) when he suggests that in "old paintings" the protagonists could not be identified unless their names were inscribed might conclude that the images of Bittē, Alexander, and others were not realistic at all, that their subjects were identified solely on the basis of the inscriptions which accompanied them. However, in the case of the portrait of Croesus' female baker at Delphi, no inscription was necessary for a correct identification. The name does not necessarily make the portrait. The name of the baker does not seem to have been known; if it was, we might expect Herodotus to have reported it.

Close in time to the end of the floruit of the Acropolis korai, the Athenian demos refused a request made by Miltiades, the victorious general at Marathon, to be granted the privilege of having his name inscribed in the painted mural depicting the Battle of Marathon located in the Stoa Poikile in the Athenian agora. Instead Miltiades was allowed to be shown at the front of the battle exhorting his men to attack by a symbolic gesture of stretching out his hand in the direction of the barbarian enemy, a gesture reminiscent, in a reversal of roles, of that of Darius III toward Alexander the Great in the famous mosaic from Pompeii which copies a painting of the Battle of Issus.[71] Miltiades was not alone in dominating the painting, however. This honor he shares with Kallimachos, the polemarch, who according to Pausanias (1.15.3) was the other conspicuous figure. While no inscription appeared under Miltiades' portrait, and Kallimachos' likely as well, the two were recognized and distinguished, presumably by differing iconographical attributes and gestures. As for individualized features, there is no way of knowing how like the men these images were. In the case of Miltiades it is probable that there was some attempt at replicating his features based on what was remembered about him, what may have been written down about his appearance and/or what was recorded in other, more contemporary portrait images.[72] The important point to be drawn from this is that an image could function well as a portrait for years and even centuries without an inscription.

In a collaboratively produced *Ilioupersis* also in the Stoa Poikile, the painter Polygnotus was responsible for a scene of a group of Trojan women, one of whom, although labeled "Laodicē," was nonetheless recognized by contemporaries to be Cimon's sister, Elpinicē.[73] An apparent aversion to the public display of portraits culminates in the indictment, conviction, imprisonment, and eventual death, if we are to believe our sources, of the sculptor Pheidias ostensibly owing to circumstances connected with the making of the gold and ivory cult statue of Athena Parthenos. The sculptor was acquitted on the charge of embezzlement, according to Plutarch (*Per.* 31.3–5), after the gold was weighed and found to be intact. Pheidias was convicted, however, in Plutarch's account, on a second unnamed charge (hubris?) of incurring jealousy by virtue of being a great artist but, more specifically, by incorporating portraits of himself and his patron Pericles among the Greeks fighting Amazons on the exterior of the Parthenos' shield:[74]

> But the reputation of his works put a burden of envy upon Pheidias, and especially the fact that, in making the battle with the Amazons on the shield, he modeled a figure like himself (αὐτοῦ τινα μορφήν) as a bald old man lifting a rock with both hands, and he also put in a very good portrait (εἰκόνα παγκάλην) of Pericles fighting an Amazon. And the *schema* of the hand, as it extends a spear in front of Pericles' face, is ingeniously arranged as if meant to conceal the likeness, which is, however, still apparent from both sides.

This and other evidence for a public distrust of portraiture which seems to emerge some time after the Persian Wars suggests, by implication, that portraits had existed without consequence until this time. Considering the fate of ideas about portraiture in the Classical period, a glimpse of which is provided above, "true" portraiture, in an ironic way, is more likely to have occurred in the Archaic period than afterward. In spite of the full institution of stylistic naturalism in the figural arts sometime after 480 B.C., on the whole, idealization, generalization, and nonspecificity—all symptoms of altered reality—preside over the art of portraiture in the Classical period and later.[75] What realism was permitted reflected, in part, the stereotypes that had settled into the artistic repertory. Verism would replace realism; idealization would replace nonidealized beauty.

After Plato and particularly after Aristotle, artists began to manipulate appearances in portraiture; coincident with the increased naturalism, but antagonistic to it, physiognomic theory and formulae for idealization began to infect the arts—this in spite of the fact that the fourth century and the subsequent Hellenistic period is commonly regarded as the age in which "true" portraiture is introduced in Greek art. The viewer cannot be sure whether he/she is seeing men as they are, men nobler than they are, or men less noble than they are,[76] but he/she can be sure that the impressions of these men that he/she takes away are not entirely his/her own. The eventual outcome was clear from the start. When character was believed to be able to be read in physical appearances, the temptation to add or to subtract character by the addition, subtraction, or enhancement of physical features would be impossible, and often inadvisable, for the would-be portraitist to resist. These "portraits" might resemble their subjects in a superficial way. However, the viewer should be wary; with the intrusion of physiognomics into the idea of likeness-making, a portrait can never again altogether be trusted.

On the evidence presented in this chapter, it is possible to conclude that intentional likeness-making thrived in the art of the Archaic period even without the attainment of full stylistic naturalism. Taken together and balanced against one another, the sources and documents just presented, literary and material, help to clarify the conceptual circumstances and attitudes toward images and image-making under which the korai from the Acropolis were conceived and created, and begin to render more intelligible the mimetic realism on display in these statues.

The Archaic period is recognized as a formative period with all of the advantages and disadvantages that a state of perpetual experimentation confers. In art this is seen in a series of false starts and dead ends, especially with regard to form—as attested by, among other things, the different sizes and scales of monumental sculptures, which range from kolossoi to under life-size, the various schemata tried and rejected for the abdominal sections, ears, and knees of kouroi, and for rendering hair on both kouroi and korai—and the unsystematic and sometimes baffling borrowings from Egypt and the Near East. It is not inconceivable that Archaic Greeks also stumbled upon a notion of likeness that has much in common with what would later be called portraiture, without qualification and with more than a little injustice. In the receptive climate of Archaic Greece an uncomplicated idea of likeness could arise and flourish in the visual arts relatively free of the compromises forced by programmatic content, ideology, and a broader range of stylistic choices overloaded with their own meaning that would beset Classical and later portraiture. In my view the message of the combined evidence for the Archaic period, verbal and visual, is so forceful that the semantic field of the term "portrait" may have to be stretched to include a category of image-making inspired by an intent-to-likeness broader than would be demanded by later standards. In the end the cumulative effect of this evidence might obligate viewers to look again, not only to the Acropolis korai, but to all Archaic images, for evidence of the kind of specificity which betrays an engagement with the idea of likeness.

conTEXTualizing the Korai

We now turn to the lyrical description of dancing maidens from Euripides' *Iphigenia in Tauris (IT)* that serves, in the poet Witter Bynner's elegant translation of 1915,[1] as the epigraph to this book. A vivid little word picture that perfectly captures a part of the spirited, carefree world of young Greek women, Euripides' verses could just as well be describing the Acropolis korai as a real-life Archaic chorus, and usefully may be enlisted, albeit somewhat anachronistically, to serve in the role of an ekphrasis of the statues in order to aid in the task of "conTEXTualizing" the korai. The well-known competitive spirit that characterized Archaic Greece, and much of Classical Greece as well—although in an altered form—is evoked, in typical Euripidean fashion, from the feminine point of view in the push toward "unrivalled radiance." A gentle spirit of competition just as easily could have motivated a "contest of graces" (ἐς ἁμίλλας χαρίτων, *IT* 1147) among the korai as among the real-life women whose physical appearances, I believe, inspired them,[2] for each element of Euripides' imagery, the motion of hands and feet, the embroidered mantle, the dense clusters of curls, braids, and crimps shading a lovely countenance, has its visual counterpart in the Acropolis statues.

The printing of "conTEXTualizing" in the title of this chapter is deliberate, for embedded within the word "context" is, significantly, the word "text"; thus, conTEXTualizing the korai shall involve the interweaving of text and image. Once interwoven, the poetry entwines its messages with those of the visual, lending the figurative substance of the verbal imagery to the literal substance of the sculptures, and transforming the latter into a visual text whose exegesis involves a sort of poetics, a poetics of appearance. However, conTEXTualizing the Acropolis korai is not an arbitrary exercise in *ut pictura poesis,* in finding delight once again in how the verbal record complements, reiterates, surpasses, or falls short of the visual, but rather it is an effort to put word and image together in a meaningful, mutually illuminating way that advances the discourse in both categories of evidence toward the common goal of illuminating the pre-Classical *mentalité*. ConTEXTualizing the korai is ultimately to do no more than to seek corroborative evidence to authenticate them further, to expose them for what they were and are, reflectors of and commentators on the milieu of their creation.

Archaic Greece was not an age that celebrated anonymity. The Lyric poets name their subjects or their targets, as the case may be. Proclamations of individuality, consciousness of the self, and self-aggrandizement dominated Archaic art and life, sacred and secular, public and private. The symptoms of a culture's emphasis on individuality at the expense of the commonweal are self-awareness, assertiveness, ostentatious and sumptuous public displays of wealth, social position, and power, both political and religious, and uninhibited pride in one's physical self, in one's descent, and in one's progeny, all of which are encountered in Lyric poetry, the literary genre most characteristic of the Archaic age. To these might be added attention to faithful portrayal of the reality of individualized physical appearances in the visual arts, in the Acropolis korai, in particular. In the sociopolitical environment for which the korai constitute important documentary evidence, the concerns of the individual rose above the needs of the populace; primary identities were with one's native region, family, or clan rather than with the developing polis; differences rather than similarities were paraded.

The Acropolis korai too are symptomatic of Archaic individualism; they would never be mistaken for products of democracy. These statues epitomize in every degree the excesses and the best of a society that equated extravagance and superiority and generously allowed for the flaunting of both. As for how this attitude affected the visual arts, Rhys Carpenter makes the pointed but often overlooked observation that monumental sculpture was utterly "unnecessary" to early Greeks and, while they had "no particular reason for making statues" for themselves, they were nonetheless enthralled by the practice when they encountered it in Egypt during the late seventh century B.C. and immediately set out to emulate the model.[3]

Not only is it reasonable to expect signs of the introduction of personal characteristics into both funerary and votive sculptures from the Archaic period, but we should probably look for them even when they are not obvious. It is commonly assumed that the law against lavish funerary monuments mentioned by Cicero (*De leg.* II.26.64–65), the so-called sumptuary legislation, was intended to curtail some of this open self-advertisement.[4] While votives are not mentioned in connection with the sumptuary laws, there is little reason to doubt that extravagance had crept into personal votive dedications as well; the Acropolis korai themselves provide an obvious example of it. Such overt, public declarations of individuality were one of the things that democratic institutions sought to stifle, marking an essential difference between the Archaic and Classical periods. Fully democratic Athens, by contrast, strove at least in principle to level the classes of society in a number of ways, which may have included a reluctance to sanction public portraits. It is then, rather than in the Archaic period, that homogeneous, nonindividualized artistic expressions might be expected to be deemed suitable for public display.

When differences are flaunted, whether in art or in life, comparison is inevitable. With every man's and woman's character and physical appearance served up for public scrutiny, evaluation, both positive and negative, invariably follows. The Lyric poets, reflecting their times, are wary of the friend who could be harboring uncharitable thoughts; hence they are keen to promote the wearing of one's heart on one's sleeve. Early Greeks preferred for others to have their characters visible at all times. It is no accident that the primary meaning of the Greek word χαρακτήρ ("character") is the stamp on the face of a coin which permitted the verification of its authenticity.[5] One was always welcome to be oneself, whether enemy or friend, but at least should make it clear which. In Archilochus' oxymoronic formulation "favoring the foe with guest-gifts of woe" (fr. 6) and other lyric warnings against the false friend, we are witnessing a developmental stage of the Classical Greek maxim "help one's friends, harm one's enemies."[6] The apparent fascination with the state of intoxication also makes sense in this context; wine makes a man honest, as in Alcaeus' fr. 366: "[Give me] wine, dear boy, and truth"; and fr. 333: "for wine is a means for seeing through a man."[7]

In earlier, simpler times, as reflected in the Homeric epics, no such stimulus was necessary. Ugliness is automatically equated with bad character, as in the case of Thersites (*Il.* 2.216–219), and greatness coincides with youthful beauty, as attested by Achilles. However, the fact that Homer's Thersites, in spite of a repulsive physical appearance matched by an ugly personality, is gifted in the use of language, suggests that visual signs are more reliable than verbal as indicators of character. Compare the ambiguity of Sappho fr. 50: "For the beautiful person is beautiful just in form, but the noble of soul will soon seem to have beauty too."[8] It is easy to imagine that when Archaic Greeks made images, they would take special care not to fall victim to the potential for deceit that false appearances could occasion. Consequently, Archaic sculptures are neither subtle nor equivocal in their messages. Sharp, precise outlines make the parts of the body clear and unmistakable; hair and accoutrements are impeccably arranged. The same qualities which define a people—in this case, open, uninhibited, clear-eyed, confident—also define their images.

In the previous chapter we saw how a sculpted image in Archaic Greece may be read first and foremost on a literalist level, that is, as a substitute for the depicted or for the dedicant him or herself. So too has this most elemental intent been ascribed to the korai from the Acropolis. We have also seen how statues need not be called "portraits" in order for them to carry out this simple function. But to sustain the argument that the korai are *Stellvertreter*, it must be assumed that, since so many of them were made for the same purpose, the statues performed this function well and properly, and to do that they must have seemed to the original audience to be mimetically accurate enough representations of real women. To ascertain to what degree this is indeed the case, logically we must try to determine what real women of the period looked like. As tempting as it is to cite them, the korai themselves cannot yet be enlisted as evidence, since that would amount to circular reasoning. However, Archaic and later poetry helpfully provides a body of evidence for the physical appearances of predemocratic-era women and shall be consulted liberally in the effort to authenticate the appearances of the Acropolis korai.

DECOROUS MOVEMENT

The Acropolis korai appear to be caught in the act of walking or processing, very like their later counterparts on the east frieze of the Parthenon. It is well to recall that the Panathenaic festival was instituted in 566 B.C., so there could be a concrete reason for the activity in Archaic statues of women on the Acropolis. While the precise nature of the korai's stance, that is, whether they are meant to be walking, taking a step, or simply standing, remains arguable, walking seems the most likely possibility.

The most common pose in the korai involves a ladylike forward step of the right or left foot, a modest reflection of the manly stride of contemporary kouroi. In the kouroi a large part of the justification for this feature is balance; the korai, with their legs physically connected by their skirts and thus offering a more stable base, did not need to have their feet as widely separated. Practical considerations aside, the male stance almost certainly derives from Egypt, where it is a virtual glyph for Pharaoh, an effective symbol of dominance, power, size, and strength that endured for centuries, carrying the message over the course of dynasties both strong and weak with amazing consistency, resilience, and effectiveness. The pose is so common an emblem in Egyptian art that the motif of a striding man also serves as the hieroglyphic determinate in words for "statue,"[9] although, considering the strong interconnections between hieroglyphs and monumental art in Egypt, the reverse direction of influence is not out of the question. For our purposes it might also be instructive to compare the convention for portraying women in two- and three-dimensional Egyptian art, seen, for example, in the double portrait of Mycerinus and Khamerernebty; he steps broadly with his left foot, while she steps also with her left in demure accord with her dominant mate.

But the early Greek habit of borrowing from the Near East does not completely account for why the korai step more lightly than their male counterparts or, more important, why they step at all. There is, closer to hand, a peculiarly Greek explanation: it is a convention for decorous walking. Attested in both literature and art, the "light step" is a sign of regal bearing, beauty, and repose in women.[10] When Astymeloisa spurns Alcman, she departs "with long strides" (διέβα ταναοῖς πο[σί], fr. 3.70), temporarily disrupting the normal delicacy of her step in order to make a quick, if flirtatious, getaway. More usually, her gait would be "lovely" (ἔρατον βᾶμα, Sappho fr. 16.17). For the woman who knows how to walk properly takes "light," moderate steps. Her feet and ankles would be but briefly on view beneath her chiton as she lifts it, to the delight of her male admirers, in order to facilitate her steps. As a signifier of genteel movement, these parts and only these parts of a woman's legs would become visible.

In the korai it is generally the feet alone to which attention could be called, since only a foolhardy sculptor would court catastrophe by carving free the narrow ankles of a woman in a life-size statue in stone; that some might have done so, with obvious results, is suggested by the many examples of korai which are broken off at the ankles. It is curious that, while the delicate step as a trope appears frequently in the literature of the Classical period, especially in the plays of Euripides, one seldom encounters its equivalent in the monumental visual arts of that period. Despite the fact that the best of the Acropolis korai were almost certainly not available for autopsy in the latter half of the fifth century, as the embodiments of a somewhat antiquated idea of feminine grace and bearing they happen to constitute a perfect visual analog to the image of young aristocratic women that appears consistently throughout the plays of Euripides, a playwright who was always attentive to the genre element.

The image in various forms is used of Creon's daughter as she dresses herself with Medea's poisoned robe (*Med.* 1164); of Helen as she approaches and boards a ship (*Hel.* 1528); of Iphigenia as she is instructed by her mother to step down from a carriage (*IA* 614); of Hecuba, in characterizing her former status at Troy as she is led away to slavery in Greece (*Tr.* 506). Helen displays an εὐσφύρου ποδός ("beautifully ankled foot," *Hel.* 1570) as she ascends a ladder to board the ship, the same formula used of a woman's lower extremities in Hesiod (*Th.* 254, 961 [εὔσφυρος]); in Sappho (fr. 103.5) a bride is εὔπους ("of beautiful foot"), a synecdoche for beauty. While their ankles are nominally covered by the transparent hems of their dresses, the exposed feet of many korai demonstrate a precocious naturalism compared with other aspects of their carving, as attested by, among others, Acr. 598 (fig. 39), 672 (fig. 17), 682 (fig. 35), and Euthydikos' Kore (Acr. 686/609, fig. 44), as well as numerous unattached foot fragments.[11] This surprising feature, already noted, now takes on added significance. The obvious beauty of the carved feet of the stepping korai, the result of a concentrated effort by the Archaic sculptor to render them as convincingly as possible, stands as yet another outward sign of the women's beauty and poised demeanor and a perfect visual correspondent to the convention of "stepping lightly" in poetry.

With feet as a measure of beauty, attention will inevitably be drawn to their shoeing. Light, colorful, and exquisitely crafted sandals connote swiftness and easy, graceful movement among goddesses and mortals in literature, as indirectly reflected in the phrase "motion of my hands and feet" of Euripides' *IT* chorus. Helen's step is "golden-sandaled" as she begins to flee an Orestes intent on murder (Eur. *Or.* 1468). Dawn, who makes a deft, quick entrance on the day, is appropriately "golden-sandaled" in Sappho (frags. 103, 123). Neither is this particular aspect of Archaic beauty left unaddressed in the Acropolis korai; in the matter of shoes, the statues do not disappoint. Sappho (fr. 39) mentions variegated colored-leather sandals of Lydian workmanship, which may have been the source of the showy polychromed sandals worn by kore 682.[12] Perhaps it was the availability of accoutrements like these and the Lydian headdresses discussed below that, if Gentili is correct, drove Lydia-hating Pittacus, ruler of Mytilene, who once refused an offer of gifts from Croesus, to issue a decree forbidding the importation of clothing and other luxury items from Lydia.[13] On the other hand, a lack of delicacy characterizes the stockinglike red boots worn by Acr. 683 (fig. 36), reiterating and underscoring the apparent lack of grace in this kore's overall demeanor. With a short, stocky body, kore 683 appears by the nature of her build incapable of graceful movement. These bulky shoes would seem to hinder rather than to enhance a lady's step; not incidentally, they also hide this kore's feet, as if to warn the viewer that they are insufficiently attractive to permit exposure.

In poetry an indelicate female gait, by contrast, announces that something is amiss; a lighthearted example is seen in Alcman fr. 3, above, but there are far more serious occasions for a woman to break from her light step. When Cassandra is described as "running" (δρομάδα) in a crazed frenzy (Eur. *Tr.* 41–42), it is clear that she has, at this point, lost all of the poise and grace that are embodied in the light step; it is not necessary to believe that she is actually running to understand the depths to which Priam's daughter has fallen.[14] The convention for running in early Greek art, less commonly found than the convention for decorous walking, has the knees far apart and bent and, usually, the skirts hiked up above the knee to expose one or both legs. For women only the most extreme circumstances warrant running, Cassandra's being a conspicuous example. In one of the earliest renditions of a running female in art, the relief decoration in the west pediment of the temple of Artemis at Corfu from ca. 600 B.C., the Gorgon Medusa flees her would-be slayer Perseus wearing a short skirt that allows for the legs to move rapidly in the so-called Knielauf position, which forces the lower body into a stylized swastika pattern. In the same spirit, or perhaps even as a direct source, a pair of running legs are used in Egyptian hieroglyphics as a determinative to mean something "in motion."[15] On the protoattic Eleusis Amphora, the Gorgon sisters each lift a completely exposed left leg as if they were in a chorus line.[16] Cassandra again runs in an Iliupersis by the Brygos Painter on a cup in the Louvre, as does a female fleeing Zeus on a kantharos in Boston, both Archaic.[17] Two metopes from one of the temples to Hera at Paestum of ca. 500 B.C. show two pairs of fleeing maidens, possibly to be identified as Nereids.[18] As they pick up their skirts with their bent right hands, the women extend their arms and legs in a modified version of the Knielauf to indicate they are moving rapidly, more rapidly than the korai, although their skirts are not pulled all the way over the knee. Female athletes are also shown in this conventional pose.[19]

The foregoing discussion may also help to shed some light on the meaning of Menelaus' strange remark at Eur. *Tr.* 1050, which has struck modern readers as an attempt at humor that is misplaced in this arguably most tragic of Euripides' extant plays.[20] Hecuba is trying to dissuade Menelaus from taking Helen aboard the same ship on which he is returning home to Greece. In response Menelaus appears to make a joke: τί δ' ἔστι; μεῖζον βρῖθος ἢ πάροιθ' ἔχει; ("Why [not let her board]? Does she have a greater weight than she had before?"). Hecuba proceeds to articulate her fear that Menelaus is still in love with his wife; unspoken is the assumption that, were Helen to accompany her husband, he would once again fall victim to her charms and forgive her, a danger that Menelaus himself is finally forced to acknowledge as he yields to Hecuba's wishes. But perhaps there is no humor at all intended in Menelaus' remark. Helen displays a properly delicate foot (ἀβρὸν πόδα τιθεῖσ') in *Helen* (1528, 1570), a play in which she is treated as something of a heroine, never having gone to Troy in the first place. The Helen of *Trojan Women* is a different character; the play's subject, the plight of the captive women, allows her little room for our sympathy. She has lost all innocence, all grace; her physical beauty may be intact but her bearing had long ago ceased to be that of a lady; now she is "heavy" by comparison, not in weight but in comportment. Priam's wife and Hector's mother, on the other hand, still preserves her dignity, although she has been brought low. We had been reminded of Hecuba's grace and bearing by the "light foot" metaphor used to describe her life at the Trojan court at *Tr.* 506; these, it seems, are things that cannot be taken away from her no matter what her life in Greece is to be.

The "light step" has a practical basis as well. Hemlines in the Archaic period were quite long, sometimes covering the feet. In order to avoid tripping and dragging the fine material along the ground as they walked, young women picked up their skirts with one hand and held them to one side as they moved, occasionally raising them to a height which exposed the ankles.[21] Often cited in connection with the ubiquitous skirt-tugging gesture of the Archaic korai is Sappho fr. 57: "And what country girl melts your sense . . . wearing rustic clothes . . . not knowing how to draw up her long robe to her ankles?" Apparently the delicacy and finesse with which a girl picked up her skirts was yet another discreet sign of her noble birth and good breeding. And the ankles which she displayed had better be graceful, as in Alcman fr. 1.78 (χ[α]λλίσφυρος, "beautiful-ankled"); contrast Archilochus fr. 206: "thick round the ankles, a hateful woman." In translating this gesture into one of the identifying characteristics of the statuary type, the korai's sculptors drew on a real-life mannerism originating within the aristocracy and surely emulated by those who aspired to their status.[22]

And while it is most commonly associated with the korai from the Acropolis, the gesture is by no means exclusive to the Acropolis examples. It makes an early appearance in the series of East Greek korai culminating in the so-called Hera of Samos (mid–sixth century) and becomes even more conspicuous as the type develops elsewhere in the Greek world throughout the second half of the sixth century B.C. and into the fifth. A perusal of the plates of Richter's *Korai* will make clear just how common this gesture is among korai of all styles, places, and dates. Chiton-wearers do this more often and more conspicuously than peplos-wearers, understandably, since chitons seem to have been worn slightly longer, to judge by the visual record. Sourvinou-Inwood distinguishes between those korai (the majority of the Acropolis group) who really do seem to be pulling their skirts—since the gesture clearly affects the drape of the fabric—and are thus to be considered represented "in action" (that is, as if walking), and those whose tug at the side of their skirts has no effect on the fall of the fabric (e.g., Phrasikleia), who are shown in a manner that is simply "emblematic" of an action or a state of being.[23]

There are several variant ways of representing hemlines affected by the pulling gesture, some more successful than others from a naturalistic point of view, even among the Acropolis group. The garment can be shown longer at the back, even on the ground, while shorter over the front, sometimes sacrificing a degree of naturalism in order to expose the fronts of the feet, as in Acr. 609, the lower half of Euthydikos' Kore (fig. 44). Sometimes the light fabric is gathered and held in the hand at front and center with its edge dropped in realistic omega folds just slightly between the feet, exposing the fronts of the feet and the sides almost to the ankle bone, as in Acr. 493, a set of fragmentary lower legs which has been connected with the kore head Acr. 696.[24] It can also be spread out at the back over the ground like a fan, while falling just over the instep of the feet, again exposing the fronts of the feet, as in Acr. 598 (fig. 39).[25] Some of the Classical processing maidens on the east frieze of the Parthenon also grasp the sides of their garments as they walk, perhaps, as we have seen, in subtle homage to the Archaic female statues that had decorated the Acropolis before the Persian Wars, although their gesture is somewhat ambiguous compared to the korai, where it is clearly an iconographical element so essential to the type's function as to be considered formulaic.[26] Even so, it is certainly based on real life.

It is not inappropriate that this aspect of the korai comes to mind in a couple of dressing scenes in Euripides, both of which will lead to fatal conclusions. At *Med.* 1136–1230 a messenger provides Medea at her request with a detailed narrative of the horrific deaths of Creon and his daughter at Medea's hands. The instrument of death is a poisoned dress and diadem that Medea has sent as a gift to Glaukē, the intended new bride of Jason. Incorporated within the narrative is a dressing scene, a poignant reminder of one of the many small tasks that filled out a young woman's day. Although the deadly gift is called a "peplos" (vv. 983, 786, 1159, 1188), the generic term for garment in tragedy, it is more likely to have been a linen chiton than a woolen peplos, since it is described as light (786, 1188) and would need to make direct contact, killing Glaukē by clinging closely to her flesh and devouring it (1188–1189); a peplos would normally require an undergarment. At 1164–1166, having donned the garment, and before the poison takes effect, Glaukē spends a few moments basking in its look and feel on her body, as would any woman trying on a new dress. She does not, however, enjoy the benefits of a full-length mirror, only a small one in which to arrange the poisoned crown in her hair (1161), but rather checks her appearance in the only way she knows, stretching her toes in every direction like a ballerina as she glances with approval at the fall of the hemline over her foot, gauging it for proper length and drape over the foot and ankle (πολλὰ πολλάκις / τένοντ' ἐς ὀρθὸν ὄμμασι σκοπουμένη, "over and over, inspecting [it] with her eyes at the straight tendon," 1165–1166).[27] Our attention had already been drawn to the girl's delicate step and appropriately pale foot (1164); the vignette of a preening young woman completes the picture of a female pantomime enacted daily over the ritual of proper dressing, the literary equivalent of the brief glimpse into a feminine world captured in the Archaic korai.[28] As a woman herself familiar with the intimate rituals of dressing, Medea, having planned it all that way, of course, knew exactly how the murder would unfold, how cruel a death in a beautiful dress would be, how quickly a young woman's vanity would evaporate and be replaced by excruciating physical torment and the realization that premature death was at hand—and therein lies the source of Medea's joy at hearing every detail of the messenger's account.

The invasion of the world of women becomes even more sinister when it is at the hands of a man, as it is in the cross-dressing scene in Euripides' *Bacchae,* an episode that is at once humorous, parodic, and disturbing in that it points up the innate feminine characteristics of its protagonist, suggesting that his obsessive interest in the activities of the Bacchae has another side in addition to the one stated. At *Bacc.* 821, when Dionysos first suggests to Pentheus that he dress as a woman in order to spy on the Bacchantes, women's garments are described as βυσσίνους πέπλους, "of fine linen," the same type used for wrapping mummies (Hdt. 2.86) and for wounds (7.181); thus, the very finest available. Their delicacy and lightness is emphasized again in the phrase στεῖλαί . . . ἀμφὶ χρωτί ("to array . . . around the skin"), an image which recalls Creon's daughter's death in a poisoned gown that clung directly to her skin; Pentheus will also die a horrible death in a fine dress.[29] It is impossible not to be reminded by these phrases that light, clinging drapery is one of the most prominent characteristics of the Archaic korai; it becomes for their sculptors a way of revealing the youthful female body without resorting to nudity, and the result is arguably more sensual than the actual nudity of the kouroi. The truth is, while the korai are frequently called "demure," they are in fact all but naked when seen from behind. These scenes would seem to require knowledge of the gossamer dress of the korai as an old-fashioned stylistic precursor of the heavy, opaque Classical peplos and chiton. One might counter that the wet-drapery look which is character-istic of the Parthenon pediments and subsequent late-fifth-century sculp-ture could also be relevant here, but, unlike the dress of the korai, the Classical "stuff," whatever its material basis, could hardly be described as light.

At *Bacc.* 833 we learn that the king's dress is also to be ποδήρεις ("foot-length"), likely an allusion to the means by which proper length is as-sessed, as we have seen.[30] That allusion is made even clearer when Pentheus (935–938), criticized in a mocking tone by Dionysos for the skewed ar-rangement of his dress, checks it by looking from one side to another at the fall of the hem of the chiton against his feet in a manner that recalls the fatal dressing scene in Medea. His brief surveillance allows him to agree with Dionysos that the right side is off, but the left falls correctly at the ankle. Pentheus' instincts here seem quite natural, leading to the sus-picion that he has done this before.[31] It seems that Pentheus is confronted with three distinct problems regarding his dress as articulated by Dionysos. His ζῶναι ("girdles") are slack (χαλῶσι), the pleats (στολίδες) are not evenly arrayed (ἑξῆς), and the hem of the dress is too long, falling below the ankles (ὑπὸ σφυροῖσι). The latter may include an implied criticism of the manner in which he is walking, since, were he lifting his skirts in properly ladylike fashion, they would not seem to be too long. The source of the trouble appears to be some sort of faulty belting or hiking, whether over the hip or perhaps at the shoulders, where a linen chiton would normally be buttoned. Hiking the skirts to the proper length and picking them up properly when walking, as the korai demonstrate, allow for the creation of both longitudinal and latitudinal pleats to which the wearer's close atten-tion must be given. The former will be judged by evenness of size and separation, while the latter might be judged in the same way that a mod-ern tailor determines the appropriate length of a man's trousers by making sure that the ends create one and only one crease as they lie on his insteps; the back will then take care of itself. Pentheus is probably to be pictured as looking down at the front and sides of the garment rather than at the back, as most commentators suggest, since he would better be able to judge the fall of the pleats without lifting his feet.

To visualize the niceties of aristocratic Archaic dress we need only con-sult again the korai, with their manifold ways of arranging the various components. Even though many of the statues no longer retain their lower extremities, there are enough examples to illustrate the basic principles involved in the *Bacchae* dressing scene. The neatness with which very narrow longitudinal pleats might be arrayed in a finely woven garment belted at the waist can best be seen on "Hera of Samos," to cite only the most outstanding example, while in the case of a heavier woolen belted garment, this feature is attested in the form of two wide lateral pleats ending in single perfect omega folds on Acr. 679. Latitudinal pleats are less common, but they can be seen in the neat stack of omega folds between the feet of Acr. 683 (fig. 36), 493, and 510, among others.[32]

All of this evidence goes to the question of movement in the korai. In lieu of real movement, which could only be bestowed on an inanimate image by a god, such as Hephaistos (e.g., *Il.* 18.417–421, the god's golden helpmates; *Od.* 7.91–94, the animate dogs that guard Alcinoös' palace), an impression of movement must suffice in an Archaic statue; Greek visual aesthetics from an early date virtually require it. The situation could not be more unlike its Near Eastern counterpart, which features the opposite, stability and immobility; these statues must not under any circumstances leave their posts. In the korai, before the invention of the *contrapposto* pose, which is less effectual in a dressed figure than in a nude anyway, the "light step," the trailing chiton, the tugging gesture, and the extended arms all work together to signify movement. Furthermore, the clinging fabric, which leaves few aspects of the young women's forms to the imagination, obviates the need for the bent leg of the *contrapposto* which would come to be essential in the peplophoroi of the Early Classical period for suggesting that there is a body under all that cloth.[33] But the illusion only worked among those viewers who were willing to suspend their disbelief and admire the ingenuity of the artist and the effectiveness of the artifice. Not all viewers were so willing, especially if there was an occasion for a *paragone* between the verbal and the visual media. Just such an opportunity was seized by Pindar (*Nem.* V.1–3) when, in a triumphant tone, he boasts that he is not a portrait-sculptor (ἀνδριαντοποιός) making statues (ἀγάλματ') that are condemned to stand still on their bases.[34] As a poet he holds this advantage over the sculptor: his work is, in a sense, portable; consequently, he can send his songs along on every vessel leaving Aegina, his patron's home port, like Keats' name, "writ on water," to announce the victor's name and recent success to distant shores. What, Pindar might be asking, can the creator of a victor's statue that is destined to remain in one place offer by comparison?

Pindar was not the first to pit the visual and verbal arts against one another in a *paragone* of their respective values as monuments. Late New Kingdom Egyptian literary encomia on scribes and the legacy of their written work by comparison with material monuments[35] offer what are likely to be the earliest extant commentaries on this particular aspect of the *ut pictura poesis* debate. It is not surprising, considering the ancient Egyptians' deep interest in the perceptions of posterity and in eternal life for the deserving, that Egyptian poets reflect on the lasting effects of their memorabilia.

Closer to home, Sappho (fr. 55) had staked a poet's claim to superiority in the matter of conveying immortality, at least on the dead, although the fragment as we have it does not include a comparison with a grave statue, which, as the Egyptians had already recognized for millennia, is the best guarantee of eternal remembrance, if not of immortality itself:

> But when you die you will lie there, and afterwards there will never be any recollection of you or any longing for you since you have no share in the roses of Pieria [i.e., in the products of the muses]; unseen in the house of Hades also, flown from our midst, you will go to and fro among the shadowy corpses.[36]

Sappho, while offering high praise to her own muse and the power of verses, does not seem to feel that her work stands in competition with funerary statues, which, in the late seventh century, had not yet developed the level of sophistication seen in Phrasikleia. It is up to Pindar to make the comparison directly, perhaps because the epinician form itself more readily invites a comparison with the other means of immortalizing victorious athletes, the portrait statue.

Pindar seems to have had two purposes in drawing the line between encomiastic poetry and sculpture. First, he could not resist poking fun at sculptors, who had a reputation for trying to achieve in their statues a semblance of real life, by reminding them of what they secretly knew, that no matter how convincing the illusion, a statue is doomed to literal immobility and silence. In his reproof of the sculptor's art Pindar invokes a common trope, which held that particularly realistic works of art could do all but move and speak.[37] On one level, the poet is a critic, arguing the relative merits of one artform over another, but in this case from a somewhat inferior position. For in Pindar's day portrait sculptures of victors already had a long history, considerably longer than that of epinician poetry; the tradition of erecting statues to honor victors at the Olympic Games goes back at least to the first half of the sixth century B.C. and probably even earlier, while Simonides (fl. mid- to late sixth century, early fifth) is believed to have been the first to formalize epinician poetry as a genre.

On another, more pragmatic, level, Pindar seems to be asking, rhetorically, where his patron might better have invested his money, a victory ode or a portrait statue, and concluding that it is the former, of course, with the implication that he continue to commission those poems from Pindar himself. The poet, it seems, would like to reassure potential patrons of what he considers the obvious advantages of his own agalma, the poem, as opposed to the other kind of agalma, the portrait statue, as an artform through which to memorialize the occasion of victory. While at this time the term "agalma" was commonly used as a synonym for statue, it is clear that Pindar thought of his poem as an exact equivalent; in *Nem.* III.12–13 and *Nem.* VIII.15–16 he explicitly refers to his composition as an ἄγαλμα, as does Bacchylides at *Ep.* V.4. We may infer that, with the appropriation of statuary language by these poets, the poem as a made "object" is being regarded as something akin to a "light, holy and winged thing,"[38] pulsing with potential animation like a statue. However, Pindar is fully aware that, while a poem may "travel" more effectively than a statue, neither words nor statues can really speak of their own accord; he is even willing to concede a level of equality when, at *Nem.* VIII.47, he refers to his ode as a λίθον Μοισαῖον ("stone of the muses").

The Greek fascination with what might be called the semiotics of movement in art, which underlies Pindar's *paragone* in *Nem.* V, may be reflected as well in the language they used to name colors, especially in poetry. Ancient Greek color terminology is a complex topic; just a few general observations are in order here. It has been noticed that a number of Greek words for colors denote movement or action along with a range of other sensate phenomena like hue, texture, grayness (tone or intensity), and value (shade); examples include αἰόλος, ἀργός, ἀμάρυγμα, αἰθύσσω.[39] Further instances of what I consider synaesthetic color language are λειριόεις and λευκός, which, according to Eleanor Irwin, "illustrate for us the unity the Greek poets saw between high, clear sounds, fine, delicate surfaces, and 'whiteness' or 'lightness.'"[40] This tendency among early Greeks seems to have developed in response to the observable fact that nature offers countless subtle and varied hues, shades, and tones within each large color class, not just one "red," one "blue," one "yellow," and so forth, while at the same time certain colors partake of the sensual characteristics of other colors even when they do not share hues. Homer's "wine-dark sea," for example, would fall in the second category. In modern times seemingly more sophisticated terminology like "scarlet," "vermilion," and "cadmium red light, medium, dark" would be applied to the colors within colors as they are manifested in paint pigments, some arbitrarily and others in reference to the actual pigmenting medium. But when the "color wheel" becomes the standard for color language rather then nature itself, the range of additional sensations associated with this second category would be lost entirely. The Greeks were more imaginative about the naming of colors within each of these two categories. The poetic language they adopted for describing colors in nature (they were less concerned with paint pigments) is impressive even today, making it all the more surprising that an old view which held that ancient Greek color perception and vocabulary is primitive in comparison with modern still has currency.[41] In a discussion of the language of Aeschylus, who can be said to be among the most "painterly" of poets, William B. Stanford makes some general remarks about the Greek way of naming things, including "their sensitive sympathy for nuances of verbal meaning, as well as . . . their love of condensed expressions and their gift for seeing many aspects of a matter at once,"[42] which could also apply to their naming of colors.

In sum, while the ancient Greek system of color terminology, if there is one, is not entirely understood, some broad conclusions may be drawn which could have resonance among the korai. Greeks took a synaesthetic approach to the naming of colors, reflecting in part their interest in sensing movement in places where others have not, to which their language, renowned for its versatility, was especially well suited. This interest in combining motion language with language that describes a range of other sensate phenomena in order to arrive at names for colors resulted, it seems, in an intelligent, sophisticated, and adaptable chromatic vocabulary that, in my view, is not surpassed even by the modern.

Interest in the semiotics of movement in art could help to explain the ancient Greeks' apparent willingness to suspend disbelief in regard to artistic representations of animate beings, and, more specifically, could provide a further rationale for the devices used to suggest movement in the korai. Until now we have been considering how these features add to the overall impression of mimetic realism. They could be even more significant, if I am correct in suspecting that the depiction of movement in the korai supplies additional evidence that these statues were not intended to represent divinities. In this regard Acr. 679 (fig. 1) may be the exception that proves the rule. As we have seen, there is a strong possibility that the Peplos Kore could be a representation of a statue of a goddess. Yet in spite of the nuances of modeling elaborated by Payne, which are markedly visible even in photographs that show the statue in three-quarter view, in the final analysis Acr. 679 stands rigid, unyielding, and motionless, a symbol rather than a real woman, or a real woman trapped beneath a symbol. Her frozen, perfect beauty exists in contrast to the imperfect beauty and apparent motion of the other Acropolis korai, and, among Attic examples, may be compared only with the Berlin Kore and Phrasikleia, which exhibit some of the same qualities—more understandably, however, since they represent the dead.

LUXURIOUS FURNISHINGS

Literary testimonia corroborating the extravagance of the korai's dress and accoutrements are abundant. To begin, Athenaeus, while a late source, is nonetheless useful for confirming the mimetic realism of the Ionian garments worn by the majority of Acropolis korai. The topic of discussion at *Deip.* 12.525c–e is luxury. The excursus on clothing from which the following is excerpted is claimed by Athenaeus to be drawn from Book 1 of a treatise on the Temple of Artemis at Ephesus by Democritus of Ephesus. Little is known about Democritus, but it is fairly certain that he lived sometime in the Hellenistic period and wrote about Ephesus and Samothrace:

> The garments of the Ionians are violet-dyed, and crimson, and yellow, woven in a lozenge pattern; but the top borders are marked at equal intervals with animal patterns. Then there are robes called *sarapeis* dyed with quince-yellow, crimson, and white, others again with sea-purple. And long robes *(kalasireis)* of Corinthian manufacture; some of these are crimson, others violet, others the colour of hyacinth; one might also buy these robes in flame-colour or sea-green. There are also Persian *kalasireis,* which are the finest of all. One might also see . . . the so-called *aktaiai,* and this in fact is the most costly among Persian wraps. It is compactly woven to give solidity and lightness, and is strewn all over with gold beads; all the beads are fastened to the inner side of the robe by a purple cord attached at the center.

In his presentation of the dress of the Samians, Athenaeus (*Deip.* 12.525f) tells us that he is quoting Duris, the Hellenistic historian, who himself is quoting Asius of Samos, a poet thought to have lived in the sixth century B.C.:

> And they, even so, whene'er they had combed their locks, would hie them to the precinct of Hera, swathed in beautiful vestments, with snowy tunics that swept the floor of wide earth; and golden head-pieces

surmounted them, like cicadas; their tresses waved in the breeze mid their golden bands, and bracelets wrought with cunning circled their arms.

While their subject is the luxurious habits of Ionian men (which contributed to their downfall), these passages, and more like them, could just as well be describing Attic women in Ionian-inspired dress from the Archaic period, especially as reflected in the Acropolis korai. The fussed-over hair, the trailing hem, and the elaborate headgear and jewelry all find their visual equivalent in the korai. The colors of garments mentioned by Athenaeus also ring true for the korai; the lozenge-shaped designs are familiar, and the "animal patterns" recall the chariot frieze which once decorated the chiton of Acr. 686. Even the intricate web of beading, while not precisely documented among the korai, is not implausible. The filigree-like design still on occasion visible on Acr. 683's chitoniskos could easily have been made of beads or seeds in real life. Worth noting in this connection is the upper part of the chiton of Acr. 685 (fig. 12), which, in common with a number of other korai, appears to be made of a different fabric from the bottom half, a portion of which is visible over the left shoulder and arm, which are not covered by the mantle, where the pattern of wrinkles is unusually fine and tight, and where, on the sleeves, it can be noticed that the sculptor has used two distinct types of parallel engraved lines to suggest wrinkles.[43] Perhaps one of these types of marking could be read as a shorthand reference to fine rows of minute beads which would have been impossible to render individually.

It is not only from Asia Minor that we find literary references that authenticate the Ionian-style dress and manners exhibited in the Acropolis korai. Thucydides (3.104), in the course of relating the story of Athens' repurification of Delos under Nicias in 426 B.C., pauses to muse on the grandeur of an Ionian festival which was once celebrated on the island with athletic and poetical contests and choirs of dancers, quoting twice from the *Homeric Hymn to Apollo*.[44] The historian then compares the lapsed Delian festival, which was in the process of being reinstituted as a result of the purification of the island, to one which, in his own day, was celebrated at Ephesus. For us, what is important is that Thucydides validates the participation of Athenians in Delian festivals of the past where luxurious Ionian festival garb, like that described by Athenaeus and mirrored in the dress of the Acropolis korai, was actually worn. Thus it is certain that young Athenian women took part in Ionian festivals on Delos and in Ephesus, the likes of which are celebrated in the Homeric Hymns and by the Lyric poets, and that they accoutered themselves extravagantly for these events.[45] Occasions like these would provide opportunities for Athenian women to dress as the korai are dressed.

In at least one place in the Archaic Greek world festival participants had become so carried away with their accoutrements that a law had to be passed in order to allow everyone sufficient time for the preparation of her festival attire. The evidence is again from Athenaeus (*Deip.* 12.521c):[46]

> "The Sybarites," [the Hellenistic historian] Phylarchus says, "after drifting into luxury passed a law that women should be invited to the public celebrations, and that those who issued the call to the sacrifices should do so a year beforehand, in order that the women might prepare their dresses and other adornments in a manner in keeping with the long time provided, before going forth in answer to the invitation."

We know that Sybaris was destroyed in 510 B.C. The passage of this law likely occurred shortly before this date, since Athenaeus/Phylarchus seems to believe that it was their luxurious habits that rendered the Sybarites victims. From this story we might deduce that the level of extravagance in festival attire had been rising as the Archaic period advanced. Further, we may surmise from this that other Ionian Greek cities, including Athens, may also have fallen into the pattern of the Sybarites, whose name eventually became synonymous with luxury. It is not difficult to place the korai from the Acropolis within this milieu. As contemporary documents of the practice at its peak, the korai provide a visual record of the kind of extravagance in dress which laws like the above were established to accommodate. In democratic Athens, when public displays of private wealth were no longer feasible and the garments worn by the Acropolis korai were out of style, the Panathenaic robe with its intricate narrative design may have served as a reminder of the earlier tradition and stood as a kind of abbreviated visual recapitulation of a way of life no longer possible.

An entire year sounds like a long time to construct a dress. It will be remembered, however, that the Panathenaic peplos took four years to renew. Among the korai, the real-life garments behind the most outstanding depicted examples (e.g., Acr. 594, 675, 681, 682, to mention those with substantial polychromy) could easily be imagined to require a year's preparation. Athenaeus' observations lend a further note of authenticity to the painted decorations of the korai. In the face of evidence like this, it is even more untenable that the korai's polychromies represent mere displays of artistic skills or flights of fancy on the parts of the painters, but rather are successful attempts to capture the effects of real, variegated garments. In fact, as colorful and decorative as they once were, the encaustic versions of brilliant woven and embroidered decorations probably did not do full justice to the originals, which must have been spectacular, especially when they were assembled in numbers. One suspects that the Panathenaic peplos, displaying the Gigantomachy aloft on a ship's mast, would have appeared coarse, ungainly, and not especially decorative in comparison to the poly-chromatic spectacle provided by a procession of young women, the love-liest of Athenian maidens, each wearing her own distinctive festival attire. As a group the Acropolis korai offer a mimetic replica of this real-life vi-sual phenomenon.

For our next examples we turn to the plays of Euripides, who yet again inadvertently supplies testimony for the niceties of Archaic female dress and behavior and thus, indirectly, for the Acropolis korai, the majority of which he probably never saw. At a climactic moment of *Ion,* a woven swaddling garment becomes one of three tokens of proof that allow Creusa finally to claim Ion as the son by Apollo whom she assumed had been exposed after birth. The mother has correctly deduced that it is the work of her own loom in the box that Ion is now carrying, a box which had been secreted away and preserved by the Pythia at Delphi in anticipation of this very recognition scene.[47] A skeptical Ion wants further proof; he asks for a description of the decoration (1418): ποῖόν τι; πολλὰ παρθένων ὑφάσματα ("What sort? Manifold are the weavings of virgins"), in one perfect line, a simple, eloquent testimonium to the ancient Greek woman's artistic prowess, no actual example of which has survived. Creusa avoids a direct answer at first, revealing only that it is not a "finished" piece, but the work of a beginner.[48] She finally acknowledges that the design is that of the gorgoneion, in the manner of Athena's aegis. At *Ion* 887–890 Creusa had recalled her encounter with Apollo, which occurred, in typical fash-ion, as she was gathering flowers and collecting them in the fold of her dress; she describes the golden stamens of the crocus flowers reflecting the god's hair also shining with gold. These might have been the very flowers she would have used for dying the wool for her weavings.

The verbal beauty of *Ion* 1418 is matched, I suggest, by the visual beau-ties of the Acropolis korai, which, in their dresses ornamented with intri-cately woven patterns expertly imitated in encaustic paint, no two alike, offer the best and most abundant visual verification that the weavings of virgins were manifold. Also among the tokens of proof in the box which Ion brings before his mother in their recognition scene (*Ion* 1427–1431) is a golden child's necklace in the form of snakes, mimicking the body of the chthonic Athenian deity, Erichthonios. While such a necklace is not precisely paralleled among the korai, who are not children, the serpentine bracelet worn by kore 670 (fig. 45) may be compared. Exactly such a bangle, in gold, is documented in Lyric poetry (Alc. fr. 1.66–67).

For an Archaic Greek woman, hair was also an accoutrement, notable for its color, texture, abundance, and arrangement. As we have seen, a full range of hair colors is represented among the korai, including blonde of varying hues and shades. We hear of "the river Crathis which dyes hair blonde" at Eur. *Tr.* 226–227.[49] The Lyric poets also verify that women had different colors of hair, although the ones attracting the most attention seem to be the fair colors, including blonde/tawny/red (ξανθός; e.g., Alcman fr. 1.101) and very bright blonde (Sappho fr. 98a; Alcman fr. 1.51–54), some of which might have been dyed with a substance called "fustic."[50] That blonde or tawny hair was something of a status symbol even in antiquity is suggested by Alcman's use of the adjective ἐπιμέρῳ ("desired," fr. 1.101) to characterize this color of hair on a young woman; compare fr. 59b, where another blonde is "a gift among *parthenoi.*" Archilochus' description of a young woman whose hair "hangs down and overshadows the shoulders and the broad of the back" (fr. 31), could only be said of an Archaic, and not a Classical, woman, and is matched visually in the weight and copious hair enveloping those very body parts on ubiquitous display in the Acropolis korai.

Even wigs are not out of the question for both men and women, and might, as we have seen, be reflected in the complex tresses of the korai. In the cross-dressing scene in *Bacchae* Dionysos announces his intention to outfit Pentheus with κόμην ταναόν ("long hair," 831). E. R. Dodds suggests that this would be a wig rather than a reference to unbinding his own long hair.[51] Whether Pentheus is to don a wig or let down his own hair, we should imagine feminine-looking hair worn in the style of the Archaic period rather than the Classical. And since he must pass for a woman, it is preferable to think of the korai rather than the kouroi, who, while they do wear their hair long, display considerably less variety and delicacy in crimping, braiding, and curling. I should emphasize that my contention that the imagery of the cross-dressing scene in *Bacc.* is drawn from real life as represented in the korai does not disregard or negate the possibility that the korai are themselves dressed for religious ritual and that real Dionysiac dress, imagery, and ritual is being evoked in the play, as commentators are careful to point out. However, since Dionysos himself was identified with women, wore women's clothes (cf. Arist. *Frogs*), and was regarded as an effeminate figure, the point almost becomes moot.

It might also be significant that one of Euripides' favorite synonyms for hair, βόστρυχος (used, for example, of Glaukē's hair as she puts on the poisoned crown at *Med.* 1160), is also used of vines or tendrils, anything twisted or curled, imagery which is more suitable to Archaic than to Classical tresses, which are more wavy than curly.

The wide variety of headgear worn by the Acropolis korai, as has already been noted, includes form-fitted caps, bow-ribbons, and various sorts of stephanai. To this list we might add "mitrai." At *Bacc.* 833, as the crowning touch of his appropriation of female attire, Pentheus is to wear a μίτρα in his hair. This accoutrement has for the most part been associated with the regalia of Dionysos and his followers, as seen on vases. But the term appears also to be used in general of any fashionable oriental type of headband, especially for women.[52] They are a highly decorated form of Lydian headdress in Lyric poetry (e.g., Sappho fr. 98a.10–11; b.1–3) and in Pindar (*Nem.* VIII.15); in Alcman (fr. 1.67–69), the Lydian μίτρα is especially appropriate for the dark-eyed (ἰανογ[λ]εφάρων), bringing to mind Acropolis korai 674 (fig. 4), 683 (fig. 3), and 684. Herodotus (1.195.1) says that the Babylonians bound up their long hair with μίτραι. And at Eur. *Hec.* 924 the term used of a headdress appears without any Dionysian associations in a *genre* scene related by the women of the chorus, who are reminiscing about their innocuous grooming rituals as they prepared for bed on the night Troy was sacked. Medea, in Euripides' play, it will be remembered, included a poisoned golden diadem along with the dress that she sent to kill Glaukē, a decision which presupposes that some type of ornamental headdress, perhaps a selection from a variety of such items, as attested among the korai, would be expected to complete an aristocratic young woman's outfit. So perhaps the term μίτρα should be thought of as a generic term for an ornate headband of vaguely Eastern inspiration exactly like those worn in great variety by the Archaic korai, any or all of which might perhaps then be called μίτραι. This would not be the first orientalizing motif that we have encountered in these statues.

Some aristocrats in Archaic Greece were known to affect "Eastern" fashions of dress and behavior. At least one tradition in Lyric poetry flaunts Medism and its attendant luxuriousness. There are ancient testimonia about influxes of foreign craftsmen into Athens. Solon is said to have offered citizenship to foreigners who would relocate to his city to practice a craft; Themistocles is said to have removed the taxes placed on metic craftsmen shortly after the Persian Wars so that they might pour into Athens to contribute to the upkeep of the navy and, it is tempting to presume, to the quality of life.[53] The presence of potters and vase-painters such as Amasis (a common Egyptian name) and Lydos ("the Lydian") attests to Solon's success for the Archaic period.[54] It is possible that some of the korai were carved by such itinerant stoneworkers, whose names are lost to us, lured to Athens by the offer of work and citizenship, or by native Greeks (e.g., Aristion of Paros, the sculptor of the kore Phrasikleia) who may have been trained or otherwise influenced by them. Thucydides (1.6.6) observes that in many respects the habits and customs of earlier Greeks were similar to those of barbarians of his own day. If we accept the picture of Greek aristocrats before the Persian Wars sporting Eastern dress, treasuring Eastern objects, emulating Eastern wealth, and commissioning and buying Greek works of art that displayed a flair for orientalizing, the orientalizing features of the Acropolis korai are readily explained.

WHO ARE THE KORAI?

Dressed to the nines, wreathed, smiling, and moving in as graceful a fashion as inanimate objects might be made to seem to move, the Acropolis korai are living ποικίλα ("variegated ornaments"). For what occasion? Two possibilities come immediately to mind: marriage or festival. Regarding the latter, examples of specific nonexclusively Athenian festivals have already been briefly considered, but the Panathenaia would be the most obvious choice. John Scheid and Jesper Svenbro have brought together ancient evidence for association of the dragging of the peplos or the chiton with a festival context (they do not, however, mention the Acropolis korai).[55] Among the ancient testimonia which they adduce are Trojan and Lesbian "peplos-draggers" in Homer (Τρῳάδας ἑλκεσιπέπλους, *Il.* 6.442; 7.297) and Alcaeus (fr. 130.32–33: Λ[εσβί]αδες ἐλκεσίπεπλοι), and Ionian "chiton-draggers" in the *Homeric Hymn to Apollo* 147 (ἑλκεχίτωνες Ἰάονες). Technically, the korai do not drag their garments; rather they lift them so that they do not drag. However, the gesture may be thought of as reminiscent both of the genteel movements of a young woman and its opposite, the ritual dragging, which could be appropriate behavior during some festivals.

In an article on representations in Greek art of *kanephoroi*, the young women who carry or wear a ritual basket (the *kanoun*) on their head as they lead the procession to the sacrifice during a typical Greek festival, Linda Roccos proposes that Acr. 593, a very early kore, wears the long festival mantle that iconographically distinguishes the *kanephoros*, and wonders whether other Archaic korai might be wearing similar festival attire that would mark them as *kanephoroi*.[56] She also identifies as *kanephoroi* the caryatid maidens from the south porch of the Erechtheum, which, as we have seen, have often been viewed as reconfigurations and visual reminders of the Archaic korai in the Classical period.[57] If the Acropolis korai are to be regarded as existing in a permanent festival mode, then together they may be said to constitute an ancient group sculpture in the form of a perennial tableau of worshiping female *Stellvertreter.*

Second, and perhaps even more appealing, is the possibility that the Acropolis korai represent nubile young women in the market for or on the verge of marriage. Since the korai are not, with the exception of their vast array of jewelry, otherwise certainly dressed in wedding attire, it would be difficult to argue that those wearing the highly ornamented stephanai reminiscent of wedding headgear are certainly meant to be brides, although it is not out of the question.[58] It is possible, however, that the korai are meant as hopeful brides or brides-to-be.[59] The long, loose hair could then be read as a sign of premarital status; it will soon be subjected to a ritual cropping and finally transformed into a bound, up-swept matronly style.[60] The mantle covering the kore's shoulders and, as it finds its way along her body, emphasizing the voluptuous forms of her breasts will be more decorously draped over her head. There will be less of a need for seduction after marriage.

John Oakley and Rebecca Sinos reproduce a drawing of a fragmentary red-figured vase by the Talos Painter from ca. 400 B.C. which shows Helen in heavily ornamented bridal attire and wearing a stephane very like that worn by many of the Acropolis korai; the figure looks also to be pulling at her chiton as she steps.[61] Oakley's and Sinos' description of the appearance of the bride as depicted in Greek vase-painting matches the general picture presented by the Archaic korai:

> Like Pandora and Hera, the Athenian bride met her bridegroom only after she had been carefully adorned and thus provided with irresistible powers of seduction. Vase paintings depicting her adornment show the bride undergoing a process of transformation, taking on the sexual role that follows her departure from childhood. . . . In the various motifs of bridal adornment we see the tools of Aphrodite, the perfumes, jewelry, crowns, shoes, and graceful garments that will make the bride powerfully attractive. On some of the vases illustrating later stages of the ceremony, we will see how the bridegroom is affected by the bride's allure.[62]

There has never been a question about the seductiveness of the korai. The contest for "unrivalled radiance" is carried out, as in the chorus of Euripides with which we opened, through the particularized accoutering, the carriage, the graceful movement, and the overall demeanor of the individual kore. The keen observer can almost, synaesthetically, smell the perfumed garments. The much touted frontality of Archaic sculpture is belied in these images. A full appreciation of their latent sexuality is available only to the viewer who walks all the way around the statue, taking in all views, but especially the back, where the poetic license of sculptors allows reality to be compromised so that the garments appear virtually transparent. Moreover, the evident robustness, which manifests itself most visibly in the strong buttocks and legs, and which symbolizes, I believe, the woman's suitability for childbirth, would also support the theory that the korai are marriageable young women. Oakley and Sinos suggest that weddings could be held in sanctuaries.[63] Might they not have taken place on the Acropolis itself?

A related possibility is that the korai are ergastinai, female weavers of the Panathenaic peplos. At Eur. *Hec.* 466–472 the chorus describes the robe that adorned the ancient image of Athena which was woven with the scene of the Gigantomachy every four years by well-born Athenian women and girls:[64]

ἢ Παλλάδος ἐν πόλει
τὰς καλλιδίφρους Ἀθα-
ναίας ἐν κροκέῳ πέπλῳ
ζεύξομαι ἆρα πώ-
λους ἐν δαιδαλέαισι ποι-
κίλλουσ᾽ ἀνθοκρόκοισι πή-
ναις ἢ Τιτάνων γενεάν . . .

(Or, in the city of Pallas, am I to weave colts yoked to beautiful chariots on the saffron peplos of Athena, or [am I to weave] the race of Titans . . . , in Daidalic, flower-dyed and spun fibers.)

At *Hec.* 485 the chorus members, who have just sung these lines, are addressed as "Trojan korai" by Talthybius, using a perhaps intentionally belittling term, since they would be recent widows,[65] but which seems nonetheless appropriate in the light of the hopeful tone of the ode and the kinds of activities which the women anticipate: singing, dancing, and weaving. Should they be sent to Athens, the chorus members wonder, and put to work on the peplos, would they be assigned to weave a god (Athena in her chariot, *Hec.* 466–470, which brings to mind the chariot frieze of kore 686) or a giant (the race of Titans, *Hec.* 472–474), implying a kind of division of labor like that of any ancient craftsmen's studio.[66] Apparently the former is favored, since the chorus' description of the work on the gods' side is more extensive than that of the giants' side. There were no pictures of flowers woven into a battle scene; ἀνθοκρόκοισι in this case refers to the threads colored by dyes made from flowers collected by the women.[67]

Similarly, in a passage to be discussed further in Chapter Five, Andromache in the *Iliad* (22.441) "strews many-colored flowers" into the fabric of a cloak she is weaving for Hector coincidentally just as he is meeting a premature death outside the city walls at the hands of Achilles, although here we might imagine the flowers to be actual design elements.[68] And in imagery directly reminiscent of that of the Panathenaic peplos, Helen weaves contemporary battle scenes into a double cloak at *Il.* 3.125–128. Barber argues that young girls, older girls, and even married women were involved in the making of the peplos.[69] This could account for the apparently varied ages of the korai (although married women are not represented) and for the fact that they display their handiwork in the *paryphai* of the very clothes that they are wearing.

A final clue that the korai are real women and not goddesses may be gleaned once more from the literary evidence. In the Archaic period the traditional Homeric depiction of the gods as human beings was being questioned, particularly and most vehemently by the presocratic philosopher and poet Xenophanes. Among the many fragments by Xenophanes that confront this issue, the best known are frags. 14–15:

But mortals believe the gods to be created by birth, and to have their own *(mortals')* raiment, voice and body. But if oxen (and horses) and lions had hands or could draw with hands and create works of art like those made by men, horses would draw pictures of gods like horses, and oxen of gods like oxen, and they would make the bodies (of their gods) in accordance with the form that each species itself possesses.[70]

On the basis of this passage and the thinking that produced it, it is tempting to wonder whether artistic portrayals of divinities based on the Homeric anthropomorphic model could have been subject to similar criticism and ridicule if they betrayed too much evidence of familiar mortal trappings.

Sculptors might just as well as poets have been the target of Xenophanes' cynical remarks. We have already had occasion to note that at precisely this time, the later sixth century B.C., gods begin to be represented with their specific attributes. Criticisms like those of Xenophanes possibly could have provided the impetus for artists to create an iconography for each god which would help to make deities readily distinguishable from humans as well as from each other—in other words, to reserve and restrict the distinctiveness of the accoutrements of divinity. If this was the case, then the mimetically realistic trueness-to-life seen in the Acropolis korai arguably served as a representational mode admissible, at the time of their creation, in images of real people but not of divinities.

The quality of godliness has always been attributed to the Acropolis korai. This is fair enough. But to recognize divine beauty in the korai is not necessarily to give credence to those theories which claim that the statues actually are representations of divinities. More likely, it is the gods who would be flattered, Xenophanes-style, by comparison with such lovely mortal women. Although, according to the popular imagination, when it came around to explaining why gods look like beautiful people, it was conveniently forgotten that people make gods to look like themselves, the very thing against which Xenophanes railed. Sappho fr. 1 makes reference to some by now familiar features:

> Colorfully-dressed [ποικιλόθρον'] immortal Aphrodite, wile-weaving daughter of Zeus, I entreat you . . . and you, blessed one, with a smile on your immortal face asked what was the matter with me this time and why I was calling this time.[71]

It may be significant that the goddess' dress is many-colored, that wiles are metaphorically woven, and that Aphrodite smiles. As for the inevitable question of which influenced which, it would seem that the evidence falls in favor of a mortally inspired, rather than a divinely inspired, direction for the movement of these motifs. Real-life Archaic garments and sculpted images are many-colored; weaving is a legitimate and commonplace mortal female occupation; and sculptures from all over the Archaic world, as well as from other ancient cultures in the Mediterranean vicinity, smile. They do not smile because Aphrodite smiles. Aphrodite smiles because they smile.[72]

Even when goddesses are described in Archaic poetry, it is young women, again, who are the models. Though the relationship was thought to be reciprocal, and that the loveliest got their loveliness from the gods, the effort to account for the unaccountable, beauty, when it occurs in very human form, is evident. Even ideal images can and should be regarded as realistic if they seem to represent appearances correctly at any given time and place; this is a beauty which exists independently of idealization, a natural, as opposed to an unnatural, beauty, an *ideal* beauty, perhaps, but not an *idealized* beauty. What the poets brought about through literary devices, the artists achieved in stone—that is, mimetically realistic portrayals of the appearances of real Archaic women. The media may be different, but the impulse is identical. The fact that it has been an effortless task to relate the specific language used by the poets directly to the korai suggests that the poets are actually describing the korai; they are not, of course, but the poetics of appearance is a testimony to the authenticity of the imagery of both media.

CHAPTER FIVE

PHRASIKLEIA

Unlike the statues under discussion thus far, the Attic kore that is the subject of this chapter neither is from the Athenian Acropolis nor, to our knowledge, was ever used as a votive dedication. But it happens to provide a unique opportunity to test the theory of the semiotics of appearance as a symptom of realism in Archaic Greek art in a case in which a statue is actually named.

The kore Phrasikleia (fig. 46) by the sculptor Aristion of Paros represents something of an anomaly, since its original inscription, which includes both the name of the individual represented and the sculptor, has also survived in its entirety. The statue is made of Parian marble; its polychromy is extensively preserved. It was excavated in Myrrhinous (modern Merenda), Attica, in 1972, having been found in a custom-designed pit carefully buried alongside a kouros, which might also be from the same hand.[1]

The circumstances of the burial of the two Archaic statues are unknown; however, the fact that it appears to have been deliberate is significant. The freshness of the statues and the lack of evidence for destruction or desecration[2] preclude the possibility of their having been buried as part of the debris associated with the Persian destruction, as were most of the Acropolis korai. Most scholars have connected the statues' burial with the exile (one or more) of the powerful Alcmaeonid family of Athens, which occurred sometime during the Peisistratid tyranny.[3] Martin Robertson, among others, sensibly speculates that Phrasikleia may have been an Alcmaeonid whose grave statue, like that of another likely member of the clan, Kroisos (Athens NM 3851), was taken down and buried before the family's departure.[4]

A less popular alternative is that the two statues from Merenda were deliberately buried before the Persian invasion in order to prevent their desecration by the enemy.[5] However, if the ceramic evidence from the burial includes black-figured pottery as the latest material, as the excavator reports, a burial date in the early fifth century seems less likely.[6]

Proposed dates for the kore have ranged from ca. 550 to ca. 530 B.C.[7] Discussion of the statue's date has often centered on the date of the accompanying inscription, but since its discovery, the opposite has also taken place, lending confusion to the entire process. The fact that the statue wears a peplos is also sometimes taken into consideration. As I have argued that the peplos may occasionally be an iconographical feature rather than an index of chronology, I believe that the advanced style of the statue alone points toward a somewhat later date, ca. 520, roughly contemporary with the kouros, Kroisos. If all of these statues are in fact Alcmaeonid grave monuments, and if, as has been argued, the family's exile from Athens occurred only once and as late as 514, the later date would still allow sufficient time for their creation, erection, dismantling, and burial.[8]

The kore represents a unique addition to the small corpus of monumental Archaic female statues that are known or suspected to have been intended for funerary use. Only two extant, substantially preserved Attic korai can definitely be connected with tombs: Phrasikleia and the Berlin Kore (fig. 40). A handful of others are either badly preserved or of uncertain, but probably funerary, function; no korai come from the Kerameikos, as Ridgway observes with some surprise.[9] Such a small sample makes it difficult to speculate about the general character of this category of monument and the intentions of the patrons and makers; nonetheless, many have tried. In general there has been a tendency to declare that all Archaic grave monuments, whether relief stelai or statues in-the-round, although less so in the case of the former, represent little more than idealized versions of the type or class of men or women to which the deceased belonged. A quotation from Robertson may suffice for what is the accepted interpretation: "[An Archaic] grave-statue shows always, so far as our evidence goes, an ideal youth. Inscriptions prove it to be thought of as in some sense representing the dead, but it is not characterized in even the most general way. The rare statues on the graves of women were probably likewise undifferentiated korai."[10] One might suspect that Robertson was writing without knowledge of the discovery of Phrasikleia, which could hardly be called an undifferentiated kore, but a footnote refers to this statue.

As an inevitable outgrowth of the tendency to assume that mimetic realism was neither a concern nor within the technical expertise of Archaic Greek artists, the view that Archaic grave statues, in common with votives, represent no more than types persists in spite of the fact that representations of men and women on grave monuments, unlike votives, are usually accompanied by some version of the person's name, even if alone and in the genitive case.[11] The fact that these statues are named should render moot the proviso that a "true" portrait must be a representation of a specific individual. Yet, following the same pattern that has characterized the historiography of the Acropolis korai, the statue of Phrasikleia has been alternately characterized as a representation of a divinity, of a heroine, and of a real woman.[12] It is important to note that the first two identifications, divinity and heroine, depend directly upon an interpretation of the inscription. In fact the most extensive argument for divinity, that of Nikolaos M. Kontoleon, was published in 1970 *before* the statue was excavated and thus was based solely on the inscription; the newly excavated statue itself appears to have had no effect on the thesis when it was republished in 1974 except, in his opinion, to solidify it.

While it is unwise to generalize about the character of funerary korai as a group, there is little reason not to particularize from this one outstanding example. Assessing the reality of appearances in the kore Phrasikleia is an easy task because the sculptor, Aristion, offering a wide array of semiotic clues, has made it so. These cannot be accidental. It shall be seen that the visual evidence alone, evaluated according to the terms laid out for the Acropolis korai, suggests that Aristion of Paros meant the statue destined to mark the woman's grave to be the best likeness of the dead that he was able to achieve within the boundaries of the conventions dictated by the tastes of the time and the skills of its sculptors. Yes, Phrasikleia is a kore, and, yes, she smiles, but what is typical about this statue is, in my view, outmatched by what is individual.

First, the presence of a name. I have argued, with Himmelmann, that intent is a key feature of likeness; therefore, if a name is attached to a statue, it is incumbent upon the viewer to presume that the image was intended to be some form of likeness rather than that it was not and, regardless of whether it is perceived to function successfully as such by modern standards, to pursue in his or her viewing the implications of that presumption. With Phrasikleia, unlike Wilhelm Uhde of Picasso's portrait, we have no means of judging the likeness, but modern viewers of an ancient image are not entirely without resources, for the intent to liken leaves visible traces. If the condition which may be identified as mimetic realism in Archaic art results from the cumulative semiotic effect of multiplying details, as I have defined it, then the more types of information a sculptor utilizes, the more specific his statue will seem, even if we are not able to read all of the signs.

Prominent among the conveyors of information in the funerary image of Phrasikleia is iconography. This "iconographical realism" might be distinguished from "mimetic realism" but equally should be considered a legitimate modality of realism in an age when naturalism had not been mastered. Both kinds of Archaic realism can coexist in a single work of art. In the case of Phrasikleia, a statue that is distinct in a number of ways from the Acropolis group of korai, we shall pursue exclusively the evidence for iconographical realism, but this is not to say that mimetic realism is not also present. What I call "iconographical likeness" is not achieved by the conventional means of portraying, which include attention to details of particularized physiognomy. Aristion of Paros has fabricated a synthetic visual identity for the dead woman through a series of iconographical signs which, in my view, would have signaled to the alert passerby the ways in which the statue differs from, rather than matches, other images of its type. These signs remain just signs unless the viewer actively participates in the semiotic process.

It is these visual signs, some recalling the woman in life, others, in death, which shall be examined below. Constantly at the forefront of the discussion and serving as its focus is, appropriately, the lotus, a timeless symbol of both life and death, featured in Phrasikleia's image in all three stages of its existence, in bud, in full flower, and in fruit, and thereby rendering her image very nearly a personification of this singular plant.

THE MONUMENT

There is slight disagreement as to whether Phrasikleia is life-size or larger. Some have argued that the kore is over life-size, at 1.76 m.[13] The question of scale is important because it has been cited as an indicator either of human or of heroic stature in support of various theories of interpretation. In any assessment of scale in a work of art the measurement itself is not as crucial as the subjective impression received when standing alongside the work (which itself must be modified to account for the slight diminution in apparent height when a statue is viewed properly on its pedestal). It is often noted that a freestanding statue must be somewhat over life-size in order to appear to be actually life-size, while a statue which is actually life-size conveys the impression of being smaller than it really is; this is the same kind of optical illusion to which Vitruvius (3.11) alludes in his discussion of architectural refinements when he advises that the corner columns of a peripteral temple must be thicker than the others because the air around them "eats" away at their apparent size. My own subjective first-hand impression of Phrasikleia is that the statue *appears* to be life-size; I will proceed on that assumption.

The kore wears a belted peplos of red or purple cloth decorated with a panel patterned with an incised and painted meander running full-length and around the neck and down the sleeves. A tongue-patterned border arranges itself decoratively over the sandaled feet at the bottom of the garment. A variety of incised and painted swastikas and several types of rosette,[14] the dominant one in the form of a stylized lotus seed-vessel, carpet the remainder of the fabric.[15] The lotus rosette represents another oriental borrowing; during the Empire of the New Kingdom, when Egypt was under the cultural sway of newly annexed Near Eastern lands, in a rare instance of influence from without, Egyptian women began to incorporate a few colorful patterns in the cloth woven for their garments. The rosette pattern that decorates the left breast of the statue of Merit-Amon, a Ramesside queen, in the Cairo Museum[16] is repeated almost verbatim over the breast of Phrasikleia. The kore's peplos is girded with an ornamental belt. She wears a necklace and earrings fashioned in the form of either fruits or flower buds, probably lotuses, and a crown of the same, real or fashioned; she holds another lotus flower or bud at her breast (unfortunately not visible in the excavation photograph reproduced here, but restored later). Again the resemblance to Merit-Amon is hard to miss; for she, too holds something at her breast with her left hand, in this case a Menat, and sports a heavy, imposing queen's crown carved in high relief made up of uraei topped with sun discs. One foot of the kore is slightly advanced.

Like the majority of the Acropolis group, Phrasikleia also smiles and gathers her skirts, although the drapery, along with the body beneath, maintains a columnar perfection in spite of its disturbed fall. While the sculptor is generally faulted for his disregard for naturalistic considerations in his portrayal of the behavior of the fabric, Ridgway's sensitive characterization of the qualities of the heavy material as portrayed makes a convincing case for exactly the opposite, an attention to mimetic realism.[17] Concerning the skirt-tugging gesture, a common feature among Archaic korai, Sourvinou-Inwood distinguishes an "emblematic" stance, signified by the undisturbed draping of pulled fabric, and an "active" stance, where the pulling gesture actually makes an impression on the fall of the drapery, suggestive of real motion.[18] Phrasikleia would fall into Sourvinou-Inwood's "emblematic" category; this makes sense in the light of the fact that she is funerary and, unlike the Acropolis korai, need not necessarily be regarded as moving or processing. Phrasikleia's hair is not abundant, but it is nonetheless delicately plaited, bound, and crimped in an elaborate arrangement that reflects the latest contemporary fashions. Her features are pointed and angular, fine rather than voluptuous. She is pretty or handsome but not beautiful.

The statue was found about 200 m north of the Church of the Panaghia in Merenda.[19] Upon discovery it was immediately associated with an inscribed base which had been known and admired since the early eighteenth century, having been built into a wall of the Church of the Panaghia.[20] Lilian H. Jeffery saw the base when it was *in situ* in the church: "The stone serves (upside-down) as the capital of an engaged column which supports the arch of the north window inside the church. The face is whitewashed, and the sides are free only for a depth of 0.45 [m]. The bottom is invisible, and little more than the edge of the top can be seen, since the top of the engaged column has been set in the plinth-cutting and plastered all around." She also notes that "the letters were carefully obliterated when the stone was re-used in the church."[21] In 1968 the base was removed and brought to Athens, where it was housed, until recently, in the Epigraphical Museum (EM 13383). Clearly visible in photographs taken of the excavation of the two Archaic statues, an irregular ring of poured lead found placed, with apparent deliberation, between the feet of the kouros and the feet of the kore became the key for securing the connection between the kore statue and this base; the lead ring fit perfectly when inserted back into its original location in the bedding of the base, where it had secured the plinth of the statue, and statue and base were reunited after nearly twenty-five centuries.[22] They are currently displayed in the National Archaeological Museum, Athens, under one inventory number (Athens NM 4889).

The principal face of the base contains an epigram in the form of a neatly ordered inscription which, in its physical presentation, approximates an epigraphical style of the Classical period known as stoichedon, in which the letters are evenly spaced and aligned vertically as well as horizontally:

> σε͂μα Φρασικλείας. / κόρε κεκλέσομαι / αἰεί,
> ἀντὶ γάμο / παρὰ θεο͂ν το͂υτο / λαχο͂σ’ ὄνομα.

[I am the grave] marker of Phrasikleia. I shall always be called "kore," this name being my fate by will of the gods who deprived me of marriage.

The left lateral side of the base is inscribed with the signature of the sculptor: Ἀριστίον Πάρι[ός μ' ἐπ]ο[ίε]σε ("Aristion of Paros made me").[23]

Phrasikleia's epigram is possibly the earliest extant Attic example of a stoichedon inscription.[24] Until the discovery of the statue in 1972, the dating of the inscribed base and of the statue it once held could only be determined by the style of the lettering. Reginald P. Austin, noting decades before that the stone itself had been seen by only a few of the scholars who had discussed it, was able to examine it and tentatively offered a date "as early as 550 B.C."[25] Jeffery's suggestion of "c. 540?" has been followed, sometimes without the question mark, by virtually all commentators on the inscription.[26] Perhaps the most circumspect appraisal is "pre-Jeffery," that of Johannes Geffcken: "2. Hälfte des 6. Jahrhunderts" ("second half of the sixth century").[27] Henry Immerwahr attempts to reconcile the statue's date with that of the base. The base is included in his 530–500 B.C. grouping as a result, it seems, of Andrew Stewart's suggestion of a date of ca. 530 for the statue. However, Immerwahr observes that the inscription is "somewhat earlier than our period, but with some forward-looking features," and grants that, if Stewart's date is followed, the inscription would then look "even more Archaic" by comparison with the statue. In a later publication Stewart dates the statue to ca. 550.[28] Given the confusion and the potential for circular reasoning, perhaps it is best to conclude that, at most, the nearly stoichedon style suggests a later rather than an earlier date. However one prefers to reconcile the dates of the statue and the inscription, since both are ultimately dependent on stylistic analysis, the fact remains that neither provides a secure touchstone for the other, yet they are undeniably connected. In the end even as much as a twenty- to thirty-year differential does not affect the present argument.

Aristion of Paros is known from a number of inscriptions, but until the discovery of Phrasikleia, no statue could be associated with him; he may have specialized in funerary monuments.[29] A primary thesis of Didier Viviers' study is that certain sculptors worked for certain families. I suspect, with Stewart, that Kroisos may also be by the hand of Aristion of Paros; if so, this would strengthen the idea of an Alcmaeonid connection for Aristion; Viviers, however, assigns Kroisos to Aristokles.[30] H. Alan Shapiro assumes that the kouros buried with her represents a relative of Phrasikleia, a brother, perhaps.[31] Carlo Gallavotti has argued that the sculptor's signature is metrical, while M. B. Wallace discusses the likelihood that Aristion himself composed the epigrams that accompanied his statues.[32] Sourvinou-Inwood argues for the sculptor's signature to be taken as a continuation of the epigram and suggests that σῆμα Φρασικλείας and Ἀριστίον Πάρι[ός μ' ἐπ]ο[ίε]σε would be "spoken" by the monument, while κόρε κεκλέσομαι / αἰεί, / ἀντὶ γάμο / παρὰ θεὸν τοῦτο / λαχōσ' ὄνομα would represent the "words" of the deceased persona behind the monument.[33]

The excavator, Euthymios Mastrokostas, correctly, I believe, identifies the vegetal crown rendered in high relief as a stephane of rare form, composed of a chain of alternating lotus buds and flowers: "la tête porte une haute stéphanè décorée d'une chaîne de perles ellipsoïdes, dont chacune porte en alternance un calice et une fleur de lotus" ("the head carries a high crown decorated with a chain of ellipsoid pearls, of which each carries alternately a calyx and a lotus flower").[34] This particular combination is found on only a handful of other Archaic monuments, among them, and most important for our purposes, the crown worn by the Berlin Kore— also from Attica and also funerary—where the motif appears in incised polychromy rather than relief.[35] A crown of alternating lotus buds and flowers is featured in a painted version on a number of terracotta sphinx acroteria; the finest and best preserved is the head in the Louvre, said to be from Thebes.[36] The sphinx itself is commonly found in funerary contexts, both in Egypt and in Greece. In Phrasikleia's plastically rendered version it is not obvious that flowers are being distinguished from buds, since both are shown in closed format; the buds would logically be the smaller ones. Typically, painted versions of the lotus flower/bud chain represent the lotus in full flower, while sculpted ones do not.[37] It is not hard to understand why an ancient sculptor would be reluctant to attempt a lotus in full flower; it would be technically difficult, worthy of a Bernini, and the results would easily be damaged. Executed in high relief, Phrasikleia's elaborate sculpted headdress is unique among korai, paralleled closely only by the painted version worn by the Berlin Kore. Mastrokostas points out that the stephane is a feminine accouterment "par excellence"; males, however, also wear them.[38]

Mastrokostas does not attempt to identify the type of flower that Phrasikleia holds in her hand, observing only that it is a "calice d'une fleur" ("calyx of a flower"),[39] or the source of inspiration, vegetal or otherwise, behind the forms of the jewelry. Nor does he comment on the iconography of the lotus. He does find meaning in the stephane, suggesting that it points to a heroine rather than a common mortal and speculates further that, if the actual tomb were discovered, we should expect to find evidence of a cult.[40] In this Mastrokostas was following up the aforementioned theory of Kontoleon, which had been based solely on a reading of the epigram. While Kontoleon had no idea that Phrasikleia had worn a stephane, he believed that the "Kore" of the inscription was a proper name referring to the daughter of Demeter, that the dead woman was being assimilated to the goddess of the underworld, bride of Hades, and that the statue represents the assimilation in concrete form.[41] That there is some commonality with Persephone cannot be denied; Phrasikleia died unmarried and will also be forced to become "a bride of Hades." However, if there were an explicit association or amalgamation intended, in my view we should expect to find Persephone's chief attribute, the pomegranate, rather than the lotus.[42] The theories of both Mastrokostas and Kontoleon have been countered by Georges Daux, who argues that the kore represents none other than the real woman: "Le miracle, c'est que nous puissions de nouveau, contre tout espoir, contempler, après deux millénaires et demi, l'image de la *jeune fille* Phrasicleia, éblouissante de grâce" ("It is a miracle that, contrary to all expectation, we are able to contemplate anew, after two and a half millennia, the image of the *young woman*, Phrasikleia, dazzling with grace").[43] Daux stops well short of calling the image a "portrait." To be sure, there is little justification for him to do so because his argument, like Kontoleon's but to a different end, is structured principally around the inscription. Daux does not discuss the iconography of the statue.

Others have commented on the stephane while neglecting to mention or to pursue the iconographical implications of the lotuses. Christoph W. Clairmont discusses the meaning of Phrasikleia's headgear without commenting on the vegetal source of its decoration.[44] In a note he wisely denies that the crown is a polos, even though it is reminiscent of one. Calling it "probably one of the most splendid stephanai worn by maidens in archaic sculpture," Clairmont goes on to suggest, citing the many examples of korai from the Acropolis and on black-figured vases that wear some form of stephane and yet are not heroines, that the accoutrement does not make Phrasikleia a heroine, it simply reflects her social status, and that the statue is nothing more or less than a beautiful memorial to a "mortal maiden." Also in this category is Stewart, who associates the "elaborate crown" with "I shall always be called 'kore'" of the epitaph and suggests that, while it "recalls" Persephone, the monument is "unequivocally a mortal's memorial."[45] Sourvinou-Inwood concludes that, on the basis of the presence of lotuses in the crown and what she believes to be pomegranates in the necklace, the emphasis on flowers throughout the image, combined with the fact that the statue is funerary, the image "could not but evoke" Persephone. Both the Berlin Kore, who possesses similar characteristics, according to Sourvinou-Inwood, and Phrasikleia "may be seen as iconographical articulations of the metaphor that eventually crystallized into the 'bride of Hades' metaphor, through the *iconographical* partial assimilation of the two statues to Persephone, the real bride of Hades."[46]

Ridgway considers Phrasikleia's headgear to be a polos; she, too, does not discuss the lotuses.[47] There are three examples of Acropolis korai that wear poloi[48] which Ridgway would like to associate with one or more Archaic structures with caryatid supports, perhaps marking the tomb of Kekrops, which had existed on the Acropolis since at least the Geometric period. These early structures, according to Ridgway, could explain the unusual choice of caryatids for the south porch of the Erechtheum, which in the Classical period stood on the site of cult activity associated with Kekrops.[49] In all of these korai, Ridgway concludes, the polos "would remain an element outside the strictly human sphere." Her emphasis on Phrasikleia's "polos" as a type of headgear which would not be worn by a mortal, combined with what she regards as "heroic size," aligns Ridgway with Kontoleon and Mastrokostas, and is in conformity as well with her views on the Acropolis korai. Ridgway regards the forms of Phrasikleia's jewelry as abstract rather than vegetal, and grants only that the kore carries a "flower."[50] She also tentatively suggests that the buds on the crown may be those of the pomegranate rather than the lotus, and that the crown "could represent a bridal crown, given the allusion to the failed marriage and the pun on the term Kore in her epitaph."[51]

Still others have loosely characterized the items under discussion as floral or as something other than lotiform. Robertson refers to the decoration of the "polos" as being of "flowers and buds," and the object in Phrasikleia's left hand is described only as a "flower." He does not take a strong stand on the issue of divine versus human; however, his repeated references to the "figure of a girl" and to a "marble girl," as well as his intriguing suggestion that the monument may be an Alcmaeonid grave statue, would seem to place Robertson in the "mortal" camp.[52] Sourvinou-Inwood notes only that Phrasikleia holds a "flower," and that, in common with the other korai that are known to have functioned as *sēmata*, or grave monuments, she holds it against her body rather than in an extended hand.[53] Stewart compares the statue of Phrasikleia with a beautiful line from the Lyric poet Mimnermos (fr. 2): "We are as leaves in jeweled springtime growing," and speaks of "life's jeweled springtime," without, however, making a direct reference to Phrasikleia's jewelry.[54] In a later publication, however, Stewart focuses more closely on the lotuses, suggesting that the closed lotus which the kore holds at her breast "would signal a girl who is unmarried and sexually unplucked, awaiting her full efflorescence into a woman."[55] But in Phrasikleia's case the marriage that would permit the unveiling of her full potential is denied; according to Stewart: "She is dead and her acclaim *(kleos)* will only flourish vicariously when someone comes by and stops to read the epigram on her base out loud." Apropos the prominence of lotuses decorating the statue, Stewart sees a "poignant metaphor of wish fulfillment."

In these conclusions Stewart echoes Svenbro's more extensive semiotic treatment of the iconography of Phrasikleia's lotuses.[56] In Svenbro's view various aspects of the lotus' physiology inspire associations with fire, dying down and rekindling, and with the sun, rising and setting. He suggests that the fire of the hearth is meant and that, being dead, Phrasikleia can no longer tend to it in a literal way. Metaphorically, however, through the symbolism of the flower which she holds, she is still her family's future, and it is through the flower/fire of the hearth that the young woman makes her inherited *kleos* ("glory") known. She cannot contribute heirs. Her image is all that remains of her, a silent sentinel who demands, in vain, to be heard for the sake of the continuity of her father's house. Without doubt Svenbro's reading offers a provocative, multilayered interpretation of the lotuses that is worthy of our attention, but in its generalizing, verbally based approach it fails to address the importance of the iconographical distinctiveness of Phrasikleia's image and the true-to-life impression which has struck many observers of this statue since its discovery and display.

While Svenbro's is the most expansive interpretation of Phrasikleia's lotuses to date, such attempts, while valid, are still, in my view, too summary to do full justice to the significance of the plant's conspicuousness in the monument. In focusing primarily on the *verbal* semiotics of the inscription, Svenbro and others have slighted the *visual* semiotics which are omnipresent in this statue. My purpose in the present chapter is to extend this kind of analysis to the semiotics of appearance, which has been our focus throughout this study.

LIFE AND DEATH

Before proceeding to the specific symbolism of the lotus, it is well to address in a more general way the significance of flowers in the lives and images, both literary and visual, of young Greek women. We have already seen some of this symbolism indirectly in the Acropolis korai; these floral themes, and the poetry which reflects them, may now be elaborated upon. Flowers were a central and one of the more engaging preoccupations of a young woman's life. Sourvinou-Inwood, discussing Phrasikleia, makes the connection between young women and flowers clear: "The schema 'young girl with flower' is common in Greek iconography. This does not mean that it carried no specific connotations; on the contrary, the ancient viewers could not but make sense of it through their assumptions concerning the association 'girls and flowers'. Flowers and flower-gathering was [*sic*] associated with the *parthenos,* prenuptial rites and marriage, and also Persephone."[57] Among the most common flower-based activities associated with young women, all familiar from literature, are the gathering of flowers, the use of gathered flowers to dye yarns for weaving, and the plaiting of flowers into garlands to wear on their heads or otherwise to bedeck themselves, frequently for religious purposes.[58] Through literary comparanda, it will be seen that Phrasikleia's statue, to an even greater extent than the Acropolis korai, and for different reasons, constitutes a mimetically faithful replica of the Archaic aristocratic young woman; *ut poesis pictura,* with the common font of information for both being reality itself. Yet this does not necessarily turn the kore into a type; that her particular flowers are lotuses specify her as an individual and set her apart as a grave image.

The activity of young women gathering brightly colored flowers and dropping them into the broad pocket *(kolpos)* formed by lifting up the overfold of the peplos is a common image in Greek literature of all periods, a few examples of which will suffice. The *Homeric Hymn to Gē* (30.5–16) includes an image of maidens engaged in a light-hearted dance carrying in their hands flowers[59] freshly plucked from the meadow in which they find themselves. The Hesiodic *Catalogue of Women,* in tracing the line of the Deukalionidai, describes Porthaon's three daughters, referred to as korai, Eurythemistē, Stratonikē, and Steropē, all ripe for marriage, in an idyllic interlude alongside the Nymphs and the Muses. The young women have searched the grounds for flowers for transforming their persons into things of ever more beauty and delight: ἄνθεα μαι[ό]μεν[αι κεφα-λῆις εὐώ]δεα κόσμον ("pursuing flowers as a fragrant decoration for their heads"), whereupon Apollo arrives with an offer of a husband for each of them.[60]

Flower-gathering was safest when conducted in groups. The trio in the Hesiodic fragment encounters a happy fate during their ramble in the woods; when a young woman engages in this activity alone, however, things can become dangerous. When Euripides (*Hel.* 243–245) describes

Helen gathering flowers and placing them in the overfold of her peplos, he evokes the earlier poets. The image appears as Helen is recounting the sorrows of her life. Hera has sent Hermes to spirit her away to Egypt. In Helen's account the god finds her "as I was culling fresh roses within my peplos." Hermes interrupts this pious, picturesque activity to carry Helen off, as it turns out, in order to save her, and to be able, in the end, to exculpate her for the Trojan War. Since Euripides' portrait of Helen in this play is favorable, we are prepared to be haunted by this picture of innocence as the action of the play unfolds, and so we are; at the end we feel that such a woman deserves her good fortune.

In another Euripidean passage which has already been mentioned in connection with the Acropolis korai, Creusa is caught by Apollo in similar circumstances, again with fateful consequences. In this case the erotic overtones of the activity are made clearer: "You came to me with your hair shining gold when I was culling into the folds of my dress crocus flowers that burst in response with their own golden light" (ἦλθές μοι χρυσῷ χαίταν / μαρμαίρων, εὖτ' ἐς κόλπους / κρόκεα πέταλα φάρεσιν ἔδρεπον / †ἀνθίζειν† χρυσανταυγῆ, *Ion* 887–890). At Eur. *Hec.* 1160–1162 the idyllic use of the *kolpos* for the collecting of flowers is perverted into something deadly by the Trojan women, the concealing of swords for murder. While one does not have to be a virgin or even virginal to pick flowers, as Helen's case demonstrates, the apparent innocence and insouciance of the activity appears to be played against the irreversible reality of losing one's virginity, the great divide in a young woman's life.[61] Neoboulē is ridiculed for her age and extensive sexual experience in Archilochus (fr. 196a.24–28) by comparing her to a flower which has lost its bloom and consequently its charm. On the other hand the fresher, virginal young girl who is the subject of the erotic poem is, appropriately, "laid down among the fresh flowers" (vv. 42–44) for her deflowering. Bowers of roses and a flowery meadow set the scene for an invitation to Aphrodite in Sappho (fr. 2.6–10).

Occasionally even a group does not protect a young woman from divine rape. In the *Homeric Hymn to Demeter* (425–433) Persephone is recounting the circumstances of her *hieros gamos* ("sacred marriage") to Hades. She and a group of twenty-three young women, members of the great brood of children of Ocean (v. 5) and among them, apparently, Athena and Artemis, are playing in the Nysian plain and gathering a variety of flowers.[62] We have already learned from the syncopated account of the story at the beginning of the hymn that one particular flower, a narcissus, had been planted ahead of time by Zeus as a favor to Hades with the specific intention of deceiving Persephone into picking it. Just as Persephone plucks this narcissus, which she mistakes for a crocus, the god of the underworld appears and bears her away against her will.

For a man, on the other hand, it can be both dangerous and perverse to gather flowers. Aegisthus (Eur. *El.* 777–778) plucks myrtle for plaiting into a wreath for his hair, perhaps as a way of alluding to an effeminacy made clearer in Electra's long tirade over his dead body (907–956); he is met by Orestes and entourage, which eventually results in Aegisthus' death. Myrtle is gathered both for festive purposes, as it is at least on the surface here, and for funerary purposes, as at *El.* 324 and also, paradoxically, as things turns out, at *El.* 777–778. We first meet Hippolytus (Eur. *Hipp.* 73–87) as the young man, a virgin, is picking flowers for the statue of his patron goddess, Artemis.[63] He, too, is fated to die by the end of the play.

Similes and metaphors allying flowers with women may also be noted.[64] So close is a maiden's association with flowers in life that in poetry she becomes a flower—it too an embodiment of beauty, youth, naiveté, and delight. Certain flowers properly characterized certain women—a golden flower for one, the rose for another—each with its own distinctive physical and allusive properties. The poetry of Sappho is rich in such imagery:

> Now she stands out among Lydian women like the rosy-fingered moon after sunset, surpassing all the stars, and its light spreads alike over the salt sea and the flowery fields; the dew is shed in beauty, and roses bloom and tender chervil and flowery melilot.   (fr. 96.6–14)[65]

Cleis, thought by some to be the poet's daughter, possesses a form similar to flowers of gold (fr. 132): "I have a beautiful child who looks like golden flowers, my darling Cleis, for whom I would not (take) all Lydia . . ."[66]

In the *Homeric Hymn to Demeter* (v. 8) Persephone is a "bud-faced" kore (καλυκῶπιδι κούρη). Nicholas J. Richardson collects the various meanings that have been suggested for this rare adjective, preferring "with eyes like buds."[67] Schneider, following a suggestion made to him in person by Bruno Snell that the word refers almost certainly to the eyes, translates "mit blütengleichen Augen" ("with eyes like buds [or flowers]").[68] This makes little sense; naturally almond-shaped eyes do not look like buds unless they are turned up on their edges. It is more likely an allusion to a face that is like a flower in its youthful loveliness. Like Persephone, with whom Phrasikleia's epigram hints the dead girl is akin, the face of the kore is surrounded by calyxes of flowers, perfectly imaging the metaphor of a bud-faced girl. Of related interest is a contemporary small bronze kore from Sparta (fig. 47) who holds an out-sized lotus bud nearly as big as her head against her cheek, forcing the viewer to juxtapose visually the bud and the face.

Flower-gathering was the necessary prelude to another activity associated with young women which has already been introduced in connection with the polychromed garments of the Acropolis korai. This is the dyeing of yarn and cloth. In Euripides' *Ion* 889, quoted above, φάρεσιν ("for garments") probably refers to this use of flowers (that is, for dyeing), and not as A. S. Owen appears to take it, to garments strewn with flowers, a mistake, I believe, which is commonly made with reference to *Hec.* 466–474 as well.[69] Crocuses were favorites for the tenacious bright yellow color produced by their stamens; because the collection and use of saffron crocuses by women was so common, the color saffron itself comes particularly to be associated with women, as Barber shows.[70] The most famous saffron-colored garment made by women was the Panathenaic peplos. Not much is known for certain about ancient dyeing processes; the evidence is sparse, and, as Barber observes, even when we do have a tantalizing clue, such as the activity shown in the Bronze Age "Saffron-gatherers" fresco from Akrotiri, we cannot always conclude that a flower or a plant was collected specifically for dyeing purposes, since it could have been collected for a number of other reasons.[71]

There is also the question of who did the dyeing. It was a complicated process. In the oriental carpet-weaving industry, which provides a useful comparison, men did the dyeing and women did the weaving, generally speaking; the compositions of colors were closely guarded secrets, and dyers were thought of as wizards or magicians.[72] It is likely, however, that in ancient Greece women did the dyeing for their own clothes and the clothes of the family, at least when it came to plant-based dyes. Even if men did some or most of the dyeing, it was still the women who did the collecting of suitable plants and who probably should be credited for the discovery of which plants and plant parts would produce the most saturated and nonfugitive dyes. Christos Doumas, the director of the excavations at Thera, claims that picking crocus stamens for saffron is "a task which even today is performed exclusively by the womenfolk of Akrotiri."[73]

The fact that crocus flowers were so readily available for picking by young women accounts for why yellow was the preferred color for many garments. Purple, on the other hand, obtained from murex and purple-fish (two different creatures, according to Pliny, *NH* 9.125), may have been less readily accessible to the majority of women, who might not have lived near a source.[74] Men were in charge of the purple-fishing industry, as we learn from Euripides (*IT* 263), where the Herdsman describes as πορφυρευτικαὶ στέγαι the hollow, cliff-enveloped cove where he and his comrades accidentally came upon Orestes and Pylades. However, while obtaining the murex in commercial quantities was men's work, it is possible that women collected some shells on their own along the shores and did some of their own purple-dyeing.[75] That purple was more costly to obtain than saffron yellow accounts for its more sparing use, for instance, primarily in wedding and funeral attire. "Crimson-dyed" robes are brought with Andromache for her wedding to Hector in Sappho (fr. 44.8–9).[76] Sappho fr. 92, too fragmentary to translate, appears to refer to peploi of each of the two colors yellow and purple, as well as to stephanai, perhaps also colored purple, although it is difficult to ascertain anything else about these garments. The purple color of funerary attire is attested throughout Greek literature. Phrasikleia wears a dress of the appropriate color for both wedding and funeral. We shall return to this point later.

Another activity regularly engaged in by young women is the plaiting of flowers and other vegetation, once gathered, into garlands to wear on their heads or otherwise to adorn themselves in individualistic ways. In this aspect of daily life the statue of Phrasikleia and the Acropolis korai reinforce, even as they are reinforced by, the literary testimonia; some of this material could as easily have been presented in Chapter Four. In Athenaeus (15.669c) one of the symposiasts, the philosopher Democritus of Nicomedia, begins a discourse on the connections between wreaths and love that is a valuable source of ancient insights on the subject, preserving and corroborating much of the evidence from the early poets.

It is Sappho who provides the richest source of information about the grooming and dressing habits of aristocratic young women of the Archaic period. Fr. 125 comes from a scholiastic note on Aristophanes (Thesm. 401) in which an unnamed woman observes that whenever a woman plaits a wreath, she is assumed to be in love. The scholiast adds that plaiting wreaths was an occupation for the young and those in love, or for those both young and in love, such as Sappho, perhaps, in this autobiographical declaration: †αυταόρα† ἐστεφαναπλόκην ("When I myself was in the bloom of my youth, I used to plait wreaths").[77] Sappho (fr. 98a) reveals that a purple-colored wrap for the head is good enough for most any young woman, unless she is blonde:

> For my mother (once said that) in her youth, if someone had her locks bound in a purple (headband), that was indeed a great ornament; but for the girl who has hair that is yellower than a torch (ξανθοτέρα⟨ι⟩ς ... κόμα⟨ι⟩ς δάιδος) (it is better to decorate it) with wreaths of flowers in bloom.[78]

This type of wrap, as we learn elsewhere from Sappho (fr. 101), is not plain but rather its color makes it an expensive and exotic accoutrement: "and handcloths [χερρόμακτρα] . . . purple, perfumed (?), (which Mnasis) sent (to you) from Phocaea, expensive gifts . . ."[79] Athenaeus (9.410e), our source for this fragment, quotes Hecataeus in saying that these χερρό-μακτρα ("handcloths") were worn by women on their heads.[80] These would be the sort of fillet or wreath shown on white-ground lekythoi of the fifth century B.C., or, for example, in a scene of Electra at the tomb of Aga-memnon on a red-figured cup of ca. 440–430 attributed to the Penelope Painter.[81] Electra is in the process of wrapping one around her father's tombstone while an attendant holds several more, including one with a chevron design. Some of the stephanai worn by the korai from the Acropolis could also be associated with this type of headgear; kouroi also wear it on occasion.[82]

However, for a young woman the decoration of the head was not solely a matter of complementing the hair color. In Sappho (fr. 81b) the sacri-fices of the woman who is wreathed with flowers are said to be more pleasing to the gods than those of the unwreathed, according to Athenaeus (15.674e), who preserves the fragment. It may be assumed that young women vied with one another to plait the most pleasing head ornament as part of the quest for "unrivalled radiance":

And you, Dica, put lovely garlands around your locks, binding together stems of anise with your soft hands; for the blessed Graces look rather on what is adorned with flowers and turn away from the ungarlanded.[83]

This sampling of the literary evidence makes it clear that a concern for the proper, beautiful, and individualized dressing of the head claimed much of a young woman's time, and that a preoccupation with the ornamenta-tion of self was part of the almost ritualistic attention to physical appear-ance that was expected of, and central to the existence of, Archaic young women like Phrasikleia. It is fair to assume that an element of personal expression was central to this ritual. In this context the sumptuous lotus flower and bud crown worn by Phrasikleia, unparalleled and unrivalled among the Archaic korai, could be read as a personal grooming statement par excellence.

Wreathed or plaited flowers were an appropriate decoration for other parts of the body as well. Athenaeus (15.674c–d), in the course of a long scholarly discourse on wreaths and wreathing, introduces a type of wreathed necklace called a ὑποθυμίς (*hypothymis*) that is worn at the throat (τὸν τράχηλον).[84] He quotes Alcaeus, Sappho, and Anacreon on its use. Alcaeus (fr. 362) describes its effects: "Come, let someone put woven *hypothymides* (πλέκταις ὑπαθύμιδας) of anise about our necks . . . and let him pour sweet perfume over our chests."[85] Most probably the "sweet perfume" comes from the aroma of the *hypothymis* necklace itself rather than from a separate, liquid source. Athenaeus takes up the subject of the *hypothymis* again at 15.678d, where he states that it can be learned from the poetry of Alcaeus and Anacreon that this type of wreath was worn around the neck (περὶ τοὺς τραχήλους), that it was used by Aeolians and Ionians, and that there was a Lesbian version which was made of myrtle-spray entwined with violets and other flowers.

Athenaeus believes that the perfuming aspect of these decorations, rather than the beautifying, was dominant. He is careful to offer an etymology that accords with his interpretation of the purpose of the *hypothymis*, claiming (15.688c) that the word owes its derivation to ἀναθυμίασις ("rising in vapor," "exhalation"), rather than to the coincidence of its placement near the *thymos* (θυμός = generally, "heart").[86] However, not only the nose but also the heart, according to Athenaeus elsewhere (15.687d–f), reaped the benefits of perfumes, since that organ, too, is soothed by pleasant odors. The *hypothymis* appears to have been a unisex ornament. While Alcaeus probably has men in mind, Sappho (fr. 94.12–20) reveals that women also wore this distinctive type of plaited garland:

> You put on many wreaths of violets and roses and (crocuses?) together by my side, and round your tender neck you put *hypothymides* (woven) with many plaits (πό[λλαις ὑπα]θύμιδας / πλέκ[ταις) made of flowers and . . . with much flowery perfume, fit for a queen, you anointed yourself . . .[87]

Finally, the *hypothymis* mentioned by Anacreon (fr. 397) brings us directly back to Phrasikleia, as it is made of her flower, the lotus: πλεκτὰς / δ᾽ ὑπο-θυμίδας περὶ στήθεσι λωτίνας ἔθεντο ("They put lotus-plaited *hypothymides* at their breasts [i.e., around their necks]").

To judge from the literary evidence, the *hypothymis* was a necklace composed of a variety of fresh plant materials. However, it is not impossible that jewelry fabricated in the form of flowers, and perhaps incorporating a small perfume vial, might have served as suitable substitutes. It is not certain whether the necklace that Phrasikleia wears is composed of organic or fabricated materials or some combination of both. Ridgway, as we have seen, deduces that the jewelry has an abstract rather than a vegetal form, although she does not specify the formal qualities which led to the deduction.[88] The question of abstract or naturalistic persists. It may be useful to compare the jewelry worn by the Berlin Kore (fig. 40), the other extant Attic funerary kore, which has iconographical affinities with Phrasikleia. The earrings and the three ornaments of the necklace of the Berlin figure look both more fabricated and less lotiform than those of Phrasikleia. Necklaces with a form of pendant somewhat more similar to Phrasikleia's are worn by two marble korai from Delos, one of which also wore, according to Richter, two plastically rendered chains across the chest, each of which once held three metal attachments, as indicated by holes.[89] Any or all of these could be interpreted as representations of various types of *hypothymis*. No kore from the Acropolis wears jewelry in this form.

Gold necklaces from the fourth century B.C. have been found whose pendants, although they are smaller, more numerous, and more tightly packed, are very close in form to the pendants of Phrasikleia's jewelry and, even more so, to that of one of the Delian korai just mentioned (Athens NM 22). The forms of the pendants of one of the real examples,[90] as is the case with Phrasikleia's necklace, could be taken as representations of either flower buds or tiny amphorae or aryballoi, while the pendants in the others are, in all likelihood, representations of beechnuts rather than lotus buds.[91] Actual examples of pendants in the form of tiny golden aryballoi or amphorae from the mid–fifth century B.C. have been found in tomb 10 at Marion, Cyprus; they could be from either a necklace or earrings.[92] A perfect example of a gold necklace made up of alternating lotuses and lotus-rosettes with lotiform bud pendants, from the late fifth/early fourth century B.C., comes from a tomb at Pantikapaion (Kertch), in the region of the Black Sea.[93] Dyfri Williams and Jack Ogden assume that the pendants are seeds, perhaps of fennel. However, the presence of other lotus motifs would seem to point in the direction of either lotus buds or lotus seeds or seedpods which look much like lotus buds.[94]

Whether the forms of Phrasikleia's jewelry are meant to be representations of abstract or of naturalistic originals may never be determined, and might not even be determinable in the first place, since we, the viewers, are already once removed from reality by the sculpted form. It is as difficult to conclude also in the cases of the stephane, the earrings, and even the offering held in hand whether we are yet again, now, twice removed from reality. However, I will venture a judgment. The stephane and the offering are made of "real" flowers, as they appear to be carved with more detail, while the earrings, to a lesser extent, and the necklace, being more simplified and stylized, could be either meant to be real or else fabricated. There is the possibility that the largest three of the five pendant ornaments are lotus buds, since they are closer in appearance to the certainly lotiform motifs which compose the stephane, while the other smaller two, more rounded and sacklike, are tiny aryballoi containing perfumes, in fulfillment of the requirements of a *hypothymis*. Regardless of whether the floral motif is meant to be real or fabricated, it seems likely that this decoration is intended to be a representation of a *hypothymis* as might be worn along with a fashionable dress and elaborate stephane at a festive, convivial occasion like that suggested by Sappho fr. 94. While not a literal rendition of a *hypothymis,* the aryballoi might be thought of as a "representation" of the idea of scent.

On this topic Schneider makes some interesting observations.[95] While he does not mention the *hypothymis* in a discussion about the ways in which a visual artist might allude to a scent, he does refer to two small terracotta Boeotian kore figurines that wear aryballoi dangling from a necklace; a bronze statuette in the Boston Museum said to be from Elis, which wears a similar necklace with a small pendant that looks like a tiny aryballos, might also be introduced here.[96] What kore Acr. 593 (Pomegranate Kore) holds in her left hand looks more like an aryballos than a fruit; the offering held by the Berlin Kore (fig. 40), which looks more like a pomegranate, and the object held by kore Acr. 677, which looks like a fruit—if not the pomegranate that it is usually claimed to be—might be compared.[97] An ivory statuette from Ephesos carries a ewer in the right hand, which is held at her side.[98] A terracotta kore statuette from Rhodes now in the British Museum wears a necklace of pouchlike forms which recall two of Phrasikleia's five necklace ornaments; Richter calls them "disk pendants," but I wonder whether they might be perfume sacks.[99] As is the case with much Archaic iconographical visual imagery, a viewer would have to have independent knowledge of the object or symbol represented in order to be able to read it as the artist intended. Both the Archaic viewer and the modern do, in fact, possess this knowledge, if from different sources, the former from life and the latter from literature.

This leads to the question of whether the young woman behind the image, Phrasikleia, could have been especially enamored of the lotus flower when she was alive and that is why her funerary image is adorned so heavily with it. It is a question which is impossible to answer, but which nonetheless invites speculation. That certain individuals prefer particular flowers above all others may safely be adduced of any period, ancient or modern. But there is some evidence in early Greek literature that young women preferred certain flowers with which they personally identified. Persephone was fooled by a narcissus made to look like a crocus, as if the crocus was known to be her favorite flower, an especially fine example of which she could be counted on to pick.

Testimonia and her own poems suggest that Sappho's favorite flower was the rose, the flower of Aphrodite.[100] This is made clear in the first poem of Meleager's *Garland*, in which a fanciful wreath is composed of different flowers, each associated with the works of a particular poet, in Sappho's case, with roses, which are introduced as if they were the most precious of all flowers: "having woven [in the garland] many white lilies of Anyte, many narcissi of Moiro, and of Sappho, few, but [these are] roses."[101] Philostratus (*Ep.* 51) similarly testifies to Sappho's "love" of the rose and her predilection for likening it to the beauty of young women, appropriately enough, according to Philostratus, because it is the most beautiful of flowers and noted for its brief blooming period in spring. At *Il.* 22.441 Andromache "strews" θρόνα ποικίλ' ("many-colored flowers") into a garment she is weaving for Hector. It has been shown convincingly that the θρόνα are flowers rather than a throne, as once thought.[102] George M. Bolling has argued further that the θρόνα are, in fact, roses and points out that "different flowers secured different blessings for their wearers; . . . roses brought back one's man safe and sound to those who wore them."[103] This interpretation also affects the meaning of πο]ικιλόθρο[ν' ἀθανάτ' Ἀφρόδιτα in Sappho (fr. 1.1), which is often translated "ornate-*throned* immortal Aphrodite,"[104] but which more logically refers to the floral decoration (roses?) of the garment the goddess wears, analogous to the garment into which Andromache is weaving flowers. Or, alternatively, Aphrodite could be wearing a garment decorated with multicolored floral-*dyed* threads, as at Eur. *Hec.* 471. Either way, the lotus-rosette–strewn and floral-dyed peplos of Phrasikleia offers a sculpted parallel.

Even when the primary purpose was ornamentation, the flowers intended for plaited wreaths were not always fortuitously gathered. Athenaeus (Bk. 15) spends many pages detailing dozens of different types of flowers and foliage appropriate for wreathmaking for which occasion and which region. In addition to the decorative, there were practical purposes, such as medicinal and ritual, behind the choice of vegetation for certain types of wreaths. The flowers or fruits which made up these specialty wreaths would not have been chosen randomly. Apparently, there were professional female wreath-makers in Athens who worked on commission. In Aristophanes (*Thesm.* 446–458) an unnamed widow who supports herself and her five children by plaiting wreaths complains that business is bad because of the prevalence of atheism; she refers to some twenty commissioned garlands that she must plait.[105]

Such evidence allows for consideration of the possibility that the preponderance of lotus flowers in the sculpted image of Phrasikleia is not incidental, but that it reflects real-life practices, and renders less likely the suggestion that the elaborate stephane is meant to confer or imply divine status. The fact that the flowers appear on her head, around her neck, dangling from her earlobes, and in the left hand held at her breast, transforming Phrasikleia's statue into a visual counterpart to the Archaic epithet "bud-faced," suggests that, aside from any other symbolism it may have, the lotus was particularly significant for this particular young woman and for those who commissioned her grave monument.

But there may be a deeper symbolic side as well, arising from either Phrasikleia's preference for choosing lotuses to ornament her person in life or of Aristion's and her family's decision to adorn her this way forever in death. Some aspects of the iconography of the lotus suggest why it was an appropriate choice for a grave monument, especially of a parthenos. Perhaps the most heavily symbolic flower in ancient art, architecture, and life, the lotus is first and foremost the quintessential Egyptian bloom. Egyptians associated the lotus with the sun, with life, and with joy, and also with death and resurrection, the kinds of things which would naturally accrue to this flower because of its habit of closing up at night and sinking into the water only to rise again the next morning.[106]

The most familiar Egyptian genus of lotus, *Nymphaea*, which includes the species *Nymphaea lotus* (white lotus) and *Nymphaea caerulea* (blue lotus), was not indigenous to Greece.[107] However, the Greeks acknowledged the special botanical character of the genus and made note of its prominence in Egyptian art and life not only in their literature but also by reproducing its stylized form in their own art and architecture. Herodotus (2.92) describes how Egyptians used parts of two different species of lotus for food.[108] Theophrastus (*HP* 4.8.9–11) describes the plants' habitats and botanical characteristics in greater detail. Athenaeus (15.677d–e), in his catalogue of wreaths, relates the origins of a type of wreath made of rose-colored lotus flowers that was worn in Alexandria; these would be the plants of the *Nelumbium* genus rather than *Nymphaea*.[109] On account of the spectacle of its flowers, the species of lotus used for these wreaths as well as the wreaths themselves was renamed "of Antinoös" after a visit by the emperor Hadrian. Presumably these wreaths as well as ones made from the blue lotus, also mentioned by Athenaeus, had been worn before Hadrian's visit and the renaming of the flower in honor of his favorite. The lotus plant is all-pervasive as a decorative motif (e.g., lotus/palmette frieze) in Greek art, especially vases, and architecture.[110] Greeks did not invent these motifs, they borrowed them; the origins and development of the stylized lotus in Near Eastern art is well documented.[111]

Images, both major and minor, from ancient Egypt, primarily of the Middle and New Kingdoms, attest to the Egyptians' intimate association with the lotus; it was in its manifold forms an all-purpose accoutrement. The most ubiquitous lotiform image, and the one upon which all other lotuses in Egyptian and subsequently Greek art depend, is the hieroglyph for lotus, which takes the form of the spiky-petaled *Nymphaea caerulea* seen in profile; Richard H. Wilkinson describes the careful attention to botanical accuracy in depictions of the various forms of this species by Egyptian artists.[112] Out of this hieroglyph developed the symbol for Upper Egypt, a stylized cluster of the plants which, when entwined with the symbol for Lower Egypt, a cluster of papyrus plants, is used as the emblem for the United Two Lands for ca. 3,000 years.[113]

The lotus is best seen in all of its naturalistic splendor as a bodily ornament for both men and women in life and in art. Among the most appealing examples of lotus-bedecked Egyptian women are the three daughters of Djehutyhotep from the 12th Dynasty of the Middle Kingdom, who are depicted in painted limestone relief in their father's tomb.[114] The two better-preserved women wear crowns made of alternating and certainly real lotus flowers and buds, just like Phrasikleia's, as well as fillets, with ends straggling, ornamented with a lotus in full flower front and back. In addition, each wafts a huge lotus in her left hand as she fans its coveted aroma toward her nostrils. Phrasikleia, too, holds a lotus in her hand. But each of the Egyptian women, rather than holding the lotus in simple bud form rigidly at her breast, like Phrasikleia, or, at most, in an awkwardly extended hand, instead wields a fan in the form of a huge, botanically correct, perfume-laden lotus in her left hand, in the more lifelike manner that the medium of painting affords. Even the separate species are discernible. The young woman in the middle prefers *Nymphaea caerulea,* and the woman on the right, *Nymphaea lotus.*

In other examples the bouquet in hand is made up of lotuses and buds combined, as in the relief of a seated couple in the banquet scene from the New Kingdom tomb of the vizier Ramose.[115] In a painted limestone relief from the tomb of Haremheb, Nefertum, the Egyptian god of ointments and pleasant odors, wears atop his wig a huge anthemium in the form of a blue lotus, suggesting that its perfume was the most powerful of all.[116]

Not only ornaments made of real lotuses but also fabricated ones are common. Dating from the reign of Amenhotep III of the New Kingdom, a faience necklace that originated as the last major row of beads from a broad collar or pectoral, perhaps of the type worn by the three Middle Kingdom ladies, is made up of pointed blue-lotus petals.[117] It is possible that the habit of wearing of earrings by youth, both male and female, among Egyptian royalty inspired a similar practice in orientalizing Greece. Phrasikleia, as well as virtually all of the korai from the Acropolis, wears earrings.

The spectacular Egyptian water lily did not grow naturally in Greece, but that did not stop Greek artists from being inspired to assimilate and recreate the flower as if it were their own. There were, however, native Greek genera of lotus. Theophrastus (*HP* 7.15.3) observes that there are many types of plant which are called by the same name, lotus, even though they have little or nothing in common, differing in the forms of their leaves, stems, flowers, and fruit as well as in the uses to which they are put. He classifies five types of lotus:[118] (1) the nettle tree, *Celtis australis,* which supplies a type of wood; (2) the "Libyan tree," *Zizyphus lotus,* another tree species that was berry-producing and native to Libya, and probably the source for the lotuses eaten in the *Odyssey* (9.91–97);[119] (3) the Nile water lily, the genus *Nymphaea,* which, from Theophrastus' silence on the matter and his detailed references to how they grow in Egypt and in the Euphrates valley, does not seem to have been found in Greece; (4) the trefoil, *Trifolium fragiferum,* which is herbaceous and native to Greece; (5) the melilotus, *Trigonella graeca,* another herbaceous species native to Greece.

As they were herbaceous and indigenous to ancient Greece, the last two are of interest to us here. Both are from the unassuming Leguminosae family, and neither bears a resemblance to the Egyptian genus.[120] Without any other redeeming qualities, *Trifolium* species served principally as food for horses. The saving grace of the humble melilotus was the aroma produced by its honey, which may have encouraged the association with the Egyptian lotus. When dried, it is said to have smelled much like the saffron crocus (Pliny, *NH* 21.53), something which can no longer be tested, since the species of crocus cultivated today are not known for their smell. It should be assumed that, in most instances in Greek literature where the word "lotus" appears in a ritual or festive context like the examples discussed above, the melilotus, or sweet clover, is meant. This is the case in Homer (*Il.* 14.348), where, during an erotic interlude, Zeus and Hera are depicted lying in a thick, soft bed of freshly grown grass, lotus, crocus, and hyacinth. Some commentators have assumed that the Egyptian variety of lotus is meant, although that would mean that the gods are lying on the water![121] The lotuses which are eaten by Achilles' horses would be trefoil or melilotus (*Il.* 2.776). It is unlikely that any of the lotuses mentioned in Homer refer to the *Nymphaea* species. In many of these literary references to the lotus, however, one senses a deliberate ambiguity about which lotus is meant; the Greeks were, after all, well acquainted with the Egyptian and other varieties as well as their own, and a conflation of the humble Greek lotus species with those of Egypt could only flatter the former.

It would be the melilotus that was typically dried and wound around the neck as a *hypothymis* (Anacreon fr. 397), or about the head as a stephane.[122] If Phrasikleia is depicted as in life, she would most likely be meant to be wearing lotuses of this genus, even though it is the Egyptian variety which the artist has opted to depict. She is unlikely to have worn freshly cut Egyptian lotuses and buds; fabrications of them were, however, possible. It must be borne in mind that, within the formal and conceptual vocabulary of the Archaic artist, there were only two ways to represent any kind of "lotus," whether Greek or Egyptian: the familiar Egyptian kind either in bud or in flower. In its own right the melilotus, its beauty residing in its perfume, would have held little ornamental interest for the Greek artist. When, however, it was desirable or necessary to represent this common plant with its unremarkable blooms, an artist might substitute instead the more famous flower with which it shared only its Hellenic name, the Egyptian lotus which has few rivals for spectacular display. If I am correct, the viewer would see and recognize the Egyptian variety, read "lotus" but understand, through homonymic recognition, "melilotus," that is, "the lotuses that we pick and wear in our hair." This semiotic process would be comparable to that of the aryballoi mentioned above, where the perfume vessels substitute for sensual perceptions like odors which the artist wants to express but which cannot be depicted.

The homonymic mode of conveying information might be extended even further in the case of the lotuses which adorn Phrasikleia. The noun λώτισμα in Greek means "flower" or, metaphorically, "fairest, choicest, best"; while the verbs λωτίζομαι and ἀπολωτίζω, by analogy, become "to cull the best." Euripides (*Hel.* 1593) has a messenger report Menelaus' command to his comrades to stop delaying and take up arms against Theoclymenus' sailors with the address: ὦ γῆς Ἑλλάδος λωτίσματα ("O choicest men of Greece").[123] The verbal forms represent a more expressive alternative to something like ἀπανθίζω/ἀνθίζομαι. It is significant that the lotus was selected to represent all flowers; for this reason, I am sure that the Egyptian flower is meant.

Two additional Euripidean examples bring us even closer to the imagery of Phrasikleia. A chorus (*IA* 790–792), anticipating the fate of the Trojan women who are destined to be led away as slaves to the Greek victors, asks: Τίς ἄρα μ᾽ . . . πατρίδος ὀλομένας ἀπολωτιεῖ; ("Who . . . will pluck me away from the destroyed fatherland?"); at *Suppl.* 448–449, Theseus, in the course of a rousing speech on the perils of totalitarian governance, says: . . . ὅταν τις ὡς λειμῶνος ἠρινοῦ στάχυν / τομαῖς ἀφαιρῇ κἀπολωτίζῃ νέους; (". . . whenever someone culls and cuts away the best of the young, like a crop from a springtime meadow?"). To call a young man "the choicest flower" could allude to his *aretē*, that is, his youth, his military prowess, and his eloquence; while for a woman, *aretē* might find outward expression in her youth, her beauty, her children, and her weaving skills, but significantly not in her eloquence; it is her choice of flowers that speaks for her.

Now there is a darker side to the symbolism of the lotus. Eating lotuses brings on forgetfulness in the *Odyssey* (9.91–97). Lotuses are associated with death in Sappho fr. 95: "and a longing grips me to die and see the dewy, lotus-covered banks of Acheron."[124] Euripides (*Ph.* 1571) uses an unusual word, λωτοτρόφον, a *hapax legomena*, according to Donald J. Mastronarde, to refer to a meadow rich in lotuses, an apt setting for the deaths of three family members, Polyneices, Eteocles, and their mother, Jocasta.[125] Mastronarde's contention that the term refers not to death but to "beautiful fertility" does not seem strong enough given the context, since immediately following the mention of the meadow, in Antigone's recounting of the tragedy, the heroes fought and bloodied each other and soon will die, and in the next few lines their mother takes her own life at the same spot. Both meanings may be intended.

The image of a fragrant field of melilotus/lotus as a site of love and death is rich and cogent and parallels the imagery of Phrasikleia. For the lotus also functions as an erotic symbol, juxtaposing love/death in a manner that is familiar from other mythic traditions. There can be no doubt that the obvious phallic characteristics of the stylized Egyptian lotus forms were noted and exploited in explicit erotic contexts in Greek art.[126] The erotic connotations of the forms of the lotus did not go unnoticed among the Egyptians, although here the Greeks did not require any source of inspiration.[127] While this kind of overt eroticism flourished on vases, it was by no means common in sculpture, and nonexistent in monumental sculpture.

Unrealized fertility and unwanted virginity, rather than overt eroticism, are more likely what the sculptor of Phrasikleia's statue had in mind. David Armstrong and Ann Ellis Hanson have collected evidence for folk beliefs about the physical signs of virginity in a young woman, which include small breasts, a thin, graceful neck which would thicken at the loss of her virginity, and a high-pitched voice which would darken afterward.[128] Phrasikleia cannot speak, but she does have small breasts, as do many of the korai from the Acropolis, and her neck is graceful, again in common with many members of that group. I would add the fact that her lower arms are bared, as are many of the Acropolis korai.[129] Sappho (fr. 53), on the "rosy-armed" (βροδοπάχεες = "forearm, wrist to elbow") Graces, "korai" of Zeus, may be related to this feature in the sculptures. The statue that memorializes Phrasikleia's real-life tragedy is, as it turns out, a perfect figuration of a paradoxical double antistasis of Euripides (*Hec.* 612), when, as an anguished Hecuba anticipates the ritual bathing of the body of her daughter, Polyxena, she calls the girl, dead before marriage, about-to-be bride of Hades: νύμφην τ' ἄνυμφον παρθένον τ' ἀπάρθενον ("both a bride without a marriage and a virgin without a maidenhead"). Similarly, Phrasikleia's lotuses direct the viewer's attention not only to the beauty of her youth, her aristocratic background, and her innocent, virginal activities in life, but also to the poignancy of her premature passing.

We now turn from the iconography of life to the iconography of death. The kore Phrasikleia is, after all, a tomb statue, and it is to be expected that she is outfitted in funerary attire. There has been some disagreement about the nature of the dress. John Pedley, for instance, leaves open the question of exactly what Phrasikleia wears, preferring to call it a "sleeved tunic." In his view the garment "is not characterized by the kolpos typical of the linen chiton nor by the overfold typical of the woolen peplos."[130] Claude Rolley refers to it as a chiton.[131] Ridgway, however, concludes that the garment is a peplos.[132] In her discussion of funerary korai she observes: "It may be a coincidence that none of the six wears the diagonal himation; certainly the fashion was already known at least by the time of the Lavrion kore [New York MMA 07.286.110]."[133] This coincidence is explained if, as I suggest, the type of dress is seen as an iconographical feature rather than as an indication of date. Although Ridgway does consider an iconographical explanation, that funerary korai may be shown in "indoors attire" or possibly bridal attire, as opposed to the "more elaborately dressed," presumably in outdoors attire, votive Acropolis group, unfortunately she does not press this interesting suggestion.[134] Stewart notes only that Phrasikleia is "dressed in all her finery for the tomb."[135] On issues relating to the accuracy of the rendering of female dress, it is often best to defer to the shopworn but still useful argument, artistic license, and assume from the texture, drape, and color of the fabric and the boxy style in which it is rendered, typically for peplophoroi, that the garment is a dark peplos.

It is true that the peplos is less commonly featured in Archaic female statues than Ionic costume. The simple, heavy drape of the coarse woolen peplos is more properly associated with the overall less-decorative statues of the Early Classical period, while the use of transparent crimped and pleated linens layered in a luxuriant manner around and about the female body is the drapery fashion associated with the Archaic. When worn by an Archaic kore, the peplos is frequently taken as an indication of early date; Acr. 679 is a case in point. That this line of argumentation has not affected discussions of Phrasikleia's date to the same extent is due to the existence of an inscription whose approximate date had already been ascertained by epigraphers, thereby limiting the range of possibilities. However, any such argument can be seen to be less than compelling in many instances if the peplos is taken as an iconographical feature instead of a stylistic indicator. The possibility has already been presented that the Peplos Kore, rather than bearing a date earlier than the majority of the finest of the Acropolis group, to which it is otherwise stylistically similar, may in fact be an archaizing representation of a statue of a goddess, but contemporary with the others. Phrasikleia, on the other hand, surely wears a peplos because she is dead. The peplos was a standard form of burial dress, documented in Greek art as far back as the Geometric period, with the depiction of a *prothesis* (lying in state) of a deceased female on the funerary Dipylon Amphora.[136] In the Archaic period and earlier, mourning women are frequently shown wearing peploi, while later in the fifth century they appear in Ionic dress on white-ground lekythoi.[137] There is also abundant literary evidence attesting to peploi as both an element of the *kosmos* of the corpse and the appropriate garments for mourners to wear.[138]

Furthermore, the red color preserved on Phrasikleia's peplos could have added significance. Many funerary stelai had red-painted backgrounds, which cannot have been anything other than symbolic, akin to the gold backgrounds of Byzantine paintings, since red is unlikely to have been used as a representation of space or sky in the way that blue is used for backgrounds in Western art. Ridgway has suggested that the red background is meant to remove the scene from "any possible connection with reality," and to make it seem "otherworldly." Red, as Ridgway notes, "predominated on the costumes of the Berlin kore and Phrasikleia, two undoubtedly funerary statues."[139] As we learned from the Acropolis korai,

it is difficult to conclude from the preserved red polychromy of Phrasikleia's peplos just what the original color was. The crucial distinction, it
seems, was not between actual hue or color but between dark and light.
Peploi in literature are routinely referred to either as yellow or purple or as
simply light or dark. There does not appear to be a great deal of consistency in the colors of the garments worn by the deceased and mourners.[140] Our best pictorial source of information about funerary ritual of
the Classical period is Attic white-ground lekythoi, where both corpses
and mourners often wear a combination of yellow chiton with a dark
green or violet/red himation, perhaps solely for the dramatic effect caused
by the light/dark juxtaposition.[141] Literary evidence reinforces the notion
that dark clothes are associated with death. In Euripides dark (purple?
red?) garments of mourning are donned by both men and women, sometimes in exchange for light-colored (yellow?).[142] In Plutarch (*Per.* 38.4)
a dying Pericles declares that no Athenian has had to put on a dark himation
because of him.

Thus, both the peplos itself and its color signal to the viewer of Phrasikleia's image that this is a grave marker. However, given the marriage/
death conflation implied by the epitaph, the dark, highly ornamental peplos
could simultaneously be interpreted as a wedding dress, perhaps converted
to funeral attire with unanticipated haste, an event which could as well
have happened before or even just after the girl's wedding; the inscription
would seem to allow for either. For wedding gowns were also purple in
color.[143] Reeder argues that this purple would have been achieved by dying with the substance obtained from the costly murex shell, and that the
color "carried connotations of wealth as well as, certainly, of blood."[144]

Phrasikleia's impressive array of jewelry, customary for weddings, as
well as the unusual high crown with prominent floral elements which is
evocative of those typically worn by brides, further contributes to the
impression of a girl having begun to dress for her marriage when death
intervened.[145] Just as men were regularly buried in their military costume,
so unmarried or recently married women were buried in wedding attire.[146]
Joan Reilly's study of the so-called mistress and maid scenes on white-
ground funerary lekythoi, previously thought to represent funerary rituals of various kinds, has shown convincingly that these scenes in fact depict a bride being prepared for a wedding which will never take place,
owing to premature death. While these objects are later, Phrasikleia's statue
might be thought of as a comparable, but much more elaborate, Archaic
response to the impulse to imagine a loved one's lost future. Helene P.
Foley also notes the similarities and consequent ambiguities between

women's wedding and funeral attire; in both cases she wore her best: "wreaths and fine jewelry as well as a special *peplos*."[147] In Euripides (*Tr.* 1220), as Hecuba is preparing her grandson, Astyanax, for burial, she remarks that the beautiful Phrygian peploi in which she is wrapping his body should have been his wedding attire. The conflation of weddings and funerals is even more forcefully exploited in *Medea,* in a passage discussed at length in Chapter Four, where a finely wrought, elaborately decorated peplos and a beaten gold headdress, wedding gifts from the jilted Medea, become literally a funeral shroud for the recipient, Jason's new bride.[148]

These special peploi would have been made with a young woman's own hands and very possibly in patterns and motifs of her own choosing. All forms of weaving were primarily a feminine occupation. Young women wove their own garments and those of other family members, and they braided their hair or wigs into complex arrangements and plaited garlands to wear around their heads and necks, all requiring a similar set of mechanical skills, including dexterity of smallish fingers and highly developed sense of pattern, shape, texture, and color.

Without the visual evidence for spectacular, woven garments on display in statues and on vases, it would be impossible to believe that Athenian women working within what amounts to a cottage industry would have had an opportunity to develop the level of skill required to weave a subject as complex as that depicted in any temple pediment or frieze, the Gigantomachy, into the Panathenaic peplos. It is conceivable that the cartoons for this design were created by studio-trained men versed in the proper techniques for rendering figures in space in two dimensions, but it is likely that women did the actual weaving.

It is not unreasonable to speculate that, as in the *paryphē* designs in the Acropolis korai, there was a degree of specificity and deliberation associated with the pattern featured in Phrasikleia's peplos, which incorporates a form of lotus-rosette, even if the idea is reflected solely in a personal choice made by those who were responsible for her grave monument. There are parallels. The roses which Andromache weaves meaningfully into Hector's garment (*Il.* 22.441) have already been noted. Preserved textiles are too few to be regarded as representative, but Barber discusses one possible example, a large, fragmentary, heavily ornamented funeral pall found placed directly over the wooden sarcophagus of an early-fourth-century B.C. Greek colonist in Pantikapaion.[149] It was decorated in the resist-painted technique (something like batik) with a number of friezes depicting an odd assortment of mythological characters, including Jocasta, Phaidra, and Mopsos, an obscure prophet from Asia Minor. Barber concludes that, while we may never be able to understand the iconography, it seems reasonable that it "held particular significance for the owner of the cloth." Part of the funerary clothing of the deceased was also found; its decoration as well involved unusual, apparently personalized iconography. It has been noted that rosettes frequently appear in funerary situations in Greek art; Donna Kurtz and John Boardman have wisely concluded that this implies "that they have a symbolic importance in funerary art," but they do not pursue the source of the symbol or the symbolism.[150]

However, a simple explanation is at hand. If one accepts W. H. Goodyear's supposition that the rosettes which are ubiquitous in Greek and Egyptian art are not flowers at all, but rather stylized representations of the seedpods of lotuses,[151] it is clear that the funerary significance of the rosette is derived from the funerary significance of the lotus itself. The form and meaning of these rosettes are ultimately Egyptian in inspiration, since that is where this flower grows and whence its symbolism is derived. Many Egyptian female statues, funerary or other, wear rosettes exactly like Phrasikleia's at their nipples; they appear, for example, over the breasts in the anthropoid coffin of a lady, Isis, from the 19th Dynasty.[152]

There is another possible visual affinity, perhaps accidental, but nonetheless worth pointing out, between the lotus-bud frieze featured in Phrasikleia's crown and a motif used by Egyptian artists to represent the gates of the underworld. In reduced form this motif can be seen in the hieroglyph for "gateway," looking like the teeth of a garden rake in profile view as they line a schematic representation of a wall depicted in bird's eye view. In the hieroglyph the motifs are thought to result from an attempt to represent some type of apotropaic crenellation or "battlements" in stylized format.[153] Yet it would not be surprising that a formal similarity with the lotus was noted and deliberately exploited by Egyptian artists, given the funerary symbolism of the lotus; Adolf Erman has shown that the ancient Egyptians seem to have enjoyed punning.[154] In its "real" form, upon which, presumably, the hieroglyph is based, this type of frieze is most frequently encountered painted at the tops of walls in New Kingdom tombs, particularly those which are decorated with illustrations from the Book of the Gates.[155] It consists of a chain of individual motifs, each composed of a circular base, exactly like the circular bases making up the individual motifs of the crown worn by Phrasikleia, topped by spear-pointed or budlike shapes. Sometimes the spear-pointed shape extends slightly below the circle. However, to the uninitiated, they look not at all distinct from stylized lotus buds. It could be that this motif was either mistaken for a lotus-bud frieze by Greek artists or else consciously conflated with the lotus as it is virtually its duplicate. Either way, the funerary significance is intact.

Phrasikleia's lotiform stephane may now be read as an aspect of funerary attire, both for the iconography of its motifs and for its form. Kurtz and Boardman discuss the custom of placing crowns on the head of the deceased.[156] A number of these burial crowns made of beaten gold and dating from the fourth century onward have been discovered; the authors illustrate an example from a Hellenistic grave in the Kerameikos that is especially appropriate for the present purposes, since it is made up of flattened but distinctly lotiform motifs.[157] The "unusually rich" wreath is composed of sixteen flattened four-petal lotiform motifs of the length of a finger made of red gold and about fifty smaller, three-petal lotiform motifs made of yellow gold. The most impressive extant examples of floral funerary wreaths are from the Macedonian royal tombs at Vergina.[158] A red-figured Attic loutrophoros shows a *prothesis* of a woman wearing an elaborate crown with a lotus-bud protome.[159] The archaeological evidence for the practice is supported by abundant literary references. Aristophanes (*Lys.* 602–604) offers a humorous reminder of the pervasiveness of the ritual crowning of the dead with vegetal and floral wreaths, a practice with which his audience could be expected to be fully conversant; as the final stroke of a general dressing-down conducted by the rebellious women, an aged but still, by his own testimony, very much alive Proboulos is crowned with a funerary garland as if he were a corpse.[160]

Garland puzzles over the reason behind this habit of crowning the dead, but concludes that there is probably very little significance to the gesture except to reflect the "dignity and lustre" of these items being worn in life during various festive occasions.[161] And there need not be anything more profound behind the practice. Phrasikleia, like her peers, wore floral crowns in life; in part, as a reflection of the short life she lived, she also wears one in death. Moreover, we need not assume in every instance that a fabricated crown rather than a crown of real flowers would have adorned the dead body just because it is only fabricated ones which, understandably, have survived. The impressive naturalism of the individual flowers and buds that make up Phrasikleia's stephane compared, for instance, to the relative abstraction of the forms of the necklace would seem to indicate that the former is meant to be composed of fresh flowers. Granted, real Egyptian lotuses would not have been available unless they were cultivated in public or private gardens, which is not out of the question. In lieu of either real flowers or fabricated ones made of precious metals, wax versions were also used, if we are to believe Aristophanes (*Ec.* 1035),[162] so we may imagine something more lifelike than metal for the original. Finally, there is the possibility, even likelihood, that the crown which actually adorned Phrasikleia's body was made of local melilotus. Whatever the circumstances, there can be no doubt that a Greek sculptor found a convincing way to recreate Egyptian lotuses for this occasion.

The funerary significance of the lotus is reiterated yet again in the bud which Phrasikleia holds at her breast. Like the girl herself, the choicest has been plucked before it could bloom. The bud will not make its way into the *kolpos* of Phrasikleia's peplos; it is destined for a more permanent semiotic role. Of all its attributes, this gesture is the one that, in my view, secures for the statue its status as a representation of a mortal. Deities in Greek art may hold objects, but it would be senseless for them to hold things in a conventional Near Eastern gesture of adoration that already has a venerable history before we see it here. A version of the gesture is documented in the Near East as far back as ca. 3000 B.C. in the votive statuettes from the Abu temple, Tell Asmar.[163] The hand held at breast or waist, frequently clasping an object, is seen in a number of korai, especially those which are thought to be earlier in date, like Acr. 593 and the Berlin Kore. Since both votive and funerary korai may feature the gesture, the meaning originally attached to it must have been either incompletely understood or loosely interpreted. Ridgway sensibly concludes: "It is probably incorrect to speak of offerings for the objects held by these funerary korai."[164] Sourvinou-Inwood sees the closely held object as a specific attribute demonstrating the "emblematic" status of funerary korai, although it is not exclusive to them.[165] It does seem more appropriate than the proffering gesture, which would force an incomprehensible reading as "offering." Among Greek examples of the latter gesture, which also may be read as "adoration," the most common variation shows the arm extended, holding an item.

The Berlin Kore features both gestures, hand held at breast in close imitation of the Near Eastern model, and hand slightly extended from side, grasping what is usually identified as a pomegranate, but what could be a small vessel. In Egyptian art little round pots with formed lips shaped much like Greek aryballoi are frequently held in hands extended out from chest level by figures making offerings of wine, ointment, or incense to the gods, especially in funerary contexts, as in a wall painting from the tomb of Haremheb, where the tomb's owner is offering two pots of wine to Osiris, the god of the Underworld.[166] In painted examples, the hands may hold the pots at chin-level, but the Egyptian sculptor was careful to represent the proffering arms only when a stable base for the isolated stone parts could be provided, such as in a squatting or seated figure, and even then the arms rest on the thighs.[167] Early Greek sculptors were more intrepid, but the extended arm presented a substantial technical challenge and, as expected, is more common among later korai and in other media. On the other hand, the lotus bud which Phrasikleia cradles is not intended for the gods; it is *her* attribute for eternity, a microcosmic reflection of her life and an emblem of the persona she takes to the grave and conveys to posterity in her image.

We have seen that the motif of the lotus-held-in-hand is Egyptian and, like the Greek examples, should be regarded as a reflection of real-life practices. However, one of the primary characteristics of Egyptian art and life is that what is symbolic of life is also symbolic of death; this is especially true with the lotus or lotus bud held in this manner. On tomb walls of the Middle and New Kingdoms the deceased and their families are routinely depicted with lotus flowers or buds in hand and a jar of perfumed ointment under their noses, and wearing various forms of lotus crown or a perfume cone atop their wigs.[168] Sometimes the lotuses at the front of the crown are drooping, only half-opened, or still in bud form, attesting to Egyptian artists' interest in naturalism as well as the greater ease of rendering details in a two-dimensional medium. It will be recalled that, of the three daughters of Djehutyhotep, two wear crowns of both flowers and buds, and that the Egyptian god, Nefertum, has the blue lotus as his attribute. The perfume of the god envelops humans in a divine odor to protect against death and the ravages it imposes on human flesh.[169]

In a somewhat neutralized form the custom carried over into Greece. While Phrasikleia and the Berlin Kore are the sole extant examples of funerary korai, and both of them do, in fact, hold objects at or near their breasts, the examples of figures holding objects on Archaic Attic grave stelai are more numerous. Several are of particular interest in that they hold flowers. In the Brother/Sister Stele in New York, the "brother" holds a pomegranate, while the "sister" holds a flower almost directly under her nostrils, enjoying its bouquet.[170] A stele from Athens, now in the Louvre, shows an incised and painted male figure holding a painted flower.[171] A youth holds a flower that looks like a lotus in a Late Archaic grave stele from Amorgos in the Cyclades which was found in poor condition, having been damaged in the process of readapting it for use in a small Hellenistic architectural monument, possibly funerary.[172] From the evidence, it seems fair to conclude that in Archaic Greek art, an object so held, whether real fruit or flower or perfume vial, is frequently an attribute of a dead person depicted as in life, enjoying its scent. However, once again, the fact that the attributes vary from monument to monument indicates some degree of personalization in the selection of a motif, in Phrasikleia's case, the lotus.[173] At the very least, this could mean that the melilotus was her favorite flower, which carried no particular associations with death. But if it is really the Egyptian lotus that is being invoked, the heavy, ancient weight of funerary symbolism cannot be avoided.

We have seen the positive linguistic associations which the lotus held for Greeks; its dark side has a linguistic counterpart as well. A further layer of connotative meaning has been proposed for the term λώτισμα, sounding an oblique note in an otherwise major key: "That which is plucked" could also mean, metaphorically, "destroyed."[174] In a Euripidean passage which was introduced earlier as a linguistic comparandum (IA 790–792), these two meanings are accentuated by the pointed juxtaposition of two words, underlined here: Τίς ἄρα μ᾽ . . . πατρίδος ὀλομένας ἀπολωτιεῖ; ("Who . . . will pluck me away from the destroyed fatherland?").[175] The female speaker, that is, the chorus as the voice of a typical Trojan woman, is anticipating that she will suffer the same fate as Troy, utter destruction, since she will be forced to complete her life as a slave of the enemy. She will be snatched like one of the flowers that she herself picked in all innocence as a young woman, not from a lush, tranquil meadow, however, but from a city in ruins. Euripides' image is characterized by a striking reversal of expectations; the young woman should be plucking flowers but it is she who is plucked. A flower plucked is a flower detached from its source of remaining life. She will be as one of those flowers, fresh and beautiful at the time of picking, but, in the end, dead before its time, like Phrasikleia.

The motif of the lotus flower comes to Greece already saturated with the powerful overtones of death and rebirth that it carried throughout its long history in Egyptian funerary art, from which it was surely borrowed. Add to this message the Greek linguistic connotations, and the lotuses with which Phrasikleia is arrayed, if I am correct, might have been read or even heard by the ancient viewer who, literally, "translated" them in this order: λωτός, "most beautiful and showiest of all flowers," λώτισμα, "finest young woman," λωτίζειν, ἀπολλύναι, "prematurely dead young woman." The silent message of the flower is a perfect parallel to the "silent names" of the gods that speak only to the knowing in a fragment of Euripides' Phaethon (fr. 781.224–226); the name of Apollo/Helios, whose etymology may be from ἀπόλλυμι, "destroy," is frightfully clear to Clymene, the speaker of these lines, whose son by Helios, Phaethon, has just been killed by Zeus' lightning bolt during a willful ride in the sun god's chariot.[176] Like Phrasikleia's lotuses, the names may actually be silent, but they speak nonetheless.

Acr. kore 683 (fig. 25) may be reintroduced to corroborate the type of reading that I am positing for Phrasikleia. It will be recalled that this kore's short stature and bodily proportions have inspired some viewers to conclude that she is a dwarf; her unusual footgear, red pointed slippers, has also received attention. There is some additional ancient literary evidence about this unusual style of footgear. Pollux (7.93 = *PCG* III, 2, 761; cf. Arist. *Lys.* 64), a scholar and rhetorician of the second century A.D., claims that Aristophanes uses the term ἀκάτια ("little boats") to refer to a type of shoe worn by women. But there may be yet another connotative association with the word ἀκάτια. According to an ancient anecdote (unattributed in Bekker 1814, 19.11–12), the term was apparently also applied in an intentionally unflattering way to individuals who are short: καὶ τοὺς μικροὺς τὰ σώματα ἀκάτια λέγουσιν ("And they call people who are short in stature 'little boats'"). It is possible that an ancient viewer of kore 683 might have apprehended the visual notation of the boat-shaped shoes, which are hard to miss, then, as with Phrasikleia's lotuses, read the motif as a word, ἀκάτια, proceed to deduce additional linguistic associations such as "dwarf," "unfortunate one," ultimately finding his or her mental deductions borne out in the image itself. The fact that kore 683 was the larger of two figural dedications on one base complicates the argument somewhat but does not invalidate it. We do not know the nature of the second figure; it, too, could have been a genre-type image which, read together with kore 683, offered the ancient visitor to the Acropolis a rare moment of humor or sympathy amid a clamor of loftier visual and verbal messages. As with the cluster of words related to λώτισμα above, this reading would depend on whether the term ἀκάτια was current at the time. In itself the existence of the shoes on an Archaic kore who happens also to have dwarfish proportions could attest to the word's being so used.

The proposed reading of two Archaic Greek statues could make sense as an early Greek attempt at a much-simplified version of the reading of Egyptian hieroglyphic writing, in which is achieved a unique marriage between the visual image and the written word, and whose direct connection with the figural arts has often been observed. For in hieroglyphs alone, the acts of writing and drawing are one. I am not in a position to push the analogy too far; Karl-Theodor Zauzich cautions: "Egyptian hieroglyphic writing is true picture writing, with agreement between the picture and its meaning, only in a very limited way."[177] While individual motifs rarely stand for entire words, the motifs were read as syllables. However, as the title and underlying thesis of Wilkinson's *Reading Egyptian Art* demonstrate, the direct transference of motifs and their meanings from hieroglyphs to artworks is an undeniable feature of Egyptian art.

It would not be surprising that some less than perfectly understood version of the Egyptian norm of making artworks which could be read as well as appreciated visually was attempted by Greek artists during their lengthy orientalizing phase, which, as the profusion of Egyptianizing and Near Eastern features treated in this study has made clear, extended well beyond the seventh century B.C. Carved forms on Archaic monumental images which are read a little like glyphs could be interpreted as a reductionist and only superficially understood reflection of a complex linguistic/visual correspondence that is borrowed from the Egyptians together with other ideas, formal characteristics, styles, and motifs. From their first encounters with hieroglyphs Greeks seem to have understood that they were both beautifully carved pictorial motifs and a written language. While Herodotus was by no means among the first Hellenic visitors to Egypt, since Greeks had been there at least since the third quarter of the seventh century, he (2.37.1) identifies correctly the two types of letters used by Egyptians, one called "sacred" and the other "demotic," indicating that the little pictures in relief had long been recognized as a sophisticated written language. Having invented the name that is still used to describe the most elevated form of the Egyptian written language, the Greeks remained fascinated with hieroglyphs throughout their history.[178]

If the "glyphs" which adorn the statue of Phrasikleia are to be translated like Egyptian hieroglyphs, it might then be more correct to interpret the first word of the inscription, σἔμα, as "portrait" or "picture" rather than "grave monument," if "sign," in this sense, is indicative of "image to be read," and the reading of the multiple glyphs results in a deduction that the whole image constitutes a coherent synthetic visual identity of one particular Archaic Greek woman.

For as long as it has been known, the metrical inscription which accompanied the grave statue of Phrasikleia has been interpreted both without and with the additional information provided by the presence of the statue.[179] This chapter has attempted the opposite, to interpret the statue with minimal reference to the inscription, in short, to find a way to permit this magnificent example of Archaic sculpture to function fully as the *sēma* that Aristion of Paros and his patron(s) intended it to be, to allow it to *become* Phrasikleia on Archaic rather than on Classical or post-Classical terms. It should now be clear that, while the inscription complements the image, the image speaks eloquently enough on its own behalf and on behalf of the deceased whom, if the visual evidence is read carefully, it was meant to replicate. The epigram is a lovely piece of simple poetry, but as a transmitter of information, it adds just one piece of crucial evidence about the subject of this funerary portrait: her name. Putting Svenbro's theory to work in reverse, an ancient viewer might have been able to deduce the content of the inscription from an intelligent viewing of the statue. The fact that the image is part of a memorial, the fact that the young woman died a kore, either unmarried or briefly married, the fact that she was the type of woman whose reputation will forever be exemplary, can all be read from the statue alone without the help of the written word. The permanence of the future perfect tense of κεκλέσομαι αἰεί ("I shall always be called")[180] and the permanence of death are reiterated in the far more salient permanence of the medium, Parian marble, belying Pindar's boast. "As doth eternity," itself, the "silent form" of Phrasikleia "teases us *into* thought,"[181] transgressing the authority of the written word. *Ut marmor poesis.*

NOTES

INTRODUCTION

1. Charbonneaux et al. 1971: 249.

2. The number catalogued by Langlotz in *AMA* 43–184. Hurwit (1999: 126; cf. Hollo-way 1992: 267) suggests that some seventy-five or more korai occupied the Acropolis by the end of the Archaic period. In referring to the korai which are currently housed in the Acropolis Museum, Athens, I follow the standard practice of using their inventory numbers. The use of the term "kore" to refer to Archaic female statues is not just a modern convention; there is justification for the term in ancient usage. On the various meanings that the word held for the Greeks, Holloway 1992: 267, with sources, observing that any statue of a standing woman, "even if given a specific identity," was called a "kore" by Archaic Greeks. As Osborne (1994: 90) has noted, just one Acropolis inscription uses the word "kore" to refer to the dedicated object. This is *DAA* no. 229 (= *IG* I³ 828), a dedica-tion of a kore to Poseidon from ca. 480 B.C. by the fisherman [Iso]lochos (Raubitschek's restoration); Raubitschek (*DAA* 262), based on the assumption that the base held a kore, believes that "in spite of the reference to Poseidon," the fisherman "made his dedication to Athena." Langlotz (*AMA* 8) believes it to be a kore dedicated to Poseidon.

3. A fact not often acknowledged; on nonaristocratic dedications on the Acropolis, Hurwit 1999: 126–127; and Camp 1994: 11, observing that none of the Archaic dedications preserves the name of any of the tyrants; rather they include "professions sounding not much like landed aristocracy: an architect, a shipbuilder, and several potters." The Moschophoros (Acr. 624: *GSA*, fig. 112), the Potter's Stele (Acr. 1332: Payne and Young 1936: pls. 129–130), and Acr. 681 (kore made by Antenor for Nearchos, a potter) are the best known of the apparently nonaristocratic dedications on the Acropolis. Holloway (1992) argues convincingly that the kore was a favorite dedication of the "business" class of Athens.

4. If one talks about korai, the Acropolis examples inevitably come to mind. This is not accidental. As Richter (1968: 6) observes: "the kore was not as popular a dedicatory offering as was the kouros. But, for some reason, a female statue was a favourite dedication in Athens during the second half of the sixth century B.C., that is, under Peisistratos and his sons; and it is these many female statues that now constitute the majority of the extant statues of that type."

5. Richter 1970a (orig. pub. 1942).

6. Richter 1968: 17 has a summary of the chronological reference points for each of her six groups. Following Richter, a floruit of ca. 550–480 for the Acropolis korai is adopted in

this study, although I believe that the majority fall within the period ca. 520–480 or possibly an even narrower time span, to judge by the uniform style of the finest examples, which constitute the great bulk of the group. While Richter's remains a useful standard for both the relative and the absolute chronologies of the korai, neither has gone unchallenged, e.g., Childs 1993: 413–414, with earlier literature. Since a determination of chronology is not central to my thesis about reading/viewing the korai, there is no need to engage this controversial issue in depth here.

7. Rolley 1994: 160–161.

8. Useful is the cautionary observation of B. S. Ridgway on p. 197 of her review of Richter's *Korai* (*AB* 52 [1970]: 195–197): "To say that all *korai* look the same is a truism comparable to the saying that all Doric temples look alike. Miss Richter has rightly stressed the similarities, laying the foundations for all future work on the subject; we can now proceed to build on them our own speculative superstructures on differences and regionalisms."

9. I am not the first to invite the reader/viewer to conceive of realism in the Archaic period; however, the few scholars who have argued on behalf of realism in Archaic art, such as N. Himmelmann, who has written recently on the subject, have tended to concentrate their efforts in the area of thematic or genre-type imagery. In his introductory overview, Himmelmann (1994: 1–22), in my view, dismisses too many occasions of subtle but genuine realism in Archaic art in his quest for more obvious, genre-type subject matter.

10. Illustrated in Rubin 1989: 181.

11. E.g., Rubin 1989: 21.

12. Translated in full in Rothschild 1991: 267–268.

13. Mimesis, one of the most discussed of all Greek terms and concepts, has generated a vast bibliography; see, recently, Benediktson 2000: esp. 41–86, with references to earlier literature. For the present purposes, there is no need to engage the philosophical side of the debate, which, as it regards the visual arts, becomes rigorous and controversial only in the fourth century with the writings of Plato and Aristotle. On the earlier history of the μῖμος family of words, Else 1958 remains a useful collection of sources with commentary; he emphasizes the performance aspect of mimicry and mimēsis in its pre-Platonic sense.

14. Mourelatos 1973.

15. Summers 1978.

16. The interpretation of ἡ τέχνη μιμεῖται τὴν φύσιν ("art imitates nature," *Physics* ii.2.194a21; and *Meteorologica* iv.3.381b6) and related statements in Aristotle is greatly debated; I follow Butcher (1951: 116 and 154) in assuming that nature here is "not the outward world of created things," but the "creative force" itself: "'Imitation' so understood is a creative act. It is the expression of the concrete thing under an image which answers to its true idea. To seize the universal, and to reproduce it in simple and sensuous form is not to reflect a reality already familiar through sense perceptions; rather it is a rivalry of nature, a completion of her unfulfilled purposes, a correction of her failures." Halliwell (1989: 158) observes: "It was as a comment on all such productive activity [i.e., *technai*], and not as the formula for the fine arts which it later became, that Aristotle enunciated the principle that 'art imitates nature,' linking the purposive and intelligible methods of artistry with the teleological workings of the natural world."

17. Childs 1988.

18. Hephaistos was the creator out of clay of Pandora, the first woman; Prometheus created the first humans. On Hephaistos and Athena as the "creators" of the autochtho-

nous Athenians, Loraux 1993: 125–127. Imhotep, the actual builder of the step-pyramid of Zoser, was later deified and honored as a creator figure sometimes conflated with Ptah, another creation deity, who was a generic craftsman. Khnum modeled the first humans on a potter's wheel.

19. The term "Attic" is applied in a general way to the korai under present discussion even though not all Attic korai are considered, because, while attention is centered on the Acropolis group, one exceptional funerary statue from the Attic countryside, Phrasikleia, is included.

20. As espoused by Dougherty and Kurke, who adopt the term (1998: 5) from Stephen Greenblatt, a specialist in English Renaissance literature. Their enterprise is described on p. 5: "This approach, starting from an emphasis on representation and power relations, offers a new way of conceptualizing the relation of art to society. Cultural poetics rejects the privileging or bracketing of a self-contained realm of art within society, which an old-fashioned historical approach to literature maintains, with its carefully articulated foreground and backdrop, the text and its context. Instead, this approach sees texts as sites for the circulation of cultural energy and for the ongoing negotiation of power relations within society." On the other hand, my study finds itself more naturally in the ongoing, and currently revitalized, *ut pictura poesis* debate, which still assumes, but does not insist on, a degree of independence of art from context.

21. Ridgway 1993: 123–124, 128–129.

22. *Contra* Ridgway (1993: 124–125), who is inclined to view the earliest of these votive korai, Nikandre (Athens NM 1), as a deity, pointing to other potential examples.

23. The term is borrowed from Himmelmann (1994: 63).

I. HISTORIOGRAPHY

1. For a recent overview of the history of the Archaic Acropolis, Hurwit 1999: 99–153, with earlier bibliography. Hurwit (1999: 62) includes a useful catalogue of the types of objects which were dedicated on the Acropolis, and gives a good sense of how crowded it was in antiquity. On the double sacks of the Acropolis by the Persians in 480/79 B.C., Hdt. 5.77; 8.53; 9.13; Thuc. 1.89; Paus. 1.27.2; 10.35.1–4. For a vivid accounting of the sacks and their toll on the monuments, architectural and sculptural, which populated the citadel, see Hurwit 1999: 135–136; in describing the desecration of statues, which included the korai, he aptly refers to a "Persian massacre of images." On the Near Eastern habit of damaging, desecrating, or removing statues during war, Shapiro 1994b: 124, with n. 19.

2. Morris (1992: 215–237) collects the testimonia and argues that there were two opposing strains of anecdotal reminiscences about Daidalos, one flattering, the other demeaning.

3. Richter 1968: figs. 587–590.

4. Most of the Acropolis korai were discovered during the excavations of the late nineteenth century by the Greek Archaeological Society under the direction of P. Cavvadias and G. Kawerau. The largest group (the so-called sensational find consisting of fourteen korai) was found packed together in fill northwest of the Erechtheum in February 1886 (*ArchEph* [1885–1886]: 78). Cavvadias and Kawerau (1907: 23–24) reproduce a photograph of the korai "graveyard" at the north wall as it was being excavated, as well as a plan and a cross-section of the findspot. Additional korai were excavated east and west of the Parthenon,

west of the Erechtheum, and near the south wall of the citadel. On the Acropolis excavations, Cavvadias and Kawerau 1907; Bundgaard 1974; Hurwit 1999: 298–302, with additional bibliography. On the careful burial of the statues: It is true that feet and ankles are often missing, but plinths could be reused for a variety of purposes and bases were often columns which could be reincorporated in either an architectural or a sculptural context. Some sculptures, korai among them, appear to have been deliberately hacked away, mostly at the back, in order to streamline the material for stacking: Acr. 595, 606, 671, 676, 697, "B," 159, 356 (595, 671, 676 being korai). But all in all, the evidence suggests an expeditious, methodical handling of statues that were essentially intact when they were buried.

5. Thucydides' (1.10) remarks on the potentially misleading impression given to future generations by the archaeological remains of Sparta and Athens make it clear that this is not just an idle thought.

6. Holloway 1992: 267: "The Athenian korai are easily the most intensively studied group of archaic Greek sculptures."

7. Wagner (2000: 383; cf. Keesling 1995: 136) has observed of the Acropolis inscriptions: "Athenian custom seems to have disapproved of incising inscriptions directly on to statues." This practice was common in Ionia and in the ancient Near East, and seems even to the modern viewer to detract from the realism of the images.

8. *DAA* 3–60, 308–336 on the inscriptions that accompanied marble korai; p. 480 lists the sixteen. Keesling (1995: 13, 134–135, 217–220, 236, 253–254) rejects three of Raubitschek's attributions, as well as Acr. 681, which she considers an Athena figure rather than a kore, and arrives at twelve examples. The nearly four hundred inscriptions have recently been re-edited in *IG* I³; Raubitschek's commentary, however, remains indispensable. Keesling's important dissertation on the *DAA* inscriptions came to my attention after this manuscript was accepted for publication; consequently, I have been able to make only limited use of it. This material has most recently been reviewed in Kissas 2000. Hurwit 1999: 57–63 contains a useful synthesis of "who dedicated what on the Acropolis" and why; see also Keesling's summary (1995: 395–435).

9. *DAA* 419; see pp. 419–431 for an overview of the formulae found in the inscriptions.

10. *DAA* 430.

11. On the problems posed by this passage, Hyde 1921: 37–40; Frazer 1965: 623–624.

12. On the *arrhephoroi* and their duties, which are not entirely understood, Parke 1977: 141–143; Hurwit 1999: 41–43, 58.

13. E.g., *IG* II² 3470, 3473, 3497, 3515, 3554, 3556; I owe these references to T. L. Shear Jr.

14. Heliodorus wrote a work of fifteen books (number given by Athenaeus, 6.229e) on the artworks on the Athenian Acropolis. The title comes down in various forms, including Περὶ τῆς Ἀθήνησιν Ἀκροπολέως and Περὶ τῶν Ἀθήνησιν Ἀναθημάτων; see *FGrH* 373. Polemon, a geographer, published works on the dedications and other monuments at major Greek sanctuaries, including Athens. He is mentioned by later writers, including Athenaeus (6.234d; 10.436d, 442e) and Strabo (1.1.2).

15. Himmelmann (1994: 84) correctly points out that Archaic sanctuaries were typically "peopled" with portrait dedications, most of which depicted the dedicants themselves. The Acropolis likely also conformed to this pattern.

16. *DAA* 426.

17. *DAA* 431.

18. Cf. Viviers 1992: 137.

19. Keesling (1995: 212–222), on the Acropolis inscriptions that can be associated with korai, comes to much the same conclusion (p. 222): "The *DAA* statue bases shed little

light upon the distribution and significance of the 'generic' kore type in marble as a dedication on the Athenian Acropolis."

20. Musée du Louvre A 20; Kozleff et al. 1992: 172–175, with illustrations.

21. On the issue and quality of literacy in the Archaic period, much has been written of late; e.g., Murray 1983: 96, where, although he admits that Archaic Greece was a "literate society in the modern sense," goes on to qualify this by noting that "writing was seldom a normal or preferred mode of communication if speech was possible." I would add visual imagery to speech as a preferred medium for communication. W. Harris (1989: 45–64) reiterates that the evidence tells against the idea that literacy was widespread in Archaic Greece. Harris distinguishes at least three levels of increasing literacy: "scribal" literacy, "craftsman's" literacy (neither of which he actually defines), and mass literacy, and concludes that "archaic Greece reached no more than a rather low level of craftsman's literacy." For a more recent comprehensive overview of the relationship between orality and literacy, Thomas 1992.

22. For a recent critical analysis of the so-called Peisistratid recension and related issues surrounding the transcription of the Homeric poems, Nagy 1996: 65–112.

23. *GSA*, fig. 107. There is much recent literature on the subject and its many ramifications for the relationships between word and image; see, e.g., Day 1989, Kassel 1983, and Sourvinou-Inwood 1995: 108–297. Day (1994) has convincingly extended this type of analysis to the study of votive inscriptions.

24. Hurwit (1999: 141–142) describes in detail the scene the Athenians confronted when they returned to their Acropolis in 479, the process and timeline of burial of the debris, and, of the few Archaic statues that went unburied, those which may have been visible to Pausanias.

25. Hurwit 1999: 21, 125, 141, with fig. 99.

26. Of the approximately 195 Archaic sculptures and fragments of various sizes catalogued in the Acropolis Museum by Dickins in 1912, on only eighteen does he observe signs of contact with flames: Acr. 1, 588, 620, 653, 655, 658 (with 293, 452), 665, 672, 673, 676, 677, 680, 686, 687, 690, 691 (of these 672, 673, 676, 677, 680, 686, and 687 are korai). Among the korai, I have been able to verify in person signs of burning on only Acr. 686. Granted that a comparison survey using also the catalogues of Langlotz in *AMA* as well as Brouskari 1974 could yield slightly different results, the number is still surprisingly paltry, given the devastating picture presented by the ancient sources, although it does seem rather heavily weighted toward korai.

27. On Panthea and her role in the *Imagines*, Jones 1986: 75–77.

28. Pollitt 1990: 47.

29. The statue's exact provenance is uncertain; Ridgway 1993: 147–148: "We can no longer tell whether the Lyons kore suffered from the Persian destruction and was buried with the other war debris since at least part of her reached France in the late Seventeenth or early Eighteenth century. Her availability in Roman times may perhaps be very tentatively confirmed by a statue in Corinth, an archaistic Athena with an owl [illustrated fig. 146 therein], who holds her dress with the same peculiar half-fisted hand as the Lyons kore." In this study I include the Lyons Kore in the Acropolis group, while acknowledging that it is different from the other korai in important ways. It now seems likely that Acr. 269 was used as a caryatid on an Archaic building on the Acropolis, as has long been believed; Hurwit (1999: 115; cf. Ridgway 1993: 147, 168, n. 4.42, with references) points to the powerful, masculine physique, the polos on the head (atypical headgear for a kore), which has been worked to receive another stone block, and the himation that covers the left shoulder

rather than the right, as was typical for freestanding korai, as evidence that Acr. 269 was a mirror image of a second caryatid, who wore her himation in the normal fashion. Hurwit, however, does not attempt to associate Acr. 269 with a specific building.

30. *DAA* no. 229 (= *IG* I³ 828).

31. *GSA* 86 and fig. 161, where the statue is nonetheless dated "no later than 480." I am in agreement with Hurwit (1999: 146), who suggests "early 470s," pointing out that "only the suspect notion that *korai* production for some reason had to shut down completely in 480/79 supports [an] earlier date."

32. A more extensive overview of the scholarship on the korai is found in Stieber 1992: 13–34, to which may now be added: Holloway 1992; Ridgway 1993: 123–179 (an important update of the material in the 1977 edition of her book); Osborne 1994; Manzelli 1994; Sourvinou-Inwood 1995: 241–252; Hurwit 1999: 125–126, among the more significant studies. The dissertations of Rohner (1993, on the hairstyles of korai as a dating tool) and Keesling (1995, on the *DAA* inscriptions) came to my attention too late for full consideration. Schneider 1975 remains the most expansive interpretative study of all of the korai.

33. Hurwit (1999: 126) does not use the term "agalma" here, but it is clear that he has it in mind. He describes all of the theories about the identities of the korai in passing, but appears to favor the divinities theory.

34. Stewart 1990: 124.

35. Osborne 1994: 90–91.

36. *DAA* 430 lists the inscriptions that contain the element, which include some that are likely to have accompanied korai (*DAA* no. 7 [where it is restored] = *IG* I³ 763 [where it is not restored]; *DAA* no. 48 = *IG* I³ 631; *DAA* no. 290 = *IG* I³ 647), as well as scribes, horses and riders, and reliefs, among other types of dedications; Raubitschek observes further that the element occurs only in verse inscriptions, not prose.

37. These are "golden" in the case of Electra, a princess. Denniston (1954: 70) notes that the word "only occurs elsewhere in tragedy at S. *El.* 211," where he translates, with Jebb, "external splendour of [their] life." Jebb (1894: 38) clearly acknowledges the essentially materialistic nature of the term, citing comparanda in Homer and Pindar.

38. E.g., Acr. 682 had bronze ornaments on the sandals and stephane; Acr. 684 had bronze buttons on the sleeves of the chiton.

39. Compare the similar views of Stewart (1990: 123–124).

40. Ridgway (1990; 1992; 1993: 147–151) remains the strongest advocate of the identification of the Acropolis korai as goddesses; nymphs: E. Harrison (1988a: 53–54).

41. Lechat 1890: 572–586; 1903: 264–277; he also observed (1890: 572–573, 584–586) that only a very few of the female statues from the Acropolis (and of the ones listed none is, technically speaking, a kore) carry "characteristic attributes" which allow them to be identified securely as representations of goddesses.

42. Cf. Graindor 1938: 203–208, who, following Lechat's reasoning, reaches a similar conclusion.

43. Acr. 681: *DAA* no. 197 (= *IG* I³ 628); Kissas 2000, no. 45, with fig. 110.

44. Ridgway 1977; 1993: 148, 159–160, n. 4.20, with bibliography on the reception of the theory.

45. Assuming that Herodotus (5.87–88) was correct in adducing a change of dress from Doric to Ionic around 560 B.C.; for the standard argument, Richter 1968: 10.

46. Kritios Boy (Acr. 698): Payne and Young 1936: pls. 109–112; Acr. 692: Payne and Young 1936: pl. 108.1–3; Acr. 697: Payne and Young 1936: pls. 139.2–140; Rampin Rider

(Acr. 590 and Louvre 3104 [head]): *GSA,* fig. 114. Attribution of the Peplos Kore to the "Rampin Master": *GSA* 75, with bibliography.

47. Payne and Young 1936: 19–21.

48. The commonly accepted date for the Peplos Kore hovers around 540–530 B.C.: Richter 1968: 72; Payne and Young 1936: 21; Langlotz in *AMA* 47; Ridgway 1977: 58.

49. Naples, Museo Nazionale 2422 (*ARFVA,* fig. 135); the Kleophrades Painter flourished ca. 505–475. A frontal statue of Aphrodite on a much later red-figured lekythos in the manner of the Meidias Painter in the Ashmolean Museum (GR 1966.714; illustrated in Oakley and Sinos 1993: fig. 4), although lacking somewhat in stiffness because it is executed in a more florid, curvilinear style, demonstrates the continuity of the idea of adopting the stereotypical trappings of archaism when representing a statue.

50. Schäfer (1986: 107) adopts the term to describe the typical Egyptian habit of rendering figures and objects as if the draughtsman were changing his viewpoint for each of the parts rendered. The most common manifestation is the familiar combination frontal/ profile rendering of the human figure.

51. E.g., Smith 1990, figs. 196, 197.

52. Ridgway 1990, aspects of which are reiterated in 1993: 147–151.

53. Ridgway 1990: 603.

54. Ridgway 1990: 610. In an article on *IG* II² 1498–1501A, an inventory list of bronze statues still on the Acropolis in the fourth century B.C., D. Harris (1992: 644) notes that "several of the statues listed in the inventory are described as wearing headpieces," and, citing Ridgway 1990, suggests that these might be heroes or gods. Inevitably, it is tempting to connect Ridgway's theory about the korai with this evidence and project it back onto the korai (which Harris, by the way, does not do). But this evidence is unlikely to constitute a remnant of an Archaic tradition of helmeted female figures on the Acropolis going back to the korai, since, as Harris points out, there is a "distinct lack of references to representations of women in this inventory." On a Panathenaic amphora in the manner of the Kleophrades Painter dated ca. 490 (Toledo Museum of Art 61.24, illustrated in Neils 1992: 170, cat. no. 38), Athena's helmet has "sprouted a visor" (Neils 1992: 170) that looks something like the stephanai worn by the korai. This element is a rarity and could actually reflect incidental acquaintance with the Acropolis korai; significantly, Neils (1992: 170) seems to consider it an "Archaizing" feature. Ridgway (1992: 131–133), however, makes much of the visor, seeing it on Acropolis korai 681 and 669, and referring to additional comparanda, including the helmet of the Pheidian Parthenos, whose elaborate visor, to judge from replicas, is very different in structure from the stephanai on the korai, since it has a prominent peak at the middle of the forehead, top and bottom (this feature would be invisible in the profile view shown on the Panathenaic vase mentioned above), and is so restored by Leipen (1971, frontispiece). I myself do not see a substantial difference between the stephanai of korai 681 and 669 and the others. While respecting Ridgway's argumentation, I am not convinced that this feature, common in the korai, can certainly be identified as the visor of a helmet.

55. Hurwit 1999: 126. In an interesting variation on the divinities theory, Stewart (1997: 135), noting that most of the Acropolis korai wear a stephane, suggests that it could be in *imitation* of a stephane, possibly in gold, worn by the ancient image of Athena Polias.

56. Ridgway 1990: 585–589 reviews the literature on *mēniskoi.* W. Miller 1929.II: 356–358 conveniently assembles the testimonia; see also Dunbar 1995: 593, with references.

57. In the case of the warrior Kroisos, Ridgway (1993: 68) speculates, unconvincingly,

that the metal rod could be evidence of the crest of a caplike helmet otherwise rendered in marble.

58. Childs 1994, followed by Hurwit (1999: 121).

59. E.g., *ABFV,* fig. 227, a black-figured calyx crater by the Rycroft Painter.

60. The most significant for our purposes are Lechat 1890, 1903, and 1904, although his observations and his ideas about the korai appeared in several other publications (see his own references). Lechat's interest in the individuality of the korai was so consuming and his study so thorough that he also wrote several long essays on the artistic "hands" in evidence among the statues, culminating in 1903: 293–383.

61. Lechat 1890: 572–586.

62. Lechat 1890: 585.

63. Lechat 1903: 264–277, 279–291; 1904: 216–250.

64. Lechat 1903: 279–291.

65. Collignon (1886: 145), citing Winckelmann as the source of the mistaken viewpoint.

66. Collignon 1892: 354–355.

67. Winter 1894: 7.

68. Lermann 1907: 67–70.

69. Graindor 1938: 203–208.

70. *AMA* 8.

71. "Ein Menschenbild verkörpert für den Griechen der Frühzeit Menschliches und Göttliches zugleich und damit das Schönste, Edelste und Kraftvollste, das er sehen, fühlen und sinnen kann" (*AMA* 8). ("For the Greeks of the early period, a representation of a human being embodies both human qualities and divine qualities at the same time, and with these, that which is most beautiful, noblest, and most powerful that one is able to see, feel, and sense.")

72. *AMA* 8.

73. Karo 1948: 263.

74. Himmelmann 1994: 63. I am not sure what he means by the use here of the substantive "Persönliches"; he could mean "personages" or "persons" or "personalities" in the sense of individuals with specific characteristics, not necessarily the way English uses "personality" to mean something like "personal temperament."

75. Himmelmann (1994: 63–64) usefully reviews the German literature on early Greek portraiture which addresses the issue of the korai. Since I am not arguing that the korai should be considered portraits, which we cannot know for sure since they are not named, but that they are nonetheless mimetically realistic images, it is not necessary here to engage directly with the extensive literature on the early history of Greek portraiture; for this, I refer the reader to Himmelmann 1994: 49–88.

76. Ridgway (1993: 154, n. 4.1), although respectfully disagreeing with his conclusions, calls Schneider's (1975) perhaps "the most ambitious study" of the korai.

77. Schneider 1975: 33 and 36.

78. Holloway 1966.

79. *IG* I³ 474.86; see the discussion in Hurwit 1999: 206, following Stewart 1990: 167–168. Some five Acropolis korai show signs of having been reworked at their backs with cuttings for mortices and clamps, suggesting reuse at some point in their history in the form of attachment to a wall somewhere on the Acropolis, which would then offer a strong parallel for the later Parthenon frieze and/or the Erechtheum korai; I owe this point to an anonymous reviewer.

80. These shallow ritual vessels are not visible on what remains of the badly damaged caryatids, which retain little of their arms; however, the full-scale copies discovered at Hadrian's villa at Tivoli reproduce a phiale in the right hand. An original now in the British Museum and a Roman copy are illustrated side by side in Richter 1969: figs. 178–179.

81. Holloway 1992: 267; further quotations are from pp. 271, 268, 272.

82. Richter 1968: 6.

83. *Kanephoroi* as well-born women: Roccos 1995: 644, citing Thuc. 6.56 on the rejection of the tyrant Hippias' sister; *arrhephoroi:* Roccos 1995: 643–644; Hurwit 1999: 58, cautioning that the theory cannot explain all of the Acropolis korai.

84. Holloway (1992: 270) cites Schneider 1975 and Richter 1968 as examples of interpretations which assume that the korai were aristocratic dedications and therefore reflections of aristocratic ideals.

85. Ridgway 1992: 142.

86. Ajootian 1996: 95, with n. 28, the inscriptional evidence.

87. As argued in Stieber 1999a.

88. Napier 1986: 46.

89. Euarchis, one of the two dedicants of *DAA* no. 292, which belongs with the double dedication that included kore 683, has a name with a traditionally female ending, -ις. The gender of this dedicant has long been debated; both Raubitschek (*DAA* 313) and Keesling (1995: 391), while reviewing the evidence, conclude that it is a man. For women as dedicants on the Acropolis, Keesling 1995: 390–394.

90. Sourvinou-Inwood 1995: 245. Males dedicating korai, e.g., *DAA* no. 56 (= *IG* I³ 758); Kissas 2000, no. 163 (Acr. 686 and 609, Euthydikos' Kore).

91. E.g., *DAA* no. 79 (= *IG* I³ 745), father and daughters; *DAA* no. 236 (= *IG* I³ 773), son and mother; see Keesling 1995: 211, 422–426.

92. Holloway 1992: 270 (following, in part, Ridgway [1990]) suggests that some sixteen Acropolis korai (that is, the ones with metal rods in their heads) "may have been *assimilated* [my emphasis] to Athena in this way." He rejects the notion of identifying any of the other korai with divinities or heroic figures.

2. THE REALITY OF APPEARANCES

1. Cf. Osborne 1994: 88–93.

2. *IG* II² 11162.

3. Munich, Antikensammlungen 2307 (*ARFVA*, fig. 33.2).

4. The initial publications of the korai from the Acropolis are found in *ArchEph* of 1885 and subsequent years, sometimes with colored illustrations. Regarding the polychromy of the korai, the early publications are still essential: Lechat 1890: 552–586: 1904: 316–334; Lermann 1907: 44–98 (especially valuable are the detailed colored renderings of the polychromal decorations then visible on the freshly excavated korai, which are more effective than any verbal description in giving a sense of the astonishing variety and distinction of these painted designs); Dickins 1912; Payne and Young 1936; in *AMA* Langlotz gives the most nuanced visual information. Also useful is later work such as Richter 1968, whose copious documentation of most of the Acropolis korai from various angles (photographs by A. Franz) has not been superseded; Brouskari 1974; Dimitriou 1947: 229–238, a still-useful catalogue of the polychromy that has been recorded for all extant Archaic korai,

where the author distills the opinions of earlier scholars in each entry; the more recent catalogue of Manzelli (1994: 159–206) is somewhat less informative, in that she does not distinguish nuances of color hues, perhaps owing to their current states of preservation; in a review of Manzelli, L. James (*CR* 46 [1996]: 126–127) cautions: "it seems that she has not had the opportunity to examine the works she catalogues."

5. On polychromal color schemes and combinations, Dimitriou 1947: 100–103; Reuterswärd 1960: 64–67; Manzelli 1994: 91–148.

6. Dimitriou 1947: 103.

7. Lermann 1907: 78–82; Reuterswärd 1960: 65–67; Karakasi (1997: 512, with n. 31) identifies some of the red on Phrasikleia as the foundation for other colors, citing these authors' conclusions.

8. Respectively, Langlotz in *AMA* 79, 46, 101, 105. Langlotz (p. 105) describes the complex polychromal articulation of Acr. 684's eyes: "Brauen, Irisrand, Pupille, Lidränder schwarz. Augensterne dunkelrot" ("Brows, iris rim, borders of the lids, black. Center of the pupil, dark red"); cf. Dimitriou 1947: 236: "black on brows, pupils, outlines of lids; dark red on irises."

9. Dickins 1912: 236: "the pupils consist of a yellow ochre ring with black centre and black outline." Langlotz in *AMA* 52: "Schwartz: Brauen, Lidränder, Pupille. Gelb: Iris." ("Black: brows, borders of the lids, pupils. Yellow: iris.") I have been unable to observe any trace of this ochre; Manzelli (1994: 173–174) does not mention any eye coloration.

10. Even the slightest exposure to light will cause olive-green–colored leather on the spine of a book to fade to brown within a very short time.

11. In the fourth century B.C. Nicias, according to Pliny (*NH* 35.133), painted the statues of Praxiteles.

12. E.g., Dickins 1912: 229, 232. Langlotz in *AMA* 81, on the eyes of Acr. 681: "Bergkristall, mit Blei umgossen, vielleicht waren Wimpern eingesetzt" ("Rock crystal, set with lead, perhaps with inserted eyelashes"). It is true that the expensive extras are in keeping with the fact that these two are the largest and, especially in the case of Acr. 682, the most elaborate of all the Acropolis korai.

13. Langlotz in *AMA* 94; cf. Lermann 1907: 83.

14. For incision, Dimitriou 1947: 232; for the "deutlich erkennbar" ("clearly recognizable") blue-grey–colored eyes of Acr. 688, Lermann 1907: 82; Langlotz (*AMA* 62) suspects traces of black lashes (cf. Lermann 1907: 82), but considers the irises red, as does Manzelli (1994: 182).

15. See Karakasi (1997: 513, with n. 37), following Brinkmann (1994: 31–33). The engraved outline that is faintly visible around the lips of kore 674 might also be mentioned.

16. Lermann 1907: 82.

17. Maxwell-Stuart 1981, *passim*.

18. Acr. 643: Langlotz in *AMA* 131; Acr. 672 and 686: Dimitriou 1947: 233.

19. Osborne (1994: 92–93), I think, overlooks this common feature of korai when he constructs an argument about female empowerment based on the "forward gaze" of Archaic korai, which then he contrasts with Classical female statues, which do not engage the male viewer. On the contrary, a great many Acropolis korai seem to avert their gaze from the viewer's, avoiding direct confrontation.

20. Reeder 1995: 123–124; she does make a point in the catalogue entry for Acr. 672, which was in the exhibit that occasioned Reeder's publication, that this kore "engages the viewer with her direct gaze" (p. 131), which, I would argue, is the exception rather than the rule on the Acropolis.

21. On the eroticism of the gaze in Greek literature, Reeder 1995: 124–126.

22. It is also remotely possible but worth mentioning that the frequency of angular, downcast eyes among the korai may be attributable to Egyptianizing. Downcast eyes are prominently featured in the portraiture of one Egyptian pharaoh in particular, Amenhotep III of the Eighteenth Dynasty. This idiosyncratic eye treatment incorporates a vertical angular slant which has been measured (app. 5 of Kozloff et al. 1992) and is consistent throughout the king's portraiture; examples: Kozloff et al. 1992, nos. 5–7, with a diagram showing the angle of the tilt. As is typical of pharaonic art, some portraits of elites made during Amenhotep III's reign also exhibit this curious tilt of the eye to some degree. Kozloff et al. (1992: 156–157) offer the following explanation: "Not surprisingly it is the colossal statuary, in all materials, that appears to look downward. These enormous images of the king gazed down on the world and, at the same time, became accessible to a petitioner." Whether it is inspired by the real-life personal appearance of the man or whether it is part of the artistic iconography of kingship during his reign, regardless of its meaning to the ancient Egyptians, the trope of downcast eyes is striking enough and plentiful enough in Egyptian art to have been noticed and perhaps imitated by Archaic Greek sculptors. If this is the case, it is curious, however, that kouroi do not feature them.

23. Respectively, Langlotz in *AMA* 79, 46, who believes that the irises and lips of 679 show the same "Eisenrot" ("iron-red"); Lermann 1907: 56.

24. See Ridgway 1993: 19, n. 1.21 for a survey of the scholarly literature on the Archaic smile, to which may be added Lermann 1907: 99–107; Fowler 1983: 167–168.

25. Cf. Ridgway 1993: 146.

26. E.g., Tuthmosis III (British Museum 986); Amenhotep III (British Museum 30448); the fragmentary colossus of Ramesses II from the temple at Luxor (British Museum 19); illustrated in James 1979, figs. 16–17 and pl. 7. Amenhotep III, the father of Akhenaten, presided over a period of great prosperity, bolstered by extensive international trade, in which all of the arts flourished at an unprecedented level; see Kozloff et al. 1992. As James (1979: 66) observes, the reputation of Ramesses II and his works was so great that "even in the Classical Period he was regarded as the great Egyptian king *par excellence*."

27. Childs 1998: 9.

28. Sumerian examples from the third millennium: Parrot 1961, figs. 138–141.

29. Robins 2001: 7; Hornung 1990: 167–168.

30. Schäfer 1986: 17; see also Wilson 1947: 235–238 on Egyptian terms for artists.

31. See also Robins 2001: 7.

32. Hornung 1990: pls. 130–132.

33. *Od.* 8.362.

34. Gentili 1988: 89, with a full discussion (216–222) of fr. 384, usually given to Alcaeus but whose authorship is uncertain in Lobel and Page 1963.

35. Maxwell-Stuart 1981: 6.

36. The precise postexcavation skin tone of Acr. 683 has not been universally agreed upon, although the uniqueness of this kore's facial demeanor has always been remarked upon. In some of the earlier publications, there seems to have been a certain reluctance to recognize the potential for seeing a different, and altogether unexpected, racial type. Dickins (1912: 237) attributes the olive tone to *ganosis* (see discussion below, with notes 43–51) and attempts to rebut, with little success, I think, the suggestion (unattributed) that the kore is "naturalistic" and possesses negroid features, the latter perhaps in reference to Collignon (1892: 354), who speaks of an "air africain." Brouskari (1974: 81) notes only that "the sur-faces of the face have been powerfully polished, a brilliant example of archaic technique";

although her language was much more forceful, curiously, in a slightly different version of her catalogue (which, while I have used it in the past, I was unable to locate as this manuscript went to press, leaving me in a state of puzzlement), where she stressed the "olive-toned face due to special treatment of the surface" and, echoing Dickins, suspected "naturalistic" features. Langlotz in *AMA* 52 claims of the complexion of kore 683: "Keine Ganosis, wie Dickins behauptet" ("No *ganosis,* as Dickins maintains"), while acknowledging that earlier writers "erwähnen mehr Farben als heute erhalten" ("mention more colors than are preserved today"). Of the face of Acr. 674, Dickins (1912: 214–215) concludes that "the expression is markedly individual," observing that "the surface of the face and neck is finely preserved, with the γάνωσις toned to a dark olive colour"; cf. Reuterswärd 1960: 73.

37. Noted by Langlotz in *AMA* 104–105, who concluded that the patina was achieved through the application of oil; see more recently Reuterswärd 1960: 68; Manzelli 1994: 110, 181.

38. Lermann 1907: 83; Langlotz in *AMA* 94; Manzelli 1994: 177–178; similarly, Acr. 679 (Lermann 1907: 56).

39. Dimitriou 1947: 147: "The nude parts of korai as of other archaic female figures in marble were largely reserved."

40. E.g., Paris, Bibliothèque Nationale, Cabinet des Médailles 222 (von Bothmer 1985, fig. 23), a neck-amphora on which Athena's flesh was in added white (now lost), while that of two maenads is outlined.

41. Richter 1928–1929; quote, p. 30; she does not discuss the Acropolis korai. The long-debated question of whether the nude parts of marble and limestone statues were painted still lacks a definitive answer; in addition to Richter, see Lermann 1907: 77–78; Dimitriou 1947: 142–150; Reuterswärd 1960: 67–74; and below. Reuterswärd (1960: 67–68) offers a list of Archaic through Hellenistic statues that exhibit evidence of skin-tone coloring, either by polychromy or by *ganosis;* however, only one kore (Acr. 684) makes the list; compare the broader list of Dimitriou (1947: 147–150), which curiously includes no korai at all.

42. See also Richter 1928–1929: 25, n. 1. Karakasi (1997: 513) believes that the incision of the decorative motifs on Phrasikleia's otherwise smooth peplos were intended to "trap" the color and keep it confined to the intended area. One thinks also of increasing the potential for absorption with a scratched surface.

43. On *ganosis,* Gardner 1911: 29–30; Richter 1928–1929; 1970b: 129–131; Dimitriou 1947: 123–125; Reuterswärd 1960: 67–74; Stewart 1990: 41–42; Manzelli 1994: 101–115; Karakasi 1997: 513, with n. 38, with additional references.

44. Homolle 1890: 498; cf. Richter 1970b: 130; Dimitriou 1947: 124–125; Manzelli 1994: 108.

45. Reuterswärd (1960: 73–74) concludes that the probable starting point for the use of *ganosis* was "die Jahrzehnte um 500 v. Chr." ("the decades around 500 B.C."). Manzelli (1994: 102) surmises that the process "already had a long history" before Vitruvius and Pliny wrote about it, noting its use in Egyptian tomb paintings; see also Dimitriou 1947: 123.

46. Richter (1970b: 129) assumes that marble "figures" specifically are meant.

47. Manzelli 1994: 107; Dimitriou 1947: 123.

48. In her discussion of *ganosis,* Manzelli (1994: 108–109), deducing from the epigraphical evidence that the process must be renewed periodically, places great emphasis on the *conservational* aspect of the process; cf. Dimitriou 1947: 124–125.

49. E.g., Pliny *NH* 36.125; *Anth.Gr.* 16.221.

50. Gardner 1911: 29.

51. Richter 1970b: 130; 1928–1929: 28–29, where she describes the test of the process on a painted marble statue that was undertaken by C. G. Fink of Columbia University. Dimitriou (1947: 124) and Manzelli (1994: 110) concur with Richter against Gardner's view, Manzelli suggesting that the paucity of statues that show variations of skin tone militates against Gardner's theory. Karakasi (1997: 513, with n. 40), who identifies *ganosis* in the funerary kore Phrasikleia, observes of its intended effect that it approximates the surface appearance of real female flesh, of the "ivory" color so admired in women like Penelope in *Od.* 18.196; cf. Reuterswärd 1960: 72, 74.

52. E.g., Reuterswärd 1960: 74.

53. Dickins (1912: 214) implies a certain customizing of the process when he notes that the *ganosis* of kore 674 is "toned to a dark olive colour."

54. The Hermes presents an interesting case. Pliny (*NH* 35.133) uses the term "circumlitio" to refer to the process which Nicias applied to the statues of Praxiteles, who preferred this painter's touch (manum) to that of any other. As Praxiteles was a specialist in nude marble statues, it is tempting to conclude that circumlitio is the Latin equivalent of *ganosis,* as Manzelli (1994: 109), pointing to this passage, surmises, and that circumlitio/*ganosis* was a process specifically associated with the nude parts of statues, as I am suggesting.

55. Robins 2001: 11, with fig. 3.

56. Dickins 1912: 246; he also (p. 215) saw dimples on Acr. 674, less convincingly.

57. Himmelmann 1994: 49.

58. Himmelmann 1994: 49.

59. Giovanni Morelli, who formulated the method which has since borne his name in *Italian Painters: Critical Studies of Their Works* (trans. C. Foulkes), 1892–1893, was a connoisseur who developed a methodology for identifying hands in early Italian Renaissance paintings, that of Botticelli in particular. Morelli believed that the artist's subconsciousness, and therefore his hand, would manifest itself in the details of those parts of the body which generally look the same on everyone; ears, for example, would be rendered differently by each artist. Among Classical archaeologists, both Richter and J. D. Beazley, each to a different end, adapted aspects of Morellian methodology.

60. Other examples: Acr. 682, 606 (bottom half of kore 686), and the fragments assembled in Richter 1968: figs. 429–434.

61. Cf. Ridgway 1993: 146.

62. E. Harrison 1988b; she does not pursue the issue for this particular group of statues, however, observing (p. 250, n. 22) only: "In general the Acropolis maidens who look youngest in either dress or proportions have uncut front hair."

63. A preserved composite wig is illustrated in Quirke and Spencer 1992, fig. 12; scenes of hairdressers at work on a woman's hair, Capel and Markoe 1996, cat. nos. 34, 39.

64. Bartman 2001.

65. Illustrated in Payne and Young 1936: pl. 61. A small headless kore from Taranto now in Berlin (Staatliche Museen, no inv. no.; Richter 1968: figs. 545–547) shows the same mysterious lack of hair, in this case, front and back, which Richter (p. 95) attributes, unconvincingly, to the statue's "unfinished state."

66. Wilkinson 1992: 212, fig. 4.

67. Quirke and Spencer 1992, fig. 12.

68. Dimitriou (1947: 140) does not associate deliberate polychromal variation in hair color exclusively with the Acropolis group of korai, although the majority of her examples are, in fact, Acropolis korai.

69. Lermann 1907: 78; cf. the scientifically based conclusions of Brinkmann (1994: 33).

70. Respectively, Langlotz in *AMA* 98, 137, 136.

71. Acr. 696: Brouskari 1974: 67; Acr. 662: Dickins 1912: 198.

72. Dickins 1912: 214; Dimitriou 1947: 140, 235; Langlotz in *AMA* 94, followed, apparently, by Manzelli (1994: 177).

73. Dimitriou 1947: 140: "The variation in the intensity of color according to the requirements of the form or style of the motif is seen in the painting with red of the thick looped hair on either side of a female head [Acr. 674] while the smoother hair surfaces were colored yellow."

74. Brinkmann (1994: 33) cites Acr. 674 in a discussion of the polychromy of the Siphnian Treasury frieze, which is the primary subject of his study; Karakasi (1997: 512) sees a similar pattern of layering on the hair of Phrasikleia.

75. Acr. 605: Dickins 1912: 138; Langlotz in *AMA* 55; Manzelli 1994: 188. Acr. 639: Langlotz in *AMA* 130; Manzelli 1994: 192. Acr. 664: Dickins 1912: 200; Langlotz in *AMA* 139; Manzelli 1994: 199.

76. Langlotz in *AMA* 85; Manzelli 1994: 186 (yellow only).

77. Acr. 687: Langlotz in *AMA* 59; Manzelli 1994: 184. Lermann (1907: 78), writing in 1907, seems quite astonished at the "richtiges Blondhaar" ("proper blond hair") of kore 687, which he associates with the ancient color term for hair, ξανθός, and suggests that the artist deliberately sought to represent a hair color "offenbar im engen Anschluss an sein Modell" ("evidently in imitation of his model"). The coloring of the hair of Acr. 687, which I was able to view in the Acropolis Museum storerooms, is still bright and unmistakably strawberry blonde.

78. Acr. 673: Dickins 1912: 212: "no remains of colour"; Dimitriou (1947: 232) does not note any hair color; but Langlotz in *AMA* 101 sees "geringe rote Farbspuren" ("slight traces of red coloration"); cf. Manzelli 1994: 172. Acr. 680: Dickins 1912: 227, noting otherwise that: "The colour-scheme of the statue is remarkably well preserved"; Langlotz in *AMA* 96 records red irises but no hair color; Dimitriou (1947: 235) and Manzelli (1994: 175) do not note any hair color. Acr. 686: Dickins 1912: 243: "There is no color preserved"; Langlotz in *AMA* 79 questions whether the "rote Farbspuren" that he sees are ancient; Dimitriou (1947: 233) does not note any hair color; Manzelli (1994: 180) records red and brown. For Acr. 684 I follow my own eye and Dickins 1912: 239: "No colour is preserved on the hair." Dickins (1912: 238) also notes, apparently in reference to the odd red splotches visible today on parts of this kore, including the triangle of hair over the right shoulder: "The spots of red on the statue are not original, but accidental." Langlotz in *AMA* 105 (cf. Dimitriou 1947: 236; Manzelli 1994: 181), however, seems to believe that these are in fact ancient: "Am Haar geringe rote Farbreste" ("On the hair, slight remains of red"). The brown discoloration at the front of the hair appears to be the result of damage. It must be acknowledged that Acr. 684 has much less polychromy preserved than the others mentioned, but there is some preserved on the drapery, and it seems that we should expect at least slight traces of the original coloration, if there were any, to have been preserved among the minutely detailed carved ridges of the hair. Of the polychromy of this statue, Brouskari (1974: 69) notes: "Earlier observers saw much more painted ornament *on the drapery* [my emphasis] as for example the patterns of chiton border and scattered motifs all over the garments." She mentions no coloration in the hair.

79. Dickins (1912: 218) does not comment on the color, while Langlotz in *AMA* 99 (cf. Manzelli 1994: 182) saw "rote Flecken" ("patches of red").

80. To Langlotz in *AMA* 118, "zinnoberrote" ("vermilion").

81. Richter 1968: 6–10 remains a useful if somewhat simplified overview of Archaic female costumes; more recent are Floren 1987: 94–96; E. Harrison 1991; Rolley 1994: 176–177. Ridgway has been the keenest and most reliable of decipherers of the dress of Archaic korai; see, e.g., 1982, 1985, and 1993: 129–134, on its many variations and frequently vexing incongruities, with corrections of Richter. Ridgway herself generally follows the categories laid out by Langlotz in *AMA*, even a simple listing of which may serve to give the reader a good sense of the variety of dress among the Acropolis korai: "Koren im Peplos" ("korai in the peplos"), "Koren im Chiton" ("korai in the chiton"), "Koren mit Mäntelchen" ("korai with the short mantel"), "Koren mit Mantel über beiden Schultern" ("korai with the mantel over both shoulders"), "Samische Koren" ("Samian korai"), "Koren mit Mantille" ("korai with the 'mantilla'"), "Koren mit auf beiden Schultern gehefteter Mantille" ("korai with the 'mantilla' fixed on both shoulders"), "Koren mit Himation" ("korai with the himation").

82. Hurwit 1985: 325.

83. Boston MFA 11.738 (illustrated in W. S. Smith 1990, fig. 108).

84. Egyptian Museum, Berlin 14145 (illustrated in W. S. Smith 1990, fig. 302).

85. Ridgway 1993: 131; cf. Langlotz in *AMA* 53–55 ("Koren mit Mäntelchen"), who sees this arrangement as well in Acr. 605.

86. Cf. Ridgway 1993: 131; Langlotz in *AMA* 100–102 ("Koren mit auf beiden Schultern gehefteter Mantille").

87. Cf. Ridgway 1993: 132–133, with n. 24, who is careful to point out, however, that there is no term in the ancient Greek sources which can be associated with a "skirt."

88. Ridgway 1985: 13.

89. Reproduced in *GSA*, fig. 129; Ridgway (1993: 159, n. 4.20) is critical of this restoration.

90. Gardner 1911: 29–30; Dimitriou 1947: 36.

91. Sturgis 1890: 546; see also Dimitriou 1947: 236, citing Sturgis: "traces of curious soft lavender color on narrow bands of belt visible at front." Manzelli (1994: 177) records "violet" on the mantle, but it is unclear whether this is her own observation. Lilac or violet is rare but not unparalleled in Archaic polychromy. According to Dimitriou (1947: 227; while seeming to contradict herself on p. 98), violet was erroneously reported at the back of the torso of the Persian Rider, Acr. 606; it is not reported by W. Schuchhardt in *AMA* 227; however, much to Schuchhardt's surprise (*AMA* 229), "lila (!)" appears on the polychromed lozenge motif on Acr. 357a, a quiver fragment.

92. Dimitriou 1947: 102.

93. See also *AMA*, pls. I–V, an artist's renderings of the polychromy of several korai, reproduced in Manzelli 1994, pls. VI–X. While Lermann's reconstructions of the korai's polychromies are not foolproof and are occasionally questioned, his observations and detailed verbal descriptions (1907: 83–96) provide a useful supplement.

94. MMA 48; von Bothmer 1985: 18–87; *ABFV,* fig. 78.

95. British Museum E-140; Barber 1991: 363–365, with fig. 16.2; and 1992: 115, with n. 34.

96. Museo Archeologico Nazionale, Chiusi 1831, Barber 1992: 104, fig. 63.

97. Vat. Mus. Gregoriano Etrusco 16757 (illustrated in Simon and Hirmer 1981, fig. 74).

98. Richter 1968: 77 has an artist's rendering.

99. Dimitriou 1947: 233; cf. Langlotz in *AMA* 79; Dickins 1912: 243; early reconstruction drawing, Winter 1887: 217.

100. Barber 1991: 363–364, with fig. 16.3.

101. Barber 1991: 365–372.

102. Barber 1991: 370, n. 10.

103. *LSJ*, s.v. II; in *Im.* 2.28 the verb is used rhetorically to extol the craft of a spider (depicted in a painting) by comparing its skills with those of Penelope and the "Seres," specialists in weaving silk.

104. Davison 1961: 21–40. This is quite distinct from the Morellian methodology adopted by Beazley to ascertain hands in black- and red-figure vase-painting, where subconscious details are thought to reveal the artist's hand.

105. For a convenient listing of the appropriate ornaments for various types of architectural moldings in Greek architecture, D. Robertson 1928: 38–39. Dimitriou (1947: 135–137) has emphasized the korai's indebtedness to architectural polychromy.

106. Summers 1981: 43.

107. On the distinctive bridal headdress with its leaflike elements rising from the rim of a broad ornamental diadem, Oakley and Sinos 1993: 16 with, e.g., fig. 2; Reeder 1995: 127 with, e.g., cat. nos. 24 and 27. On some of the korai (e.g., Acr. 670, 680, 682) the stephanai have a series of holes along the top or bottom edge which could have been used for attachments like those shown on the bride's stephane in wedding scenes on Greek vases.

108. Richter does not distinguish this as a separate type, although she observes that, in cases like these, the individual strands of hair are not rendered but carved smooth or nearly smooth over the cap of the head. With the more typical form of stephane there is no interruption in the manner of rendering of the individual strands of the hair in this area. The "cap" is reminiscent of a so-called *sakkos*, but the latter is worn by mature women over bound-up hair. Perhaps, if it is a *sakkos*, atypically worn, it is meant as an allusion to the girl's future as a wife. Ridgway (1990: 602–603) interprets this feature in Acr. 681 and 669 as evidence of a helmet, and therefore, an identification as Athena.

109. Foot fragments include some with sandals, Acr. 4907 and 483, which has been associated with Acr. 679; *contra*, Morrow 1985: 25, who would like to disassociate this fragment from Acr. 679, and suggests that the Peplos Kore was barefoot. In general, on Archaic footwear, Morrow 1985: 23–43.

110. Morrow (1985: 191, n. 42) points to shod foot fragments Acr. 505 and 506 as comparanda on the Acropolis; Langlotz in *AMA* 117 (with fig. 72:a–b), 92 (with fig. 58) associates the latter with kore 675, and the former, citing the opinion of Schrader, with Nike figure Acr. 694. The photograph of Acr. 506 is not conclusive; while Acr. 505 seems to show the same type of shoe, the attribution to the Nike figure is not convincing, and the fragment is perhaps best left unattributed and possibly belongs to a kore. These are surely the shoes that Morrow (1985: 38, 42, 147–148) identifies as *akatia* ("little boats") on account of their distinctive high-beaked-boat–like shape, although she does not say so directly in reference to Acr. 683. This style of shoe is sometimes referred to as Ionic, although Etruscan might be more accurate; according to Morrow (1985: 147–148): "The form originates in the Near East and frequently appears on Etruscan monuments of the Archaic period. There are a few examples from mainland Greece but only one from East Greece. Their use generally points to foreign influence on local fashion in the place of manufacture." The reclining female figure in the famous terracotta Archaic Etruscan sar-

cophagus from Cerveteri now in the Museo Nazionale di Villa Giulia, Rome, wears this style of footgear. Non-Assyrians bringing tribute to the Assyrian king in a relief from the Northwest Palace at Nimrud wear the open version of the shoe (illustrated in *AB* 80 [1998]: 215, fig. 8). For additional Archaic examples of footgear similar, although not identical to that worn by Acr. 683, Matt and Zanotti-Bianco 1967, pls. 62, 87, and *Metropolitan Museum of Art Acquisitions Bulletin* (fall 1993): 10.

111. According to Richter (1968: 79); while a pomegranate is commonly associated with youthful death, it is paralleled on the Acropolis by Acr. 593 (Pomegranate Kore), if that is indeed what this kore holds (it looks also like a small vessel). It is not entirely certain what Acr. 680 is holding; D. Harris (1992: 644) calls it "abstract," suggesting that the term ἀκροθίνια, meaning "first fruits," in an Acropolis inventory list of the fourth century (*IG* II² 1498–1501A, which tallies bronze statues, none of which survives) refers to these objects when they are held by korai.

112. It is clear that *kosmēsis* was regarded as a process separate from sculpting and polychroming; cf. the list of articles intended for *kosmēsis* in Delian inscriptions of 279 B.C., cited in Richter 1970b: 130. We do not know for certain that the procedure was the same in the Archaic period, or whether it was done for all statues or just statues of divinities.

113. *AMA* 8.

114. Richter 1968: 73.

115. Sinos (1998) has reinterpreted the propagandistic content of the Phye episode, emphasizing its performance aspect.

116. Heubeck, West, and Hainsworth 1990: 272.

117. *GSA* 89.

118. E.g., Brouskari 1974: 81. Although there are numerous representations of male dwarfs in Greek art, Dazen (1994: 173–174) could find only one representation (pl. 51) of a female dwarf, that on a red-figured skyphos in Munich, suggesting that "the rendering of female deformity was under some kind of taboo." She does not mention Acr. 683.

119. Graindor 1938: 205.

120. Ancient Greeks did concern themselves with the genetic problems associated with small physical stature, especially where aristocratic progeny were concerned; cf. Plut. *Aeg.* 2. Aristotle (*EN* 1123b7) declares that small people cannot be beautiful.

121. *DAA* no. 292 (= *IG* I³ 644); Kissas 2000, no. 81, with figs. 164–166.

122. *DAA* 314; cf. the comments of Kissas (2000: 145–146), who finishes Raubitschek's thought by suggesting that the second, smaller figure would have had its left foot advanced.

123. Cf. Ridgway 1993: 172, n. 4.63; she speculates also that further knowledge about the entire monument could shed light as well on the significance of the unusual footgear worn by kore 683.

3. THE IDEA OF LIKENESS

1. Himmelmann (1994: 49–88, with earlier references), who treats the issue of the origins of "realistic portraiture" in Greek art, places it sometime in the Early Classical period with the named portraits of Themistocles and Pindar and the anonymous Portocello "philosopher" (see esp. 18, 66–77). Frel (1981: 19), echoing a commonly held opinion, calls the

portrait of Lysimachē from the early fourth century B.C. (Pliny *NH* 34.76) "the first female portrait"; according to Hurwit (1999: 251, with n. 23 and fig. 205), who discusses fourth-century portraiture on the Acropolis, the original probably stood on the Athenian Acropolis.

2. Trans. Oldfather (1946), with some spelling modifications.

3. For a review of the sources on Daidalos, Morris 1992: 215–237; for a full discussion of the language of the *Theoroi* fragment and the art-historical issues it raises, Stieber 1994.

4. Lessing 1962: 111. That this is the case is more or less directly stated at *Il.* 3.156–158.

5. As Thalmann (1988: 15, n. 37) observes, detailed physical descriptions of individuals are scarce in Homer, the only others being that of Odysseus when he is turned into a beggar (*Od.* 13.397–403, 430–433) and of Eurybates (*Od.* 19.244–246).

6. Trans. Campbell (1982: 429).

7. Trans. Freeman (1956: 160).

8. Trans. West (1993: 9).

9. Gentili 1988: 179–196, on "Archilochus and the levels of reality"; quote here from p. 182.

10. I have discussed Hipponax's portrait in Stieber 1994: 102–103; some parts of that discussion are repeated here.

11. Crofton 1988: 172.

12. On Boupalis and Athenis and on Archaic Greek sculpture in Rome, see the comments of P. Zanker (1988: 240–245), who points to a fragment of an Archaic Athena statuette recently discovered on the Palatine (fig. 188), and of Isager (1991: 149–150). Henig (2000: 132), in a discussion of the adaptation of Greek statuary types on Roman coins, notes that "an Archaic kore often seen on coins as well as gems was identified by the Romans as Spes."

13. Rosen 1988: 31, n. 10, and 32.

14. E.g., temple of Artemis at Corfu (illustrated in *GSA*, fig. 187); Eleusis Amphora (illustrated in M. Robertson 1975: pl. 4:b).

15. Richter/Smith 1984: 80, with fig. 44; see also Frel 1981: 4–5.

16. For portraits of Socrates, Richter/Smith 1984: 198–204.

17. My translation; on the role played by the baker in Croesus' life, How and Wells 1912.I: 75. For Herodotus' usage of various words for statues, Donohue 1988: 26–27, with notes 64–65.

18. Cf. Denniston 1966: 255: "and in particular."

19. How and Wells 1912.I: 75.

20. The introduction of Croesus' baker-woman's portrait into Plutarch's account at *De Pyth.* 401e–f is prompted by its unusualness; a rather extensive discussion of the image follows.

21. Another Archaic example has been found in Boeotia; on these little-known objects, see now Theodossiev 1998, with earlier references.

22. Delphi Museum 467, 1524 (*GSA*, fig. 70). The identification has not gone unchallenged; one theory, that they are the Dioskouroi, continues to have its adherents, e.g., Vatin (1982).

23. Transcription and discussion, *GSA*, fig. 70.

24. Berlin and Samos (Vathy) Museum; Stewart 1990: 117, with figs. 97–99; Walter-Karydi 1985: 101–103. As Stewart's fig. 97 shows, the base survives, with the bottom half of the seated Phileia, the headless Philippe, and much of a headless reclining male. A new restoration of the figures has been proposed by Walter-Karydi (1985: fig. 4).

25. Walter-Karydi 1985: 95–97.

26. Walter-Karydi 1985: 98–101, followed by Stewart (1990: 117); on the evidence for the flute, Walter-Karydi 1985: 94–95.

27. The details of the career of Antenor, culminating in the commission for the Tyrannicides group at the end of the sixth century, have recently been argued by Childs (1993: 411–412, with n. 72, and 441).

28. The ancient sources for the Tyrannicides are collected by Wycherley (1957: 93–98).

29. *GSC,* figs. 7–9.

30. *DAA* 481–483.

31. Naples G103–104 (illustrated in *GSC,* fig. 3).

32. Cf. Hurwit 1985: 277: "possibly no more than two metal *kouroi* standing side by side."

33. Akurgal 1986: 9–14, with pls. 4–5.

34. *AJA* 92 (1988): 610.

35. Akurgal 1986: 9–10, 13.

36. Akurgal 1986: 13; M. Robertson 1975: 98; Cahn and Gerin 1988: 20. Robertson, in a comment appended to Akurgal's article, reaffirms his earlier position on the Sabouroff Head's being a portrait of an oriental potentate by a Greek sculptor, an attribution which he now considers strengthened by the new find; Himmelmann (1994: 65) remains skeptical about either head as a portrait.

37. Boardman 1994: 47, with fig. 2.35. Against the identification of these figures as portraits of Persian individuals, and in favor of an identification with divinities, C. M. Harrison 1982: 20–32.

38. Cf. Morris 1992: 297–298; Cahn and Gerin 1988: 20.

39. Cahn and Gerin 1988, with illustrations.

40. Cahn and Gerin 1988: 18–19, with n. 25.

41. Cahn and Gerin 1988: 19. The ancient evidence for the dates of these statues is not unequivocal. The μνημεῖον reported by Thucydides to have been erected in the Magnesian agora, given his choice of language, may refer to a monument set up after Themistocles' death. The same is the case with the statue of Themistocles that Plutarch tells us he saw in the temple of Artemis Aristoboulē in Athens. At most Plutarch's statement that the statuette stood "even down to my own day" indicates that it had been there awhile.

42. Portraits of Themistocles, Richter/Smith 210–212.

43. Richter/Smith, fig. 173.

44. E.g., Himmelmann 1994: 18, 66–70.

45. Ober and Strauss 1990: 254; they do not, however, mention the portraiture issue in this context.

46. Hammond in Hammond and Griffith 1979: 109.

47. Hammond 1992: 46.

48. Hammond in Hammond and Griffith 1979: 109. Raymond's is the standard study of Macedonian royal coinage (1953); groups I and II are illustrated in pls. 3–9.

49. Hammond in Hammond and Griffith 1979: 109, with n. 1, citing ancient references to the Nesaean breed of horses, which were famed in antiquity.

50. Raymond 1953: 93–94.

51. The evidence for the coincidence of occurrence of the Battles of Himera and Salamis is discussed by Gauthier (1966).

52. Obviously the "crown" was symbolic; Diodorus (11.26.3), who relates the story, does not refer to an object, but to a "crowning" (στεφανωθεῖσα).

53. The ancient sources for the Damareteion and the circumstances surrounding its

issue: Diod. (11.26.3); Poll. (9.85); Hesych., s.v. Δημαρέτειον. Diodorus and Pollux provide somewhat conflicting accounts; Hesychios affirms Pollux' account, with one variation. Pollux and Hesychios mention the jewelry; Diodorus does not. Pollux states that Damarete herself had the jewelry converted into the coins, while Hesychios says that Gelon did the coining. Diodorus claims that the coining happened after and as a direct consequence of the bestowing of the crown on Damarete. These differences do not, however, substantially affect the present discussion. For discussion of the dating of the Damareteion, with earlier references, Arnold-Biucchi 1990: 32–34, 46–47, and Mattingly 1992.

54. Arnold-Biucchi 1990: pl. 1:1–10; p. 18 for the date of this issue. The mule cart appears on the coins of Rhegium as well as of nearby Messana: Arnold-Biucchi 1990: 26, with pls. 5–9.

55. Kraay and Hirmer 1966: 280, Rutter 1983: 28, for examples of foreign coins modeled directly on Syracusan Arethusa heads of the later fifth century. These included Carthaginian coins issued in Sicily for the payment of mercenaries.

56. Lessing 1962: 13–14.

57. Hyde 1921: 54.

58. Habicht 1998: 150.

59. Kurke 1998: 141–142; on victors' statues not exceeding life-size, Lucian, *Pr. Im.* 11.

60. Kurke 1999: 314–316.

61. We know of the statue at Olympia from the Pseudo-Demosthenic "Letter of Philip" (12.21). Hammond (Hammond and Griffith 1979: 102, n. 1) points out that some of the words in the letter (τῶν αἰχμαλώτων Μήδων ἀπαρχήν) "probably echo the words of the dedication." Hammond (103) also concludes that portraiture existed in the Late Archaic/ Early Classical period in that the statues of Alexander I at Delphi and Olympia "must have been among the earliest portrait sculptures at any Greek shrine."

62. Shapiro 1994a: 29–30, with figs. 16–17.

63. Kelly 1976: 123–125.

64. W. Miller (1929: II.338, n. 25) cites in reference to this passage a colossal golden statue of Zeus dedicated in the temple of Zeus at Olympia by the Corinthian tyrant Cypselus, which we know of only from literary sources (e.g., Paus. 5.2.3). The life-size golden Nike held in the hand of the Parthenos comes also to mind, as do Herodotus' "golden Alexander" and the golden statues which served as a form of punishment for archons who broke their oaths. For additional documented golden statues, Kurke 1999: 316, n. 43.

65. *IG* I³ 1240 (= *CEG* no. 27); Kissas 2000, no. 20, with figs. 28–30; *GSA*, fig. 107; on the statue and its authorship, Viviers 1992: 104–105, n. 8, with further bibliography on the inscription, 121–124, 187–189.

66. For a convenient summary of the questions surrounding the identity and meaning of the Kroisos kouros, Ridgway 1993: 68–69, with n. 20, with further references. Ridgway is herself expansive on the subject of iconography in the statue but does not, in the end, believe that the image can be a likeness of the deceased; she does, however, cite others who believe differently.

67. Ridgway (1993: 68) speculates that the "meniskos" could be evidence of a helmet's crest; I am unconvinced, although it is not impossible.

68. Leaf 1886–1888: 338: "a word of uncertain derivation, known only from the present line." On the cap underneath the helmet in the Archaic period, Ridgway 1993: 100. For caps worn underneath helmets in the art of the Classical period, Knauer 1992.

69. Ridgway (1993: 68–69) associates the nudity with heroization.

70. *CEG* no. 153.

71. Aeschin. *Ktes.*, 186, together with schol. Aristid. 46.174, both cited in Wycherley 1957, nos. 49 and 54; Wycherley believes, however, that "the story of [Miltiades'] asking the privilege of an inscription is no doubt a rhetorical invention."

72. Richter/Smith (169), in discussing the possibility of likeness in the only extant portrait of Miltiades, the Ravenna herm, reach similar conclusions.

73. Plut. *Cim.* 4.5; works in the Stoa Poikile, Paus. 1.15.1.

74. The two portraits have been identified in extant copies of the exterior of the Parthenos' shield; Leipen (1971: 41–46) assembles and analyzes the ancient testimonia on the exterior of the shield and the alleged portraits; see also her reconstructions, figs. 81–82.

75. Himmelmann (1994: 88) also notes that ideal depictions go hand in hand with the equalizing tendency of democracy.

76. Arist. *Poet.* 1448a: "Since those who imitate, imitate people who do things, it is necessary that the doers be either serious or paltry . . . or indeed better or as they are or worse, or even the sorts which the painters [depict]; Polygnotus [depicted men as] better, Pauson, worse; Dionysios likened them to what they are." G. Zanker (2000) has argued that Aristotle's distinctions refer to social classes of men represented, rather than to moral categories, the usual interpretation. Cf. *Pol.* 1340a36–38: "It is necessary for young men to look, not at the works of Pauson, but at those of Polygnotus, or any other of the painters or sculptors who is ethical." Related is Pliny (*NH* 34.65), on earlier sculptors depicting "men as they were" (quales essent) and Lysippos of Sikyon depicting "men as they appeared to be" (quales viderentur esse), although this comparison surely lacks the moral overtones present in Aristotle. In the same spirit is Sophocles' purported statement that he himself depicted men as they ought to be while Euripides depicted men as they are (οἷον καὶ Σ. ἔφη αὐτὸς μὲν οἵους δεῖ ποιεῖν, Ε. δὲ οἷοι εἰσίν), quoted by Aristotle (*Poet.* 1460b34–36).

4. ConTEXTualizing the Korai

1. Grene and Lattimore 1969: 392; *IT* 1145–1150 are obelized by Diggle in his recent Oxford Classical Text edition, but not by others.

2. Such a contest appears to be taking place in Alcaeus fr. 1.

3. Carpenter 1960: 8.

4. The precise date and conditions of this legislation are controversial; for a reconsideration, Morris 1992: 305–307, with further bibliography.

5. Campbell (1983: 126) has conveniently collected and translated selected examples of Attic *scholia* (symposiastic songs) on friendship which document the Archaic demand for openness. Euripides' fondness for the simile of the counterfeit coin—some form of which appears in *Hipp.* 616–617, 925–931, 1115–1116; *Med.* 516–519; *El.* 550, 558–559; and *Bacc.* 475—might be compared.

6. For the theme, Blundell 1989. Fr. 6, trans. Fowler (1992); on the perils of false friendship, Archil. frags. 15, 23, 26.5–6, 126, 129, and more.

7. The trope of wine and drinking in the poetry of Alcaeus is treated in depth by Trumpf (1973); cf. Gentili 1988: 197: "Within the fraternity of the symposium, the great spyglass or 'speculum' of the friend's sincerity and loyalty is wine."

8. Trans. West (1993: 41).

9. Wilkinson 1992: 23.

10. Although not exclusively women; some variant of the expression is used of the "sons of Erechtheus" at Eur. *Med.* 830; Ganymede at Eur. *Tr.* 821; a fawn, at Eur. *Alc.* 586, among others.

11. Fragments, Richter 1968: figs. 429–434. Also worthy of mention is the statue of Philē by Phaidimos (Athens NM 81; Richter 1968: figs. 284–285; Kissas 2000, no. 13, with figs. 16–17), whose exquisite feet are all that remain of what must have been a splendid Archaic funerary statue.

12. For an early description of the polychromy of Acr. 682's sandals, Dickins 1912: 234.

13. Gentili 1988: 80–81, with notes 48–49, citing the ancient sources for Pittacus' "ill-concealed aversion" to Lydia and his refusal of riches from King Croesus. On the decree, Gentili (1988: 80, with n. 46 [a reference to previous bibliography]) cites Sappho fr. 98b, where she bemoans being unable to procure a decorated headband for Cleis, as a poetic "echo" of this decree.

14. Cf. Soph. *Tr.* 927: δρομαία, said of the distraught nurse describing her own actions during the murder of Heracles by his wife.

15. Zauzich 1992: 27.

16. Illustrated in M. Robertson 1975: fig. 4:b.

17. Louvre G 152 (illustrated in M. Robertson 1992: fig. 87; on p. 95 Robertson identifies this woman running with her skirt hiked over her knee as Cassandra); Boston 95.36, discussed in Robertson 1992: 99.

18. Langlotz and Hirmer 1963, figs. 30–31, with p. 64 for the identification.

19. Serwint 1993, with figs. 1 and 4.

20. Barlow 1997: 214: "This feeble joke by Menelaus is almost too heavy-footed even to be appropriate to him! It is a very rare instance of a joke in tragedy"; Lee 1997: 244: "This is one of the rare instances in tragedy of a joke spoken by a tragic character."

21. When the feminine habits of men like Alcibiades are pilloried, as in Plut. *Alc.* (1.4, 16.1), the trailing robe is cited as evidence; see M. Miller 1999: 250–251, with n. 108.

22. Schneider 1975: 29–30, with n. 142, includes additional evidence to equate the pulling gesture of the korai with walking.

23. Sourvinou-Inwood 1995: 241–242, 247–248, anticipating the distinction I make between mimetic and iconographic realism in Chapter Five.

24. Richter 1968: figs. 405–406.

25. Richter 1968: figs. 358–361.

26. Parthenon maidens: Stewart 1990: fig. 346.

27. Page (1955: 158) associates τένοντ᾽ ἐς ὀρθόν precisely with the Achilles tendon at the heel of the foot. This would seem an appropriate length for a peplos (e.g., Acr. 679), but too short for a chiton.

28. Cf. Page (1955: 158): "Eur. alone of the Tragedians could introduce and dignify these delicate instances of feminine vanity."

29. Dodds (1960: 176–177) emphasizes the oriental (= effeminate) overtones of the description of the dress. Heracles dies in a clinging poisoned chiton, a gift of Deianira, at Soph. *Tr.* 767–769.

30. Both Dodds (1960: 177) and Seaford (1997: 214–215), citing ancient sources, note that the term is used specifically of the costume of maenads and of Dionysos himself almost as if it were a technical term, but this does not eliminate the possibility of an additional touch of realism by way of an allusion to daily life, as represented in the korai.

Seaford's suggestion that in tragedy this term used of male dress connotes the garment worn by a corpse is also appropriate in the present context.

31. On transvestism, M. Miller 1999, *passim*.

32. Omega folds on Acr. 679 visible in Richter 1968: figs. 349–350; Acr. 493: Richter 1968: figs. 405–406; Acr. 510: Richter 1968: fig. 431. For a different interpretation of *Bacc.* 935–938, see the comments by Seaford (1997: 224–225), who focuses on the ritualistic significance of the dress, as opposed to the genre element, which I am emphasizing.

33. There may be at least one exception among the korai: from behind, it appears that Acr. 613 features a very subtle hip shift, reflected in the asymmetrical pattern of folds over her buttocks, as visible in Richter 1968: figs. 385–386.

34. Stieber 1999b: 142 contains an earlier version of parts of this discussion; on Pindar's use of artifacts as metaphors, Steiner 1993, with different conclusions.

35. E.g., Parkinson 1991, no. 60a.

36. Trans. Campbell (1982: 99).

37. I argue (Stieber 1994) that Pindar's contemporary, Aeschylus, does something similar in *Theoroi*.

38. If I may invoke Socrates' unforgettable but controversial characterization of the poet at Pl. *Ion* 534b.

39. Irwin (1974: 205–216) explains each of these terms.

40. Irwin 1974: 213.

41. Keuls 1997: 137–139, citing earlier opinions.

42. Stanford 1942: 72–73; cf. Mourelatos' (1973) "naive metaphysics of things."

43. Visible in Richter 1968: figs. 573–574.

44. Hornblower 1991: 517–525, for a concise introduction to the issues surrounding this important event, including the possibility of its awakening antiquarian interests in Thucydides' contemporary, Euripides, which lends a note of support to my own repeated appeal to the works of Euripides in a study of Archaic art.

45. See Schneider 1975: 5–7.

46. See Schneider 1975: 11.

47. Compare Eur. *El.* 538–540, where the old man asks Electra if she could identify the swaddling clothes she herself wove for her brother, Orestes.

48. Barber (1991: 360, with n. 3) translates: "Not a finished piece, but a sort of sampler of the shuttle," noting that a κερκίς is literally a pin-beater, since the true shuttle had not yet been invented.

49. Lee (1997: 108) cites additional ancient sources for this river's dying properties, including Pliny *NH* 31.13–14; Strabo 6.263; and Ovid *Met.* 15.315–316, where the river is mentioned as a source for lightening the color of hair whether by bathing in it or drinking from it.

50. Photius defines fustic (θάψος) as "a wood used to dye both wool and hair yellow," adding that "Sappho speaks of Scythian wood" (C. Theodoridis, ed., *Photii Patriarchae Lexicon* II [Berlin and New York 1998], 286). On the significance of hair color in Archaic poetry, Schneider 1975: 22, with n. 111.

51. Dodds (1960: 177) thinks that ἐπὶ σῷ κρατί "would have little point" if the loosening of long hair is meant; Seaford (1997: 214), citing the Kritios Boy for long hair bound up at the back in the Late Archaic/Early Classical manner, concludes that either a wig or loosened hair is possible.

52. Dodds 1960: 177–178; Seaford 1997: 215; M. Miller 1999: 230–232, n. 28, 240. At least two very different types of female headgear have been commonly identified on vases

as "mitrai": a band worn around the head and a more substantial, turbanlike structure, sometimes with the hair pulled through the crown; on this debate, M. Miller 1999: 230–232, n. 28, with further references. An even more specific type of long-flapped headgear, identified as a Persian mitra and worn under a helmet by Athena, Amazons, and warriors in the Early Classical period, is isolated by Knauer (1992), and its iconography associated with the Persian Wars. Only the headband-type applies to the korai.

53. Plut. *Sol.* 24.4; Diod. 11.43.3.

54. On these ideas, Burkert 1992: 23, with further references.

55. Scheid and Svenbro 1996: 197–198, n. 145.

56. Acr. 593: Richter 1968: figs. 147–150; Roccos 1995: 647–648; cf. Sourvinou-Inwood 1995: 246, who briefly suggests the same.

57. Roccos (1995: 659) notes that the grouping of two behind four echoes the pattern of *kanephoroi* on the Parthenon east frieze, that is, four coming from the north, two from the south. I have never been convinced that the Erechtheum caryatids carry a basket on their heads; a capital and an entablature would seem to be enough of a burden, visually as well as metaphorically. Nothing about this building is conventional. The order of the south porch is technically Ionic, but the capital has a Doric abacus and the swelling member between the heads of the statues and the abacus represents, I think, a highly ornamented echinus, a fitting departure from the norm for this unusual, ornate building.

58. Cf. Ridgway 1993: 174; on bridal attire, Oakley and Sinos 1993: 16; Reeder 1995: 127.

59. Cf. Sourvinou-Inwood 1995: 245: "The korai, then, represented young maidens of the 'marriageable *parthenos*' age, an important social category in ancient Greece; the richness of their dress and jewellery corresponds to, and articulates iconographically, the fact that in Greek mentality the marriageable *parthenos* was symbolically associated with beauty and beautification."

60. Oakley and Sinos 1993: 14, 17, with figs. 5–8; significance of short hair in front, E. Harrison 1988b.

61. Serra di Vaglio 51532, 54622, 54623; Oakley and Sinos 1993: fig. 2, and pp. 12–13; Reeder's (1995) cat. no. 27 might also be compared.

62. Oakley and Sinos 1993: 19–20; 16–21, for the evidence summarized here.

63. Oakley and Sinos 1993: 22–23.

64. On the *Hec.* passage, see Barber 1991: 362. I leave aside the vexed questions about whether one or two peploi were woven and presented to Athena during the Greater (every four years) and Lesser (every year) Panathenaic festivals, and whether men were involved in the weaving; Barber (1992, with further references) opts for two peploi, the larger "sail-peplos" being woven by professional male weavers.

65. Ecker (1990: 198, n. 695) claims that in Attic poetry and prose κόρη can mean only an unmarried woman; but at Eur. *Andr.* 489 Andromache is referred to as τὰν τάλαιναν Ἰλιάδα κόραν, perhaps as an allusion to her prime of life as a marriageable girl in Troy.

66. Cf. Eur. *IT* 222–224, where a simplified version of the same periphrasis is used again to allude to the Panathenaic peplos.

67. Cf. Barber 1991: 362; 1992: 103; *LSJ*, s.v., has "worked with flowers."

68. Cf. Scheid and Svenbro 1996: 54; their interpretation of this passage is similar to mine. They do not, however, distinguish clearly enough between the two very different conditions implied by the use of "ornately flowered" in reference to garments, that of flowered designs and that of multicolored dyes, at least some of which would have a floral base. In this case, both are possible.

69. Barber (1992: 117), believing in two peploi, refers to the yearly peplos.

70. Trans. Freeman (1956: 22); on Xenophanes and the gods, Podlecki 1984: 169–170.

71. Trans. Campbell (1982: 53–55), with minor modifications. Scheid and Svenbro (1996: 53–58) discuss the meaning of the epithet *poikilothronos* used of Aphrodite at Sappho fr. 1.1 and argue convincingly for "dressed in a cloak with flowered designs" rather than for the more usual translation, "seated on a richly worked throne"; thence my slight alteration of Campbell's translation.

72. *Contra* Schneider 1975: 27–29.

5. PHRASIKLEIA

1. At press, the kore awaits official publication. The circumstances of its discovery and photographic documentation of the excavation by Nikos Kontos are laid out in a preliminary report by E. I. Mastrokostas (1972). Kontos (1983) himself publishes additional photographs of the excavation of the two statues; his brief, lively description of the circumstances in which his services were solicited by the excavator offers a glimpse of the excitement which accompanied the discovery. For rare color photographs, Mastrokostas 1972: frontispiece and pl. 3; Biers 1996: pl. 3 (cf. *GSA*, fig. 108:a), although the polychromy does not reproduce well; it is still best to visit the statue in person. For a reconstruction of the sumptuous polychromy of Phrasikleia, Karakasi 1997: pls. 7–8, drawings by H. Meinhold. Pedley 1976: 44–45; Floren 1987: 164; and Karakasi 1997: 510–511 are good on the style.

2. *Contra* D'Onofrio (1982: 151–152), who does, however, rightly draw attention to the possible significance of the separation of the statues from their bases, only one of which has been recovered.

3. For a convenient summary of this controversial issue, Fornara and Samons 1991: 17–21.

4. M. Robertson 1975: 106; cf. Svenbro 1993: 12–13; Hornblower 1991: 210, apropos of Thuc. 1.126.12 (καὶ τῶν τεθνεώτων τὰ ὀστᾶ ἀνελόντες ἐξέβαλον ["after having taken up the bones of the dead, they threw them out"]), followed by Sourvinou-Inwood 1995: 146, n. 133. While the kouros buried with Phrasikleia has not been associated with an inscription that could helpfully supply his name, if this theory is correct, it is possible that he, too, was an Alcmaeonid and this was his grave statue.

5. Karakasi 1997: 509, citing Mastrokostas (1972: 314), who seems to me to be uncommitted on the issue.

6. On the ceramic evidence, Mastrokostas 1972: 324; Svenbro (1993: 12) comes to much the same conclusion.

7. A sampling: Mastrokostas 1972: 318: not earlier than 540; Catling 1973: 6: not earlier than 590; Travlos 1988: 365: ca. 540; M. Robertson 1975: 101: between the Berlin Kore and Acr. 679; Stewart 1976: 262: ca. 530, and 1990: 119: ca. 550; Floren 1987: 164: ca. 570; *GSA*, fig. 108:a: ca. 550; Ecker 1990: 195–196: following Mastrokostas, ca. 540; Ridgway 1993: 142: ca. 530; Rolley 1994: 282–283: ca. 530; Karakasi 1997: 511: ca. 540.

8. Fornara and Samons (1991: 21), after sifting through the evidence, conclude that there was only one exile, not two, and that it began as late as 514, "when the murder of Hipparchus ended the truce between tyrant and aristocracy, resulting in the exile of many of the clans."

9. Ridgway (1993: 141–142, with ns. 50–51) lists the six or so certain and probable Attic examples, and, in n. 51, a few extremely uncertain potential additions to the list.

Cf. Sourvinou-Inwood 1995: 247, following D'Onofrio 1982: 142, 144–145, for a somewhat more broadly based list. The strange absence of examples from the Kerameikos is perhaps due, according to Ridgway, to the fact that "it became a public cemetery after the early Sixth century when it could still house monumental funerary kouroi" (p. 142) or "because of different funerary practices at an early stage" (p. 169, n. 4.50; cf. p. 124).

10. M. Robertson 1975: 108, with n. 80.

11. For the genitive alone, the stele of Aristion (Athens NM 29); Aristodikos (Athens NM 3938), both Attic; Kroisos, as we have already seen, is named in a more informative inscription.

12. Divinity: Kontoleon (1974), Schefold (1973: 155), Neumann (1979: 227); heroine: Mastrokostas (1972), Ridgway (1993), D'Onofrio (1982); real woman or symbol thereof: Daux (1973 and 1973–1974), Catling (1973: 7), Clairmont (1974), Stewart (1990), Svenbro (1993), Sourvinou-Inwood (1995). The views of the writers for whom page numbers are not given here are addressed below, where full citations may be found.

13. For the measurement, Mastrokostas 1972: 316, calling the statue life-size; Catling (1973: 6) and M. Robertson (1975: 100) concur. Over life-size: Clairmont (1975: 221); Floren (1987: 164); Ridgway (1993: 148) ("heroic"). Karakasi (1997: 509) curiously gives the height as 1.79 m, calling the statue "slightly over life-size."

14. Karakasi 1997: 511–512.

15. On the derivation of this version of the rosette, I follow Goodyear (1891: 99–107, with numerous line-drawings of Egyptian examples), who discusses the stylization process at 103–104; and Koch-Harnack (1989: 24–32), who uses Goodyear as a starting point for identifying the far more numerous Greek examples. More below.

16. Saleh and Sourouzian 1987, no. 208.

17. Ridgway 1993: 139: "Yet the sculptor may have felt the need to emphasize the difference between the thin Samian chiton which the hand could grasp almost like a rope, and the heavier peplos which should have more vertical pull. . . . The resultant effect suggests stretchable material that can momentarily be pulled out of shape before it returns to cling immediately below the hand."

18. Sourvinou-Inwood 1995: 241–242, 247.

19. Mastrokostas 1972: 318–319.

20. Both inscribed sides illustrated in Mastrokostas 1972: figs. 17–18.

21. Jeffery 1962: 138–139; cf. Kontoleon 1970: 91, n. 10, which acknowledges that the damage was inflicted when the stone was re-employed for use in the church during the twelfth or thirteenth centuries and adds some interesting observations about the base's modern history.

22. Mastrokostas 1972: figs. 7–8; fig. 16, for the lead ring inserted into the bedding of the base.

23. The epigram and signature are published together as *IG* I³ 1261 (= *CEG* no. 24; Jeffery and Johnston 1990, no. 29 [Attica] and Jeffery 1962, no. 46; Kissas 2000, no. 14).

24. Austin 1938: 12; Jeffery 1962: 139.

25. Austin 1938: 12.

26. Jeffery 1962: 139.

27. Geffcken 1916: 16.

28. Immerwahr 1990, no. 460; Stewart 1976: 262; 1990: 119.

29. On the career of Aristion of Paros, Ridgway 1993: 433; *GSA* 75–76; Stewart 1976; 1990: 119. The burial stele of Aristion by Aristokles (Athens NM 29: *GSA*, fig. 235; Kissas 2000, no. 17) is assumed to show this sculptor as a warrior.

30. Stewart 1976; Viviers 1992: 187–196; Frel (1973) unconvincingly attributes the Merenda kouros to a different hand, the master of the Lyons Kore (Acr. 269).

31. Shapiro 1991: 633; cf. Humphreys 1980: 105.

32. Gallavotti 1979: 78; Wallace 1970: 100–101; cf. Webster 1960: 259: "the vase-painter Kleimachos signs with a phalaecean and Exekias with an iambic trimeter." Pausanias (3.17.2) mentions a Late Archaic Spartan, Gitiadas, who was both a bronze-worker and a poet.

33. Sourvinou-Inwood 1995: 281.

34. Mastrokostas 1972: 316–317.

35. Visible in Lullies and Hirmer 1956: pls. 20–21. A list may be found in Mastrokostas 1972: 317, n. 3. On the alternating lotus/bud chain design in Greek art, Kurtz 1975: figs. 1–2; Elderkin 1936: 128, 138; Payne 1931: 153–156. Also Cook 1965: 776–785; Jacobsthal 1906: 13–32, on the various combinations of lotus flower/bud used to represent the thunderbolt of Zeus. On the lotus as a comparable symbol of power in Egyptian art: Wilkinson 1992: 22–23, fig. 2, an "unnaturally erect" lotus bud and stem held in the right hand of the wife of Sa-Inheret on a Middle Kingdom funerary stele; Wilkinson suggests that this lotus, with the rest of its stem hanging naturally limp as it emerges from the back of her hand, is stiffened in front to mimic "the scepter held by her husband," thereby imparting "a measure of authority and prestige to her also."

36. Rolley 1994: figs. 13 and 158, a Calydonian example.

37. Cook 1965: 776.

38. Mastrokostas (1972: 317, n. 3) points to a head of a kouros in the Delphi Museum (inv. 7534: Richter 1970a: figs. 169–171) that wears a diadem decorated, according to Richter (1970a: 69), with lotus buds and circles. Compare also the "flamelike" arrangement of hair at the forehead that is the most conspicuous feature of the Volomandra Kouros (Athens NM 1906: Richter 1970a: figs. 208–216) and that of the kouros head in New York (MMA 21.88.16: Richter 1970a: figs. 217–218; Richter [pp. 80–81] wisely suggests that this arrangement is more likely to represent a fillet than locks of hair).

39. Mastrokostas 1972: 316; Karakasi throughout her article refers to the bloom in hand simply as a "Knospe" ("bud"), just once (1997: 512) calling it a "Lotosknospe," without comment.

40. Mastrokostas 1972: 319; cf. the related thesis of D'Onofrio (1982: 151), who does not argue for a cult per se, but comes very close; *contra,* Daux 1973–1974: 241. Ridgway (1993: 174) agrees that there is an element of "heroization" in the statue, but wisely does not speculate about cult, and rejects (p. 247, n. 6.6) D'Onofrio's thesis as regards Phrasikleia, but tentatively accepts it for the kouros; Sourvinou-Inwood (1995: 145–146) also rejects D'Onofrio's attempt to bestow votive status on the two Merenda statues.

41. Kontoleon 1970: 53–55, 89–92, reiterated in 1974; Hansen (*CEG* no. 24) rejects Kontoleon's thesis out of hand.

42. On the pomegranate and Persephone, Garland 1985: 158. I disagree with Sourvinou-Inwood (1995: 249) that "her necklace is surely made of pomegranates," thus certifying a connection with Persephone, "especially in her persona as bride of Hades." On the contrary, as I argue below, I do not believe that the forms comprising the necklace can be securely identified.

43. Daux 1973–1974: 241; cf. Clairmont 1974: 220–223, 237. Floren (1987: 164) is noncommittal on the identity of the depicted, noting only that: "Als Braut des Hades ist P. reich mit Armreifen, Halskette und Ohrringen geschmückt." ("As the bride of Hades, P. is richly ornamented with armbands, necklace, and earrings.")

44. Clairmont 1974: 222; cf. Pedley 1976: 44; *GSA* 73.

45. Stewart (1990: 119–120) makes no mention of the vegetal motif, but in 1997: 115 considers the significance of the lotuses.

46. Sourvinou-Inwood 1995: 249–250, who (p. 251) also suggests that a fragmentary kore in New York (MMA 07.286.110) is a "metaphorical Persephone."

47. Ridgway 1993: 148. The full discussion of Attic korai who wear poloi is found in Ridgway 1993: 147–148, from which my remarks are drawn; for details and further bibliography on the issues briefly raised here, Ridgway's footnotes may be consulted.

48. Acr. 654, probably a sphinx; Acr. 269, almost certainly a caryatid; Acr. 696, a kore's head, to which some body parts have also been attached (Richter 1968: figs. 405–410).

49. Cf. Hurwit (1999: 204), who observes: "Perhaps the Karyatids themselves, with their *phialai* or libation-bowls, were to be thought of as participants in the cult of Kekrops."

50. Ridgway 1993: 139 (on the flower), 143, with n. 54.

51. Ridgway 1990: 602 (cf. 1993: 174), citing a manuscript on pomegranate buds by Louise Clark.

52. M. Robertson 1975: 100–101, 106.

53. Sourvinou-Inwood 1995: 247, 249.

54. Stewart 1990: 49, 120.

55. Stewart 1997: 115.

56. Svenbro 1993: 20–24.

57. Sourvinou-Inwood 1995: 249.

58. On the religious associations of flower-gathering for use in garlands, Lilja 1972: 179–180.

59. Reading φερεσανθέσιν with Allen and Sikes (1904: 297); see also Schneider 1975: 13–14.

60. Fr. 26.21 (West 1985).

61. On which see Burnett 1970: 85.

62. The women are not characterized in any way except by their names; however, the list has much in common with Hes. *Th.* 346–361, where they are referred to as "a holy race of korai," a periphrasis for nymphs, according to West (1966: 263). Richardson (1974: 140–144) and Foley (1994: 33–34) discuss the associations between flower-picking and abduction of young women as well as the symbolic significance of the types of flowers gathered in the *Homeric Hymn to Demeter.*

63. On the significance of the flowery meadow as an occasion for erotic encounters in Greek literature, Bremer 1975; on the dangers to young women gathering flowers, with additional bibliography, Loraux 1993: 228.

64. For young people, especially women, compared to plants, West 1966: 264, pointing to Aesch. *Suppl.* 281; Fränkel (1968: 44–45) shows how widespread the motif is in early Greek poetry.

65. Trans. Campbell (1982: 121).

66. Trans. Campbell (1982: 149). According to information given to Owen (1939: 129) by D. Page, Sappho fr. 132 "is the only passage in Greek literature which speaks of golden flowers." It appears, however, that Owen would like to include the χρυσανταυγῆ ("reflecting golden light") of Eur. *Ion* 890 as a reference, if only an oblique one, to a golden flower.

67. Richardson 1974: 144; on this colorful epithet, also Allen and Sikes 1904: 16; Foley 1994: 34.

68. Schneider 1975: 63, n. 122.

69. Owen (1939: 129) takes φάρεσιν two ways: (1) almost equivalent to a subjective

genitive with κόλπους ("pouches") or (2) "to deck my robes," which sounds as if he is suggesting that the robes somehow be decked with the actual flowers. While a robe could be decorated with woven floral motifs which might qualify it as being "decked" with flowers, I do not believe this to be the case here.

70. Barber 1992: 116–117.

71. For a survey of the dyes and dyeing processes used in ancient fabrics, primarily prehistoric, Barber 1991: 223–243, esp. 233 on the use of crocus stamens to produce a yellow dye; Baumann 1993: 154–162 also has a good overview. The fresco (Doumas 1983: pls. 30–32) is from Room 3 of Xestē 3 at Akrotiri.

72. Bosly 1980: 23–65.

73. Doumas 1983: at fig. 32.

74. Purple-fishery: Pliny, *NH* 9.125–127, 133–137; Hdt. 4.151.2; Athenaeus 3.89b–c; Pollux 1.47–49.

75. For a description of contemporary Central American women engaged in hand dyeing skeins of yarn with the dyes of living purple-snails, Barber 1991: 228, n. 4.

76. On the purple color of the wedding gown, Oakley and Sinos 1993: 16, with n. 43.

77. The first word is garbled; the sense of my translation follows the reading αὖτα δ' ὡράα suggested by Ahrens, according to Campbell (1982: 144).

78. Trans. Campbell (1982: 123).

79. Trans. Campbell (1982: 127).

80. He also cites Hdt. 2.122.

81. Shapiro 1994a: fig. 91.

82. Compare, for example, one style of wearing it on the New York Kouros (Richter 1970a: figs. 25–32), and another on the Volomandra (Richter 1970a: figs. 245–250).

83. Trans. Campbell (1982: 109).

84. Here the word τράχηλον certainly refers to the neck and not the head or both the neck and head, as it does elsewhere; Powell (1938: 58) cites examples where it would be impossible to translate "neck."

85. Trans. Campbell (1982: 395), with slight modification; lines 3–4 are quoted by Athenaeus later (15.687d), in his discussion of scents.

86. Cf. Plut. *Qu. Conv.* 647e–f, for the same etymology.

87. Trans. Campbell (1982: 117), with modifications.

88. Ridgway 1993: 143, with n. 54, where, in support of her remark that "Phrasikleia's Attic inheritance is particularly visible in her high-sloping feet and her jewelry," Ridgway cites L. Blanck, *Studien zum griechischen Halsschmuck der archaischen und klassischen Zeit* (Cologne 1974): 129, a work I was unable to consult, as a source for the conclusion that "Attica and Boiotia prefer abstract forms and objects, such as vessels, for their jewelry pendants, instead of the vegetal motifs favored in the East Greek area."

89. Athens NM 22 (Richter 1968: figs. 472–475, with pp. 88–89, comparing the chains worn across the chest with her nos. 47, 49, terracotta statuettes—one from Acarnania, and the other from Rhodes—which appear to have metal discs as pendants); Delos Museum A4067 (Richter 1968: figs. 476–479).

90. *Treasures of Ancient Macedonia*, Archaeological Museum of Thessalonike, n.d., fig. 254, from grave Z at Derveni.

91. *Treasures of Ancient Macedonia*, figs. 79, from Pella, and 253, from grave Z at Derveni. They are called beechnuts in similar examples illustrated in Williams and Ogden 1994, nos. 30, 53, 123.

92. Williams and Ogden 1994, nos. 181–182.

93. Williams and Ogden 1994, no. 94.

94. See Goodyear 1891: fig. 7 for a line drawing of a *Nymphaea* species seedpod. Williams and Ogden (1994, nos. 46, 69) call the identical form when they are opened "asphodel seed-pods." (The asphodel flower was well known in ancient Greece and looks much like a tiny lotus bud when its many flowers, which are carried on umbels, are in full bloom; perhaps for this reason it was planted around graves; see A. M. Coats, *The Treasury of Flowers* [London 1975]: pl. 1.) In Williams and Ogden 1994, no. 46, however, rosettes appearing inside the open head would seem to indicate that they are meant to be lotus seedpods. A very similar, but less completely open form of seed or bud appears in no. 69; Williams and Ogden are uncertain in this case whether they are seeds or buds; they look to me more like the latter; cf. the pendants on a necklace from Egypt, Saleh and Sourouzian 1987, no. 240.

95. Schneider 1975: 63–64, n. 125.

96. Illustrated in Richter 1968: figs. 313–316, 456–459.

97. Acr. 593: Richter 1968: figs. 147–150; Acr. 677: Richter 1968: figs. 198–200.

98. Richter 1968: figs. 259–262.

99. Richter 1968: figs. 168–169, with p. 42.

100. Cf. Lilja 1972: 176.

101. Text is from Gow and Page 1965 I.214; the editors note in vol. II.593 the long history of association between flowers and poetry (cf. "anthology"), a theme elaborated upon in Gutzwiller 1998: 78–79, 87, where it is seen to originate with Sappho.

102. Bolling 1958; Scheid and Svenbro 1996: 53–82.

103. Bolling 1958: 281; cf. Barber 1991: 372; further on the symbolism of the rose, Richardson 1974: 142; Stulz 1990: 181–201.

104. E.g., Campbell (1982: 53).

105. Cf. Athenaeus 15.680d; Pollux 7.200.

106. Goodyear 1891: esp. 3–41; Cook 1965: 772–774; Wilkinson 1992: 27, 121.

107. There is a third, quite different, species of lotus that was also common in ancient Egypt; H. E. Steier in *RE* XIII.2, cols. 1518–1520; Goodyear 1891: 25–39; and Murr 1890: 281–283. This is the so-called Indian lotus, or "rose lotus," actually plants of the genus *Nelumbium,* which, like the genus *Nymphaea,* is also in the Nymphaeaceae family, but, unlike *Nymphaea,* bears its uncleft leaves on stems four to five feet above water level. The leaves of the *Nymphaea* species, on the other hand, are single-clefted and float on the surface of the water. This species no longer flourishes in Egypt and furthermore was not native to Egypt in ancient times but had been introduced from the East, while it stopped being cultivated at the end of antiquity and disappeared, according to Murr (1890: 282); Wilkinson (1992: 121) claims it was introduced from Persia in the Late period. This is the Nile plant that was eventually associated with Heracles (Murr 1890: 282–283). Goodyear (1891) argues that the *Nelumbium* species does not appear in Egyptian art by demonstrating how the *Nymphaea* species underwent the process of stylization. The "Indian lotus" seems, at least in contemporary photographs which show a peony-type flower, to be less well suited for stylization in art than the more angular, and generally showier, *Nymphaea* species. For an illustration of *Nelumbium nelumbo album plenum,* still called the "Sacred Lotus," Graf 1978: 1192; cf. the *Nymphaea* species, 1191–1193.

108. How and Wells 1912.I: 212–213.

109. Goodyear 1891: 29–39; Steier, *RE* XIII.2, col. 1519, for testimony on the rose coloration of this genus' flowers; col. 1521 for the identification of Athenaeus' rose-colored lotuses as of this genus.

110. Koch-Harnack 1989: 11–108, with illustrations.

111. E.g., Goodyear 1891, *passim*.

112. Wilkinson 1992: 121.

113. On the individual hieroglyphs for Upper and Lower Egypt, as well as the combined form, which frequently appears on the sides of thrones of royal seated figures, Wilkinson 1992: 80–81, 122–123; examples: Saleh and Sourouzian 1987, nos. 87 and 167. There is controversy over what plant forms are represented in both cases; Goodyear (1891: 43–65) thinks that the "papyri" are lotuses.

114. Cairo Museum, JE 30199 (Saleh and Sourouzian 1987, no. 99).

115. Michalowski n.d.: pl. 98.

116. Hornung 1990: 59–60, with pl. 39.

117. Kozloff et al. 1992, no. 126; unlike the Greek examples already introduced, there appears to be no doubt that these motifs are lotiform.

118. The types are conveniently distinguished in the index of Hort 1916: 460–463.

119. Heubeck and Hoekstra (1989: 19) make no attempt to identify precisely the kind of lotus which Odysseus' men are thought to have eaten, believing it "pointless to attempt . . . to identify either the λωτός plant itself or the country where it grows." The preoccupation with coordinating the places that Odysseus visited with a real map is bound to be frustrating, but we are on stronger ground when it comes to identifying the type of lotus eaten in *Od.* 9. It seems unlikely that the species of *Nymphaea* were intended, the evidence of Hdt. 2.92, that they were used for food, notwithstanding. More likely it is the Libyan variety of lotus, an arborescent rather than a herbaceous species, that is meant, as recognized as long ago as 1876, the original publication date of Autenrieth; see also Steier in *RE* XIII.2, cols. 1526–1530; How and Wells 1912.I: 212.

120. For photographs of other *Trifolium* species, see Graf 1978: 1042. For a concise, thorough account of all the species of lotus that grew in antiquity, Steier in *RE* XIII.2, cols. 1515–1532.

121. Cf. Koch-Harnack 1989: 71–72.

122. For stephanai made of melilotus, Athenaeus 15.678c and 685a; Theocritus 18.43 (a crown of melilotus made for Helen); and other examples cited by Gow (1956: 359). Most likely it is a crown of melilotus rather than of Egyptian lotus that is indicated by the term λωτίη, which in the Suidias is a crown of lotus (Adler 1967: l. 741).

123. Cf. Ἑλλάδος λωτίσματα, from a fragment of Aeschylus (*TrGF* 3, F 99.17). The expression is paralleled by the ἄνθος Ἀργείων ("flower of the Argives") of Aesch. *Ag.* 197 and comparable examples at Hes. *Th.* 988, fr. 132; Eur. *Tr.* 809, *El.* 15, *Ph.* 88. Kannicht (1969: II.415–416, upon which my discussion is largely based) also suggests that the association of λώτισμα (Hesych., Latte l. 1525) with "chosen," "select," is a result of word play with λῷων (= "better").

124. Trans. Campbell (1982: 119).

125. Mastronarde 1994: 587.

126. Koch-Harnack 1989: esp. 72–83; figs. 29, 36, 40, 61, 62, 73, 74, and 88a illustrate in its most extreme form the exploitation of the stylized lotus' similarity to the phallus.

127. E.g., a spoon composed of a nearly naked, tattooed swimming young woman holding a huge lotus, Kozloff et al. 1992, pl. 74; a lotus-diademed, splay-legged courtesan depicted in the so-called erotic papyrus, Peck 1978: fig. 21; and from the interior of a faience bowl, a nearly naked, tattooed, lute-playing lady (another courtesan?) afloat and surrounded by lotus stems, leaves, buds, and flowers, Peck 1978: pl. XV. On the lotus as a symbol of eroticism and reproductive power in Egypt, Cook 1965: 772, n. 1.

128. Armstrong and Hanson 1986.

129. Noted also by Schneider (1975: 63, n. 124).

130. Pedley 1976: 44.

131. Rolley 1994: 282.

132. Ridgway 1993: 139.

133. Ridgway 1993: 142.

134. Ridgway 1993: 142.

135. Stewart 1990: 119.

136. Athens NM 804 (M. Robertson 1975: pl. 4:a). Garland (1985: 24) characterizes the woman's dress only as "a long ankle-length robe." Ahlberg (1971) does not use the term "peplos" to describe the garments worn by the dead in Geometric art. The presence of fibulae in many Submycenaean and Geometric graves would seem to point to burial in a peplos; Kurtz and Boardman 1971: 33–34, 62.

137. Kurtz and Boardman (1971: figs. 14–16, 43) illustrate several examples, including a sixth-century clay figure of a mourner wearing what looks like a peplos; cf. Shapiro 1991: figs. 3, 5 (black-figured vases depicting the *prothesis*, in which the women are wearing fancy peploi); Havelock 1981: fig. 88; Zschietzschmann 1928: pl. IX, fig. 84. Boardman (1955: 55), on Archaic funerary plaques ("both the finest and the fullest representations and which in the early sixth century are the only monuments figuring the *prothesis*"), refers to the shroud as "patterned stuff."

138. Corpses wrapped in peploi: Eur. *HF* 702–703; *Tr.* 378, 627, 1143–1144, which refers to crowns as well. Mourners wearing peploi: *IA* 1438, 1448; *Alc.* 216, 923; *Hel.* 1088. It is true that "peplos" is used rather loosely by the tragedians; as is the case with its representation in works of art, there seems to be little consistency to its application. The term cannot in all cases be assumed to refer either to a woolen garment or to a particular style of wearing a garment, but may be used as a generic term for "garment"; cf. Studniczka 1886: 133–143.

139. Ridgway 1993: 238, with n. 50, with references to opposing viewpoints on the question of whether colors have significance in Archaic art, to which may be added Manzelli 1994: 33–90, arguing on behalf of significance (for a critique of Manzelli's approach, L. James, *CR* 46 [1996]: 126–128). See further on the association of red with funerary paraphernalia, Kurtz and Boardman 1971: 71, on a red-painted interior of a coffin from the Kerameikos, and 217 and 318, for the practice of smearing red paint on the body or bones to simulate the lost blood "in many early cultures."

140. Garland 1985: 24; Zschietzschmann 1928: 34–35.

141. E.g., Athens NM 1818 (Fairbanks 1907, group C: class V, 49).

142. *Hel.* 1088; cf. *Alc.* 216, 923; *Or.* 457; Ar. *Frogs* 1336.

143. Oakley and Sinos 1993: 16, with n. 43.

144. Reeder 1995: 127.

145. Cf. E. Harrison 1988a: 53; Ridgway 1990: 602 (and more forcefully in 1993: 142 and 174), although she considers this theory stronger if the buds are pomegranates rather than lotuses. On bridal jewelry and headdress, Oakley and Sinos 1993: 16; Reeder 1995: 127.

146. Garland 1985: 25, 139; cf. Reilly 1989: 431. On Greek marriage customs, Sissa 1990: 93–99; Oakley and Sinos 1993, *passim*, with numerous illustrations. On the relationship between marriage and death, Armstrong and Ratchford 1985: esp. p. 9 with n. 31; and Connelly 1996: 62–63, for a parthenos being dressed for death as if for marriage. In general, on the evidence for the connections between weddings and funerals, Rehm 1994: esp.

pp. 30–42 on the visual record. In rural Greece today there is a close association between the rites of burial and marriage; Danforth 1982: esp. pp. 79–90.

147. Foley 1992: 138–139.

148. Cf. *Ph.* 1485–1492; Foley (1992: 139) also cites *Suppl.* 1054–1058, where "Evadne . . . dresses in wedding attire to prepare for her suicide over her husband's pyre."

149. Barber 1991: 206–208, 379–380, with figs. 7.11, 16.15.

150. Kurtz and Boardman 1971: 126, 357, with pl. 35, a black-figured kantharos which shows an *ekphora* (carrying away) with the corpse and all mourners wrapped in lotus-rosette–covered garments; on rosettes in funerary contexts, Ahlberg 1971: 151–152, 235; Boardman 1955: pls. 4, 7, where mourners wear rosettes; Havelock 1981: figs. 91–92, a red-figured vase with a dead young man wearing a rosette-covered shroud; Zschietzschmann 1928: pl. XV, fig. 91, where both mourners and the dead wear rosette-strewn garments. A plastic rendering of a life-size lotus-rosette is featured prominently perched atop the handle of a funerary oinochoe from the Kerameikos (Ker. Mus. inv. 149). The vessel is abundantly ornamented with funerary iconography: its body has a painted *prothesis,* the neck has painted lions or sphinxes, two molded clay snakes slither right through the neck and emerge from the trefoil mouth, and plastically rendered women wearing peploi stand upon the shoulder and, with arms raised in lamentation, support the broad lip of the vessel; Richter 1968: no. 3, figs. VIa–c, 31–32; Kubler 1979: no. 49, pls. 38–42 and 410–411, on the funerary significance of the rosette. Examples of incised and painted lotus-rosette and lotus designs decorating the abacuses of the crowning capitals of Archaic grave stelai: Richter 1961: figs. 66–67, 68–69, 73–76.

151. The term "lotus-rosettes" is used by Williams and Ogden (e.g., 1994: 152–153) for a rosette superimposed on a lotus flower. I use the term to refer to the rosette on its own, following Goodyear (1891: 99–107). The lotus seedpod, or "rosette," may be examined in person at any water lily pond.

152. Saleh and Sourouzian 1987, no. 218, cf. no. 208; Kozloff et al. 1992, no. 34.

153. Wilkinson 1992: 138–139.

154. Erman 1971: 396.

155. Hornung 1990: 45, pls. 22 (mislabeled 23), 33, 37, pp. 72, 125.

156. Kurtz and Boardman 1971: 207.

157. Kurtz and Boardman 1971: pl. 39; the wreath as shown is apparently incomplete; cf. K. Gebauer, "Ausgrabungen im Kerameikos," *AA* 57 (1942): 244, with pl. 21.

158. Andronicos 1984: figs. 35, 137, 183–184; cf. Williams and Ogden 1994: fig. 60, an example made of oak leaves, fig. 105, of olive, found wrapped around the skull of a male skeleton, and fig. 115, of olive, from a woman's burial.

159. Athens NM 1170 (Garland 1985: fig. 7). Burial crowns: Havelock 1981: fig. 90; Kurtz and Boardman 1971: pls. 34, 37 (vase-paintings); Richter 1961: figs. 80–81, a youth wearing an (olive?) wreath on an Archaic grave stele. Reilly (1989: 417–420) discusses the use of wreaths in wedding, funerary, and festive contexts.

160. Henderson (1987: 147) discusses the dramatic context; for additional literary references, Garland 1985: 139; Kurtz and Boardman 1971: 207.

161. Garland 1985: 26.

162. Henderson 1987: 147.

163. Now in Baghdad, Chicago, and New York (Frankfort 1970: figs. 39–46).

164. Ridgway 1993: 170, n. 4.52.

165. Sourvinou-Inwood 1995: 246–248.

166. Hornung 1990: pl. 84.

167. Saleh and Sourouzian 1987, no. 135.

168. E.g., Hornung 1990: 172–174; Michalowski n.d.: pls. 95–98.

169. Wilkinson 1992: 121.

170. MMA 11.185 (illustrated in Richter 1961: figs. 99, 107–109).

171. Louvre, MND 1863 (illustrated in Richter 1961: figs. 138–139).

172. Zapheiropolou 1973, *passim*.

173. Phrasikleia is not the only kore to feature the lotus; for additional examples, Richter 1968: figs. 288, 306–308.

174. Kannicht 1969: II.415, apropos Eur. *Hel.* 1593.

175. Hesych., s.v. λωτίζειν (Schmidt 1965: l. 1529), glosses the word ἀπανθίζεσθαι ("to pluck a flower"), ἀπολλύειν ("to destroy"). Latte (l. 1522) replaces the latter with ἀπολαύειν ("to have enjoyment of"), Heinsius' conjecture, found in Schmidt's apparatus, perhaps rejecting the negative connotation of the word.

176. Diggle 1970: 146–148, on the etymology of Apollo and the interpretation of this passage; for a different view of the origins of Apollo's name, Nagy 1994.

177. Zauzich 1992: 5–6.

178. On the Greek experience of the art and hieroglyphs of Egypt, Iversen 1993: 38–52; Davies 1990: 119. In general, on the early Greek presence in Egypt, see Boardman 1999: 111–153; the topic is treated extensively by Möller (2000).

179. Even in 1990, Ecker (1990: 195–202), who offers the fullest treatment of the language and style of the epigram, virtually ignores the statue.

180. For use of the future perfect to convey permanence, Goodwin 1965: §78. Because this tense of καλέω ("call") expresses a permanent state in future time, it is most often used of a state of being that transcends death, and thus is popular in epitaphs; cf. Eur. *Hec.* 480–481, where Hecuba says she will always be called a slave, and *Hec.* 1271, where κεκλήσεται appears in a funerary context used by Polymestor, who is gleefully characterizing the future tomb of Hecuba (κυνὸς σῆμα, "tomb of a dog"); Ecker (1990: 199, n. 697) collects additional examples.

181. My language is borrowed and respectfully adapted from the last stanza of John Keats' "Ode on a Grecian Urn," where it is said of a work of art: "Thou, silent form, dost tease us out of thought as doth eternity" (text, Garrod 1972: 210).

REFERENCES

The numbering and texts of the fragments of Sappho and Alcaeus are from Lobel and Page 1963. Hesiod's *Theogony* is from West 1966, and the fragments from Merkelbach and West 1967. Pindar and Bacchylides are from Snell and Maehler 1987 and 1970, respectively; other Lyric poets are from *PMG*. For other ancient authors, where available, the latest Oxford Classical Text edition is used. Citations of Euripides' fragments are from Collard, Crop, and Lee 1995. Unless stated otherwise, translations of Homer's *Iliad* are from Lattimore 1951; of Herodotus, from Sélincourt 1972; of Thucydides, from Warner 1972, sometimes with slight modifications. Texts and translations of Athenaeus, Pausanias, and Theophrastus are from the Loeb Classical Library editions (respectively, Gulick 1928–1951; Jones, Ormerod, and Wycherley 1918–1935; and Hort 1916); of Pliny, from Jex Blake/Sellers, sometimes with slight modifications.

Adler, A. 1928–1938. *Suidae Lexicon*. Stuttgart.

Ahlberg, G. 1971. *Prothesis and Ekphora in Greek Geometric Art*. Göteborg.

Ajootian, A. 1996. "Praxiteles." In *Personal Styles in Greek Sculpture*, ed. O. Palagia and J. J. Pollitt. *YCS* 30. Cambridge: 91–129.

Akurgal, E. 1986. "Neue archaische Skulpturen aus Anatolien." In *Archaische und klassische griechische Plastik* I, ed. H. Kyrieleis. Mainz: 1–14.

Allen, T. W., and E. E. Sikes. 1904. *The Homeric Hymns*. London.

Andronicos, M. 1984. *Vergina: The Royal Tombs and the Ancient City*. Athens.

Armstrong, D., and A. E. Hanson. 1986. "Two Notes on Greek Tragedy." *BICS* 33: 97–100.

Armstrong, D., and E. A. Ratchford. 1985. "Iphigenia's Veil: Aeschylus, *Agamemnon* 228–248." *BICS* 32: 1–12.

Arnold-Biucchi, C. 1990. *The Randazzo Hoard 1980 and Sicilian Chronology in the Early Fifth Century B.C.* American Numismatic Society, Numismatic Studies 18. New York.

Austin, R. P. 1938. *The Stoichedon Style in Greek Inscriptions*. Oxford.

Autenrieth, G. 1982. *A Homeric Dictionary*. Trans. R. P. Keep, rev. I. Flagg. Norman, Okla.

Barber, E. J. W. 1991. *Prehistoric Textiles: The Development of Cloth in the Neolithic and Bronze Ages*. Princeton.

———. 1992. "The Peplos of Athena." In Neils 1992: 103–117.

Barlow, S. A. 1997. *Euripides Trojan Women*. Warminster, Wiltshire.

Bartman, E. 2001. "Hair and the Artifice of Roman Female Adornment." *AJA* 105: 1–25.

Baumann, H. 1993. *The Greek Plant World in Myth, Art, and Literature*. Trans. W. T. Stearn and E. R. Stearn. Portland, Ore.

Bekker, I. 1814. *Anecdota Graeca* I. Berlin.

Benediktson, D. T. 2000. *Literature and the Visual Arts in Ancient Greece and Rome*. Norman, Okla.

Biers, W. 1996. *The Archaeology of Greece: An Introduction*. 2nd ed. Ithaca, N.Y.

Blundell, M. W. 1989. *Helping Friends and Harming Enemies*. Cambridge.

Boardman, J. 1955. "Painted Funerary Plaques and Some Remarks on Prothesis." *BSA* 1: 51–66.

———. 1994. *The Diffusion of Classical Art in Antiquity*. Princeton.

———. 1999. *The Greeks Overseas: Their Early Colonies and Trade*. 4th ed. London.

Bolling, G. M. 1958. "*Poikilos* and *Throna*." *AJP* 79: 275–282.

Bosly, C. 1980. *Rugs to Riches*. New York.

Bremer, J. M. 1975. "The Meadow of Love and Two Passages in Euripides' *Hippolytus*." *Mnemosyne* 28: 268–280.

Brinkmann, V. 1994. *Beobachtungen zum formalen Aufbau und zum Sinngehalt der Friese des Siphnierschatzhauses*. Munich.

Brouskari, M. S. 1974. *The Acropolis Museum: A Descriptive Catalogue*. Trans. J. Binder. Athens.

Bundgaard, J. A. 1974. *The Excavation of the Athenian Acropolis, 1882–1890*. 2 vols. Copenhagen.

Burkert, W. 1992. *The Orientalizing Revolution: Near Eastern Influence on Greek Culture in the Early Archaic Age*. Trans. M. E. Pinder, W. Burkert. Cambridge, Mass.

Burnett, A. P. 1970. *Ion by Euripides*. Englewood Cliffs, N.J.

Butcher, S. H. 1951. *Aristotle's Theory of Poetry and Fine Art*. New York.

Cahn, H. A., and D. Gerin. 1988. "Themistocles at Magnesia." *NC* 48: 13–20.

Camp, J. M. 1994. "Before Democracy: Alkmaionidai and Peisistratidai." In Coulson et al. 1994: 7–12.

Campbell, D. A. 1982. *Greek Lyric*. 4 vols. Loeb Classical Library. Cambridge, Mass.

———. 1983. *The Golden Lyre: The Themes of the Greek Lyric Poets*. London.

Capel, A. K., and G. E. Markoe, eds. 1996. *Mistress of the House, Mistress of Heaven: Women in Ancient Egypt*. New York.

Carpenter, R. 1960. *Greek Sculpture*. Chicago.

Catling, H. 1973. "Archaeology in Greece, 1972–1973." *Archaeological Reports* 1972–1973: 3–32.

Cavvadias, P., and G. Kawerau. 1907. Ἡ Ἀνασκαφὴ τῆς Ἀκροπόλεως (*Die Ausgrabung der Akropolis*). Athens.

Charbonneaux, J., R. Martin, and F. Villard. 1971. *Archaic Greek Art, 620–480 B.C.* New York.

Childs, W. A. P. 1988. "The Classic as Realism in Greek Art." *Art Journal* 47: 10–14.

———. 1993. "Herodotos, Archaic Chronology, and the Temple of Apollo at Delphi," *JDI* 108: 399–441.

———. 1994. "The Date of the Old Temple of Athena on the Athenian Acropolis." In Coulson et al. 1994: 1–6.

———, ed. 1998. *Reading Greek Art: Essays by Nikolaus Himmelmann*. Princeton.

Clairmont, C. 1974. "Gravestone and Epigram." *AA* 89: 219–238.

Collard, C., M. J. Cropp, and K. H. Lee. 1995. *Euripides: Selected Fragmentary Plays* I. Warminster, Wiltshire.

Collignon, M. 1886. *A Manual of Greek Archaeology.* Trans. J. H. Wright. London.

———. 1892. *Histoire de la sculpture greque* I. Paris.

Connelly, J. B. 1996. "Parthenon and *Parthenoi:* A Mythological Interpretation of the Parthenon Frieze." *AJA* 100: 53–80.

Cook, A. B. 1965. *Zeus: A Study in Ancient Religion.* New York.

Coulson, W. D. E., O. Palagia, T. L. Shear Jr., H. A. Shapiro, and F. J. Frost, eds. 1994. *The Archaeology of Athens and Attica under the Democracy.* Oxbow Monograph 37. Oxford.

Crofton, I. 1988. *A Dictionary of Art Quotations.* New York.

Danforth, L. M. 1982. *The Death Rituals of Rural Greece.* Princeton.

Daux, G. 1973. "Les ambiguïtés du *grec* KORH." *Comptes rendus des séances de l'Académie des inscriptions et belles-lettres:* 382–393.

———. 1973–1974. "Sur quelques stèles funéraires grecques d'époque archaïque." *Archeologia classica* 25–26: 238–249.

Davies, W. V. 1990. "Egyptian Hieroglyphs." In *Reading the Past: Ancient Writing from Cuneiform to the Alphabet.* Berkeley: 75–135.

Davison, J. M. 1961. "Attic Geometric Workshops." *YCS* 16.

Day, J. W. 1989. "Rituals in Stone: Early Greek Grave Epigrams and Monuments." *JHS* 91: 16–28.

———. 1994. "Interactive Offerings: Early Greek Dedicatory Epigrams and Ritual." *HSCP* 96: 37–74.

Dazen, V. 1994. *Dwarfs in Ancient Egypt and Greece.* Oxford.

Denniston, J. D. 1954. *Euripides Electra.* Oxford.

———. 1966. *The Greek Particles.* Oxford.

Dickins, G. 1912. *Catalogue of the Acropolis Museum* I: *Archaic Sculpture.* Cambridge.

Diggle, J. 1970. *Euripides Phaethon.* Cambridge.

———. 1981–1994. *Euripidis Fabulae.* 3 vols. Oxford.

Dimitriou, P. 1947. *The Polychromy of Greek Sculpture to the Beginning of the Hellenistic Period.* Diss., Columbia University.

Dodds, E. R. 1960. *Euripides Bacchae.* Oxford.

D'Onofrio, A. M. 1982. "*Korai* e *Kouroi* funerari attici." *Annali dell'Istituto universitario orientale di Napoli. Departimento di studi del mondo classico e del Mediterraneo antico. Sezione di archeologia e storia antica* 4: 135–170.

Donohue, A. A. 1988. *"Xoana" and the Origins of Greek Sculpture.* American Classical Studies 15. Atlanta, Ga.

Dougherty, C., and L. Kurke, eds. 1998. *Cultural Poetics in Archaic Greece: Cult, Performance, Politics.* New York.

Doumas, C. G. 1983. *Thera, Pompeii of the Ancient Aegean.* London.

Dunbar, N. 1995. *Aristophanes Birds.* Oxford.

Ecker, U. 1990. *Grabmal und Epigramm.* Stuttgart.

Elderkin, K. M. 1936. "The Contribution of Women to Ornament in Antiquity." In *Classical Studies Presented to Edward Capps on His Seventieth Birthday.* Princeton: 124–143.

Else, G. F. 1958. "'Imitation' in the Fifth Century." *Classical Philology* 53: 73–90, 245.

Erman, A. 1971. *Life in Ancient Egypt.* Trans. H. M. Tirard. Orig. pub. 1894. New York.

Fairbanks, A. 1907. *Athenian Lekythoi with Outline Drawing in Glaze Varnish on a White Ground.* New York.

Floren, J. 1987. *Die geometrische und archaische Plastik* (in W. Fuchs/J. Floren. *Die griechische Plastik, 1.* Handbuch der Archäologie.) Munich.

Foley, H. P. 1992. "*Anodos* Dramas: Euripides' *Alcestis* and *Helen.*" In *Innovations of Antiquity,* ed. R. Hexter and D. Selden. New York: 133–160.

———. 1994. *The Homeric Hymn to Demeter.* Princeton.

Fornara, C. W., and L. J. Samons II. 1991. *Athens from Cleisthenes to Pericles.* Berkeley.

Fowler, B. H. 1983. "The Centaur's Smile: Pindar and the Archaic Aesthetic." In *Ancient Greek Art and Iconography,* ed. W. G. Moon. Madison, Wisc.: 159–170.

———. 1992. *Archaic Greek Poetry: An Anthology.* Madison, Wisc.

Fränkel, H. 1968. *Wege und Formen frühgriechischen Denkens.* Munich.

Frankfort, H. 1970. *The Art and Architecture of the Ancient Orient.* 4th ed. New Haven.

Frazer, J. G. 1965. *Pausanias' Description of Greece* III. New York.

Freeman, K. 1956. *Ancilla to the Pre-Socratic Philosophers.* Oxford.

Frel, J. 1973. "The Sculptor of the Kouros from Myrrhinous." *AAA* 6: 367–369.

———. 1981. *Greek Portraits in the J. Paul Getty Museum.* Malibu.

Gallavotti, C. 1979. *Metri e ritmi nelle iscrizioni greche.* Bollettino dei classici, Accademia Nazionale dei Lincei, suppl. 2. Rome.

Gardner, E. A. 1911. *A Handbook of Greek Sculpture.* London.

Garland, R. 1985. *The Greek Way of Death.* Ithaca, N.Y.

Garrod, H. W. 1972. *Keats Poetical Works.* Oxford.

Gauthier, P. 1966. "Le parallèle Himère-Salamine." *Revue des études anciennes* 68: 5–32.

Geffcken, J. 1916. *Griechische Epigramme.* Heidelberg.

Gentili, B. 1988. *Poetry and Its Public in Ancient Greece: From Homer to the Fifth Century.* Trans. A. T. Cole. Baltimore.

Goodwin, W. W. 1965. *Syntax of the Moods and Tenses of the Greek Verb.* London.

Goodyear, W. H. 1891. *The Grammar of the Lotus.* London.

Gow, A. S. F. 1965. *Theocritus.* 2 vols. Cambridge.

Gow, A. S. F., and D. L. Page. 1965. *The Greek Anthology: Hellenistic Epigrams.* 2 vols. Cambridge.

Graf, A. B. 1978. *Exotica: Pictorial Cyclopedia of Exotic Plants.* 9th ed. East Rutherford, N.J.

Graindor, P. 1938. "Parthénon et Corés." *Revue archéologique* 11: 193–211.

Grene, D., and R. Lattimore, eds. 1959. *The Complete Greek Tragedies,* vol. 3. Chicago.

Gulick, C. B. 1928–1951. *Athenaeus, the Deipnosophists.* 7 vols. Loeb Classical Library. Cambridge, Mass.

Gutzwiller, K. J. 1998. *Poetic Garlands: Hellenistic Epigrams in Context.* Berkeley.

Habicht, C. 1998. *Pausanias' Guide to Ancient Greece.* Berkeley.

Halliwell, S. 1989. "Aristotle's Poetics." In *The Cambridge History of Literary Criticism* I: *Classical Criticism,* ed. G. A. Kennedy. Cambridge: 149–183.

Hammond, N. G. L. 1992. *The Macedonian State.* Oxford.

Hammond, N. G. L., and G. T. Griffith. 1979. *A History of Macedonia* II: *550–336 B.C.* Oxford.

Harris, D. 1992. "Bronze Statues on the Athenian Acropolis." *AJA* 96: 637–652.

Harris, W. V. 1989. *Ancient Literacy.* Cambridge, Mass.

Harrison, C. M. 1982. *Coins of the Persian Satraps.* Diss., University of Pennsylvania.

Harrison, E. 1988a. "Sculpture in Stone." In Sweeney, Curry, and Tzedakis 1988: 50–54.

———. 1988b. "Greek Sculptured Coiffures and Ritual Haircuts." In *Early Greek Cult Practice. Proceedings of the Fifth International Symposium at the Swedish Institute at Athens, 26–29 June 1986,* ed. R. Hägg, N. Marinatos, and G. C. Nordquist. Stockholm: 247–254.

———. 1991. "The Dress of the Archaic Greek Korai." In *New Perspectives in Early Greek Art,* ed. D. Buitron-Oliver. Hanover: 217–239.

Havelock, C. M. 1981. "Mourners on Greek Vases: Remarks on the Social History of Women." In *The Greek Vase,* ed. S. L. Hyatt. Latham, N.Y.: 103–118.

Henderson, J. 1987. *Aristophanes Lysistrata.* Oxford.

Henig, M. 2000. "From Classical Greece to Roman Britain: Some Hellenic Themes in Provincial Art and Glyptics." In Tsetskhladze, Prag, and Snodgrass 2000: 124–135.

Heubeck, A., and A. Hoekstra. 1989. *A Commentary on Homer's Odyssey* II. Oxford.

Heubeck, A., S. West, and J. B. Hainsworth. 1990. *A Commentary on Homer's Odyssey* I. Oxford.

Himmelmann, N. 1994. *Realistische Themen in der griechischen Kunst der archaischen und klassischen Zeit.* Berlin.

Holloway, R. R. 1966. "The Archaic Acropolis and the Parthenon Frieze." *AB* 48: 223–226.

———. 1992. "Why Korai?" *OJA* 11: 267–274.

Homolle, T. 1890. "Comptes & inventaires des temples déliens en l'année 279." *BCH* 14: 389–511.

Hornblower, S. 1991. *A Commentary on Thucydides* I: *Books I–III.* Oxford.

Hornung, E. 1990. *The Valley of the Kings: Horizon of Eternity.* New York.

Hort, A. 1916. *Theophrastus Enquiry into Plants* II. Loeb Classical Library. Cambridge, Mass.

How, W. W., and J. Wells. 1912. *A Commentary on Herodotus.* 2 vols. Oxford.

Humphreys, S. C. 1980. "Family Tombs and Tomb Cult in Ancient Athens: Tradition or Traditionalism?" *JHS* 100: 96–126.

Hurwit, J. M. 1985. *The Art and Culture of Early Greece, 1100–480 B.C.* Ithaca, N.Y.

———. 1999. *The Athenian Acropolis: History, Mythology, and Archaeology from the Neolithic Era to the Present.* Cambridge.

Hyde, W. W. 1921. *Olympic Victor Monuments and Greek Athletic Art.* Washington, D.C.

Immerwahr, H. R. 1990. *Attic Script: A Survey.* Oxford.

Irwin, E. 1974. *Colour Terms in Greek Poetry.* Toronto.

Isager, J. 1991. *Pliny on Art and Society.* London.

Iversen, E. 1993. *The Myth of Egypt and Its Hieroglyphs.* Princeton.

Jacobsthal, P. 1906. *Der Blitz in der orientalischen und griechischen Kunst.* Berlin.

James, T. G. H. 1979. *An Introduction to Ancient Egypt.* New York.

Jebb, R. C. 1894. *Sophocles, the Plays and Fragments,* VI: *The Electra.* Cambridge.

Jeffery, L. H. 1962. "The Inscribed Gravestones of Archaic Attica." *BSA* 57: 115–153.

———. 1990. *The Local Scripts of Archaic Greece.* Rev. ed. with a suppl. by A. W. Johnston. Oxford.

Jex-Blake/Sellers = Jex-Blake, K., trans., with commentary and historical introduction by E. Sellers, *The Elder Pliny's Chapters on the History of Art.* Repr. with preface by R. V. Schoder. Chicago, Ill., 1976.

Jones, C. P. 1986. *Culture and Society in Lucian.* Cambridge, Mass.

Jones, W. H. S., H. A. Ormerod, and R. E. Wycherley. 1918–1935. *Pausanias, Description of Greece.* 5 vols. Loeb Classical Library. Cambridge, Mass.

Kannicht, R. 1969. *Euripides Helena.* 2 vols. Heidelberg.

Karakasi, E. 1997. "Die prachtvolle Erscheinung der Phrasikleia." *Antike Welt* 28: 509–517.

Karo, G. 1948. *Greek Personality in Archaic Sculpture.* Martin Classical Lectures XI. Cambridge, Mass.

Kassel, R. 1983. "Dialoge mit Statuen." *ZPE* 51: 1–12.

Keesling, C. M. 1995. *Monumental Private Votive Dedications on the Athenian Acropolis, ca. 600–400 B.C.* Diss., University of Michigan.

Kelly, T. 1976. *A History of Argos to 500 B.C.* Minneapolis, Minn.

Keuls, E. C. 1997. "Skiagraphia Once Again." In E. C. Keuls, *Painter and Poet in Ancient Greece: Iconography and the Literary Arts.* Stuttgart: 107–144. Orig. publ. in *AJA* 79 [1975]: 1–16.

Kissas, K. 2000. *Die attischen Statuen- und Stelenbasen archaischer Zeit.* Bonn.

Knauer, E. R. 1992. "Mitra and Kerykeion: Some Reflections on Symbolic Attributes in the Art of the Classical Period." *AA:* 373–399.

Koch-Harnack, G. 1989. *Erotische Symbole: Lotosblüte und gemeinsamer Mantel auf antiken Vasen.* Berlin.

Kontoleon, N. M. 1970. *Aspects de la Grèce préclassique.* Paris.

———. 1974. "Περὶ τὸ σῆμα τῆς Φρασίκλειας." *ArchEph:* 1–12.

Kontos, N. 1983. "From a Photographer's Scrapbook." *Zygos* 2: 190–195.

Kozloff, A. P., and B. M. Bryan, with L. M. Berman. 1992. *Egypt's Dazzling Sun: Amenhotep III and His World.* Cleveland, Ohio.

Kraay, C. M., and M. Hirmer. 1966. *Greek Coins.* London.

Kubler, K. 1970. *Die Nekropole des späten 8. bis frühen 6. Jahrhunderts (Kerameikos* VI.1.2). Berlin.

Kurke, L. 1998. "The Economy of *Kudos.*" In Dougherty and Kurke 1998: 131–163.

———. 1999. *Coins, Bodies, Games, and Gold: The Politics of Meaning in Archaic Greece.* Princeton.

Kurtz, D. C. 1975. *Athenian White Lekythoi: Patterns and Painters.* Oxford.

Kurtz, D. C., and J. Boardman. 1971. *Greek Burial Customs.* Ithaca, N.Y.

Langlotz, E. 1969 [1939]. "Die Koren." In *AMA* 3–184.

Langlotz, E., and M. Hirmer. 1963. *Die Kunst der Westgriechen in Sizilien und Unteritalien.* Munich.

Latte, K. 1953–1966. *Hesychii Alexandrini Lexicon.* 2 vols. Hauniae.

Lattimore, R. 1951. *The Iliad of Homer.* Chicago.

Leaf, W. 1886–1888. *The Iliad.* 2 vols. London.

Lechat, H. 1890. "Observations sur les statues archaïques de type féminin du Musée de l'Acropole." *BCH* 14: 301–362 and 552–586.

———. 1903. *Au Musée de l'Acropole d'Athènes: Études sur la sculpture en Attique avant la ruine de l'Acropole lors de l'invasion de Xerxès.* Lyon.

———. 1904. *La sculpture attique avant Phidias.* Paris.

Lee, K. H. 1997. *Euripides Troades.* London.

Leipen, N. 1971. *Athena Parthenos: A Reconstruction.* Toronto.

Lermann, W. 1907. *Altgriechische Plastik: Eine Einführung in die griechische Kunst des archaischen und gebundenen Stils.* Munich.

Lessing, G. E. 1962. *Laocoön: An Essay on the Limits of Painting and Poetry.* Trans. E. A. McCormick. Baltimore.

Lilja, S. 1972. *The Treatment of Odours in the Poetry of Antiquity.* Societas Scientiarum Fennica, Commentationes Humanarum Litterarum 49. Helsinki.

Lobel, E., and D. Page. 1963. *Poetarum Lesbiorum Fragmenta.* Oxford.

Loraux, N. 1993. *The Children of Athena: Athenian Ideas about Citizenship and the Division between the Sexes.* Trans. C. Levine. Princeton.

Lullies, R., and M. Hirmer. 1956. *Griechische Plastik.* Munich.

Manzelli, V. 1994. *La policromia nella statuaria greca arcaica.* Studia Archaeologica 69. Rome.

Mastrokostas, E. I. 1972. "Ἡ κόρη Φρασίκλεια Ἀριστίωνος τοῦ Παρίου καὶ κοῦρος μαρμάρινος ἀνεκαλύφθησαν ἐν Μυρρινοῦντι." *AAA* 5: 298–324.

Mastronarde, D. J. 1994. *Euripides: Phoenissae.* Cambridge.

Matt, L. von, and U. Zanotti-Bianco. 1967. *Magna Graecia.* New York.

Mattingly, H. B. 1992. "The Damareteion Controversy—A New Approach." *Chiron* 22: 1–11.

Maxwell-Stuart, P. G. 1981. "Studies in Greek Colour Terminology." (1: "Glaukos" and 2: "Charapos."). *Mnemosyne,* suppls. 65 and 67. Leiden.

Merkelbach, R., and M. L. West. 1967. *Fragmenta Hesiodea.* Oxford.

Michalowski, K. n.d. *Art of Ancient Egypt.* New York.

Miller, M. C. 1999. "Reexamining Transvestism in Archaic and Classical Athens: The Zewadski Stamnos." *AJA* 103: 223–253.

Miller, W. 1929. *Daedalus and Thespis: The Contributions of the Ancient Dramatic Poets to Our Knowledge of the Arts and Crafts of Greece.* 3 vols. New York.

Möller, A. 2000. *Naukratis: Trade in Archaic Greece.* Oxford.

Morris, S. P. 1992. *Daidalos and the Origins of Greek Art.* Princeton.

Morrow, K. D. 1985. *Greek Footwear and the Dating of Sculpture.* Madison, Wisc.

Mourelatos, A. P. D. 1973. "Heraclitus, Parmenides, and the Naïve Metaphysics of Things." In *Exegesis and Argument: Studies in Greek Philosophy Presented to Gregory Vlastos,* ed. E. N. Lee, A. P. D. Mourelatos, and R. M. Rorty. Assen, the Netherlands: 16–48.

Murr, J. 1890. *Die Phlanzenwelt in der griechischen Mythologie.* Innsbruck.

Murray, O. 1983. *Early Greece.* Stanford, Calif.

Nagy, G. 1994. "The Name of Apollo: Etymology and Essence." In *Apollo: Origins and Influences,* ed. J. Solomon. Tucson, Ariz.: 3–7.

———. 1996. *Homeric Questions.* Austin.

Napier, A. D. 1986. *Masks, Transformation, and Paradox.* Berkeley.

Neils, J., ed. 1992. *Goddess and Polis: The Panathenaic Festival in Ancient Athens.* Princeton.

Neumann, G. 1979. "Zum Verhältnis von Grabdenkmal und Grabinschrift in der archaischen und klassischen Zeit Griechenlands." In *Wort und Bild,* ed. H. Brunner, R. Kannicht, and K. Schwager. Munich: 219–235.

Oakley, J. H., and R. H. Sinos. 1993. *The Wedding in Ancient Athens.* Madison, Wisc.

Ober, J., and B. Strauss. 1990. "Drama, Political Rhetoric, and the Discourse of Athenian Democracy." In *Nothing to Do with Dionysos? Athenian Drama in Its Social Context,* ed. J. J. Winkler and F. I. Zeitlin. Princeton: 237–270.

Oldfather, C. H. 1946. *Diodorus of Sicily* I. Loeb Classical Library. Cambridge, Mass.

Osborne, R. 1994. "Looking on—Greek Style: Does the Sculpted Girl Speak to Women Too?" In *Classical Greece: Ancient Histories and Modern Archaeologies,* ed. I. Morris. Cambridge: 81–96.

Owen, A. S. 1939. *Euripides Ion.* Oxford.

Page, D. L. 1955. *Euripides Medea.* Oxford.

Parke, H. W. 1977. *Festivals of the Athenians.* Ithaca, N.Y.

Parkinson, R. B. 1991. *Voices from Ancient Egypt: An Anthology of Middle Kingdom Writings.* Norman, Okla.

Parrot, A. 1961. *Sumer: The Dawn of Art.* Trans. S. Gilbert, J. Emmons. New York.

Payne, H. 1931. *Necrocorinthia: A Study of Corinthian Art in the Archaic Period.* Oxford.

Payne, H., and G. M. Young. 1936. *Archaic Marble Sculpture from the Acropolis.* Rev. ed. 1950. London.

Peck, W. H. 1978. *Egyptian Drawings.* New York.

Pedley, J. G. 1976. *Greek Sculpture of the Archaic Period: The Island Workshops.* Mainz.

Podlecki, A. J. 1984. *The Early Greek Poets and Their Times.* Vancouver.

Pollitt, J. J. 1990. *The Art of Ancient Greece: Sources and Documents.* Cambridge.

Powell, J. E. 1939. "Τράχηλος 'Head.'" *CR* 53: 58.

Quirke, S., and J. Spencer, eds. 1992. *The British Museum Book of Ancient Egypt.* London.

Raymond, D. 1953. *Macedonian Regal Coinage to 413 B.C.* American Numismatic Society, Numismatic Notes and Monographs 126. New York.

Reeder, E. D. 1995. *Pandora: Women in Classical Greece.* Baltimore, Md.

Rehm, R. 1994. *Marriage to Death: The Conflation of Wedding and Funeral Rituals in Greek Tragedy.* Princeton.

Reilly, J. 1989. "Many Brides: 'Mistress and Maid' on Athenian Lekythoi." *Hesperia* 56: 411–444.

Reuterswärd, P. 1960. *Studien zur Polychromie der Plastik.* Stockholm.

Richardson, N. J. 1974. *The Homeric Hymn to Demeter.* Oxford.

Richter, G. M. A. 1928–1929. "Were the Nude Parts in Greek Marble Sculpture Painted?" *Metropolitan Museum Studies* 1: 25–31.

———. 1961. *The Archaic Gravestones of Attica.* London.

———. 1968. *Korai, Archaic Greek Maidens: A Study of the Development of the Kore Type in Greek Sculpture.* London.

———. 1969. *A Handbook of Greek Art.* 6th ed. London.

———. 1970a. *Kouroi, Archaic Greek Youths: A Study of the Development of the Kouros Type in Greek Sculpture.* 3rd ed. London.

———. 1970b. *The Sculpture and Sculptors of the Greeks.* Rev. 4th ed. New Haven.

Richter/Smith = G. M. A. Richter. *The Portraits of the Greeks.* Abr. and rev. R. R. R. Smith. Ithaca, N.Y., 1984.

Ridgway, B. S. 1977. "The Peplos Kore, Akropolis 679." *Journal of the Walters Art Gallery* 36: 49–61.

———. 1982. "Of Kouroi and Korai—Attic Variety." In *Studies in Athenian Architecture, Sculpture, and Topography Presented to Homer A. Thompson. Hesperia,* suppl. 20: 118–127.

———. 1985. "Late Archaic Sculpture." In *Greek Art: Archaic into Classical,* ed. C. G. Boulter. Leiden: 1–17.

———. 1990. "Birds, 'Meniskoi,' and Head Attributes in Archaic Greece." *AJA* 94: 583–612.

———. 1992. "Images of Athena on the Akropolis." In Neils 1992: 119–142.

———. 1993. *The Archaic Style in Greek Sculpture.* 2nd ed. Chicago, Ill.

Robertson, D. S. 1929. *A Handbook of Greek and Roman Architecture.* Cambridge.

Robertson, M. 1975. *A History of Greek Art.* 2 vols. Cambridge.

———. 1992. *The Art of Vase-Painting in Classical Athens.* Cambridge.

Robins, G. 2001. *Egyptian Statues.* Haverfordwest, Pembrokeshire.

Roccos, L. J. 1995. "The Kanephoros and Her Festival Mantle in Greek Art." *AJA* 99: 641–666.

Rohner, D. D. 1993. *A Study of the Hair Styles on Greek Korai and Other Female Figures from 650–480 B.C.: A Dating Tool to Clarify Workshops, Regional Styles, and Chronology.* Diss., University of Colorado.

Rolley, C. 1994. *La sculpture grecque: Des origines au milieu du Ve siècle.* Paris.

Rosen, R. M. 1988. "Hipponax, Boupalos, and the Conventions of the *Psogos.*" *TAPA* 118: 29–41.

Rothschild, D. M. 1991. *Picasso's "Parade."* London.

Rubin, W. 1989. *Picasso and Braque: Pioneering Cubism.* New York.

Rutter, N. K. 1983. *Greek Coinage.* Aylesbury.

Saleh, M., and H. Sourouzian. 1987. *Official Catalog: The Egyptian Museum Cairo.* Mainz.

Schäfer, H. 1986 [1919]. *The Principles of Egyptian Art.* Ed. E. Brunner-Traut and J. Baines. Trans. J. Baines. Oxford.

Schefold, K. 1973. "Neue Funde und Forschungen." *Antike Kunst* 16: 155–158.

Scheid, J., and J. Svenbro. 1996. *The Craft of Zeus: Myths of Weaving and Fabric.* Cambridge, Mass.

Schmidt, M. 1965. *Hesychii Alexandrini Lexicon.* Amsterdam.

Schneider, L. A. 1975. *Zur sozialen Bedeutung der archaischen Korenstatuen.* Hamburg.

Seaford, R. 1997. *Euripides Bacchae.* Warminster, Wiltshire.

Sélincourt, A. de. 1972. *Herodotus, the Histories.* Hammondsworth, Middlesex.

Serwint, N. 1993. "The Female Athletic Costume at the Heraia and Prenuptial Initiation Rites." *AJA* 97: 403–422.

Shapiro, H. A. 1991. "The Iconography of Mourning in Athenian Art." *AJA* 95: 629–656.

———. 1994a. *Myth into Art: Poet and Painter in Classical Greece.* London.

———. 1994b. "Religion and Politics in Democratic Athens." In Coulson et al. 1994: 123–129.

Simon, E. M., and A. Hirmer. 1981. *Die griechischen Vasen.* Munich.

Sinos, R. H. 1998. "Divine Selection: Epiphany and Politics in Archaic Greece." In Dougherty and Kurke 1998: 73–91.

Sissa, G. 1990. *Greek Virginity.* Cambridge, Mass.

Smith, W. S. 1990. *The Art and Architecture of Ancient Egypt.* Repr. of the 2nd [integrated] ed., rev. W. K. Simpson. London.

Snell, B., and H. Maehler. 1970. *Bacchylidis Carmina cum Fragmentis.* Leipzig.

———. 1987. *Pindari Carmina cum Fragmentis, pars I: Epinicia.* Leipzig.

Sourvinou-Inwood, C. 1995. *"Reading" Greek Death: To the End of the Classical Period.* Oxford.

Stanford, W. B. 1942. *Aeschylus in His Style: A Study in Language and Personality.* Dublin.

Steiner, D. 1993. "Pindar's 'oggetti parlanti.'" *HSCP* 95: 159–180.

Stewart, A. F. 1976. "Aristion." *AAA* 9: 257–266.

———. 1990. *Greek Sculpture: An Exploration.* 2 vols. New Haven.

———. 1997. *Art, Desire, and the Body in Ancient Greece.* Cambridge.

Stieber, M. 1992. *Realism in Greek Art of the Archaic Period.* Diss., Princeton University.

———. 1994. "Aeschylus' *Theoroi* and Realism in Greek Art." *TAPA* 124: 85–119.

———. 1996. "Phrasikleia's Lotuses." *Boreas* 19: 69–99.

———. 1999a. "A Note on A. *Ag.* 410–428 and E. *Alc.* 347–356." *Mnemosyne* ser. iv: 150–158.

———. 1999b. "'Clear Messengers, Voiceless Heralds': The Verbally Encoded Object in Greek Literature and Art." *Annals of Scholarship* 13: 37–48.

Studniczka, F. 1886. *Beiträge zur Geschichte der altgriechischen Tracht.* Vienna.

Stulz, H. 1990. *Die Farbe Purpur im frühen Griechentum.* Stuttgart.

Sturgis, R. 1890. "Recent Discoveries of Painted Greek Sculpture." *Harper's New Monthly Magazine* 81: 538–550.

Summers, D. 1978. "David's Scowl." In *Collaboration in Italian Renaissance Art*, ed. W. S. Sheard and J. T. Paoletti. New Haven: 113–120.

———. 1981. *Michelangelo and the Language of Art*. Princeton.

Svenbro, J. 1993. *Phrasikleia: An Anthropology of Reading in Ancient Greece*. Trans. J. Lloyd. Ithaca, N.Y.

Thalmann, W. G. 1988. "Thersites: Comedy, Scapegoats, and Heroic Ideology in the *Iliad*." *TAPA* 118: 1–28.

Theodossiev, N. 1998. "The Dead with Golden Faces: Dasaretian, Pelagonian, Mygdonian, and Boeotian Funeral Masks." *OJA* 17: 345–367.

Thomas, R. 1992. *Literacy and Orality in Ancient Greece*. Cambridge.

Travlos, J. 1988. *Bildlexikon zur Topographie des antiken Attika*. Tübingen.

Trumpf, J. 1973. "Über das Trinken in der Poesie des Alkaios." *ZPE* 12: 139–160.

Tsetskhladze, G. R., A. J. N. W. Prag, and A. M. Snodgrass, eds. 2000. *Periplous: Papers on Classical Art and Archaeology Presented to Sir John Boardman*. London.

Vatin, C. 1982. "Monuments votifs de Delphes." *BCH* 106: 509–525.

Viviers, D. 1992. *Recherches sur les ateliers de sculpteurs et la cité d'Athènes à l'époque archaïque: Endoios, Philergos, Aristoklès*. Académie Royale de Belgique, Classe des Beaux-Arts. Brussels.

von Bothmer, D. 1985. *The Amasis Painter and His World: Vase-Painting in Sixth-Century B.C. Athens*. Malibu.

Wagner, C. 2000. "The Potters and Athena: Dedications on the Athenian Acropolis." In Tsetskhladze, Prag, and Snodgrass 2000: 383–387.

Wallace, M. B. 1970. "Notes on Early Greek Grave Epigrams." *Phoenix* 24: 95–105.

Walter-Karydi, E. 1985. "Geneleos." *AM* 100: 91–104.

Warner, R. 1972. *Thucydides History of the Peloponnesian War*. Hammondsworth, Middlesex.

Webster, T. B. L. 1960. "Notes on the Writing of Early Greek Poetry." *Glotta* 38: 251–263.

West, M. L. 1966. *Hesiod Theogony*. Oxford.

———. 1985. *The Hesiodic Catalogue of Women*. Oxford.

———. 1993. *Greek Lyric Poetry*. Oxford.

Wilkinson, R. H. 1992. *Reading Egyptian Art: A Hieroglyphic Guide to Ancient Egyptian Painting and Sculpture*. London.

Williams, D., and J. Ogden. 1994. *Greek Gold: Jewelry of the Classical World*. New York.

Wilson, J. A. 1947. "The Artist of the Egyptian Old Kingdom." *Journal of Near Eastern Studies* 6: 231–249.

Winter, F. 1887. "Zur Altattischen Kunst." *JDI* 2: 217–237.

———. 1894. *Über die Griechische Porträtkunst*. Berlin.

Wycherley, R. E. 1957. *The Athenian Agora* III: *Literary and Epigraphical Testimonia*. Princeton.

Zanker, G. 2000. "Aristotle's *Poetics* and the Painters." *AJP* 121: 225–235.

Zanker, P. 1988. *The Power of Images in the Age of Augustus*. Ann Arbor.

Zapheiropoulou, P. 1973. "A Grave Stele from Amorgos." *AAA* 6: 351–355.

Zauzich, K.-T. 1992. *Hieroglyphs without Mystery*. Austin.

Zschietzschmann, W. 1928. "Die Darstellung der Prothesis in der griechischen Kunst." *AM* 53: 17–47.

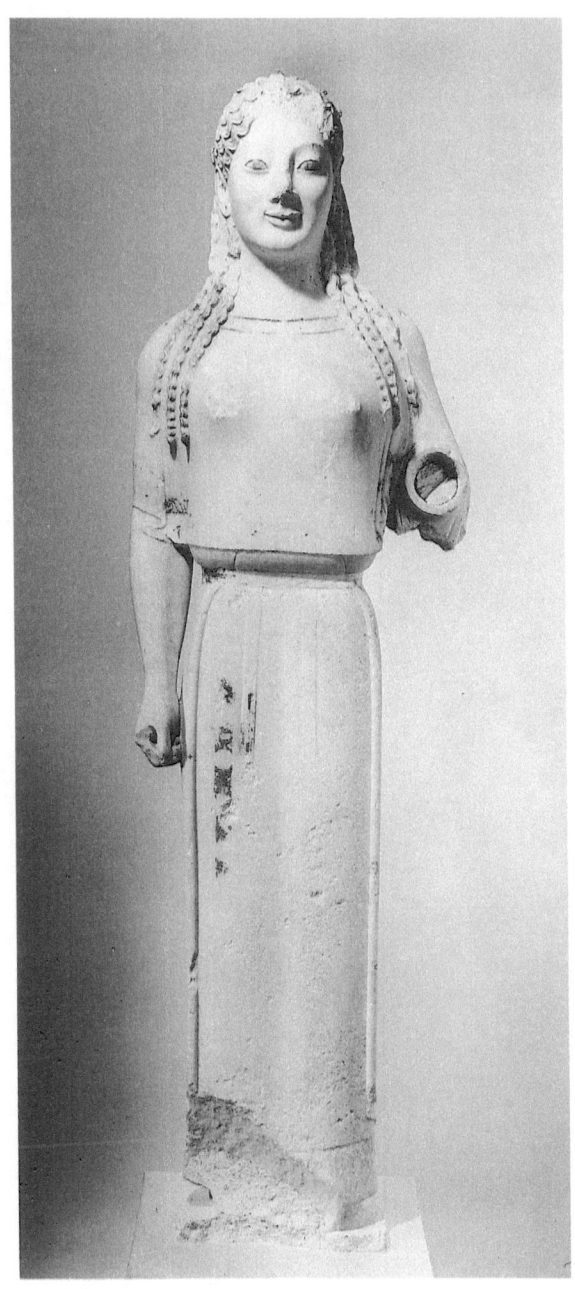

Figure 1. Acropolis Museum 679 ("Peplos Kore"), kore from the Acropolis of Athens, marble. Photo courtesy of the Alison Frantz Collection, American School of Classical Studies at Athens, neg. no. AT 359.

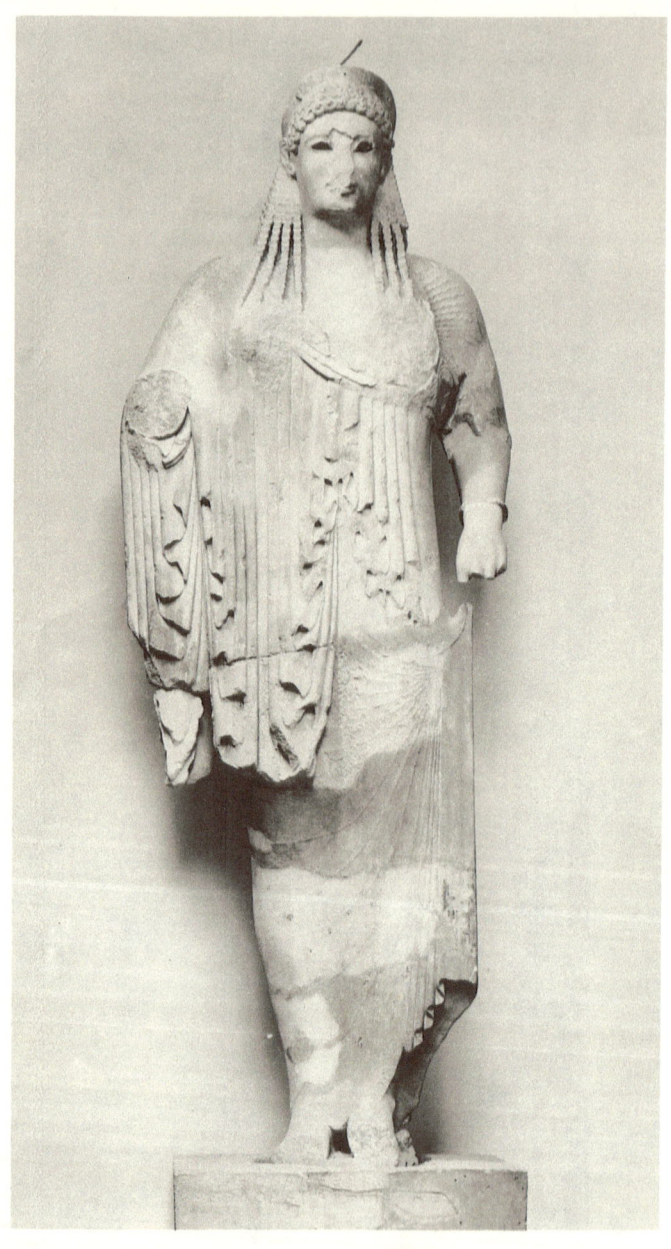

Figure 2. Acropolis Museum 681 ("Antenor's Kore"), kore from the Acropolis of Athens, marble. Photo by Wagner courtesy of the DAI (Deutsches Archäologisches Institut), Athens, neg. no. Akr. 1674.

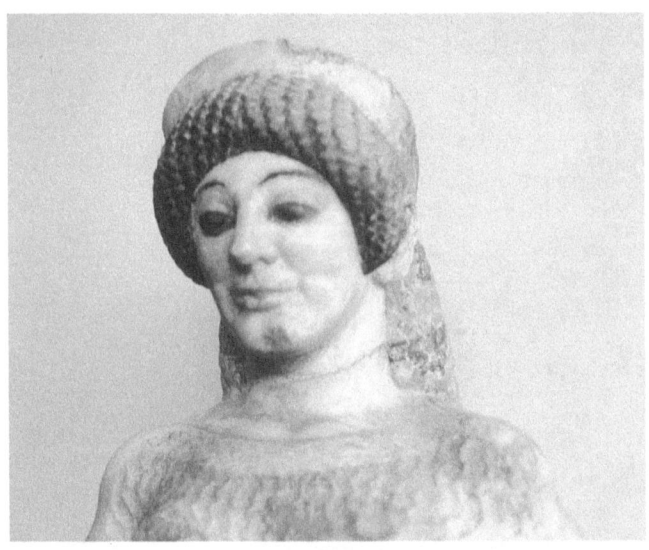

*Figure 3. Acropolis Museum 683 (**detail**), kore from the Acropolis of Athens, marble. Photo: author.*

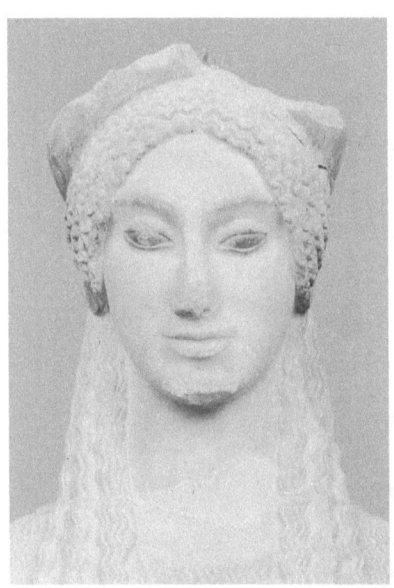

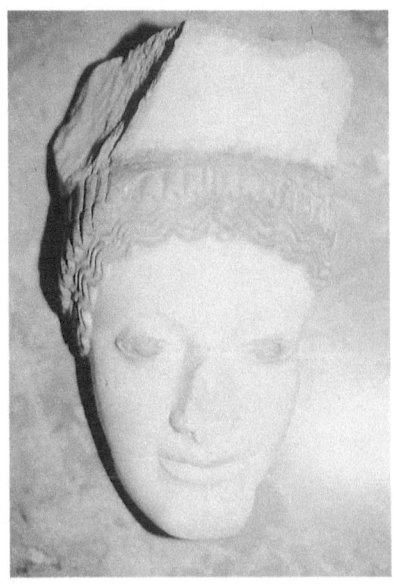

*Figure 4. Acropolis Museum 674 (**detail**), kore from the Acropolis of Athens, marble. Photo courtesy of the Hellenic Republic Ministry of Culture, Archaeological Receipts Fund (TAP Service).*

Figure 5. Acropolis Museum 696, head of kore from the Acropolis of Athens, marble. Photo: author.

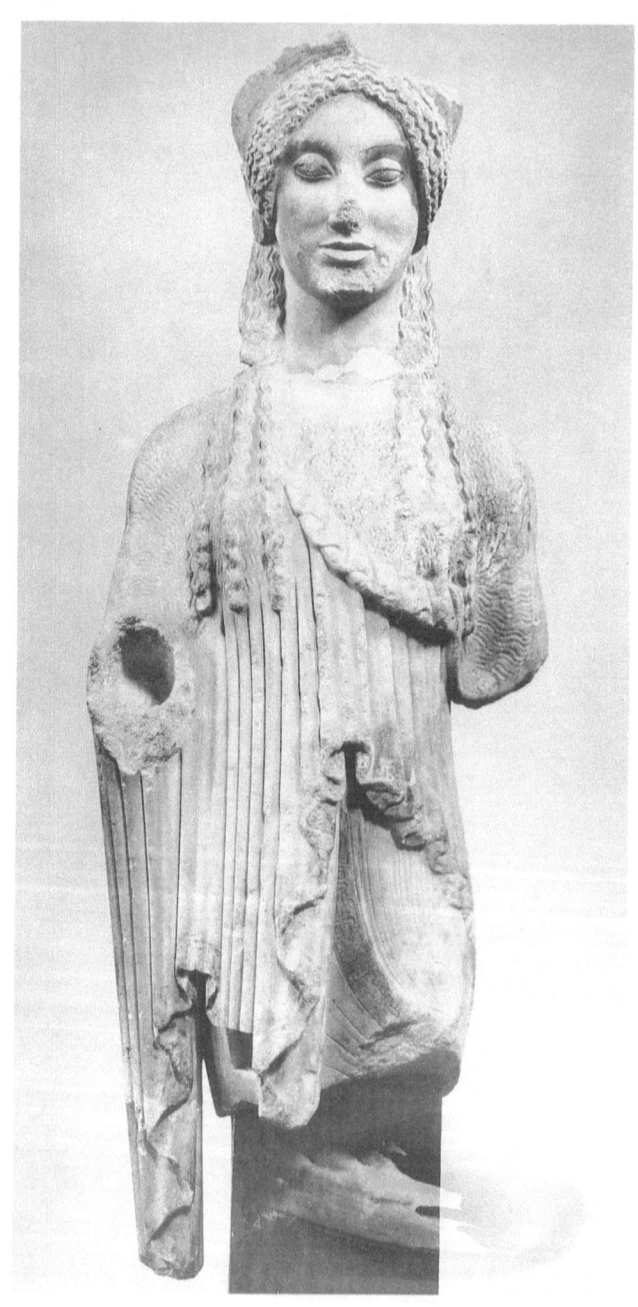

Figure 6. Acropolis Museum 674. Photo by Wagner courtesy of the DAI, Athens, neg. no. Akr. 1794.

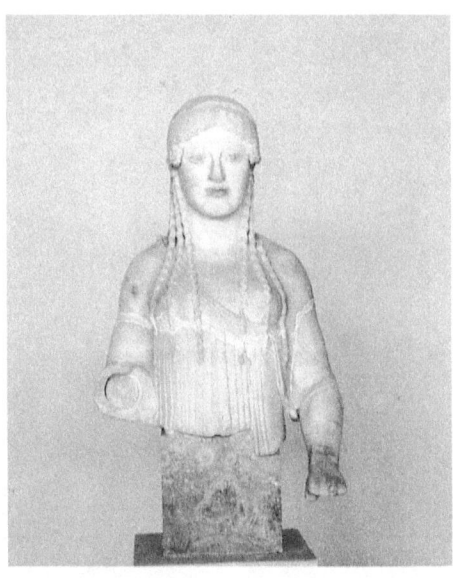

Figure 7. Acropolis Museum 686 ("Euthydikos' Kore"), kore from the Acropolis of Athens, marble. Photo: author.

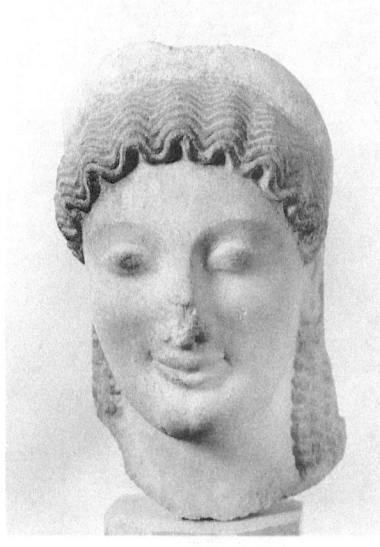

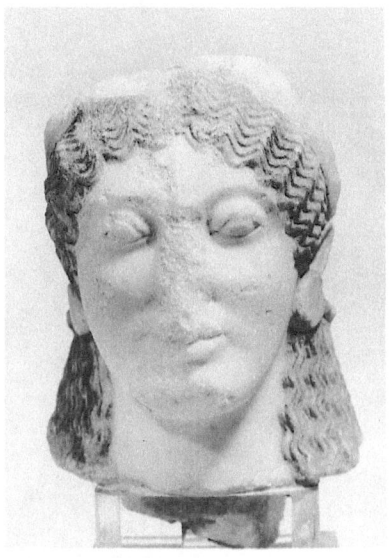

Figure 8. Acropolis Museum 616, head of kore from the Acropolis of Athens, marble. Photo courtesy of the Alison Frantz Collection, American School of Classical Studies at Athens, neg. no. AT 501.

Figure 9. Acropolis Museum 661, head of kore from the Acropolis of Athens, marble. Photo courtesy of the Alison Frantz Collection, American School of Classical Studies at Athens, neg. no. AT 504.

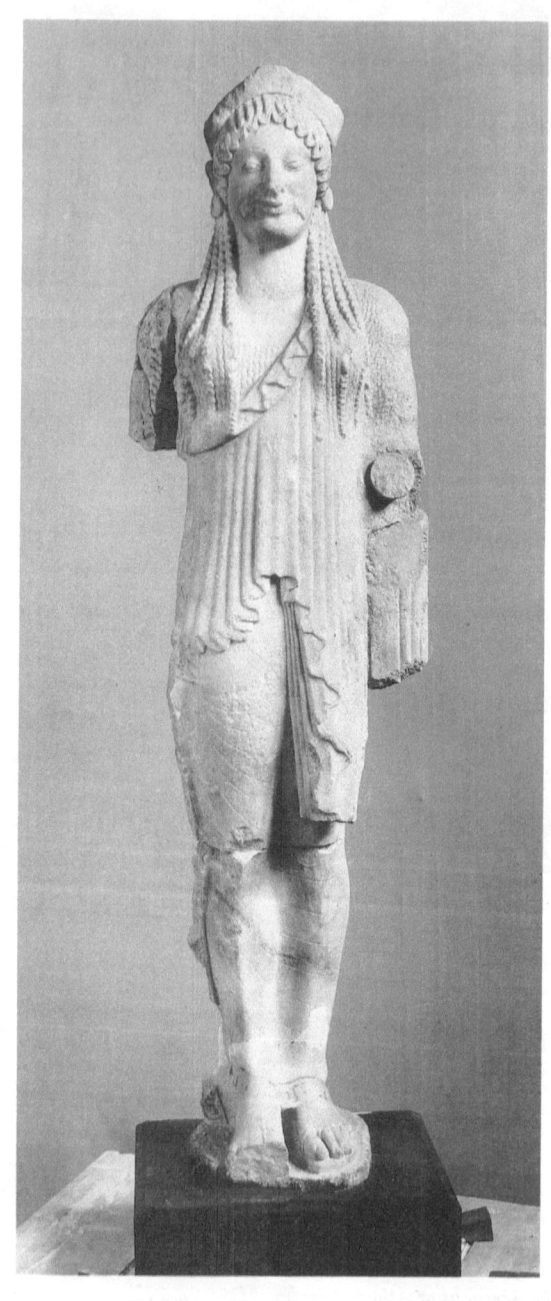

Figure 10. Acropolis Museum 672,
kore from the Acropolis of Athens, marble.
Photo by Schrader courtesy of the DAI, Athens, neg. no. Schrader 46.

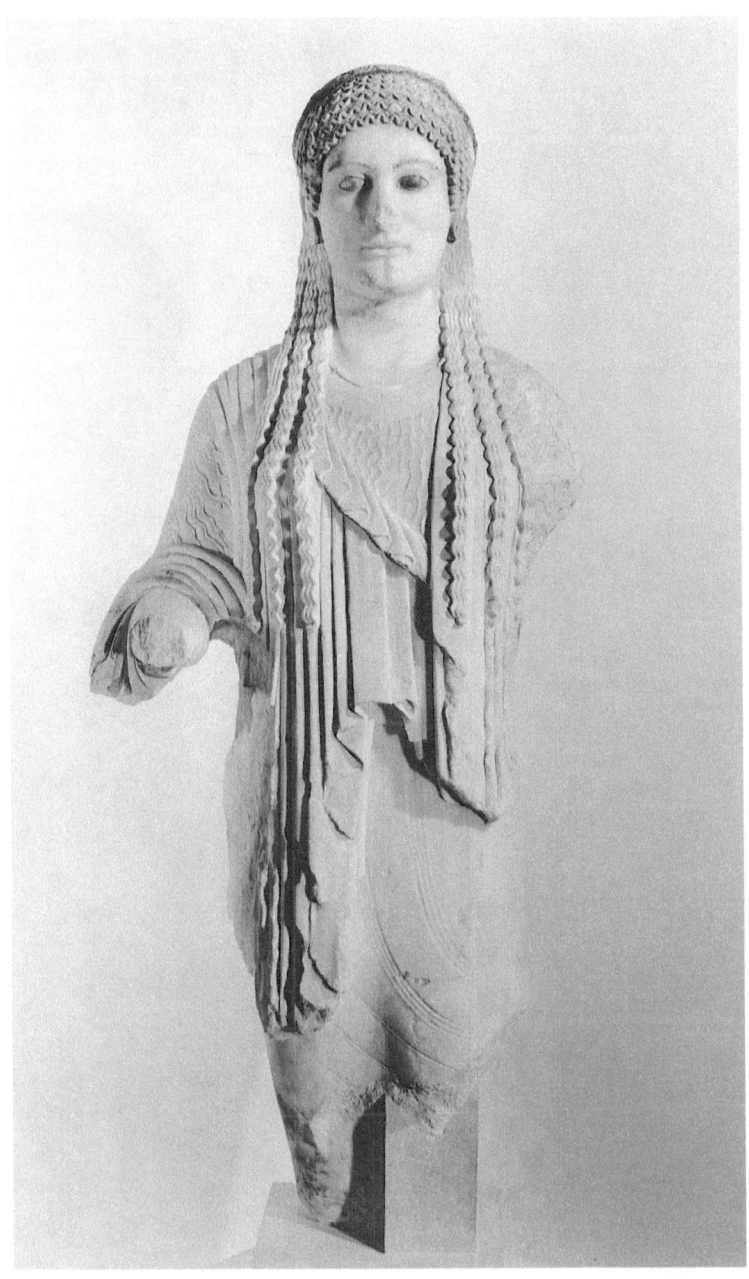

*Figure 11. Acropolis Museum 684, kore from the Acropolis of Athens, marble.
Photo courtesy of the Alison Frantz Collection,
American School of Classical Studies at Athens, neg. no. AT 524.*

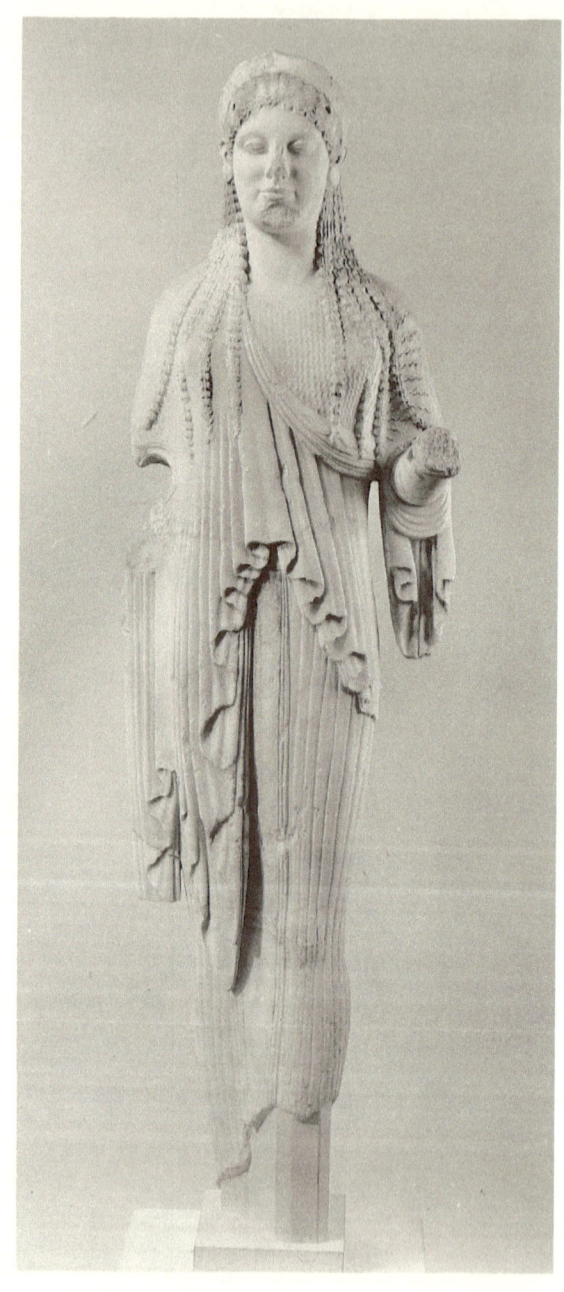

*Figure 12. Acropolis Museum 685, kore from the Acropolis of Athens, marble.
Photo courtesy of the Alison Frantz Collection,
American School of Classical Studies at Athens, neg. no. AT 521.*

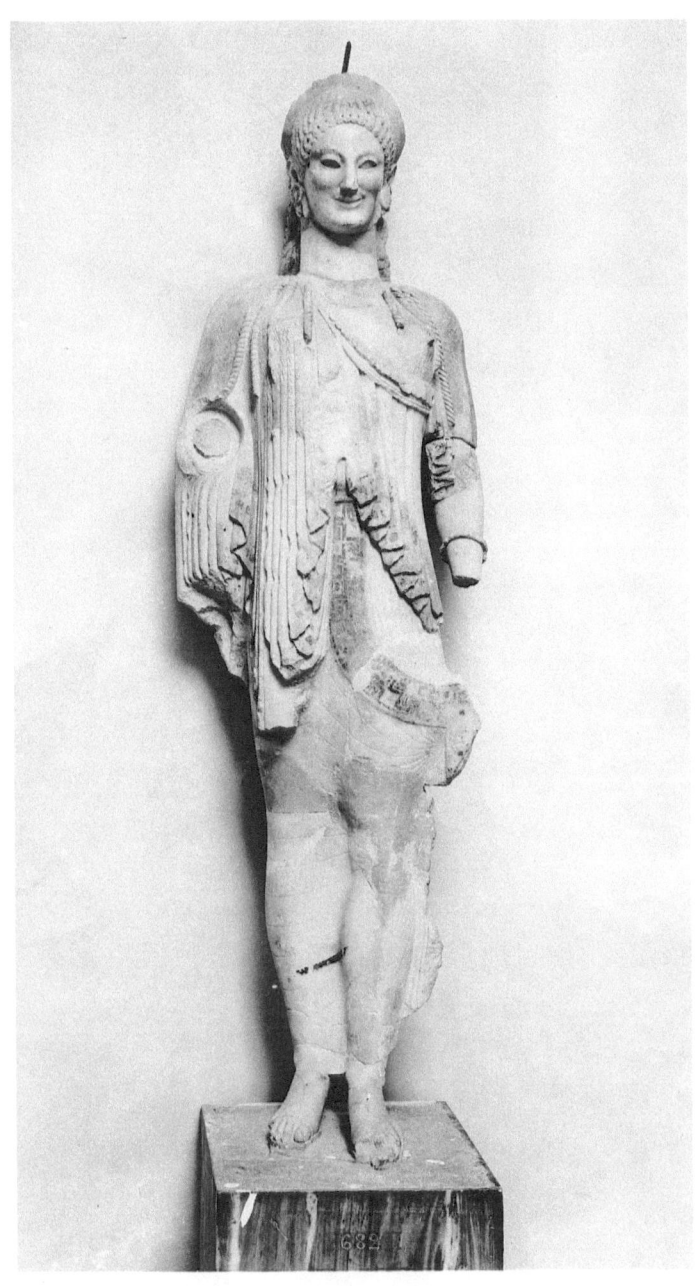

Figure 13. Acropolis Museum 682,
kore from the Acropolis of Athens, marble.
Photo by Wagner courtesy of the DAI, Athens, neg. no. Akr. 1670.

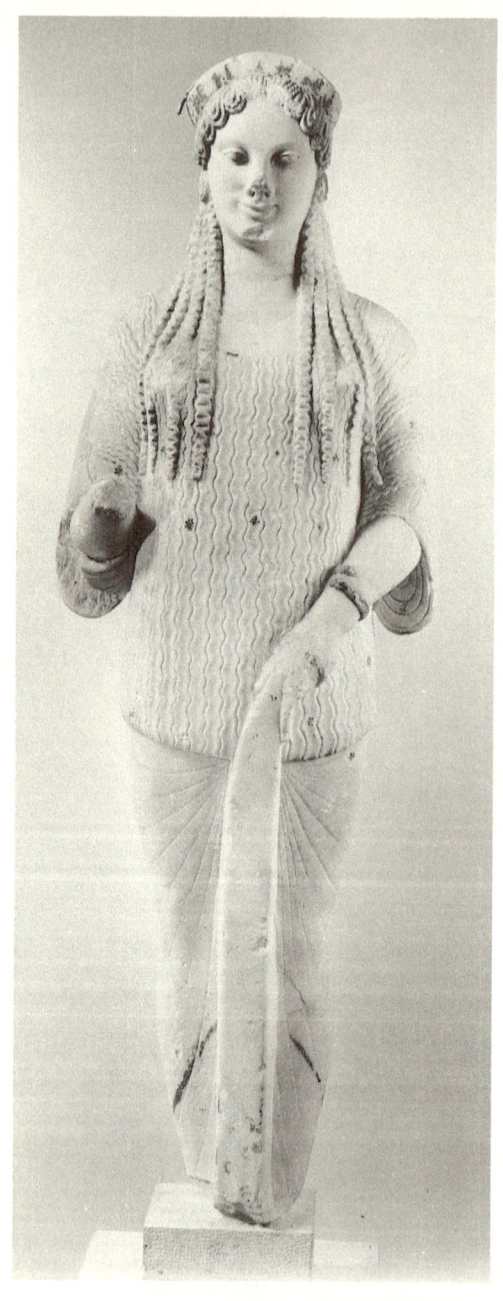

*Figure 14. Acropolis Museum 670, kore from the Acropolis of Athens, marble.
Photo courtesy of the Alison Frantz Collection,
American School of Classical Studies at Athens, neg. no. AT 467.*

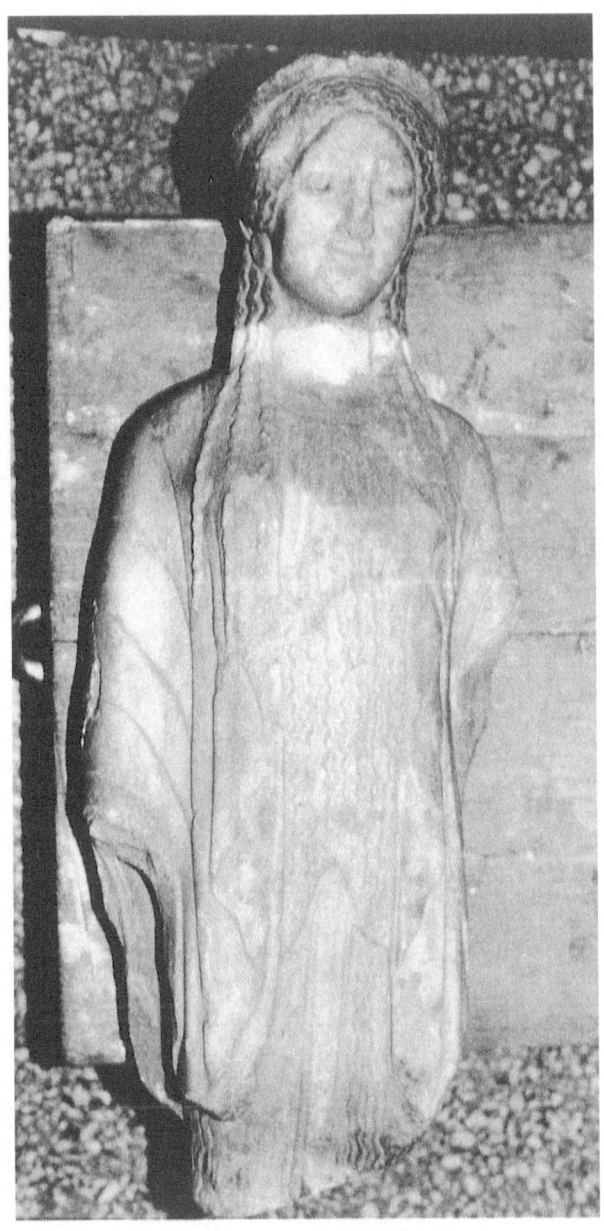

Figure 15. Acropolis Museum 687, kore from the Acropolis of Athens, marble. Photo: author.

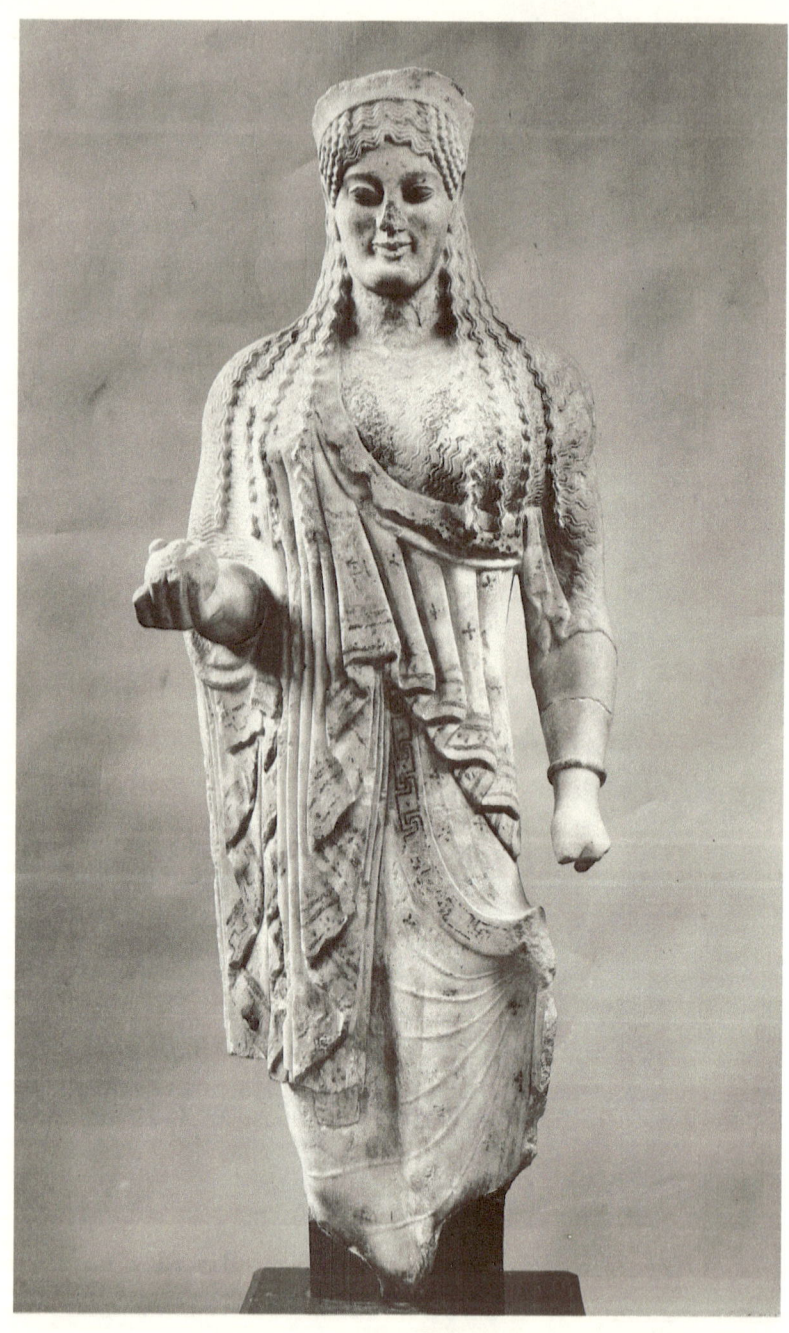

Figure 16. Acropolis Museum 680, kore from the Acropolis of Athens, marble. Photo by Wagner courtesy of the DAI, Athens, neg. no. Akr. 1787.

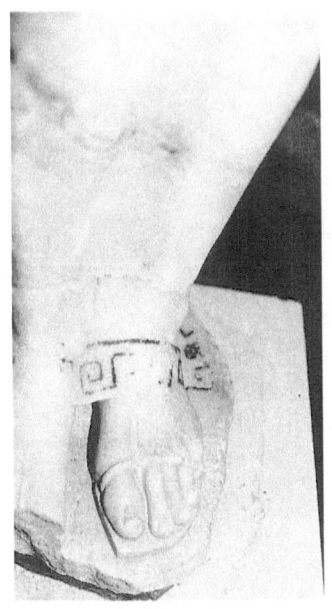

*Figure 17. Acropolis Museum 672 (**detail**). Photo: author.*

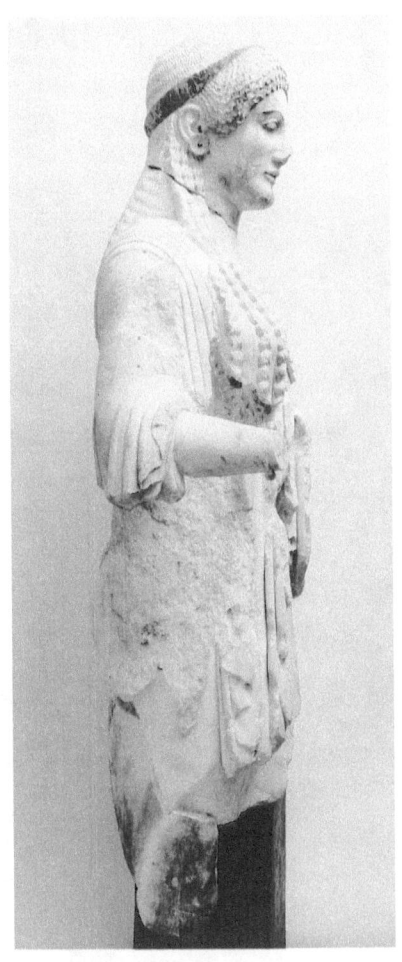

*Figure 18. Acropolis Museum 684 (**right side**). Photo by Wagner courtesy of the DAI, Athens, neg. no. Akr. 1531.*

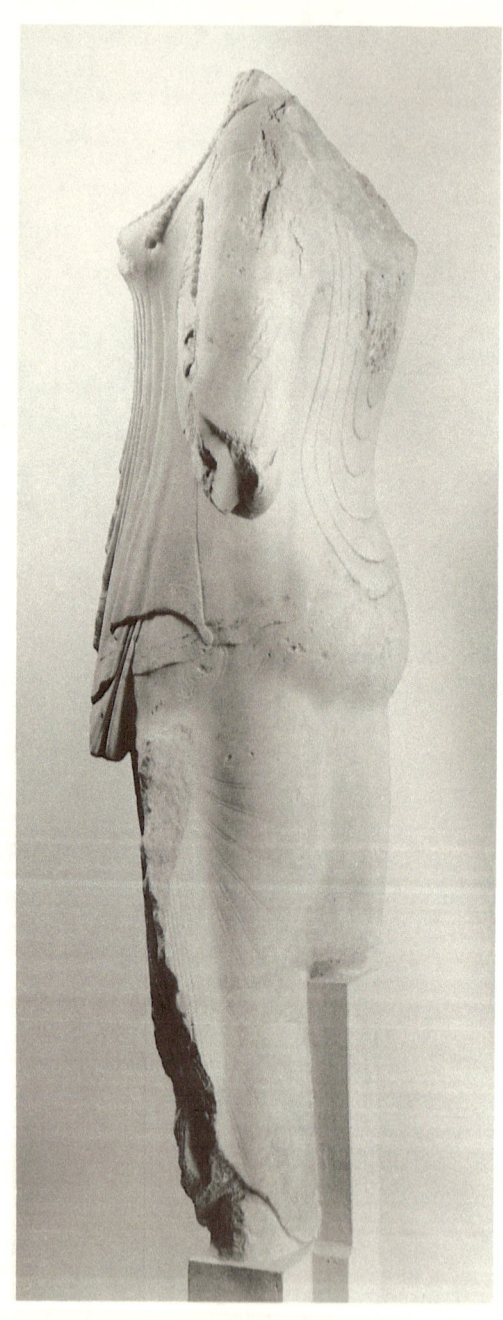

Figure 19. Acropolis Museum 594 *(three-quarter view from back)*, kore from the
Acropolis of Athens, marble. Photo courtesy of the Alison Frantz Collection,
American School of Classical Studies at Athens, neg. no. AT 489.

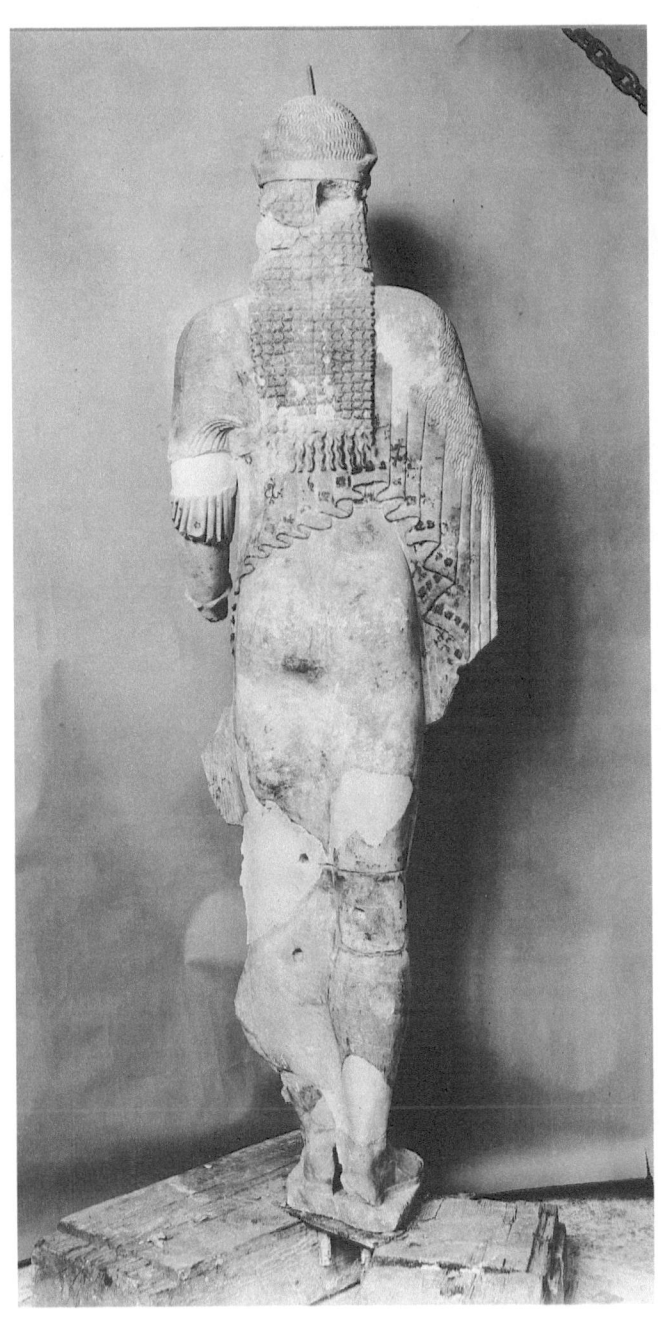

*Figure 20. Acropolis Museum 682 (**back view**).*
Photo by Schuchhardt courtesy of the DAI, Athens,
neg. no. Akr. 824.

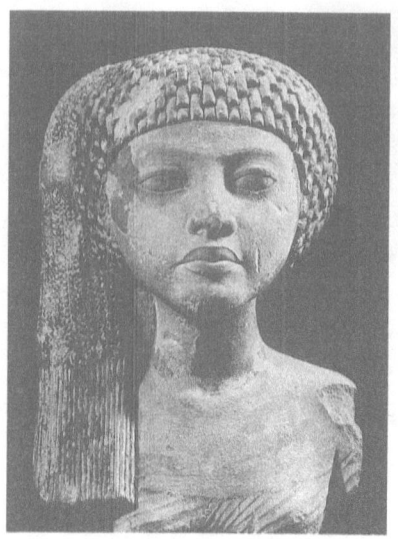 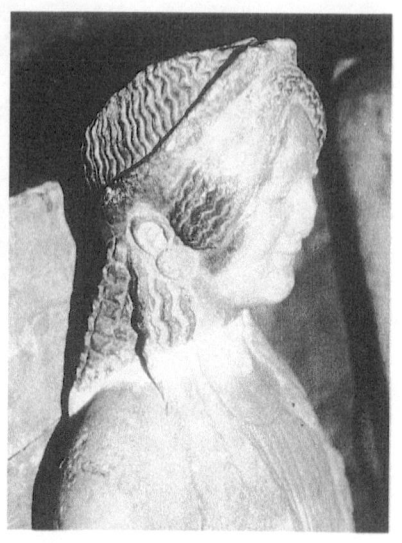

Figure 21. Princess of Amarna, from the
family of Amenhotep IV (Akhenaten),
New Kingdom, 1350–1300 B.C., painted
limestone, Musée du Louvre, Paris,
E 14715. Photo by Erich Lessing courtesy
of Art Resource, New York.

Figure 22. Acropolis Museum 687
(detail). Photo: author.

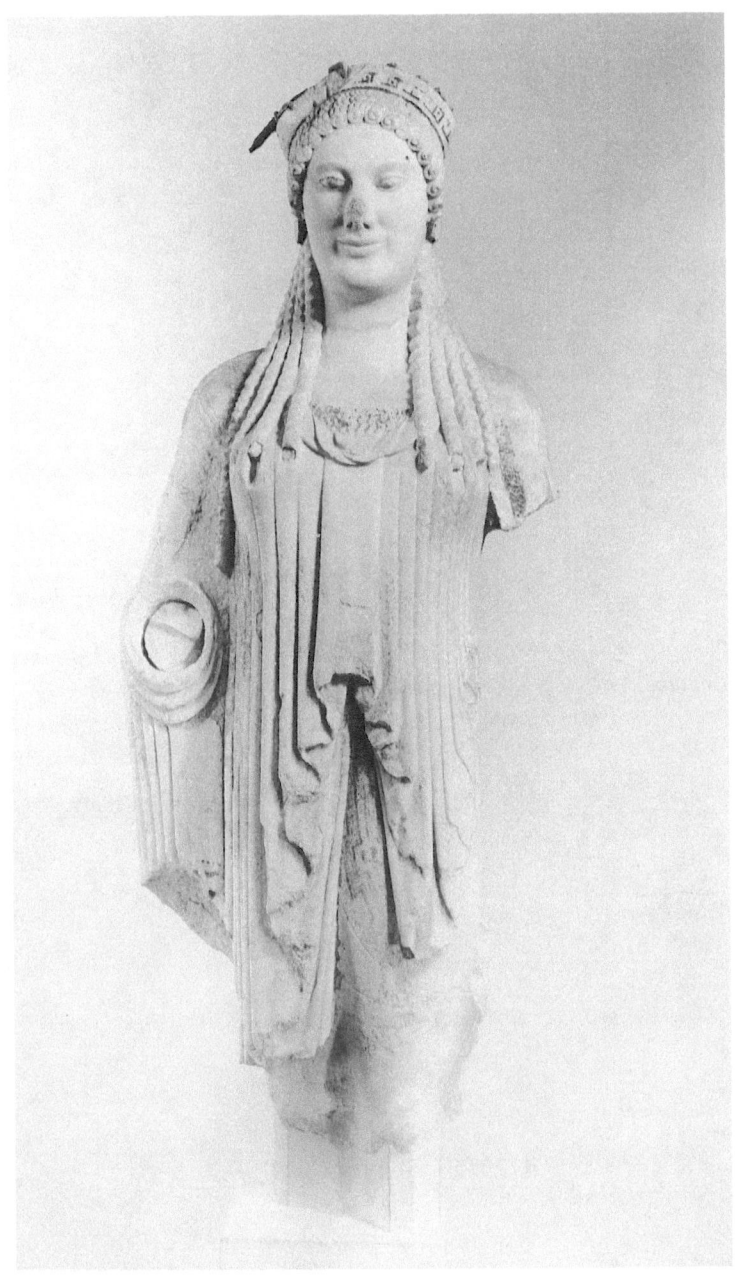

*Figure 23. Acropolis Museum 673, kore from the Acropolis of Athens, marble.
Photo courtesy of the Alison Frantz Collection, American School of
Classical Studies at Athens, neg. no. AT 459.*

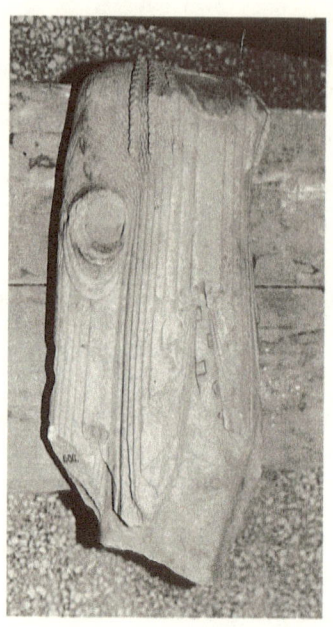

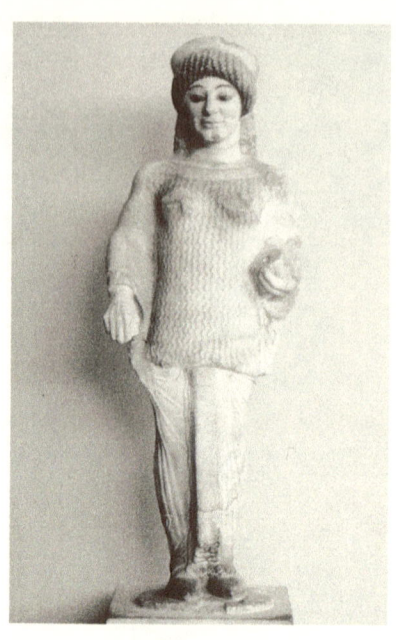

Figure 24. Acropolis Museum 600, kore from the Acropolis of Athens, marble. Photo: author.

Figure 25. Acropolis Museum 683. Photo: author.

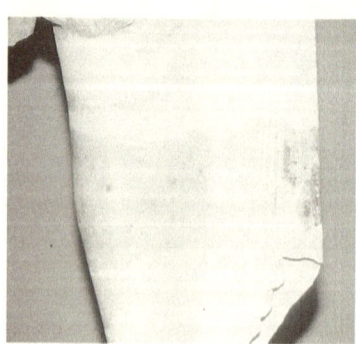

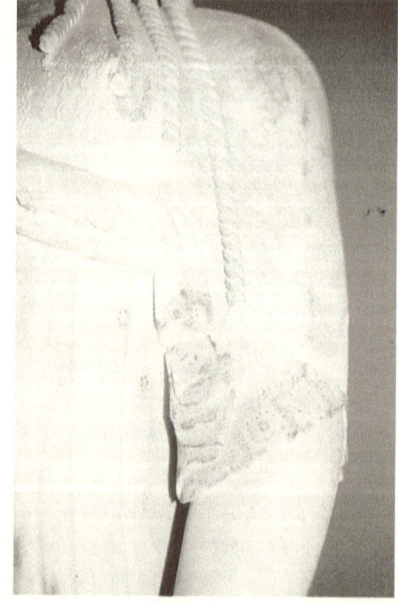

*Figure 26. Acropolis Museum 681 (**detail**). Photo: author.*

*Figure 27. Acropolis Museum 682 (**detail**). Photo: author.*

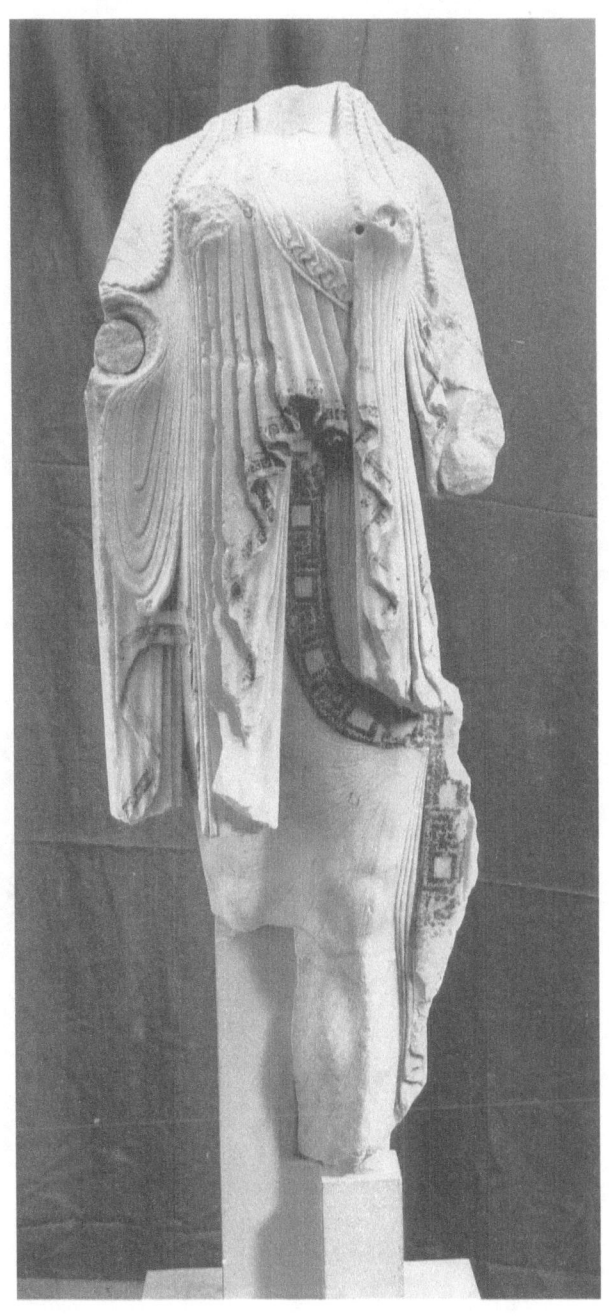

Figure 28. Acropolis Museum 594. Photo by Hellner courtesy of the DAI, Athens, neg. no. 1972/2918.

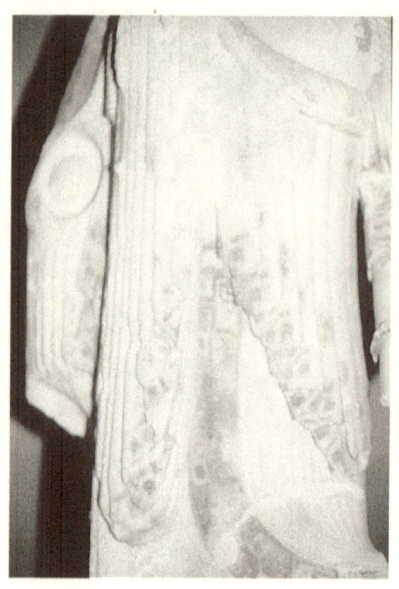 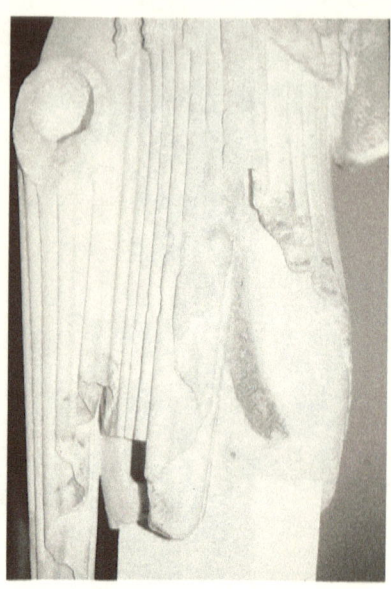

*Figure 29. Acropolis Museum 682
(detail). Photo: author.*

*Figure 31. Acropolis Museum 674
(detail). Photo: author.*

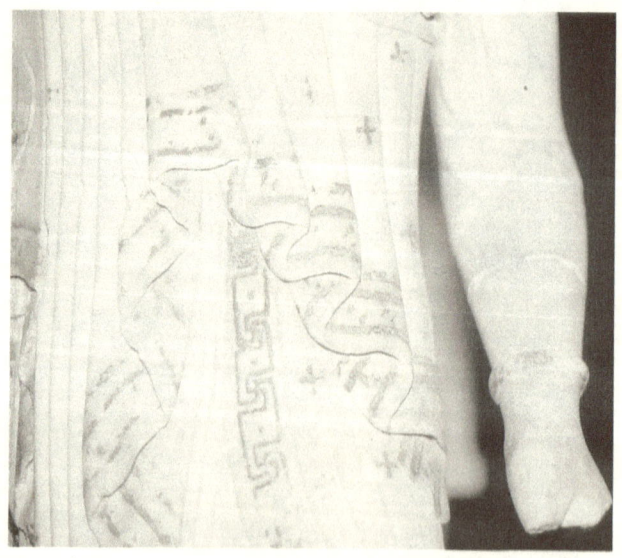

Figure 30. Acropolis Museum 680 (detail). Photo: author.

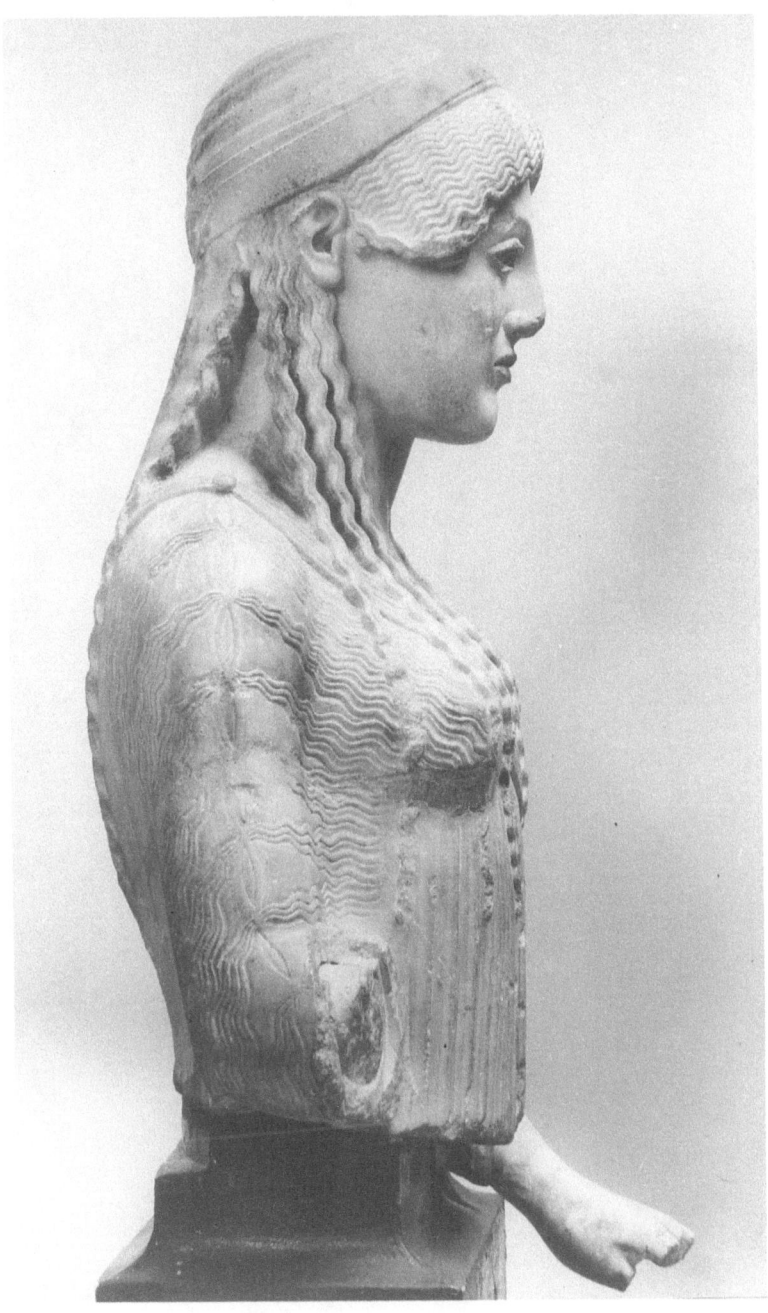

*Figure 32. Acropolis Museum 686 ("Euthydikos' Kore") (**right side**). Photo by Wagner courtesy of the DAI, Athens, neg. no. Akr. 1379.*

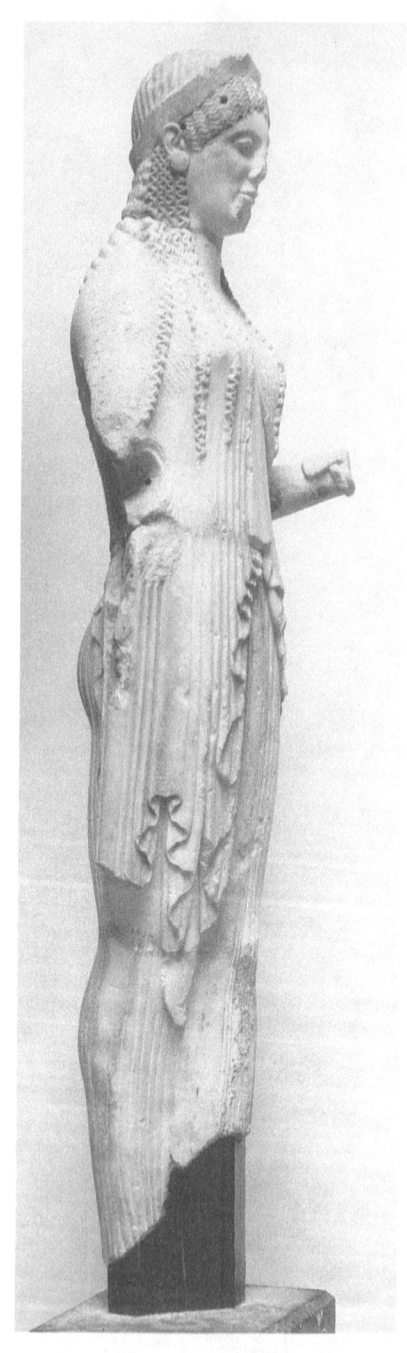

Figure 33. Acropolis Museum 685 (three-quarter view from front).
Photo by Wagner courtesy of the DAI, Athens, neg. no. Akr. 1593.

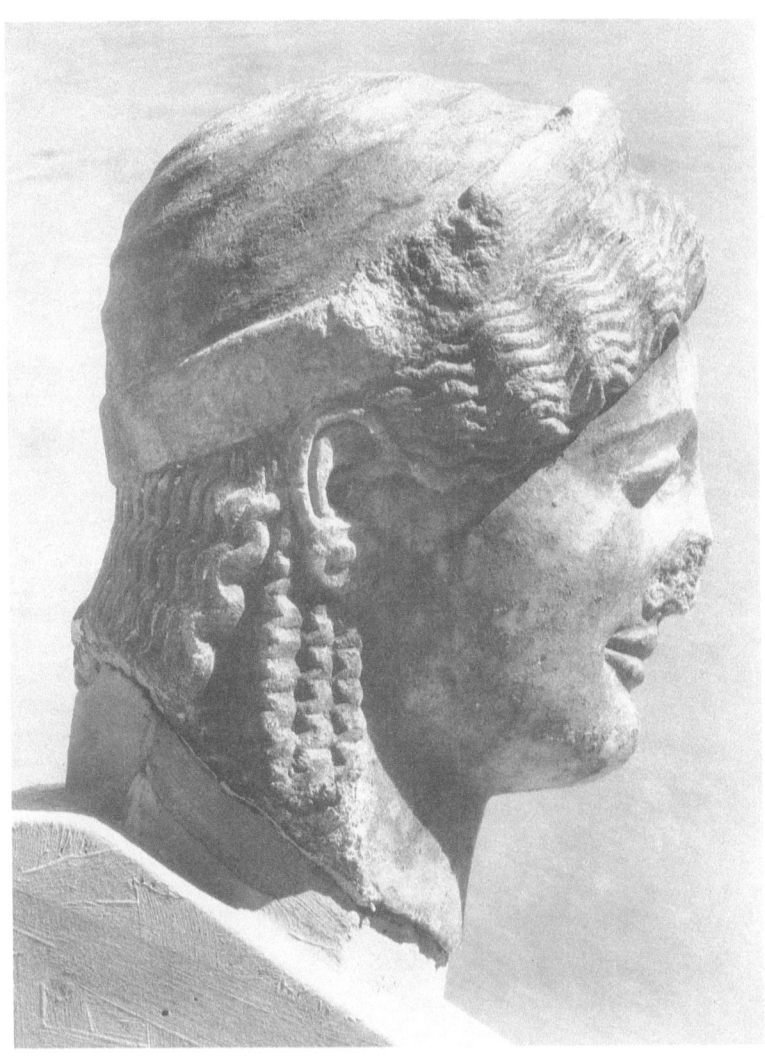

*Figure 34. Acropolis Museum 616 (**right side**). Photo by Hege courtesy of the DAI, Athens, neg. no. Hege 1365.*

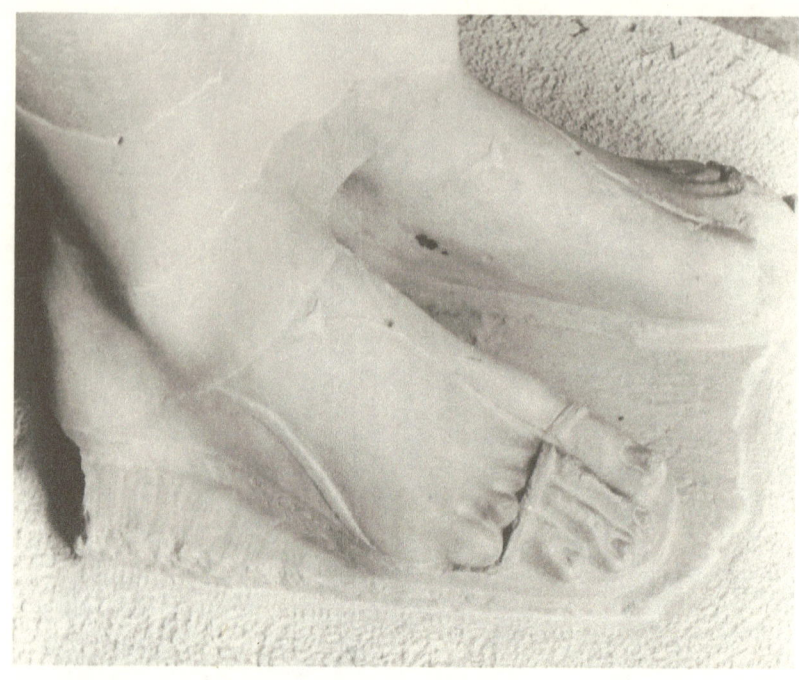

*Figure 35. Acropolis Museum 682
(detail). Photo courtesy of the
Hellenic Republic Ministry of Culture,
Archaeological Receipts Fund
(TAP Service).*

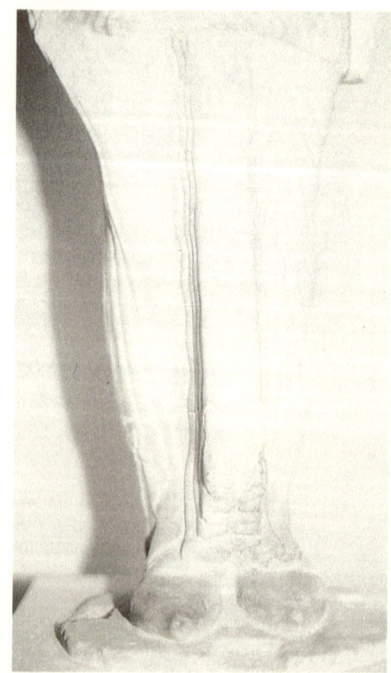

*Figure 36. Acropolis Museum 683
(detail). Photo: author.*

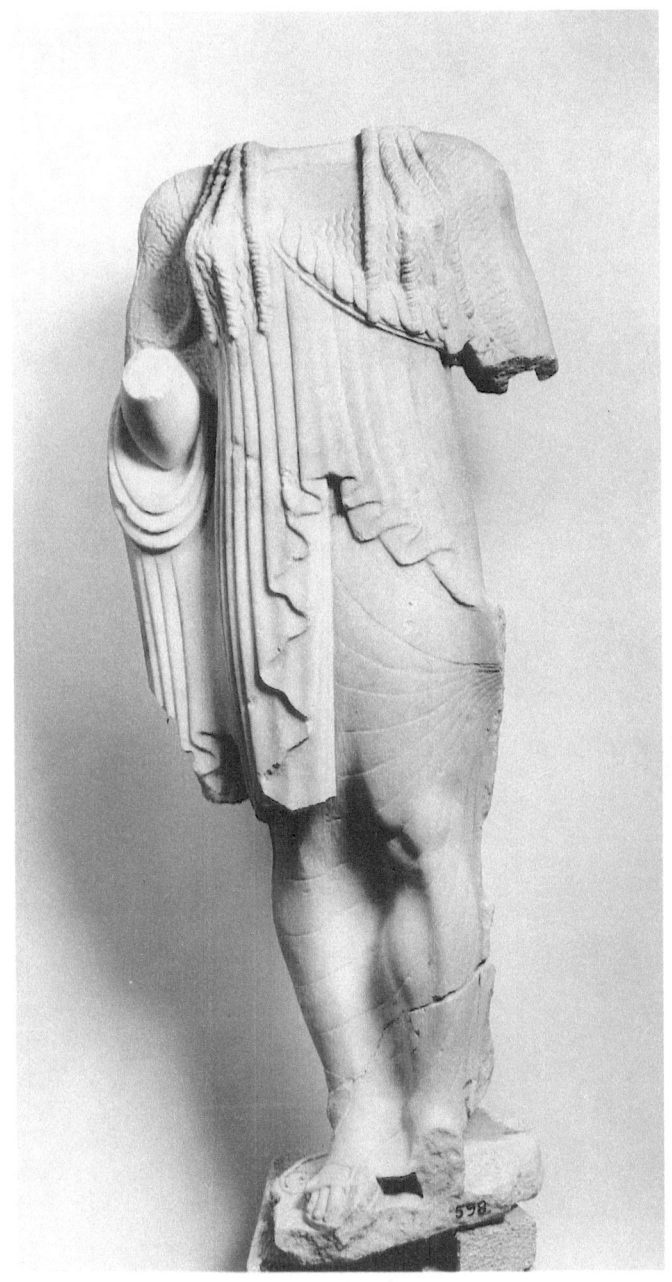

*Figure 37. Acropolis Museum 598, kore from the Acropolis of Athens, marble.
Photo courtesy of the Alison Frantz Collection, American School of
Classical Studies at Athens, neg. no. AT 450.*

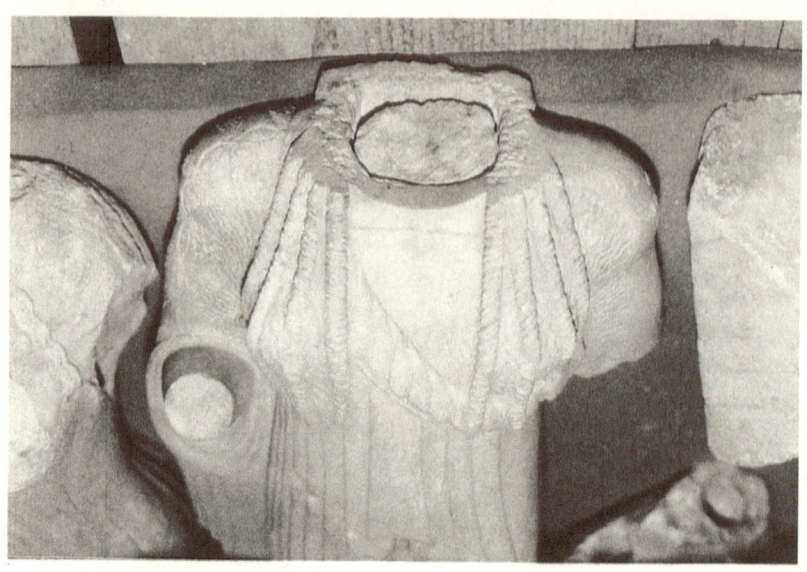

*Figure 38. Acropolis Museum 598
(**detail**). Photo: author.*

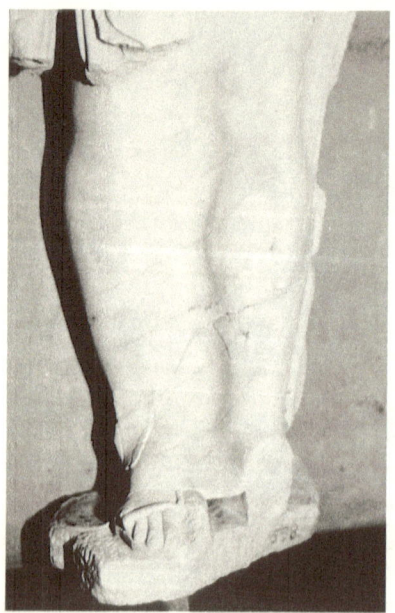

*Figure 39. Acropolis Museum 598
(**detail**). Photo: author.*

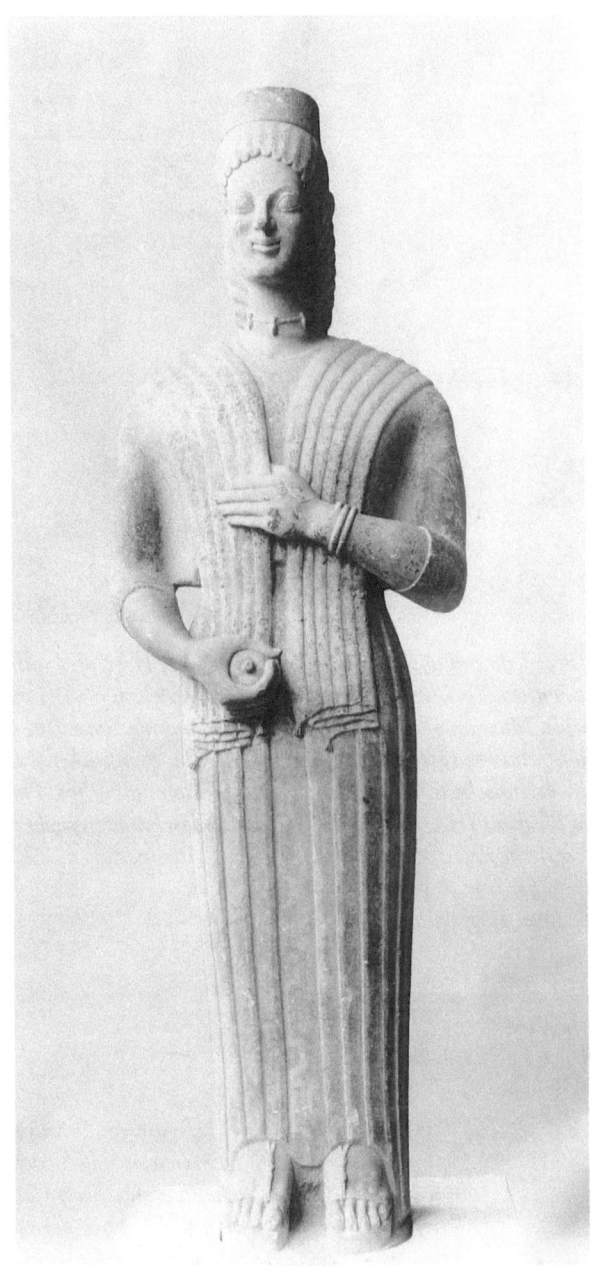

*Figure 40. Kore from Attica ("Berlin Kore"), marble, Staatliche Museen
zu Berlin, Preussischer Kulturbesitz, Antikensammlung 1800. Photo courtesy
of the Bildarchiv Preussischer Kulturbesitz, Berlin, neg. no. SK 7120.*

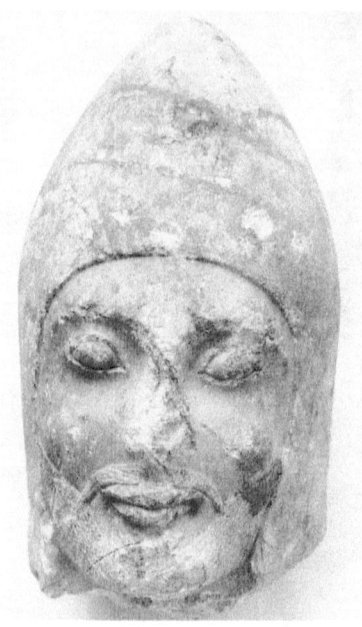

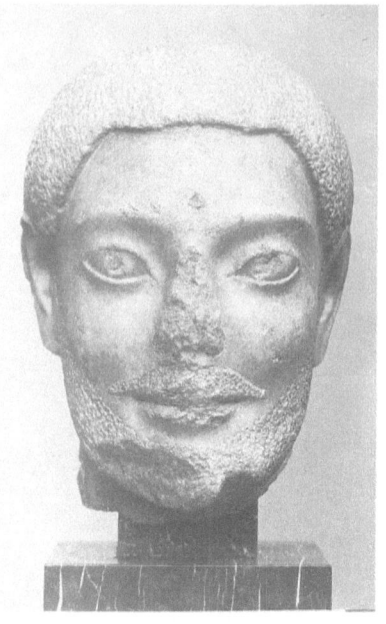

Figure 41. Bearded head with tiara from Herakleia Pontica, Turkey, ca. 540–530 B.C., marble, Museum of Anatolian Civilizations, Ankara 19367. Photo: E. Akurgal in **Archaische und klassische griechische Plastik** *I (H. Kyrieleis, ed.), Deutsches Archäologisches Institut, Mainz: 1986, fig. 1, with permission of Emel Yurttagül.*

Figure 42. Head of a man ("Sabouroff Head"), Athens or Aegina, ca. 550–540 B.C., marble, Staatliche Museen zu Berlin, Preussischer Kulturbesitz, Antikensammlung 308. Photo courtesy of the Bildarchiv Preussischer Kulturbesitz, Berlin, neg. no. SK 5944.

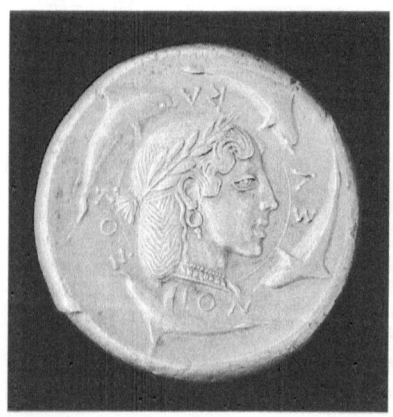

Figure 43. Decadrachm ("Damareteion") of Syracuse, mint of Syracuse, Sicily, Early Classic Period, 480–479 B.C., silver, diameter 35 mm, weight 43.39 gm. Museum of Fine Arts, Boston; Theodora Wilbour Fund in Memory of Zoë Wilbour; 35.21. Photo courtesy of the MFA, © Museum of Fine Arts, Boston.

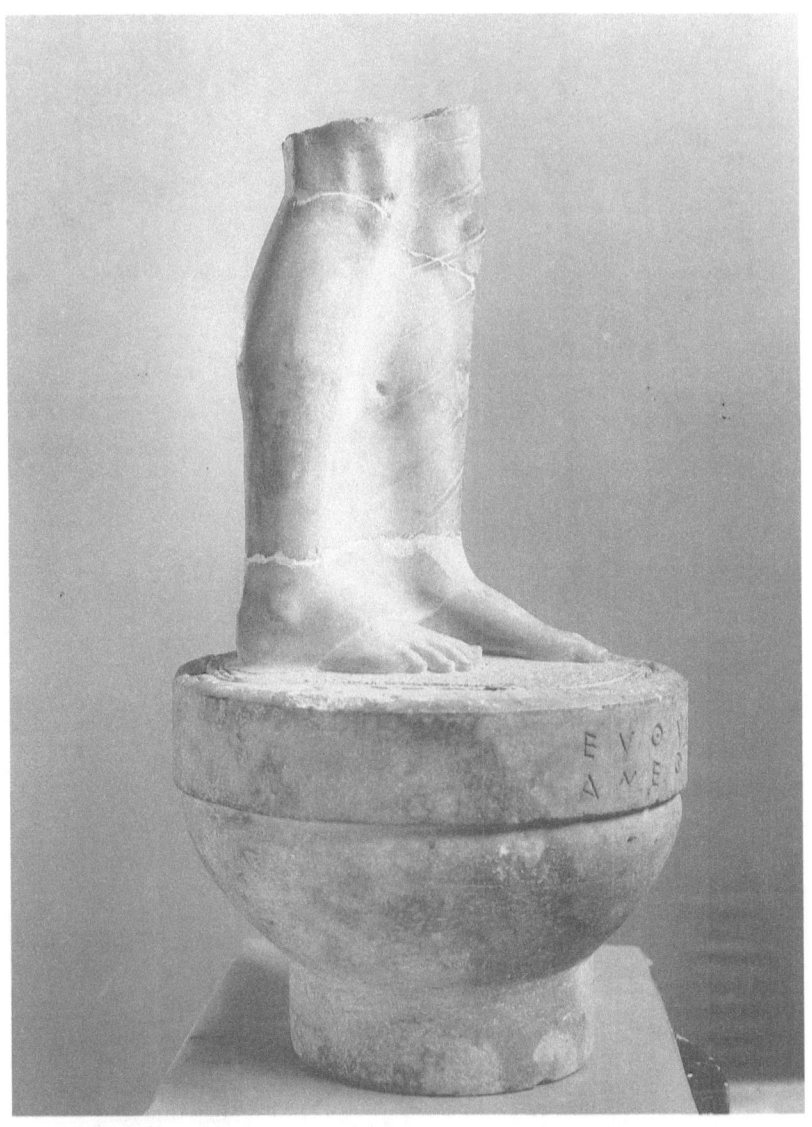

Figure 44. Acropolis Museum 609 (lower half of "Euthydikos' Kore").
Photo by Schrader courtesy of the DAI, Athens, neg. no. Schrader 40.

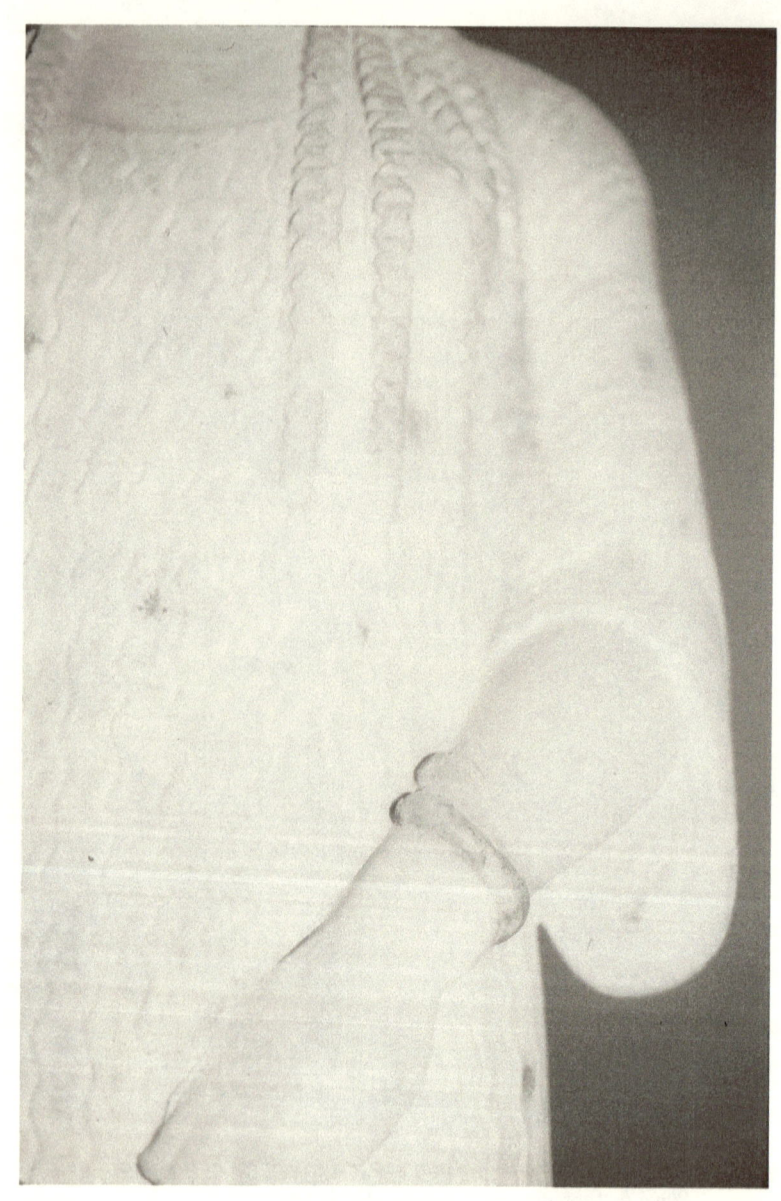

*Figure 45. Acropolis Museum 670 (**detail**). Photo: author.*

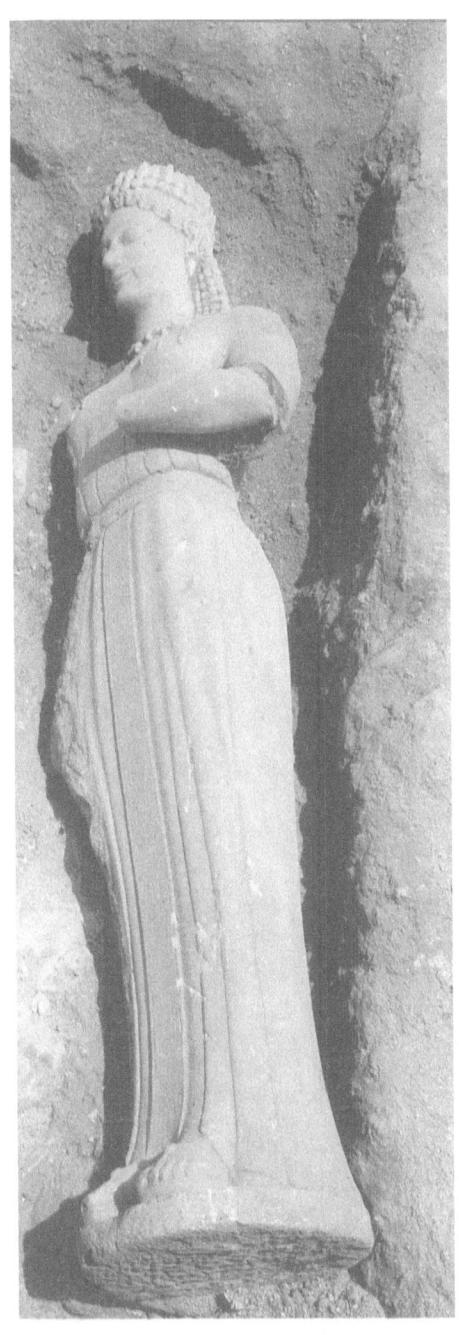

Figure 46. Kore from Merenda, Attica ("Phrasikleia"), marble, Athens, National Archaeological Museum 4889. Photo courtesy of Kontos Studio.

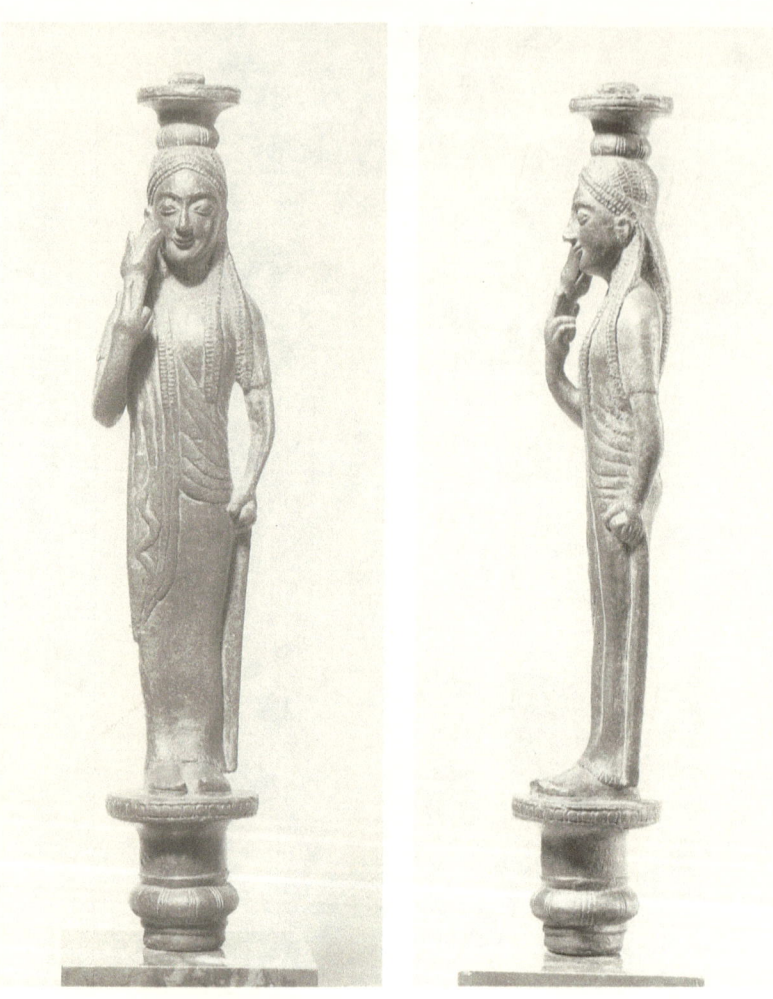

*Figure 47. Kore statuette from Sparta, bronze, Staatliche Museen zu Berlin,
Preussischer Kulturbesitz, Antikensammlung 7933. Photos courtesy of the
Bildarchiv Preussischer Kulturbesitz, Berlin.*

INDEX

I wish to thank Aura Davies for preparing this index.

www.ingramcontent.com/pod-product-compliance
Lightning Source LLC
Chambersburg PA
CBHW020734180526
45163CB00001B/230